Symmetry in Mathematical Analysis and Functional Analysis

Editors

Octav Olteanu
Savin Treanta

MDPI • Basel • Beijing • Wuhan • Barcelona • Belgrade • Manchester • Tokyo • Cluj • Tianjin

Editors

Octav Olteanu
Mathematics and Informatics
University Politehnica
of Bucharest
Bucharest
Romania

Savin Treanta
Applied Mathematics
University Politehnica
of Bucharest
Bucharest
Romania

Editorial Office
MDPI
St. Alban-Anlage 66
4052 Basel, Switzerland

This is a reprint of articles from the Special Issue published online in the open access journal *Symmetry* (ISSN 2073-8994) (available at: www.mdpi.com/journal/symmetry/special_issues/Symmetry_Mathematical_Analysis_Functional_Analysis).

For citation purposes, cite each article independently as indicated on the article page online and as indicated below:

LastName, A.A.; LastName, B.B.; LastName, C.C. Article Title. *Journal Name* **Year**, *Volume Number*, Page Range.

ISBN 978-3-0365-6591-0 (Hbk)
ISBN 978-3-0365-6590-3 (PDF)

Contents

Octav Olteanu
Special Issue of Symmetry: "Symmetry in Mathematical Analysis and Functional Analysis"
Reprinted from: *Symmetry* **2022**, *14*, 2665, doi:10.3390/sym14122665 1

Yan Sun and Xiaolan Liu
Relation-Theoretic Coincidence and Common Fixed Point Results in Extended Rectangular b-Metric Spaces with Applications
Reprinted from: *Symmetry* **2022**, *14*, 1588, doi:10.3390/sym14081588 7

Gerardo Sánchez Licea
Sufficiency for Weak Minima in Optimal Control Subject to Mixed Constraints
Reprinted from: *Symmetry* **2022**, *14*, 1520, doi:10.3390/sym14081520 31

Monairah Alansari and Muhammad Usman Ali
Abstraction of Interpolative Reich-Rus-Ćirić-Type Contractions and Simplest Proof Technique
Reprinted from: *Symmetry* **2022**, *14*, 1504, doi:10.3390/sym14081504 51

Hasanen A. Hammad and Mohra Zayed
Solving a System of Differential Equations with Infinite Delayby Using Tripled Fixed Point Techniques on Graphs
Reprinted from: *Symmetry* **2022**, *14*, 1388, doi:10.3390/sym14071388 67

Octav Olteanu
On Special Properties for Continuous Convex Operators and Related Linear Operators
Reprinted from: *Symmetry* **2022**, *14*, 1390, doi:10.3390/sym14071390 81

Vuk Stojiljković, Slobodan Radojević, Eyüp Çetin, Vesna Šešum Čavić and Stojan Radenović
Sharp Bounds for Trigonometric and Hyperbolic Functions with Application to Fractional Calculus
Reprinted from: *Symmetry* **2022**, *14*, 1260, doi:10.3390/sym14061260 93

Kin Keung Lai, Shashi Kant Mishra, Jaya Bisht and Mohd Hassan
Hermite–Hadamard Type Inclusions for Interval-Valued Coordinated Preinvex Functions
Reprinted from: *Symmetry* **2022**, *14*, 771, doi:10.3390/sym14040771 103

Muhammad Bilal Khan, Hatim Ghazi Zaini, Savin Treanţă, Gustavo Santos-García, Jorge E. Macías-Díaz and Mohamed S. Soliman
Fractional Calculus for Convex Functions in Interval-Valued Settings and Inequalities
Reprinted from: *Symmetry* **2022**, *14*, 341, doi:10.3390/sym14020341 121

Muhammad Bilal Khan, Hatim Ghazi Zaini, Jorge E. Macías-Díaz, Savin Treanţă and Mohamed S. Soliman
Some Fuzzy Riemann–Liouville Fractional Integral Inequalities for Preinvex Fuzzy Interval-Valued Functions
Reprinted from: *Symmetry* **2022**, *14*, 313, doi:10.3390/sym14020313 137

Kin Keung Lai, Mohd Hassan, Jitendra Kumar Maurya, Sanjeev Kumar Singh and Shashi Kant Mishra
Multiobjective Convex Optimization in Real Banach Space
Reprinted from: *Symmetry* **2021**, *13*, 2148, doi:10.3390/sym13112148 159

Yan Liu and Baiping Ouyang
The Well Posedness for Nonhomogeneous Boussinesq Equations
Reprinted from: *Symmetry* **2021**, *13*, 2110, doi:10.3390/sym13112110 169

symmetry

Editorial

Special Issue of Symmetry: "Symmetry in Mathematical Analysis and Functional Analysis"

Octav Olteanu

Department of Mathematics and Informatics, University Politehnica of Bucharest, 060042 Bucharest, Romania; octav.olteanu50@gmail.com

Citation: Olteanu, O. Special Issue of Symmetry: "Symmetry in Mathematical Analysis and Functional Analysis". *Symmetry* **2022**, *14*, 2665. https://doi.org/10.3390/sym14122665

Received: 13 December 2022
Accepted: 14 December 2022
Published: 16 December 2022

This Special Issue consists of 11 papers recently published in MDPI's journal *Symmetry* under the general thematic title "Symmetry in Mathematical Analysis and Functional Analysis" (see [1–11]). The deadline for manuscript submissions was 31 July 2022. This Special Issue belongs to the section of the journal entitled "Mathematics and Symmetry/Asymmetry".

Among other aspects of the theory underlying this area of research, the content of these 11 published papers (and their references) covers, but is not limited to, the following subjects:

1. Common fixed-point results in general metric space settings and applications.
2. Constrained optimization.
3. Optimal control.
4. Solving systems of special differential equations.
5. Applications of fractional calculus.
6. Inclusion and inequalities in interval-valued pre-invex and convex functions.
7. Fuzzy fractional integral inequalities in pre-invex fuzzy interval-valued functions.
8. Multi-objective convex optimization in real Banach space.
9. Well-posedness for certain classes of equations.
10. Families of convex operators and related linear operators.
11. Symmetry of sublinear continuous operators and its applications (see [11]).

In the first part of paper [11], the symmetry of sublinear continuous operators $P : X \to Y$ ($P(x) = P(-x)\ \forall x \in X$) appears in Theorem 2 and in some of its consequences. Of note, if X, Y are Banach lattices, with Y being an order complete, then the norm of a continuous sublinear operator from X into Y controls the norm of all its subgradients. In the second part of the same paper, elements of the theory of the Markov moment problem are explored. Since this thematic area is closely related to many other fields of mathematics, here, we briefly review some of the notions regarding the classical one dimensional and, in particular, the multidimensional moment problem and its relationship with other areas of research, such as the explicit form of any non-negative polynomial on a closed subset of $\mathbb{R}^n$ in terms of the sums of the squares of some polynomials; the extension of positive linear functionals and operators; the extension of linear operators dominated by a convex continuous operator and dominating a given continuous concave operator (these constraints might hold only on the positive cone of the domain space); measure theory; the notion of a moment determinate measure and study of determinacy; matrix theory; spaces of commuting self-adjoint operators (in particular, spaces of commuting symmetric matrices with real entries); inequalities; the Banach lattices of functions and self-adjoint operators; existence, uniqueness, and the eventual construction of the linear solution to an interpolation problem with one or two constraints; and examples of continuous sublinear (or only convex) operators, operator theory, and the complex functions of complex variables. In the present editorial, only the analysis and functional analysis of the real field are addressed. As is well-known and pointed out by the authors of [12], symmetric matrices with real entries have special properties, and there exits a natural order relation with respect to the real vector space $Sym(n \times n, \mathbb{R})$ of all such matrices. With respect to this order relation, for $n \geq 2$, the ordered vector space $Sym(n \times n, \mathbb{R})$ is not a lattice. On the other hand, the multiplication operation of such $n \times n$ matrices is not commutative for $n \geq 2$. Clearly, the corresponding assertions hold true regarding the space $\mathcal{A}(H)$ of all the self-adjoint operators acting on a real or complex Hilbert space H, where $\dim(H) \geq 2$. The same article [12] contains simple proof of the fact that any positive linear operator applying an ordered Banach space X to an ordered Banach space Y is continuous. In particular, any positive linear operator mapping an arbitrary Banach lattice onto a Banach lattice is continuous. In order to avoid the two main difficulties mentioned above, regarding the space $\mathcal{A}(H)$ for any $A \in \mathcal{A}(H)$, as demonstrated in [13], one must construct a commutative real Banach algebra over the real field, denoted by $Y(A)$, which is also an order complete Banach lattice (endowed with the operatorial norm on $\mathcal{A}(H)$). In this Banach lattice, we have $|U| := sup\{U, -U\} = \sqrt{U^2}$ for all $U \in Y(A)$. In other words, the modulus of U in this Banach lattice equals the positive square root of the positive self-adjoint operator U^2. Moreover, due to the order completeness of the vector lattice $Y(A)$, Hahn–Banach-type extension theorems for linear operators have $Y(A)$ as a codomain hold. In the classical one-dimensional moment problem, given a sequence $(y_j)_{j \in \mathbb{N}}$ of real numbers, we should find necessary and sufficient conditions for the existence of a positive regular Borel measure ν on the closed subset $F \subseteq \mathbb{R}$, which satisfies the interpolation conditions $\int_F t^j d\nu(t) = y_j$, $j \in \mathbb{N} := \{0, 1, 2, \ldots\}$. This is an inverse problem, because the measure ν is not known. Thus, it must be identified starting with its moments $\int_F t^j d\nu(t)$, $j \in \mathbb{N}$. If such a measure does exist, its uniqueness and, eventually, its construction can be studied. The multidimensional real moment problem can be formulated in a similar way. In the case of an $n-$ dimensional moment problem, we have $j = (j_1, \ldots, j_n) \in \mathbb{N}^n$, $t = (t_1, \ldots, t_n) \in F \subseteq \mathbb{R}^n$, $n \geq 2$, n, being a fixed integer. Considering the unique linear form L_0 on the space of all the polynomials with real coefficients, satisfying the interpolation condition $L_0(\varphi_j) = y_j$, $j \in \mathbb{N}^n$, the existence of a solution is reduced to the representation of L_0 by a positive measure $d\nu$. Namely, through linearity, the following equality is true for $d\nu : L_0(p) = \int_F p(t) d\nu(t)$ for all the polynomials $p \in \mathbb{R}[t_1, \ldots, t_n]$. This is a motivation for the terminology *representing measure* for L_0. According to the Haviland theorem [14], the sufficient (and necessary) condition for the existence of the representing positive measure $d\nu$ for L_0 is $L_0(p) \geq 0$ for any polynomial $p \in \mathbb{R}[t_1, \ldots, t_n]$ satisfying $p(t) \geq 0$ for all $t = (t_1, \ldots, t_n) \in F$. In the important case of $n = 1$, $F = \mathbb{R}$, this positivity condition can be expressed in terms of the semi-positiveness of quadratic forms, since each polynomial (with real coefficients) which is non-negative on the entirety of the real axes is the sum of two squares of the polynomials from $\mathbb{R}[t]$ (see [15,16]). With the abovementioned notations, the coefficients of the quadratic forms are y_{i+j}. This is the one-dimensional Hamburger moment problem. It represents a good example of symmetry, given by the symmetric matrices $(y_{i+j})_{0 \leq i,j \leq m}$ and $m \in \mathbb{N}$. A similar remark is valid for the one-dimensional moment problem on $[0, +\infty) : p \in \mathbb{R}[t]$, $p(t) \geq 0$ for all $t \in [0, +\infty) \Longleftrightarrow p(t) = q^2(t) + tr^2(t)\ \forall t \in [0, +\infty)$ for some polynomials $q, r \in \mathbb{R}[t]$. Unlike the one-dimensional case, there are non-negative polynomials on $\mathbb{R}^2$, which are not sums of the squares of the polynomials in $\mathbb{R}[t_1, t_2]$ (see [16]). Up to now, the terms of the sequence $(y_j)_{j \in \mathbb{N}^n}$ have been numbers. This is the scalar moment problem. Next, we consider a sequence $(y_j)_{j \in \mathbb{N}^n}$ of elements of an ordered vector space Y and, with the notation forms above, we study the existence of a linear positive operator $T : X_1 \to Y$, such that $T(\varphi_j) = y_j$ for all $j \in \mathbb{N}^n$. Here, X_1 is an ordered vector space of real functions, containing the polynomials and the space $C_c(F)$ of all the continuous compactly supported functions on F, such that the subspace of the polynomials is a majorizing subspace in X_1. For example, if $X := L^p_\nu(F)$, $p \in [1, +\infty)$, the space X_1 will be the sublattice of X formed by all the functions f from X, possessing the modulus $|f|$ dominated by a polynomial on the entire subset F. Then, it is easy to observe that the subspace of the polynomials is a majorizing subspace in X_1 and, clearly, X_1 contains $C_c(F)$ and the space of the polynomials. Assuming that Y is order complete, we consider the unique linear operator T_0 mapping the space of the polynomials to Y, $T_0\left(\sum_{j\in J_0}\alpha_j\varphi_j\right) := \sum_{j\in J_0}\alpha_j y_j$, $J_0 \subset \mathbb{N}^n$, being an arbitrary finite subset. Additionally, assume that $T_0(p) \in Y_+$ for all the non-negative polynomials p on F. The application of the Kantorovich extension theorem for positive linear operators (see [17]) leads to the existence of a linear positive extension T_1 of T_0, where T_1 is mapped X_1 to Y. If we prove the continuity of T_1 on X_1, then there exists a unique continuous positive extension $T : X \to Y$ of T_1. This follows from the density of $C_c(F)$ in $X = L^p_\nu(F)$, $p \in [1, +\infty)$ (see [18]). When an upper constraint on the solution T is required, we have a Markov moment problem. Usually, the following constraints on the solution T of the interpolation problem are required: $0 \le T \le T_2$ on the positive cone X_+, where T_2 is a given linear positive operator mapping the Banach lattice X to the order complete Banach lattice Y. In [19], the explicit form of non-negative polynomials on a strip is highlighted in terms of the sums of squares. In the papers [20–36], various results on the full and truncated moment problem are provided. These results refer to connection with fixed-point theory (see [23]), the moment problem on compact subsets with a nonempty interior in $\mathbb{R}^n$, (see [25]), and the decomposition of positive polynomials on such compact subsets, the moment problem, and the decomposition of positive polynomials on compact semi-algebraic subsets (see [26–29]. In [29], a class of moment problems on unbounded semi-algebraic sets are also discussed. The truncated Markov moment problem, including the construction of a solution, is emphasized in the articles [30,31]. For optimization related to the truncated moment problem, see [32,33]. A solution to a full moment problem obtained as a limit of the solutions for the associated truncated moment problem is provided by the authors of [34]. In [35], an operator-valued moment problem is solved, while an L-moment problem is discussed in [36]. The geometric aspects of functional analysis in nonstandard spaces are discussed in the papers [37,38], without any connection with the moment problem. Iterative methods regarding fixed-point and related optimization problems are discussed in [39–41]. In the monograph [42], the authors study the sandwich condition $T_1 \le T \le T_2$ on the positive cone of the domain space, where T_1, T_2 are given linear functionals and T is a solution for a finite number of the interpolation moment conditions. The article [43] provides the necessary and sufficient conditions for the existence of a positive linear operator solution dominated by a convex operator. A result of G. Cassier (see [25]) is applied in order to apply the first theorem in [43] to the classical multidimensional Markov moment problem on a compact with a nonempty interior in $\mathbb{R}^n$. A characterization of the existence of a linear operator solution T for an arbitrary infinite number of moment conditions, such that the sandwich constraint $T_1 \le T \le T_2$ on X_+ holds, is also provided. Here, T_1, T_2 are the given linear operators. In the article [44], sufficient conditions for the determinacy of probability distributions on $\mathbb{R}$ or respectively on $[0, +\infty)$ are studied. We recall that a measure is a determinate measure on the closed subset F if it is uniquely determined by its moments on F. In the paper [45], the notion of a finite simplicial set is reviewed and applied to a non-standard sandwich theorem on that set. Notably, a finite simplicial set can be unbounded in the case of any locally convex topology on the vector space in which the set is contained. As we have already seen, the non-negative polynomials on $\mathbb{R}^n$ are not expressible in terms of the sums of squares. This is the motivation for the polynomial approximation results provided in [46,47] and applied to the Markov moment problem with the operator solution in [46–49]. These results are essentially based on the notion of a moment determinate measure. In [46], it was proved that for a moment determinate measure ν, the non-negative polynomials on F are dense in the positive cone of $L^1_\nu(F)$. Consequently, the subspace of the polynomials is dense in $L^1_\nu(F)$. Notably, if $n \ge 2$, there exist moment determinate measures ν on $\mathbb{R}^n$, such that the polynomials are not dense in $L^2_\nu(\mathbb{R}^n)$ (see [22]). We can assume that all the measures are positive Borel regular measures on F, with finite moments of all the orders. In [47–49], the authors prove that for the products $\nu = \nu_1 \times \cdots \times \nu_n$ of n moment determinate measures ν_i on $\mathbb{R}$, any function of the positive cone of $L^1_\nu(F)$ can be approximated by finite sums of special products of polynomials, $p(t) = p_1(t_1) \cdots p_n(t_n)$, where each p_i is non-negative on $\mathbb{R}$, which, hence, is a sum of (two) squares, $i = 1, \ldots, n$. For such measures ν, this enables us to solve the multidimensional Markov moment problems on $\mathbb{R}^n$ mentioned above in terms of the quadratic forms. The corresponding result for the products of the n moment determinate measures on $[0, +\infty)^n$ holds. Here, assume that Y is an order complete Banach lattice and T_1, T_2 are bounded linear operators applying $L^1_\nu(F)$ to T. In this case, the linear solution T of the problem under investigation is also bounded due to the constraint $T_1 \leq T \leq T_2$ on the positive cone of $L^1_\nu(F)$. The uniqueness of the solution follows according to the density of the polynomials in $L^1_\nu(F)$. To conclude, we can observe that polynomial approximation on bounded subsets solves the existence, as well as the uniqueness, of the solution to a large class of Markov moment problems on $\mathbb{R}^n$ or on $[0, +\infty)^n$, $n \geq 2$.

Data Availability Statement: This study uses only theoretical results and their applications published in the cited references.

Conflicts of Interest: The author declares no conflict of interest.

References

1. Sun, Y.; Liu, X. Relation-theoretic coincidence and common fixed-point results in extended rectangular *b*—Metric spaces with applications. *Symmetry* **2022**, *14*, 1588. [CrossRef]
2. Licea, G.S. Sufficiency for weak minima in optimal control subject to mixed constraints. *Symmetry* **2022**, *14*, 1520. [CrossRef]
3. Alansari, M.; Ali, M.U. Abstraction of interpolative Reich-Rus Ćirić-type contractions and simplest proof technique. *Symmetry* **2022**, *14*, 1504. [CrossRef]
4. Hammad, H.A.; Zayed, M. Solving a system of differential equations with infinite delay by using tripled fix point techniques on graphs. *Symmetry* **2022**, *14*, 1388. [CrossRef]
5. Stojiljcović, V.; Radojević, S.; Çetin, E.; Čavić, V.S.; Radenović, S. Sharp bounds for trigonometric and hyperbolic functions with applications to fractional calculus. *Symmetry* **2022**, *14*, 1260. [CrossRef]
6. Lai, K.K.; Mishra, S.K.; Bisht, J.; Hassan, M. Hermite-Hadamard type inclusions for interval-valued coordinated preinvex functions. *Symmetry* **2022**, *14*, 771. [CrossRef]
7. Khan, M.B.; Zaini, H.G.; Treanţă, S.; Santos-Garcia, G.; Macias-Diaz, J.E.; Soliman, M.S. Fractional calculus for convex functions in interval-valued settings and inequalities. *Symmetry* **2022**, *14*, 341. [CrossRef]
8. Khan, M.B.; Zaini, H.G.; Macias-Diaz, J.E.; Treanţă, S.; Soliman, M.S. Some fuzzy Riemann-Louville fractional integral inequalities for preinvex fuzzy interval-valued functions. *Symmetry* **2022**, *14*, 313. [CrossRef]
9. Lai, K.K.; Hassan, M.; Maurya, J.K.; Singh, J.K.; Mishra, S.K. Multiobjective convex optimization in real Banach space. *Symmetry* **2021**, *13*, 2148. [CrossRef]
10. Liu, Y.; Ouyang, B. The well posedness for nonhomogeneous Boussinesq equations. *Symmetry* **2021**, *13*, 2110. [CrossRef]
11. Olteanu, O. On special properties for continuous convex operators and related linear operators. *Symmetry* **2022**, *14*, 1390. [CrossRef]
12. Niculescu, C.P.; Olteanu, O. From the Hahn-Banach extension theorem to the isotonicity of convex functions and the majorization theory. *Rev. R. Acad. Cienc. Exactas Fis. Nat.* **2020**, *114*, 171. [CrossRef]
13. Cristescu, R. *Ordered Vector Spaces and Linear Operators*; Academiei: Bucharest, Romania; Abacus Press: Tunbridge Wells, UK, 1976.
14. Haviland, E.K. On the momentum problem for distributions in more than one dimension. *Am. J. Math.* **1936**, *58*, 164–168. [CrossRef]
15. Akhiezer, N.I. *The Classical Moment Problem and Some Related Questions in Analysis*; Oliver and Boyd: Edinburgh, UK, 1965.
16. Schmüdgen, K. The Moment Problem. In *Graduate Texts in Mathematics*; Springer International Publishing AG: Cham, Switzerland, 2017.
17. Kutateladze, S.S. Convex operators. *Russ. Math. Surv.* **1979**, *34*, 181–214. [CrossRef]
18. Rudin, W. *Real and Complex Analysis*, 3rd ed.; McGraw-Hill Book Company: Singapore, 1987.
19. Marshall, M. Polynomials non-negative on a strip. *Proc. Am. Math. Soc.* **2010**, *138*, 1559–1567. [CrossRef]
20. Berg, C.; Christensen, J.P.R.; Jensen, C.U. A remark on the multidimensional moment problem. *Math. Ann.* **1979**, *243*, 163–169. [CrossRef]
21. Berg, C.; Christensen, J.P.R.; Ressel, P. *Harmonic Analysis on Semigroups*; Theory of Positive Definite and Related Functions; Springer: New York, NY, USA, 1984.
22. Berg, C.; Thill, M. Rotation invariant moment problems. *Acta Math.* **1991**, *167*, 207–227. [CrossRef]
23. Berg, C.; Durán, A.J. The fixed point for a transformation of Hausdorff moment sequences and iteration of a rational function. *Math. Scand.* **2008**, *103*, 11–39. [CrossRef]
24. Fuglede, B. The multidimensional moment problem. *Exp. Math.* **1983**, *1*, 47–65.
25. Cassier, G. Problèmes des moments sur un compact de $\mathbb{R}^n$ et décomposition des polynômes à plusieurs variables (Moment problems on a compact subset of $\mathbb{R}^n$ and decomposition of polynomials of several variables). *J. Funct. Anal.* **1984**, *58*, 254–266. [CrossRef]

26. Schmüdgen, K. The K-moment problem for compact semi-algebraic sets. *Math. Ann.* **1991**, *289*, 203–206. [CrossRef]
27. Putinar, M. Positive polynomials on compact semi-algebraic sets. *IU Math. J.* **1993**, *42*, 969–984. [CrossRef]
28. Putinar, M.; Vasilescu, F.H. Problème des moments sur les compacts semi-algébriques (The moment problem on semi-algebraic compacts). *Comptes Rendus Acad. Sci. Paris Ser. I* **1996**, *323*, 787–791.
29. Vasilescu, F.H. Spectral measures and moment problems. In *Spectral Analysis and Its Applications (Ion Colojoară Anniversary Volume)*; Theta: Bucharest, Romania, 2003; pp. 173–215.
30. Gosse, L.; Runborg, O. Resolution of the finite Markov moment problem. *Comptes Rendus Acad. Sci. Paris* **2005**, *341*, 775–780. [CrossRef]
31. Gosse, L.; Runborg, O. Existence, uniqueness, and a constructive solution algorithm for a class of finite Markov moment problems. *SIAM J. Appl. Math.* **2008**, *68*, 16181640. [CrossRef]
32. Tagliani, A. Maximum entropy solutions and moment problem in unbounded domains. *Appl. Math. Lett.* **2003**, *16*, 519–524. [CrossRef]
33. Inverardi, P.L.N.; Tagliani, A. Stieltjies and Hamburger reduced moment problem when MaxEnt solution does not exist. *Mathematics* **2021**, *9*, 309. [CrossRef]
34. Stochel, J. Solving the truncated moment problem solves the full moment problem. *Glasg. Math. J.* **2001**, *43*, 335–341. [CrossRef]
35. Lemnete, L. An operator-valued moment problem. *Proc. Am. Math. Soc.* **1991**, *112*, 1023–1028. [CrossRef]
36. Lemnete-Ninulescu, L.; Zlătescu, A. Some new aspects of the L-moment problem. *Rev. Roum. Math. Pures Appl.* **2010**, *55*, 197–204.
37. Cobzaş, Ş. Geometric properties of Banach spaces and the existence of nearest and farthest points. *Abstr. Appl. Anal.* **2005**, *2005*, 424030. [CrossRef]
38. Cobzaş, Ş. Ekeland variational principle and its equivalents in T_1 quasi-uniform spaces. *Optimization* **2022**, 1–32. [CrossRef]
39. Pakkaranang, N.; Kumam, P.; Cho, Y.J. Proximal point algorithms for solving convex minimization problem and common fixed points of asymptotically quasi-nonexpansive mappings in in CAT(0) spaces with convergenece analysis. *Numer Algorithms* **2018**, *78*, 827–845. [CrossRef]
40. Dong, Q.-L.; Cho, Y.J.; Rassias, T.M. The projection and contraction methods for finding common solutions for variational inequalitiy problems. *Optim. Lett.* **2018**, *12*, 1871–1896. [CrossRef]
41. Sahu, D.R.; Cho, Y.J.; Dong, Q.L.; Kashyap, M.R.; Li, X.H. Inertial relaxed *CQ* algorithms for solving a split feasibility problem in Hilbert spaces. *Numer Algorithms* **2021**, *87*, 1075–1095. [CrossRef]
42. Krein, M.G.; Nudelman, A.A. *Markov Moment Problem and Extremal Problems*; American Mathematical Society: Providence, RI, USA, 1977.
43. Olteanu, O. Application de théorèmes de prolongement d'opérateurs linéaires au problème des moments e à une generalization d'un théorème de Mazur-Orlicz (Applications of theorems on extension of linear operators to the moment problem and to a generalization of Mazur-Orlicz theorem). *Comptes Rendus Acad. Sci. Paris* **1991**, *313*, 739–742.
44. Stoyanov, J.M.; Lin, G.D.; Kopanov, P. New checkable conditions for moment determinacy of probability distributions. *SIAM Theory Probab. Appl.* **2020**, *65*, 497–509. [CrossRef]
45. Olteanu, O. From Hahn-Banach type theorems to the Markov moment problem, sandwich theorems and further applications. *Mathematics* **2020**, *8*, 1328. [CrossRef]
46. Olteanu, O. Polynomial approximation on unbounded subsets, Markov moment problem and other applications. *Mathematics* **2020**, *8*, 1654. [CrossRef]
47. Olteanu, O. On Markov moment problem and related results. *Symmetry* **2021**, *13*, 986. [CrossRef]
48. Olteanu, O. On Hahn-Banach theorem and some of its applications. *Open Math.* **2022**, *20*, 366–390. [CrossRef]
49. Olteanu, O. *Convexity, Extension of Linear Operators, Approximation and Applications*; Cambridge Scholars Publishing: Newcastle upon Tyne, UK; Lady Stephenson Library: Newcastle upon Tyne, UK, 2022.

symmetry

Article

Relation-Theoretic Coincidence and Common Fixed Point Results in Extended Rectangular b-Metric Spaces with Applications

Yan Sun [1] and Xiaolan Liu [1,2,*]

1 College of Mathematics and Statistics, Sichuan University of Science and Engineering, Zigong 643000, China; 320070108107@stu.suse.edu.cn
2 South Sichuan Center for Applied Mathematics, Zigong 643000, China
* Correspondence: xiaolanliu@suse.edu.cn or stellalwp@163.com

Abstract: The objective of this paper is to obtain new relation-theoretic coincidence and common fixed point results for some mappings F and g via hybrid contractions and auxiliary functions in extended rectangular b-metric spaces, which improve the existing results and give some relevant results. Finally, some nontrivial examples and applications to justify the main results.

Keywords: coincidence point; common fixed point; relation-theoretic; auxiliary functions; hybrid contractions; extended rectangular b-metric space

MSC: 47H10; 54H25

Citation: Sun, Y.; Liu, X. Relation-Theoretic Coincidence and Common Fixed Point Results in Extended Rectangular b-Metric Spaces with Applications. *Symmetry* **2022**, *14*, 1588. https://doi.org/10.3390/sym14081588

Academic Editors: Savin Treanta and Juan Luis García Guirao

Received: 30 June 2022
Accepted: 28 July 2022
Published: 2 August 2022

1. Introduction and Preliminaries

Throughout the article, we denote, by $\mathbb{R}$, the set of all real numbers; by $\mathbb{R}_+$, the set of all non-negative real numbers; and by $\mathbb{N}$, the set of all non-negative integers. At the beginning, we retrace several known metric-type spaces, which will be useful in the following.

In 1993, Czerwik [1] formally introduced and studied this interesting generalized metric space named b-metric space . Since then, many scholars have extended and developed fixed point theorems in b-metric spaces. Recent studies of fixed point theorems in b-metric spaces can be seen in [2–4].

Definition 1 ([1]). *Let $\Omega \neq \emptyset$ and $s \geqslant 1$ be a given real number. If a function $d : \Omega \times \Omega \to \mathbb{R}_+$ satisfies the following conditions:*
(d_1) $d(u,v) = 0$ *if and only if* $u = v$;
(d_2) $d(u,v) = d(v,u)$, *for all* $u, v \in \Omega$;
(d_3) $d(u,v) \leqslant s[d(u,w) + d(w,v)]$, *for all* $u, v, w \in \Omega$,
then d is said to be a b-metric, and (Ω, d) is said to be a b-metric space with the coefficient s.

In 2000, a generalized metric that replaces the triangular inequality with quadrilateral inequality was proposed by Branciari [5].

Definition 2 ([5]). *Let $\Omega \neq \emptyset$. For all $u, v \in \Omega$ and all distinct points $w, t \in \Omega \setminus \{u, v\}$, if a function $d_r : \Omega \times \Omega \to [0, \infty)$ satisfies the following conditions:*
$(d1)$ $d_r(u,v) = 0 \Leftrightarrow u = v$;
$(d2)$ $d_r(u,v) = d_r(v,u)$; *and*
$(d3)$ $d_r(u,v) \leqslant d_r(u,w) + d_r(w,t) + d_r(t,v)$,
then d_r is said to be a rectangular metric and (Ω, d_r) is said to be a rectangular metric space (Branciari distance space).

In 2015, rectangular b-metric was raised by George et al. [6], which is a development of b-metric and rectangular metric.

Definition 3 ([6]). *Let $\Omega \neq \emptyset$ and $s \geqslant 1$ be a given real number. If, for all $u, v \in \Omega$ and for all distinct points $w, t \in \Omega \backslash \{u, v\}$, a function $d_{rb} : \Omega \times \Omega \to \mathbb{R}_+$ satisfies the following conditions:*

$(d_{rb}1)$ $d_{rb}(u, v) = 0$ *if and only if* $u = v$;

$(d_{rb}2)$ $d_{rb}(u, v) = d_{rb}(v, u)$; *and*

$(d_{rb}3)$ $d_{rb}(u, v) \leqslant s[d_{rb}(u, w) + d_{rb}(w, t) + d_{rb}(t, v)]$,

then d_{rb} is said to be a rectangular b-metric and (Ω, d_{rb}) is said to be a rectangular b-metric space with the coefficient s.

In 2017, a binary function proposed by Kamran et al. [7] was used to introduce a novel metric-type space.

Definition 4 ([7]). *Let $\Omega \neq \emptyset$ and $\theta : \Omega \times \Omega \to [1, \infty)$. A function $d_\theta : \Omega \times \Omega \to [0, \infty)$ is said to be an extended b-metric if it satisfies the following conditions:*

$(d_\theta 1)$ $d_\theta(u, v) = 0$ *if and only if* $u = v$;

$(d_\theta 2)$ $d_\theta(u, v) = d_\theta(v, u)$, *for all* $u, v \in \Omega$;

$(d_\theta 3)$ $d_\theta(u, v) \leqslant \theta(u, v)[d_\theta(u, w) + d_\theta(w, v)]$, *for all* $u, v, w \in \Omega$,

then (Ω, d_θ) is said to be an extended b-metric space with θ.

In 2019, inspired by [5,7], Asim et al. [8] presented a more generalized metric space called extended rectangular *b*-metric space(also extended Branciari *b*-distance in [9]).

Definition 5 ([8]). *Let $\Omega \neq \emptyset$ and $\xi : \Omega \times \Omega \to [1, \infty)$. A function $d_\xi : \Omega \times \Omega \to [0, \infty)$ is said to be an extended rectangular b-metric, if for all $u, v \in \Omega$ and all distinct points $w, t \in \Omega \setminus \{u, v\}$, d_ξ satisfies the following conditions:*

$(d_\xi 1)$ $d_\xi(u, v) = 0 \Leftrightarrow u = v$;

$(d_\xi 2)$ $d_\xi(u, v) = d_\xi(v, u)$; *and*

$(d_\xi 3)$ $d_\xi(u, v) \leqslant \xi(u, v)[d_\xi(u, w) + d_\xi(w, t) + d_\xi(t, v)]$,

then (Ω, d_ξ) is said to be an extended rectangular b-metric space.

Remark 1. *The relationship between these types of metric spaces are shown in Figure 1.*

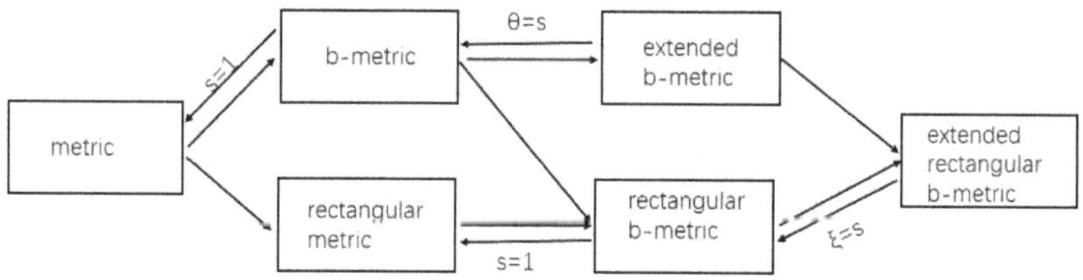

Figure 1. The relationship between these types of metric spaces.

Now, we review some topological properties of the extended rectangular *b*-metric space.

Definition 6 ([8]). *Let (Ω, d_ξ) be an extended rectangular b-metric space.*

(i) *a sequence $\{u_n\}$ in Ω is said to be a Cauchy sequence if* $\lim_{n,m\to\infty} d_\xi(u_n, u_m) = 0$;

(ii) *a sequence $\{u_n\}$ in Ω is said to be convergent to u if* $\lim_{n\to\infty} d_\xi(u_n, u) = 0$; *and*

(iii) *(Ω, d_ξ) is said to be complete if every Cauchy sequence in Ω convergent to some point in Ω.*

Next, we introduce the simulation function was introduced by Khojasteh et al. [10]. It plays an important role in recent studies on the fixed point theory, which has inspired many scholars. Some results via simulation functions can be referred to [11–14].

Definition 7 ([10]). *A function $\eta : \mathbb{R}_+ \times \mathbb{R}_+ \to \mathbb{R}$ is said to be a simulation function, if it satisfies the following conditions:*
$(\eta 1)$ $\eta(0,0) = 0$;
$(\eta 2)$ $\eta(u,v) < v - u$, for $u, v > 0$; *and which*
$(\eta 3)$ *if $\{u_n\}, \{v_n\}$ are sequences in $(0,\infty)$ such that $\lim_{n\to\infty} u_n = \lim_{n\to\infty} v_n > 0$, then*

$$\limsup_{n\to\infty} \eta(u_n, v_n) < 0.$$

We denote the set of all simulation functions by $\mathcal{Z}$.

Definition 8 ([10]). *Let (Ω, d) be a metric space, $F : \Omega \to \Omega$ be a mapping and $\eta \in \mathcal{Z}$. Then, T is called a $\mathcal{Z}$-contraction with respect to η if the following condition holds:*

$$\eta(d(Fu, Fv), d(u,v)) \geqslant 0,$$

where $u, v \in \Omega$, with $u \neq v$.

Theorem 1 ([10]). *Every $\mathcal{Z}$-contraction on a complete metric space has a unique fixed point.*

Another new variant of Banach contraction principle with binary relation is proposed by Alam and Imdad [15] on complete metric spaces. In this case, the contraction condition is relatively weaker than the usual contraction, since it only needs to keep those elements that are related under the binary relation, not the whole space. With the introduction of binary relations, the study of fixed point theory is more colorful.

For instance, Al-Sulami et al. [15] raised $(\theta, \Re)$ contraction by binary relation and applied it to nonlinear matrix equations, Alfaqih et al. [16] proposed $(F, \Re)_g$-contraction in the metric space with a binary relation and investigated the existence and uniqueness of a solution of integral equation of Volterra type, Zadal and Sarwar [17] obtained common fixed point for two mappings in the case of binary relation. Now, we recall some basic definitions of binary relations, which play an important role in our main results.

Definition 9 ([18]). *Let $\Omega \neq \emptyset$ and $\Re$ be a binary relation on Ω. For any $u\Re v$ or $(u,v) \in \Re$, where $u, v \in \Omega$, we say that "u is $\Re$-related to v" or "u relates to v under $\Re$".*

Definition 10 ([18]). *Let $\Omega \neq \emptyset$, $\Re$ be a binary relation on Ω and $F : \Omega \to \Omega$ be a mapping.*
(i) A sequence $\{u_n\}$ is called an $\Re$-preserving sequence if $u_n \Re u_{n+1}$, for all $n \in \mathbb{N}$.
(ii) A binary relation $\Re$ on Ω is said to be F-closed if $Fu\Re Fv$, whenever $u\Re v$.
(iii) A binary relation $\Re$ on Ω is said to be d-self-closed if for any sequence $\{u_n\} \subseteq \Omega$ such that $\{u_n\}$ is $\Re$-preserving with $u_n \to u \in \Omega$, there exists a subsequence $\{u_{n_k}\}$ of $\{u_n\}$ such that $u_{n_k}\Re u$ or $u\Re u_{n_k}$, for all $k \in \mathbb{N}$.
(iv) A binary relation $\Re$ on Ω is said to be transitive if $u\Re v$ and $v\Re w$ implies that $u\Re w$.

Definition 11 ([18]). *For $u, v \in \Omega$, a path of length $p \in \mathbb{N}$ in $\Re$ from u to v is a finite sequence $\{u_0, u_1, \cdots, u_p\}$ such that $u_0 = u$, $u_p = v$ and $u_i \Re u_{i+1}$ for all $i \in \{0, 1, \cdots, p-1\}$.*

In addition, Alam and Imdad [19] utilized some relatively weaker notions to prove results on the existence and uniqueness of coincidence points involving a pair of mappings defined on a metric space endowed with an arbitrary binary relation. For completeness, we first review some of the relevant definitions that are known.

Definition 12 ([19]). *Let (Ω, d) be a metric space , $\Re$ be a binary relation on Ω and $F, g : \Omega \to \Omega$ be two mappings.*

(i) The set Ω is $\Re$-complete if every $\Re$-preserving Cauchy sequence in Ω converges to a limit in Ω.

(ii) A binary relation $\Re$ on Ω is said to be (F,g)-closed if $Fu\Re Fv$, whenever $gu\Re gv$.

(iii) A binary relation $\Re$ on Ω is said to be (g,d)-self-closed if for any sequence $\{u_n\} \subseteq \Omega$ such that $\{u_n\}$ is $\Re$-preserving with $\lim_{n\to\infty} u_n = u$, there exists a subsequence $\{u_{n_k}\}$ of u_n such that $gu_{n_k}\Re gu$ or $gu\Re gu_{n_k}$, for all $k \in \mathbb{N}$.

(iv) F is $\Re$-continuous at $u \in \Omega$ if, for any $\Re$-preserving sequence, such that $\lim_{n\to\infty} u_n = u$, we have $\lim_{n\to\infty} Fu_n = Fu$. Moreover, F is called $\Re$-continuous if it is $\Re$-continuous at each point of Ω.

(v) F is $(g,\Re)$-continuous at x if for any sequence $\{u_n\} \subseteq \Omega$ such that $\{gu_n\}$ is $\Re$-preserving with $\lim_{n\to\infty} gu_n = gu$, we have $\lim_{n\to\infty} Fu_n = Fu$. Moreover, F is called $(g,\Re)$-continuous if it is $(g,\Re)$-continuous at each point of Ω.

(vi) (F,g) is $\Re$-compatible if for any sequence $\{u_n\} \subseteq \Omega$ such that $\{gu_n\}$ and $\{Fu_n\}$ are $\Re$-preserving and $\lim_{n\to\infty} gu_n = \lim_{n\to\infty} Fu_n = u \in \Omega$, we have $\lim_{n\to\infty} d(Fgu_n, gFu_n) = 0$.

(vii) A subset $E \subseteq \Omega$ is said to be $\Re$-connected, if for any $u, v \in E$, there exists a path in $\Re$ from u to v.

Definition 13 ([19])**.** *Let (Ω, d) be a metric space and F and g are two self-mappings on Ω. Then,*

(i) a point $u \in \Omega$ is called a coincidence point of F and g if $gu = Fu$;

(ii) if $u \in \Omega$ is a coincidence point of F and g, and there exists a point $\bar{u}$ such that $\bar{u} = gu = Fu$, then $\bar{u}$ is called a point of coincidence of F and g;

(iii) if $u \in \Omega$ is a coincidence fixed point of F and g and $u = gu = Fu$, then u is called a common fixed point of F and g; and

(iv) F and g are called weakly compatible if for all $u \in \Omega$ with $Fu = gu$ implies $F(gu) = g(Fu)$.

Theorem 2 ([19])**.** *Let (Ω, d) be a metric space with a binary relation $\Re$, and $\triangle$ be an $\Re$-complete subspace of Ω. F and g are two self-mappings on Ω, which satisfy*

$$d(Fu, Fv) \leqslant kd(gu, gv), \text{ for all } gu\Re gv,$$

where $k \in (0,1)$. In addition, if F and g satisfy the following conditions:

(i) there exists $v_0 \in \Omega$ such that $gv_0\Re Fv_0$;

(ii) $\Re$ is (F,g)-closed;

(iii) $F(\Omega) \subseteq (\triangle \cap g(\Omega))$; and

(iv) (a) $\triangle \subseteq g(\Omega)$ is $\Re$-complete; and

(b) one of the conditions satisfies:

(1) F is $(g,\Re)$-continuous;

(2) F and g are continuous; and

(3) $\Re|_\Omega$ is d-self-closed,

or alternatively,

(iv′) (a′) F and g are $\Re$-compatible;

(b′) g is $\Re$-continuous; and

(c) one of the conditions satisfies:

(1′) f is $\Re$-continuous; and

(2′) $\Re$ is (g,d)-self-closed,

then F and g have a coincidence point.

The following lemma plays a crucial role in proving the main results of this paper.

Lemma 1 ([19])**.** *Let Ω be a nonempty set and $g : \Omega \to \Omega$. Then, there exists a subset E of Ω such that $g(E) = g(\Omega)$ and $g : E \to E$ is one to one.*

Through the above inspiration, we can understand that the extended rectangular b-metric spaces are a type of generalized metric spaces including metric spaces, rectangular metric spaces and b-metric spaces. As far as we know, in metric space, rectangular metric and b-metric space, there are also some contractions that have not been studied; thus, we intend to study the coincidence point and common fixed point results for some mappings F and g in the extended rectangular b-metric with a binary relation $\Re$, which develops the results of [1,6,8,14,18–23].

2. Main Results

In this section, we introduce an auxiliary function before we begin our discussion of the main results. Let Ψ be the set of all increasing functions $\psi : [0,\infty) \to [0,\infty)$ satisfying the following condition: $\lim_{n\to\infty} \psi^n(t) = 0$, for all $t > 0$.

Remark 2. *If $\psi \in \Psi$, then $\psi(t) < t$, for all $t > 0$.*

Theorem 3. *Let (Ω, d_ξ) be an extended rectangular b-metric space with a binary relation $\Re$ such that $\Re$ is (F,g)-closed, and $\triangle$ be an $\Re$-complete subspace of Ω. F and g are two self-mappings on Ω, which satisfy $F(\Omega) \subseteq (\triangle \cap g(\Omega))$ and*

$$\eta(d_\xi(Fu,Fv), \psi(M_{F,g}(u,v))) \geqslant 0, \text{ for all } gu\Re gv, \tag{1}$$

where $\eta \in \mathcal{Z}$, $\psi \in \Psi$ and

$$M_{F,g}(u,v) = \max\{d_\xi(gu,gv), d_\xi(gu,Fu), d_\xi(Fv,gv), \frac{d_\xi(gv,Fv)(1+d_\xi(gu,Fu))}{1+d_\xi(gu,gv)}, \frac{d_\xi(gu,Fu)(1+d_\xi(gv,Fv))}{1+d_\xi(gu,gv)}\}.$$

In addition, if F and g satisfy the following conditions:
(i) there exists $v_0 \in \Omega$ such that $gv_0\Re Fv_0$ and $gv_0\Re Fv_1$, where v_1 is such that $gv_1 = Fv_0$;
(ii) for v_0 in (i), we have $\limsup_{n\to\infty} \frac{\psi^{n+1}(t)}{\psi^n(t)} \xi(u_{n+1}, u_p) < 1$, where for all $p, n \in \mathbb{N}$, $u_n = Fv_n = gv_{n+1}$ and $t \in (0, d_\xi(u_0,u_1)]$ with $u_0 \neq u_1$;
(iii) (a) $\triangle \subseteq g(\Omega)$;
(b) F is $(g,\Re)$-continuous or F and g are continuous or $\Re|_{g(\Omega)}$ is d_ξ-self-closed and $d_\xi(gw,Fw) > 0$, where $w \in \Omega$, such that

$$\limsup_{t\to d_\xi(gw,Fw)} \psi(t) < \frac{d_\xi(gw,Fw)}{\xi(Fw,gw)} \text{ or } \limsup_{t\to d_\xi(gw,Fw)} \psi(t) < \frac{d_\xi(gw,Fw)}{\xi(gw,Fw)};$$

or alternatively,
(iii') if d_ξ is continuous, (F,g) is $\Re$-compatible, and g and F are $\Re$-continuous, then F and g have a coincidence point.

Proof. For $gu\Re gv$, by (1) and $(\eta 1)$, it is easy to show that

$$d_\xi(Fu,Fv) \leqslant \psi(M_{F,g}(u,v)), \text{ for } M_{F,g}(u,v) \neq 0. \tag{2}$$

Considering $F(\Omega) \subseteq (\triangle \cap g(\Omega))$, we deduce that $F(\Omega) \subseteq g(\Omega)$. Now, we define two sequences $\{u_n\}$ and $\{v_n\}$ by $u_n = Fv_n = gv_{n+1}$. By $gv_0\Re Fv_0$ and $\Re$ is (F,g)-closed, it follows that

$$gv_0\Re Fv_0 \Rightarrow gv_0\Re gv_1 \Rightarrow Fv_0\Re Fv_1 \Rightarrow gv_1\Re gv_2. \tag{3}$$

Combining (3) with $\Re$ is (F,g)-closed, we have

$$gv_1\Re gv_2 \Rightarrow Fv_1\Re Fv_2 \Rightarrow gv_2\Re gv_3. \tag{4}$$

Repeating the above process, we can find

$$Fv_n\Re Fv_{n+1} \tag{5}$$

and

$$gv_n \Re g v_{n+1}. \tag{6}$$

By $gv_0 \Re F v_1$ and $\Re$ is (F, g)-closed , we obtain

$$gv_0 \Re F v_1 \Rightarrow gv_0 \Re g v_2 \Rightarrow F v_0 \Re F v_2 \Rightarrow g v_1 \Re g v_3. \tag{7}$$

Taking (7), (i) and $\Re$ is (F, g)-closed in mind, we find

$$gv_1 \Re g v_3 \Rightarrow F v_1 \Re F v_3 \Rightarrow g v_2 \Re g v_4. \tag{8}$$

Repeating the above process, it follows that

$$F v_n \Re F v_{n+2} \tag{9}$$

and

$$g v_n \Re g v_{n+2}. \tag{10}$$

If there exists $n_0 \in \mathbb{N}$ such that $u_{n_0} = u_{n_0+1}$, that is, $gv_{n_0+1} = Fv_{n_0+1}$, then v_{n_0+1} is the coincidence point of F and g. The proof is complete.

Now, suppose that $u_n \neq u_{n+1}$, for all $n \in \mathbb{N}$. Let $u = v_n$, $v = v_{n+1}$ in (2), by (6), we have

$$\begin{aligned}
d_\xi(u_n, u_{n+1}) &= d_\xi(Fv_n, Fv_{n+1}) \\
&\leqslant \psi(M_{F,g}(v_n, v_{n+1})) \\
&= \psi(\max\{d_\xi(gv_n, gv_{n+1}), d_\xi(gv_n, Fv_n), d_\xi(Fv_{n+1}, gv_{n+1}), \\
&\quad \frac{d_\xi(gv_{n+1}, Fv_{n+1})(1 + d_\xi(gv_n, Fv_n))}{1 + d_\xi(gv_n, gv_{n+1})}, \\
&\quad \frac{d_\xi(gv_n, Fv_n)(1 + d_\xi(gv_{n+1}, Fv_{n+1}))}{1 + d_\xi(gv_n, gv_{n+1})}\}) \\
&= \psi(\max\{d_\xi(u_{n-1}, u_n), d_\xi(u_{n-1}, u_n), d_\xi(u_{n+1}, u_n), \\
&\quad \frac{d_\xi(u_n, u_{n+1})(1 + d_\xi(u_{n-1}, u_n))}{1 + d_\xi(u_{n-1}, u_n)}, \\
&\quad \frac{d_\xi(u_{n-1}, u_n)(1 + d_\xi(u_n, u_{n+1}))}{1 + d_\xi(u_{n-1}, u_n)}\}) \\
&= \psi(\max\{d_\xi(u_{n-1}, u_n), d_\xi(u_n, u_{n+1})).
\end{aligned} \tag{11}$$

If

$$\max\{d_\xi(u_{n-1}, u_n), d_\xi(u_n, u_{n+1})\} = d_\xi(u_n, u_{n+1}),$$

by (11) and Remark 2, we gain

$$d_\xi(u_n, u_{n+1}) \leqslant \psi(d_\xi(u_n, u_{n+1})) < d_\xi(u_n, u_{n+1}).$$

This is a contradiction. Thus,

$$\max\{d_\xi(u_{n-1}, u_n), d_\xi(u_n, u_{n+1})\} = d_\xi(u_{n-1}, u_n).$$

In view of (11), we can deduce that

$$d_\xi(u_n, u_{n+1}) \leqslant \psi(d_\xi(u_{n-1}, u_n)). \tag{12}$$

By (12), we acquire

$$d_\xi(u_n, u_{n+1}) \leqslant \psi(d_\xi(u_{n-1}, u_n)) \leqslant \cdots \leqslant \psi^n(d_\xi(u_0, u_1)). \tag{13}$$

Taking the limits on the both sides of (13), we have

$$\lim_{n\to\infty} d_\xi(u_n, u_{n+1}) = 0. \tag{14}$$

Now, we show that $u_n \neq u_m$, for all $n \neq m \in \mathbb{N}$. If there exist $n_0, m_0 \in \mathbb{N}$ such that $u_{n_0} = u_{m_0}$ with $n_0 < m_0$, we have

$$\begin{aligned}
d_\xi(u_{n_0}, u_{n_0+1}) &= d_\xi(u_{n_0}, Fv_{n_0+1}) \\
&= d_\xi(u_{m_0}, Fv_{n_0+1}) \\
&= d_\xi(Fv_{m_0}, Fv_{n_0+1}) \\
&\leqslant \psi(M_{F,g}(v_{m_0}, v_{n_0+1})) \\
&= \psi(\max\{d_\xi(gv_{m_0}, gv_{n_0+1}), d_\xi(gv_{m_0}, Fv_{m_0}), d_\xi(Fv_{n_0+1}, gv_{n_0+1}), \\
&\quad \frac{d_\xi(gv_{n_0+1}, Fv_{n_0+1})(1 + d_\xi(gv_{m_0}, Fv_{m_0}))}{1 + d_\xi(gv_{m_0}, gv_{n_0+1})}, \\
&\quad \frac{d_\xi(gv_{m_0}, Fv_{m_0})(1 + d_\xi(gv_{n_0+1}, Fv_{n_0+1}))}{1 + d_\xi(gv_{m_0}, gv_{n_0+1})}\}) \\
&= \psi(\max\{d_\xi(u_{m_0-1}, u_{m_0}), d_\xi(u_{m_0-1}, u_{m_0}), d_\xi(u_{n_0+1}, u_{n_0}), \\
&\quad \frac{d_\xi(u_{n_0}, u_{n_0+1})(1 + d_\xi(u_{m_0-1}, u_{m_0}))}{1 + d_\xi(u_{m_0-1}, u_{m_0})}, \\
&\quad \frac{d_\xi(u_{m_0-1}, u_{m_0})(1 + d_\xi(u_{n_0}, u_{n_0+1}))}{1 + d_\xi(u_{m_0-1}, u_{m_0})}\}) \\
&= \psi(d_\xi(u_{n_0}, u_{n_0+1}) \\
&< d_\xi(u_{n_0}, u_{n_0+1}),
\end{aligned}$$

which contradicts $d_\xi(u_{n_0}, u_{n_0+1}) > 0$. Thus, $u_n \neq u_m$, for all $n,\ m \in \mathbb{N}$.

Letting $u = v_n, v = v_{n+2}$ in (2), by (10), we obtain

$$\begin{aligned}
d_\xi(u_n, u_{n+2}) &= d_\xi(Fv_n, Fv_{n+2}) \\
&\leqslant \psi(M_{F,g}(v_n, v_{n+2})) \\
&= \psi(\max\{d_\xi(gv_n, gv_{n+2}), d_\xi(gv_n, Fv_n), d_\xi(Fv_{n+2}, gv_{n+2}), \\
&\quad \frac{d_\xi(gv_{n+2}, Fv_{n+2})(1 + d_\xi(gv_n, Fv_n))}{1 + d_\xi(gv_n, gv_{n+2})}, \\
&\quad \frac{d_\xi(gv_n, Fv_n)(1 + d_\xi(gv_{n+2}, Fv_{n+2}))}{1 + d_\xi(gv_n, gv_{n+2})}\}) \\
&= \psi(\max\{d_\xi(u_{n-1}, u_{n+1}), d_\xi(u_{n-1}, u_n), d_\xi(u_{n+2}, u_{n+1}), \\
&\quad \frac{d_\xi(u_{n+2}, u_{n+1})(1 + d_\xi(u_{n-1}, u_n))}{1 + d_\xi(u_{n-1}, u_{n+1})}, \\
&\quad \frac{d_\xi(u_{n-1}, u_n)(1 + d_\xi(u_{n+2}, u_{n+1}))}{1 + d_\xi(u_{n-1}, u_{n+1})}\}) \\
&\leqslant \psi(\max\{d_\xi(u_{n-1}, u_{n+1}), d_\xi(u_{n-1}, u_n), \\
&\quad \frac{d_\xi(u_{n-1}, u_n)(1 + d_\xi(u_{n-1}, u_n))}{1 + d_\xi(u_{n-1}, u_{n+1})}\}) \\
&= \psi(A_n),
\end{aligned} \tag{15}$$

where

$$A_n = \max\{d_\xi(u_{n-1}, u_{n+1}), d_\xi(u_{n-1}, u_n), \frac{d_\xi(u_{n-1}, u_n)(1 + d_\xi(u_{n-1}, u_n))}{1 + d_\xi(u_{n-1}, u_{n+1})}\}.$$

If $A_n = d_\xi(u_{n-1}, u_{n+1})$.

By (15), we have

$$d_\xi(u_n,u_{n+2}) \leqslant \psi(d_\xi(u_{n-1},u_{n+1})) \leqslant \cdots \leqslant \psi^n(d_\xi(u_0,u_2)). \tag{16}$$

If $A_n = d_\xi(u_{n-1},u_n)$, from (13) and (15), we gain

$$d_\xi(u_n,u_{n+2}) \leqslant \psi(d_\xi(u_{n-1},u_n)) \leqslant \psi^{n-1}(d_\xi(u_0,u_1)). \tag{17}$$

If $A_n = \frac{d_\xi(u_{n-1},u_n)(1+d_\xi(u_{n-1},u_n))}{1+d_\xi(u_{n-1},u_{n+1})}$, combining (13), (15) with Remark 2, we acquire

$$\begin{aligned} d_\xi(u_n,u_{n+2}) &\leqslant \psi(\frac{d_\xi(u_{n-1},u_n)(1+d_\xi(u_{n-1},u_n))}{1+d_\xi(u_{n-1},u_{n+1})}) \\ &< \frac{d_\xi(u_{n-1},u_n)(1+d_\xi(u_{n-1},u_n))}{1+d_\xi(u_{n-1},u_{n+1})} \\ &< d_\xi(u_{n-1},u_n)(1+d_\xi(u_{n-1},u_n)) \\ &\leqslant \psi^{n-1}(d_\xi(u_0,u_1))(1+\psi^{n-1}(d_\xi(u_0,u_1))). \end{aligned} \tag{18}$$

Taking the limits on the both sides of (16), (17) and (18), by $\lim_{n\to\infty}\psi^n(t)=0$, for all $t>0$, we find

$$\lim_{n\to\infty} d_\xi(u_n,u_{n+2}) = 0. \tag{19}$$

Now, we show that $\{u_n\}$ is a Cauchy sequence. The next discussion can be divided into the following cases.

Case I: when $m = n+2k+1$ with $k \geqslant 1$. By $(d_\xi 3)$ and (13), for all $n \in \mathbb{N}$, we have

$$\begin{aligned} d_\xi(u_n,u_{n+2k+1}) &\leqslant \xi(u_n,u_{n+2k+1})[(d_\xi(u_n,u_{n+1})+d_\xi(u_{n+1},u_{n+2})+d_\xi(u_{n+2},u_{n+2k+1})] \\ &= \xi(u_n,u_{n+2k+1})[d_\xi(u_n,u_{n+1})+d_\xi(u_{n+1},u_{n+2})]+\xi(u_n,u_{n+2k+1})d_\xi(u_{n+2},u_{n+2k+1}) \\ &\leqslant \xi(u_n,u_{n+2k+1})(d_n+d_{n+1})+\xi(u_n,u_{n+2k+1})\xi(u_{n+2},u_{n+2k+1})(d_{n+2}+d_{n+3}) \\ &\quad +\xi(u_n,u_{n+2k+1})\xi(u_{n+2},u_{n+2k+1})d_\xi(u_{n+2},u_{n+2k+1}) \\ &\leqslant \xi(u_n,u_{n+2k+1})(d_n+d_{n+1})+\xi(u_n,u_{n+2k+1})\xi(u_{n+2},u_{n+2k+1})(d_{n+2}+d_{n+3})+\cdots \\ &\quad +\xi(u_n,u_{n+2k+1})\xi(u_{n+2},u_{n+2k+1})\cdots\xi(u_{n+2k-2},u_{n+2k+1})(d_{n+2k-2}+d_{n+2k-1}) \\ &\quad +\xi(u_n,u_{n+2k+1})\xi(u_{n+2},u_{n+2k+1})\cdots\xi(u_{n+2k-2},u_{n+2k+1})d_\xi(u_{n+2k},u_{n+2k+1}) \\ &\leqslant \xi(u_n,u_{n+2k+1})(\psi^n(G_0)+\psi^{n+1}(G_0))+\xi(u_{n+2},u_{n+2m+1})(\psi^{n+2}(G_0)+\psi^{n+3}(G_0))+\cdots \\ &\quad +\xi(u_n,u_{n+2k+1})\xi(u_{n+2},u_{n+2k+1})\cdots\xi(u_{n+2k-2},u_{n+2k+1})(\psi^{n+2k-2}(G_0)+\psi^{n+2k-1}(G_0)) \\ &\quad +\xi(u_n,u_{n+2k+1})\xi(u_{n+2},u_{n+2k+1})\cdots\xi(u_{n+2k-2},u_{n+2k+1})\psi^{n+2k}(G_0) \\ &\leqslant \xi(u_0,u_{n+2k+1})\xi(u_1,u_{n+2k+1})\xi(u_2,u_{n+2k+1})\cdots\xi(u_n,u_{n+2k+1})[\psi^n(G_0) \\ &\quad +\xi(u_{n+1},u_{n+2k+1})\psi^{n+1}(G_0)]+\xi(u_0,u_{n+2k+1})\xi(u_1,u_{n+2k+1})\xi(u_2,u_{n+2k+1})\cdots \\ &\quad \times\xi(u_{n+2},u_{n+2k+1})[\psi^{n+2}(G_0)+\xi(u_{n+3},u_{n+2k+1})\psi^{n+3}(G_0)]+\cdots+\xi(u_0,u_{n+2k+1}) \\ &\quad \times\xi(u_1,u_{n+2k+1})\xi(u_2,u_{n+2k+1})\cdots\xi(u_{n+2k-2},u_{n+2k+1})[\psi^{n+2k-2}(G_0) \\ &\quad +\xi(u_{n+2k-1},u_{n+2k+1})\psi^{n+2k-1}(G_0)]+\xi(u_0,u_{n+2k+1})\xi(u_1,u_{n+2k+1})\xi(u_2,u_{n+2k+1}) \\ &\quad \times\cdots\xi(u_{n+2k},u_{n+2k+1})\psi^{n+2k}(G_0) \\ &= \sum_{i=n}^{n+2k}\psi^i(G_0)\prod_{j=0}^{i}\xi(u_j,u_{n+2k+1}), \end{aligned} \tag{20}$$

where $d_n = d_\xi(u_n,u_{n+1})$ and $\psi^n(G_0) = \psi^n(d_\xi(u_0,u_1))$, for all $n \in \mathbb{N}$. Let

$$S_n = \sum_{i=0}^{n}\psi^i(G_0)\prod_{j=0}^{i}\xi(u_j,u_{n+2k+1}).$$

By (20), we obtain

$$d_{\xi}(u_n, u_{n+2k+1}) \leqslant S_{n+2k} - S_{n-1}. \quad (21)$$

Suppose that $u_n = \psi^n(G_0) \prod_{j=0}^{n} \xi(u_j, u_{n+2k+1})$. We have

$$\frac{u_{n+1}}{u_n} = \frac{\psi^{n+1}(G_0) \prod_{j=0}^{n+1} \xi(u_j, u_{n+2k+1})}{\psi^n(G_0) \prod_{j=0}^{n} \xi(u_j, u_{n+2k+1})} = \frac{\psi^{n+1}(G_0)}{\psi^n(G_0)} \xi(u_{n+1}, u_{n+2k+1}).$$

By (ii) and Ratio test, we deduce that the series $\sum_{i=0}^{\infty} \psi^i(G_0) \prod_{j=0}^{i} \xi(u_j, u_{n+2k+1})$ is convergent. Letting $n \to \infty$ in (21), we have

$$d_{\xi}(u_n, u_m) \to 0,\ n \to \infty.$$

Case II: when $m = n + 2k$ with $k \geqslant 1$. By $(d_{\xi}3)$ and (13), for all $n \in \mathbb{N}$, we obtain

$$\begin{aligned}
d_{\xi}(u_n, u_{n+2k}) &\leqslant \xi(u_n, u_{n+2k})[(d_{\xi}(u_n, u_{n+2}) + d_{\xi}(u_{n+2}, u_{n+3}) + d_{\xi}(u_{n+3}, u_{n+2k})] \\
&= \xi(u_n, u_{n+2k})[d_{\xi}(u_n, u_{n+2}) + d_{\xi}(u_{n+2}, u_{n+3})] + \xi(u_n, u_{n+2k}) d_{\xi}(u_{n+3}, u_{n+2k}) \\
&\leqslant \xi(u_n, u_{n+2k})(d_{\xi}(u_n, u_{n+2}) + d_{n+2}) + \xi(u_n, u_{n+2k})\xi(u_{n+3}, u_{n+2k})(d_{n+3} + d_{n+4}) \\
&\quad + \xi(u_n, u_{n+2k})\xi(u_{n+3}, u_{n+2k}) d_{\xi}(u_{n+5}, u_{n+2k}) \\
&\leqslant \xi(u_n, u_{n+2k})(d_{\xi}(u_n, u_{n+2}) + d_{n+2}) + \xi(u_n, u_{n+2k})\xi(u_{n+3}, u_{n+2k})(d_{n+3} + d_{n+4}) + \cdots \\
&\quad + \xi(u_n, u_{n+2k})\xi(u_{n+3}, u_{n+2k}) \cdots \xi(u_{n+2k-3}, u_{n+2k})(d_{n+2k-3} + d_{n+2k-2} + d_{n+2k-1}) \\
&\leqslant \xi(u_n, u_{n+2k})(d_{\xi}(u_n, u_{n+2}) + \psi^{n+2}(G_0)) + \xi(x_n, u_{n+2k})\xi(u_{n+3}, u_{n+2k}) \\
&\quad (\psi^{n+3}(G_0) + \psi^{n+4}(G_0)) + \cdots + \xi(u_n, u_{n+2k}) \\
&\quad \xi(u_{n+3}, u_{n+2k}) \cdots \xi(u_{n+2k-3}, u_{n+2k})(\psi^{n+2k-3}(G_0) + \psi^{n+2k-2}(G_0) + \psi^{n+2k-1}(G_0)) \\
&< \xi(u_n, u_{n+2k}) d_{\xi}(u_n, u_{n+2}) + \xi(u_0, u_{n+2k})\xi(u_1, u_{n+2k})\xi(u_2, u_{n+2k}) \cdots \\
&\quad \xi(u_{n+2}, u_{n+2k})\psi^{n+2}(G_0) + \xi(u_0, u_{n+2k})\xi(u_1, u_{n+2k})\xi(x_2, u_{n+2k}) \cdots \\
&\quad \xi(u_{n+3}, u_{n+2k})[\psi^{n+3}(G_0) + \xi(u_{n+4}, u_{n+2k})\psi^{n+4}(G_0)] + \cdots + \\
&\quad \xi(u_0, u_{n+2k})\xi(u_1, u_{n+2k})\xi(u_2, u_{n+2k}) \cdots \xi(u_{n+2k-3}, u_{n+2k})[\psi^{n+2k-3}(G_0) \\
&\quad + \xi(u_{n+2k-2}, u_{n+2k})\psi^{n+2k-2}(G_0)] + \xi(u_0, u_{n+2k})\xi(u_1, u_{n+2k}) \\
&\quad \xi(u_2, u_{n+2k}) \cdots \xi(u_{n+2k-1}, u_{n+2k})\psi^{n+2k-1}(G_0) \\
&= \xi(u_n, u_{n+2k}) d_{\xi}(u_n, u_{n+2}) + \sum_{i=n+2}^{n+2k-1} \psi^i(G_0) \prod_{j=0}^{i} \xi(u_j, u_{n+2k}),
\end{aligned} \quad (22)$$

where $\psi^n(G_0) = \psi^n(d_{\xi}(u_0, u_1))$ and $d_n = d_{\xi}(u_n, u_{n+1})$. For all $n \in \mathbb{N}$, assume that

$$R_n = \sum_{i=0}^{n} \psi^i(G_0) \prod_{j=0}^{i} \xi(u_j, u_{n+2k}).$$

According to (22), we find

$$d_{\xi}(u_n, u_{n+2k}) < \xi(u_n, u_{n+2k}) d_{\xi}(u_n, u_{n+2}) + R_{n+2k-1} - R_{n+1}. \quad (23)$$

Now, let $w_n = \psi^n(G_0) \prod_{j=0}^{n} \xi(u_j, u_{n+2k})$. It follows that

$$\frac{w_{n+1}}{w_n} = \frac{\psi^{n+1}(G_0)\prod_{j=0}^{n+1}\xi(u_j, u_{n+2k})}{\psi^{n}(G_0)\prod_{j=0}^{n}\xi(u_j, u_{n+2k})} = \frac{\psi^{n+1}(G_0)}{\psi^{n}(G_0)}\xi(u_{n+1}, u_{n+2k}).$$

In a similar way as in thecase I, we deduce that the series $\sum_{i=0}^{\infty}\psi^i(G_0)\prod_{j=0}^{i}\xi(u_j, u_{n+2k})$ is convergent. Taking the limits on the both sides of (23), by (19), we have

$$d_\xi(u_n, u_m) \to 0, n \to \infty.$$

In both Cases, $\lim_{n,m\to\infty} d_\xi(u_n, u_m) = 0$.

Thus, $\{u_n\}$ is a Cauchy sequence.

Now, we show that F and g have a coincidence point. We discuss the following cases:

Case I: (iii) holds.

Since $(\triangle, d_\xi)$ is $\Re$-complete, $F(\Omega) \subseteq \triangle$, $u_n = Fv_n = gv_{n+1}$ and (6), there exists $u \in \triangle$ such that

$$\lim_{n\to\infty} d_\xi(gv_n, u) = 0. \tag{24}$$

Considering $\triangle \subseteq g(\Omega)$; thus, there exists $v \in \Omega$ such that $u = gv$. That is,

$$\lim_{n\to\infty} d_\xi(gv_n, gv) = 0. \tag{25}$$

By $u_n = Fv_n = gv_{n+1}$, we have

$$\lim_{n\to\infty} d_\xi(Fv_n, gv) = 0. \tag{26}$$

If there exists an infinite subsequence $\{u_{n_k}\}$ of $\{u_n\}$ such that $u_{n_k} = Fv$ or $u_{n_k} = gv$, then it will lead to a contradiction with $u_n \neq u_m$, for all $n \neq m \in \mathbb{N}$. Thus, we assume that $u_n \neq Fv$ and $u_n \neq gv$ for all $n \in \mathbb{N}$.

If F is $(g, \Re)$-continuous. Thinking about (6) and (25), we obtain

$$\lim_{n\to\infty} d_\xi(Fv_n, Fv) = 0. \tag{27}$$

By $(d_\xi 3)$, it follows that

$$\begin{aligned} d_\xi(\Gamma v, gv) &\leqslant \xi(\Gamma v, gv)[d_\xi(\Gamma v, \Gamma v_n) + d_\xi(\Gamma v_n, \Gamma v_{n+1}) + d_\xi(\Gamma v_{n+1}, gv)] \\ &= \xi(Fv, gv)[d_\xi(Fv, Fv_n) + d_\xi(u_n, u_{n+1}) + d_\xi(Fv_{n+1}, gv)] \end{aligned} \tag{28}$$

Taking the limits on the both sides of (28), keep (14), (26) and (27) in mind, we deduce that

$$d_\xi(Fv, gv) = 0.$$

Thus, v is a coincidence point of F and g.

Assume that F and g are continuous. By Lemma 1, it is not difficult to find that there exists $E \subset \Omega$ such that $g(E) = g(\Omega)$ and $g : E \to E$ is one to one. Define a function $T : g(E) \to g(E)$ by $Fe = Tge$, where $e \in E$. Clearly, T is well-defined. Since F and g are continuous , we deduce that, T is continuous as well. Without loss of generality, we choose $\{v_n\} \subseteq E$ and $v \in E$. By (25), we obtain

$$\begin{aligned} \lim_{n\to\infty} d_\xi(Fv_n, Fv) &= \lim_{n\to\infty} d_\xi(Tgv_n, Fv) \\ &= \lim_{n\to\infty} d_\xi(Tgv_n, Tgv) \\ &= 0, \end{aligned}$$

that is (27) holds. Taking the limits on the both sides of (28), keep (14), (26) and (27) in mind, we deduce that

$$d_\xi(Fv, gv) = 0.$$

Then, v is a coincidence point of F and g.

If $\Re|_{g\Omega}$ is d_ξ-self closed, form (6) and (25), there exists a subsequence $\{gv_{n_k}\}$ of $\{gv_n\}$ satisfying

$$gv_{n_k}\Re gv \text{ or } gv\Re gv_{n_k}. \tag{29}$$

Assume that $gv_{n_k}\Re gv$. Let $u = v_{n_k}$ in (2), keep (29) in mind, we have

$$\begin{aligned} d_\xi(Fv_{n_k}, Fv) &\leqslant \psi(M_{F,g}(v_{n_k}, v)) \\ &= \psi(\max\{d_\xi(gv_{n_k}, gv), d_\xi(gv_{n_k}, Fv_{n_k}), d_\xi(Fv, gv), \\ &\quad \frac{d_\xi(gv, Fv)(1 + d_\xi(gv_{n_k}, Fv_{n_k}))}{1 + d_\xi(gv_{n_k}, gv)}, \frac{d_\xi(gv_{n_k}, Fv_{n_k})(1 + d_\xi(gv, Fv))}{1 + d_\xi(gv_{n_k}, gv)}\}) \\ &= \psi(\max\{d_\xi(gv_{n_k}, gx), d_\xi(u_{n_k-1}, u_{n_k}), d_\xi(Fv, gv), \\ &\quad \frac{d_\xi(gv, Fv)(1 + d_\xi(u_{n_k-1}, u_{n_k}))}{1 + d_\xi(gv_{n_k}, gv)}, \frac{d_\xi(u_{n_k-1}, u_{n_k})(1 + d_\xi(gv, Fv))}{1 + d_\xi(gv_{n_k}, gv)}\}). \end{aligned} \tag{30}$$

Taking the super limits on the both sides of (30), we gain

$$\limsup_{k\to\infty} d_\xi(Fv_{n_k}, Fv) \leqslant \limsup_{t\to d_\xi(gv,Fv)} \psi(t). \tag{31}$$

Taking the super limits on the both sides of (28), according to (14), (25) and (31), we have

$$d_\xi(Fv, gv) \leqslant \xi(Fv, gv) \limsup_{t\to d_\xi(gv,Fv)} \psi(t).$$

This leads to a contradiction with

$$\limsup_{t\to d_\xi(gv,Fv)} \psi(t) < \frac{d_\xi(gv, Fv)}{\xi(Fv, gv)}.$$

Thus, $d_\xi(gv, Fv) = 0$.

If $gv\Re gv_{n_k}$, by the similar discussion and keep

$$\limsup_{t\to d_\xi(gw,Fw)} \psi(t) < \frac{d_\xi(gw, Fw)}{\xi(gw, Fw)}$$

in mind, we can also find $d_\xi(gv, Fv) = 0$.

Case II: (iii') holds.

By $F(\Omega) \subseteq (\triangle \cap g(\Omega))$, $\triangle$ being an $\Re$-complete and the construction of the sequence $\{u_n\}$, there exists $u \in (\Delta \cap g\Omega)$ such that

$$\lim_{n\to\infty} Fv_n = u \tag{32}$$

and

$$\lim_{n\to\infty} gv_n = u. \tag{33}$$

If F and g are $\Re$-continuous, we obtain

$$\lim_{n\to\infty} gFv_n = gu \tag{34}$$

and

$$\lim_{n\to\infty} Fgv_n = Fu. \tag{35}$$

Considering (32), (33) and (F, g) is $\Re$-compatible, we gain

$$\lim_{n\to\infty} d_\xi(Fgv_n, gFv_n) = 0. \tag{36}$$

Clearly, by (34)–(36) and d_ξ is continuous, we have

$$d_\xi(Fu, gu) = 0.$$

The proof is complete. □

Example 1. *Let $\Omega = [0,1]$ with $u\Re v$ if and only if $u, v \in [\frac{1}{32}, \frac{1}{16}]$ and $d_\xi(u,v) = \frac{(u-v)^2}{2}$ with $\xi(u,v) = u + v + 4$ for all $u, v \in \Omega$. Suppose that $\Delta = [0, \frac{5}{32}]$, clearly, (Ω, d_ξ) is an extended rectangular b-metric space and Δ is $\Re$-complete. Indeed, d_ξ is generated from standard metric, for every $\Re$-preserving Cauchy sequence $\{u_n\}$ in Ω, we acquire sequence $\{u_n\}$ converges to a point in Ω. Define the mappings $F, g : \Omega \to \Omega$ by*

$$Fu = \begin{cases} \frac{u}{2}, & \text{if } u \in [0, \frac{1}{4}], \\ \frac{1}{8}, & \text{otherwise.} \end{cases}$$

and

$$gu = \begin{cases} \frac{u}{2}, & \text{if } u \in [0, \frac{1}{2}], \\ \frac{1}{4}, & \text{otherwise.} \end{cases}$$

Clearly, $F(\Omega) \subseteq \Delta \subseteq g(\Omega)$, $\Re$ is (F,g)-closed. Indeed, for all $gu\Re gv$, we obtain $u, v \in [\frac{1}{16}, \frac{1}{8}]$, then $Fu, Fv \in [\frac{1}{32}, \frac{1}{16}]$, that is $Fu\Re Fv$. Suppose that a sequence $\{u_n\} \subseteq \Omega$ and a point $u \in \Omega$ such that $\lim_{n\to\infty} u_n = u$. For mapping F, if $u_n \in [0, \frac{1}{4}]$, by the definitions of function d_ξ and mapping F, we have $u \in [0, \frac{1}{4}]$, $Fu_n = \frac{u_n}{2}$ and $Fu = \frac{u}{2}$. Then, $\lim_{n\to\infty} Fu_n = Fu$. If $u_n \in (\frac{1}{4}, 1]$, by the definitions of function d_ξ and mapping F, we have $u \in [\frac{1}{4}, 1]$ and $Fu_n = \frac{1}{8}$ and $Fu = \frac{1}{8}$. Then, $\lim_{n\to\infty} Fu_n = Fu$. Thus, mapping F is continuous. By similarly discuss, we can also find g is continuous. In addition, there exists $v_0 = \frac{1}{32}$ such that $gv_0\Re Fv_0$ and $gv_0\Re Fv_1$, where v_1 is such that $gv_1 = Fv_0$. Take $\eta(u,v) = \frac{1}{2}v - u$ and

$$\psi(t) = \begin{cases} \frac{2}{9}t, & \text{if } t \in [0,1], \\ \frac{260}{1161}, & \text{otherwise.} \end{cases}$$

For all $t \in (0, d_\xi(u_0, u_1)]$ and for all $p \in \mathbb{N}$, we have

$$\begin{aligned} \limsup_{n\to\infty} \frac{\psi^{n+1}(t)}{\psi^n(t)} \xi(u_{n+1}, u_p) &= \limsup_{n\to\infty} \frac{2}{9}(4 + u_{n+1} + u_p) \\ &= \limsup_{n\to\infty} \frac{2}{9}(4 + \frac{v_0}{2} + \frac{v_0}{2}) \\ &= \frac{2}{9}(4 + \frac{1}{32}) \\ &< 1. \end{aligned}$$

Now, we show that F and g satisfy condition (1). *Indeed, for all* $gu\Re gv$,

$$
\begin{aligned}
\frac{1}{2}\psi(M_{F,g}(u,v)) - d_\xi(Fu,Fv) &\geqslant \frac{1}{9}\max\{d_\xi(gu,Fu), d_\xi(gv,Fv)\} - \frac{(\frac{u}{2}-\frac{v}{2})^2}{2} \\
&= \frac{1}{9}\max\{\frac{9u^2}{8}, \frac{9v^2}{8}\} - \frac{(u-v)^2}{8} \\
&\geqslant (\frac{1\times 9}{9} - 1)d_\xi(Fu,Fv) \\
&\geqslant 0.
\end{aligned}
$$

Thus, by Theorem 3, there exists $v = \frac{1}{32}$ *such that* $F(\frac{1}{32}) = g(\frac{1}{32})$.

Example 2. *Let* $\Omega = [0,3)$, $u\Re v$ *if and only if* $(u,v) \in [0,\frac{1}{8}] \times [0,\frac{1}{8}]$ *and* $d_\xi(u,v) = (u-v)^2$ *with* $\xi(u,v) = u+v+4$, *for all* $u,v \in \Omega$. *Define the mappings* $F, g : \Omega \to \Omega$ *by*

$$
Fu = \begin{cases} \frac{u}{4}, & \text{if } u \in [0,\frac{1}{2}], \\ 2, & \text{if } u \in (\frac{1}{2},3). \end{cases}
$$

and

$$
gu = \begin{cases} u, & \text{if } u \in [0,\frac{1}{2}], \\ 2, & \text{if } u \in (\frac{1}{2},3). \end{cases}
$$

Clearly, $F(\Omega) \subseteq \Delta \subseteq g(\Omega)$, $\Re$ *is* (F,g)*-closed and F is* $(g,\Re)$*-continuous. Indeed, for all* $gu\Re gv$, *we obtain* $u,v \in [0,\frac{1}{8}]$, *then* $Fu, Fv \in [0,\frac{1}{32}]$, *that is* $Fu\Re Fv$. *For any sequence* $\{u_n\} \subseteq \Omega$ *such that* $\{gu_n\}$ *is* $\Re$*-preserving with* $\lim_{n\to\infty} gu_n = gu$, *we have sequence* $\{u_n\} \subseteq [0,\frac{1}{32}]$ *and* $u \in [0,\frac{1}{32}]$, *so* $\lim_{n\to\infty} Fu_n = Fu$. *We can find that both F and g are not continuous at* $u = \frac{1}{2}$, *and* Δ *is* $\Re$*-complete via* d_ξ *is generated from standard metrics, where* $\Delta = [0,\frac{1}{2}] \cup \{2\}$. *In addition, there exists* $v_0 = \frac{1}{8}$ *such that* $gv_0\Re Fv_0$ *and* $gv_0\Re Fv_1$, *where* v_1 *with* $gv_1 = Fv_0$. *Take* $\eta(u,v) = \frac{1}{2}v - u$ *and* $\psi(t) = \frac{4}{17}t$, *for all* $t \in [0,\infty)$.
For every $t \in (0, d_\xi(u_0,u_1)]$, *we have*

$$
\begin{aligned}
\limsup_{n\to\infty} \frac{\psi^{n+1}(t)}{\psi^n(t)}\xi(u_{n+1},u_p) &= \limsup_{n\to\infty} \frac{4}{17}(4 + u_{n+1} + u_p) \\
&= \limsup_{n\to\infty} \frac{4}{17}(4 + \frac{v_0}{4^{n+1}} + \frac{v_0}{4^{p+1}}) \\
&= \frac{4}{17}(4 + \frac{1}{8}) \\
&< 1.
\end{aligned}
$$

Now, we show that condition (1) *for F and g holds. Indeed, for all* $gu\Re gv$,

$$
\begin{aligned}
\eta(d_\xi(Fu,Fv), M_{F,g}(u,v)) &= \frac{1}{2}\psi(M_{F,g}(u,v)) - d_\xi(Fu,Fv) \\
&\geqslant \frac{2}{17}d_\xi(gu,gv) - (\frac{u}{4} - \frac{v}{4})^2 \\
&= (\frac{2}{17} - \frac{1}{16})d_\xi(gu,gv) \\
&\geqslant 0.
\end{aligned}
$$

So, by Theorem 3, there exists $v = 0$ such that $F0 = g0$. Further, we claim that the common fixed point theorems in [20,21] are not valid in proving the existence of common fixed points of F and g. Indeed, for $u = 0, v = 2$, $d_\xi(Fu, Fv) > k_1 d_\xi(gu, gv)$ and $d_\xi(Fu, Fv) > k_2[d_\xi(gu, Fu) + d_\xi(gv, Fv)]$, where $k_1 \in (0,1)$, $k_2 \in (0, \frac{1}{2})$.

According to Examples 1 and 2, we find that the coincidence point of F and g is not unique. Thus, Theorem 3 shows only the existence of coincidence point of F and g. Now, we add some conditions to show that the point of coincidence of F and g is unique.

Theorem 4. *In addition the assumption in Theorem 3, we also suppose the following condition:*
(iv) If $gu\Re gv$ or $gv\Re gu$, for all $u, v \in C(F,g)$, where $C(F,g) = \{u \in \Omega : Fu = gu\}$, then the point of coincidence of F and g is unique.

Proof. Assume that there exist $u, v \in C(F,g)$ with $d_\xi(Fu, Fv) > 0$. If $gu\Re gv$, by (2), we have

$$
\begin{aligned}
d_\xi(Fu, Fv) &\leqslant \psi(M_{F,g}(u,v)) \\
&= \psi(\max\{d_\xi(gu,gv), d_\xi(gu,Fu), d_\xi(Fv,gv), \\
&\quad \frac{d_\xi(gv,Fv)(1+d_\xi(gu,Fu))}{1+d_\xi(gu,gv)}, \frac{d_\xi(gu,Fu)(1+d_\xi(gv,Fv))}{1+d_\xi(gu,gv)}\}) \\
&= \psi(\max\{d_\xi(Fu,Fv), 0, 0, 0, 0\}) \\
&= \psi(d_\xi(Fu,Fv)) \\
&< d_\xi(Fu,Fv),
\end{aligned}
$$

which leads to a contradiction with $d_\xi(Fu, Fv) > 0$. Thus, $d_\xi(Fu, Fv) = 0$. If $gv\Re gu$, by the similar discussion, we have $d_\xi(Fu, Fv) = 0$. The proof is complete. □

Theorem 4 shows that the point of coincidence of F and g is unique. Now, we add a condition to show that F and g have a unique common fixed point.

Theorem 5. *Except for the assumption in Theorem 4, if (F, g) is weakly compatible, then F and g have a unique common fixed point.*

Proof. By Theorem 3, there exists $v \in \Omega$ such that $Fv = gv$. Assume that $u = Fv = gv$. Since (F, g) is weakly compatible, we have $Fu = Fgv = gFv = gu$. By Theorem 4, we have $Fu = gu = Fv = gv = u$. Thus, u is the common point of F and g. Suppose that there exists s such that $s = Fs = gs$ and $s \neq u$. By $s \neq u$, we have $Fs \neq Fu$—a contradiction. Thus, $s = u$. The proof is complete. □

Remark 3. *(i) By the proof of Theorem 3, we only use the property $(\eta 1)$ of function η.*
(ii) In the proofs of Theorem 3, Theorem 4 and Theorem 5, we can find that we mainly use (2) *instead of* (1). *Thus, if we replace* (1) *with*

$$d_\xi(Fu, Fv) \leqslant \psi(M_{F,g}(u,v)), \text{ for all } gu\Re gv,$$

in Theorem 3, these results still hold.

(*iii*) *We observe that*

$$\frac{d_\xi(gv_n, gv_{n+1})d_\xi(gv_{n+1}, Fv_{n+1})}{1+d_\xi(gv_n, Fv_n)} \leqslant d_\xi(u_n, u_{n+1});$$
$$\frac{d_\xi(gv_n, gv_{n+2})d_\xi(gv_{n+2}, Fv_{n+2})}{1+d_\xi(gv_n, Fv_n)} = \frac{d_\xi(u_{n-1}, u_{n+1})d_\xi(u_{n+1}, u_{n+2})}{1+d_\xi(u_{n-1}, u_n)};$$
$$\frac{d_\xi(gv_{n_k}, gv)d_\xi(gv, Fv)}{1+d_\xi(gv_{n_k}, Fv_{n_k})} = \frac{d_\xi(u_{n_k-1}, gv)d_\xi(gv, Fv)}{1+d_\xi(u_{n_k-1}, u_{n_k})};$$
$$\frac{d_\xi(gv_n, Fv_n)d_\xi(gv_{n+1}, Fv_{n+1})}{1+d_\xi(Fv_n, Fv_{n+1})} \leqslant d_\xi(u_{n-1}, u_n);$$
$$\frac{d_\xi(gv_n, Fv_n)d_\xi(gv_{n+2}, Fv_{n+2})}{1+d_\xi(Fv_n, Fv_{n+2})} = \frac{d_\xi(u_{n-1}, u_n)d_\xi(u_{n+1}, u_{n+2})}{1+d_\xi(u_n, u_{n+2})};$$
$$\frac{d_\xi(gv_n, Fv_n)d_\xi(gv, Fv)}{1+d_\xi(Fv_n, Fv)} = \frac{d_\xi(u_{n-1}, u_n)d_\xi(gv, Fv)}{1+d_\xi(u_n, Fv)}.$$

Thus, we add $\frac{d_\xi(gu,gv)d_\xi(gv,Fv)}{1+d_\xi(gu,Fu)}$ *and* $\frac{d_\xi(gu,Fu)d_\xi(gv,Fv)}{1+d_\xi(Fu,Fv)}$ *to* $M_{F,g}(u,v)$, *the above results still hold.*

3. Corollaries

Corollary 1. *Let* (Ω, d_ξ) *be an extended rectangular b-metric space with a binary relation* $\Re$. *F is a self-mapping on* Ω, *which satisfies*

$$\eta(d_\xi(Fu, Fv), \psi(M(u,v))) \geqslant 0, \text{ for all } u\Re v, \tag{37}$$

where $\eta \in \mathcal{Z}$, $\psi \in \Psi$ *and*

$$M(u,v) = \max\{d_\xi(u,v), d_\xi(u,Fu), d_\xi(Fv,v), \frac{d_\xi(v,Fv)(1+d_\xi(u,Fu))}{1+d_\xi(u,v)}, \frac{d_\xi(u,Fu)(1+d_\xi(v,Fv))}{1+d_\xi(u,v)}\}.$$

In addition, if F satisfies the following conditions:

(*i*) *There exists* $v_0 \in \Omega$ *such that* $v_0 \Re F v_0$ *and* $v_0 \Re F^2 v_0$.

(*ii*) $\Re$ *is F-closed.*

(*iii*) *For* v_0 *in* (*i*), *we have* $\limsup_{n\to\infty} \frac{\psi^{n+1}(t)}{\psi^n(t)} \xi(v_{n+1}, v_p) < 1$, *where* $p \in \mathbb{N}$, $v_{n+1} = Fv_n$ *and* $t \in (0, d_\xi(v_0, v_1)]$ *with* $v_0 \neq v_1$.

(*iv*) *There exists* $\triangle \subseteq \Omega$ *such that* $F(\Omega) \subseteq \triangle$ *and* $(\triangle, d_\xi)$ *is* $\Re$*-complete.*

(*v*) *One of the conditions holds:*

(*a*) *F is* $\Re$*-continuous; or*

(*b*) $\Re|_\Omega$ *is* d_ξ*-self-closed and for all* $w \in \Omega$ *with* $d_\xi(w, Fw) > 0$ *such that*

$$\limsup_{t\to d_\xi(w,Fw)} \psi(t) < \frac{d_\xi(w,Fw)}{\xi(Fw,w)} \text{ or } \limsup_{t\to d_\xi(w,Fw)} \psi(t) < \frac{d_\xi(w,Fw)}{\xi(w,Fw)},$$

then F has a fixed point.

In addition, if

(*vi*) $u\Re v$ *or* $v\Re u$, *for all u, v with* $u = Fu$ *and* $v = Fv$,

then F has a unique fixed point.

Proof. Take $g = I$ (the identity map) in Theorem 5, it is clear that the result is true. □

Corollary 2. *Let (Ω, d_ξ) be an extended rectangular b-metric space with a binary relation $\Re$ and $\triangle$ be an $\Re$-complete subspace of Ω. F and g are self-mappings on Ω, which satisfy $F(\Omega) \subseteq (g(\Omega) \cap \triangle)$, and*

$$d_\xi(Fu, Fv) \leqslant kM_{F,g}(u,v), \text{ for all } gu\Re gv, \tag{38}$$

where $k \in (0,1)$ and

$$M_{F,g}(u,v) = \max\{d_\xi(gu,gv), d_\xi(gu,Fu), d_\xi(Fv,gv), \frac{d_\xi(gv,Fv)(1+d_\xi(gu,Fu))}{1+d_\xi(gu,gv)}, \frac{d_\xi(gu,Fu)(1+d_\xi(gv,Fv))}{1+d_\xi(gu,gv)}\}.$$

In addition, if F and g satisfy the following conditions:

(i) there exists $v_0 \in \Omega$ such that $gv_0 \Re Fv_0$ and $gv_0 \Re Fv_1$, where v_1 is such that $gv_1 = Fv_0$;

(ii) $\Re$ is (F,g)-closed;

(iii) for v_0 in (i), we have $\limsup_{n\to\infty} \xi(u_{n+1}, u_p) < \frac{1}{k}$, where $p \in \mathbb{N}$, $u_n = Fv_n = gv_{n+1}$ and $t \in (0, d_\xi(u_0, u_1)]$ with $u_0 \neq u_1$; and

(iv) (a) $\triangle \subseteq g(\Omega)$; and

(b) F is $(g,\Re)$-continuous or F and g are continuous or $\Re|_{g(\Omega)}$ is d_ξ-self-closed and $d_\xi(gw, Fw) > 0$, where $w \in \Omega$, such that $\xi(Fw, w) < \frac{1}{k}$ or $\xi(w, Fw) < \frac{1}{k}$;

or alternatively,

(iv′) d_ξ is continuous and (F,g) is $\Re$-compatible, and g and F are $\Re$-continuous;

(v) if $gu\Re gv$ or $gv\Re gu$, for all u, v with $gu = Fu$ and $gv = Fv$; and

(vi) (F,g) is weakly compatible,

then F and g have a unique fixed point.

Proof. By Remark 3, if $\psi(u) = ku$, where $k \in (0,1)$, it is clear that the result is true. □

Remark 4. *Let $\Re = \Omega^2$ and $M_{F,g}(u,v) = d_\xi(gu,gv)$ in Corollary 2, we can find the results of Hassen et al. [20].*

Corollary 3. *Let (Ω, d_ξ) be an extended rectangular b-metric space with a binary relation $\Re$. F is a self-mappings on Ω, which satisfies*

$$d_\xi(Fu, Fv) \leqslant kM(u,v), \text{ for all } u\Re v,$$

where $k \in (0,1)$ and

$$M(u,v) = \max\{d_\xi(u,v), d_\xi(u,Fu), d_\xi(Fv,v), \frac{d_\xi(v,Fv)(1+d_\xi(u,Fu))}{1+d_\xi(u,v)}, \frac{d_\xi(u,Fu)(1+d_\xi(v,Fv))}{1+d_\xi(u,v)}\}.$$

In addition, if F satisfies the following conditions:

(i) there exists $v_0 \in \Omega$ such that $v_0 \Re Fv_0$ and $v_0 \Re F^2 v_0$;

(ii) $\Re$ is F-closed;

(iii) for v_0 in (i), we have $\limsup_{n\to\infty} \xi(v_{n+1}, v_p) < \frac{1}{k}$, where $p \in \mathbb{N}$, $v_{n+1} = Fv_n$;

(iv) (a) there exists $\triangle$ such that $F(\Omega) \subseteq \triangle$ and $(\triangle, d_\xi)$ is $\Re$-complete; and

(b) F is $\Re$-continuous or $\Re|_\Omega$ is d_ξ-self-closed and $d_\xi(w, Fw) > 0$, where $w \in \Omega$, such that $\xi(Fw, w) < \frac{1}{k}$ or $\xi(w, Fw) < \frac{1}{k}$; and

(v) if $u\Re v$ or $v\Re u$, for all u, v with $u = Fu$ and $v = Fv$,

then F has a unique fixed point.

Proof. By Corollary 2, let $g = I$, it is clear that the result is true. □

Example 3. *Let* $\Omega = [1,4]$ *with* $\Re = [1,2]^2$, $d_\xi(u,v) = |u-v|$ *with* $\xi(u,v) = u+v+1$ *for all* $u,v \in \Omega$. *Clearly,* (Ω, d_ξ) *be an* $\Re$*-complete extended rectangular b-metric space. Consider that the mapping* $F : \Omega \to \Omega$ *is defined by*

$$F(u) = \begin{cases} \frac{7}{4}, & \text{if } u \in [1,2]; \\ \frac{u}{10}, & \text{otherwise.} \end{cases}$$

Then, for all $u\Re v$, *we obtain* $u,v \in [1,2]^2$, *then* $Fu = Fv = \frac{7}{4} \in [1,2]$, *that is* $Fu\Re Fv$. *Since* $\Re$ *is F-closed. for any sequence* $\{u_n\} \subseteq \Omega$ *such that* $\{u_n\}$ *is* $\Re$*-preserving with* $\lim_{n\to\infty} u_n = u$, *we obtain that* $u_n \in [1,2]$, *for all* $n \in \mathbb{N}$ *and* $u \in [1,2]$, *then* $Fu = Fu_n = \frac{7}{4}$, *for all* $n \in \mathbb{N}$, *that is,* $\Re|_\Omega$ *is* d_ξ*-self-closed. Moreover, there exists* $v_0 = \frac{7}{4}$ *such that* $v_0\Re Fv_0$ *and* $v_0\Re F^2 v_0$. *Clearly,*

$$d_\xi(Fu, Fv) \leqslant \frac{1}{10}(M(u,v)), \text{ for all } u\Re v,$$

and for all $w \in \Omega$ *with* $d_\xi(w, Fw) > 0$ *satisfies* $\xi(Fw, w) < 10$ *and* $\limsup_{n\to\infty} \xi(v_{n+1}, v_p) < 10$. *Thus, by Corollary 3,* $\frac{7}{4}$ *is the unique fixed point of F.*

Corollary 4. *Let* (Ω, d_ξ) *be an extended rectangular b-metric space. F is a self-mapping on* Ω, *which satisfies*

$$d_\xi(Fu, Fv) \leqslant kM(u,v), \text{ for all } u, v \in \Omega,$$

where $k \in [0,1)$ *and*

$$M(u,v) = \max\{d_\xi(u,v), d_\xi(u,Fu), d_\xi(Fv,v), \frac{d_\xi(v,Fv)(1+d_\xi(u,Fu))}{1+d_\xi(u,v)}, \frac{d_\xi(u,Fu)(1+d_\xi(v,Fv))}{1+d_\xi(u,v)}\}.$$

In addition, if F satisfies the following conditions:
(i) there exists $v_0 \in \Omega$ *such that* $\limsup_{n\to\infty} \xi(v_{n+1}, v_p) < \frac{1}{k}$, *where* $p \in \mathbb{N}$ *and* $v_{n+1} = Fv_n$;
(ii) there exists $\triangle \subseteq \Omega$ *such that* $F(\Omega) \subseteq \triangle$ *and* $(\triangle, d_\xi)$ *is complete; and*
(iii) one of the conditions holds:
(a) F is continuous; or
(b) for all $w \in \Omega$ *with* $d_\xi(w, Fw) > 0$ *such that* $k < \frac{1}{\xi(Fw,w)}$ *or* $k < \frac{1}{\xi(w,Fw)}$,
then F has a unique fixed point.

Proof. Let $\Re = \Omega^2$, by Corollary 3, the proof is complete. □

Corollary 5. *Let* (Ω, d_ξ) *be an extended rectangular b-metric space with a binary relation* $\Re$. *Assume that F is a self-mapping on* Ω, *which satisfies*

$$d_\xi(Fu,Fv) \leqslant a_1 d_\xi(u,v) + a_2 d_\xi(u,Fu) + a_3 d_\xi(Fv,v) + a_4\frac{d_\xi(v,Fv)(1+d_\xi(u,Fu))}{1+d_\xi(u,v)} + a_5\frac{d_\xi(u,Fu)(1+d_\xi(v,Fv))}{1+d_\xi(u,v)}, \text{ for all } u\Re v,$$

where $\sum_{i=1}^{5} a_i \in (0,1)$. *In addition, if F satisfies the following conditions:*
(i) there exists $v_0 \in \Omega$ *such that* $v_0\Re Fv_0$ *and* $v_0\Re F^2v_0$;
(ii) $\Re$ *is F-closed;*
(iii) for v_0 *in (i), we have* $\limsup_{n\to\infty} \xi(v_{n+1}, v_p) < \frac{1}{\sum_{i=1}^{5} a_i}$, *where* $p \in \mathbb{N}$ *and* $v_{n+1} = Fv_n$;
(iv) there exists $\triangle \subseteq \Omega$ *such that* $F(\Omega) \subseteq \triangle$ *and* $(\triangle, d_\xi)$ *is* $\Re$*-complete;*
(v) one of the conditions holds:

(a) F is $\Re$-continuous; or

(b) $\Re|_{\Omega}$ is d_{ξ}-self-closed and for all $w \in \Omega$ with $d_{\xi}(w, Fw) > 0$ such that

$$\sum_{i=1}^{5} a_i < \frac{1}{\xi(Fw, w)} \text{ or } \sum_{i=1}^{5} a_i < \frac{1}{\xi(w, Fw)};$$

and

(vi) if $u\Re v$ or $v\Re u$, for all u, v with $Fu = u$ and $Fv = v$,
then F has a unique fixed point.

Proof. For all $u\Re v$,

$$\begin{aligned} d_{\xi}(Fu, Fv) &\leqslant a_1 d_{\xi}(u,v) + a_2 d_{\xi}(u, Fu) + a_3 d_{\xi}(Fv, v) + \\ &\quad a_4 \frac{d_{\xi}(v, Fv)(1 + d_{\xi}(u, Fu))}{1 + d_{\xi}(u,v)} + a_5 \frac{d_{\xi}(u, Fu)(1 + d_{\xi}(v, Fv))}{1 + d_{\xi}(u,v)} \\ &\leqslant \sum_{i=1}^{5} a_i \max\{d_{\xi}(u,v), d_{\xi}(u, Fu), d_{\xi}(Fv, v), \\ &\quad \frac{d_{\xi}(v, Fv)(1 + d_{\xi}(u, Fu))}{1 + d_{\xi}(u,v)}, \frac{d_{\xi}(u, Fu)(1 + d_{\xi}(v, Fv))}{1 + d_{\xi}(u,v)}\} \\ &= kM(u,v), \end{aligned}$$

where $k = \sum_{i=1}^{5} a_i$. By Corollary 4, the proof is complete. □

Remark 5. *(i) In Corollary 5, take $a_i = 0,\ i = 2,3,4,5$, our results generalized the results of Alam et al. [18] to extended rectangular b-metric spaces.*

(ii) In Corollary 5, if $a_i = 0,\ i = 2,3,5$, then we develop the result of Hossain et al. [23] into extended rectangular b-metric space.

Corollary 6. *Let (Ω, d_{ξ}) be an extended rectangular b-metric space. F is a self-mapping on Ω, which satisfies*

$$\begin{aligned} d_{\xi}(Fu, Fv) &\leqslant a_1 d_{\xi}(u,v) + a_2 d_{\xi}(u, Fu) + a_3 d_{\xi}(Fv, v) + \\ &\quad a_4 \frac{d_{\xi}(v, Fv)(1 + d_{\xi}(u, Fu))}{1 + d_{\xi}(u,v)} + a_5 \frac{d_{\xi}(u, Fu)(1 + d_{\xi}(v, Fv))}{1 + d_{\xi}(u,v)}, \text{ for all } u, v \in \Omega, \end{aligned}$$

where $\sum_{i=1}^{5} a_i \in (0,1)$. In addition, if F satisfies the following conditions:

(i) there exists $v_0 \in \Omega$ such that $\limsup_{n\to\infty} \xi(v_{n+1}, v_p) < \frac{1}{\sum_{i=1}^{5} a_i}$, where $p \in \mathbb{N}$ and $v_{n+1} = Fv_n$;

(ii) there exists a set $\triangle \subseteq \Omega$ such that $F(\Omega) \subseteq \triangle$ and $(\triangle, d_{\xi})$ is complete; and

(iii) one of the conditions holds:

(a) F is continuous; or

(b) for all $w \in \Omega$ with $d_{\xi}(w, Fw) > 0$ such that $\sum_{i=1}^{5} a_i < \frac{1}{\xi(Fw,w)}$ or $\sum_{i=1}^{5} a_i < \frac{1}{\xi(w,Fw)}$,

then F has a unique fixed point.

Proof. Let $\Re = \Omega^2$, by Corollary 5, the proof is complete. □

Remark 6. *(i) In Corollary 6, if $a_i = 0,\ i = 2,3,4,5$, we can obtain the Banach type fixed point theorem.*

(ii) In Corollary 6, if $a_i = 0,\ i = 1,4,5$, we can find the Kannan type fixed point theorem.

(iii) In Corollary 6, if $a_i = 0,\ i = 2,3,5$, we can develop the result of Dass et al. [22] into extended rectangular b-metric space.

4. Applications

4.1. Application to Ordinary Differential Equations with Periodic Boundary Value

In this section, we apply our results to show the existence of solutions to the following ordinary differential equations with periodic boundary value.

$$\begin{cases} u'(t) = f(t,u(t)), & t \in [0,T], \\ u(0) = u(T), \end{cases} \tag{39}$$

where $T \in (0,\infty)$ is a constant, $u(t) : [0,T] \to \mathbb{R}$ and $f : [0,T] \times \mathbb{R} \to \mathbb{R}$ is continuous. It is clear that the solution of (39) is equivalent to the following integral equation

$$u(t) = \int_0^T G(t,s)[f(s,u(s)) + \lambda u(s)]ds,\ t \in [0,T], \tag{40}$$

where $\lambda > 0$ and

$$G(t,s) = \begin{cases} \dfrac{e^{\lambda(T+s-t)}}{e^{\lambda T} - 1}, & 0 \leqslant s < t \leqslant T, \\ \dfrac{e^{\lambda(s-t)}}{e^{\lambda T} - 1}, & 0 \leqslant t < s \leqslant T. \end{cases}$$

Let $C([0,T],\mathbb{R})$ be the set of all continuous real value functions defined on $[0,T]$. For all $u,v \in C([0,T],\mathbb{R})$, we define two functions $\xi(u,v)$, $d_\xi(u,v)$ and a mapping F by $\xi(u,v) = |u| + |v| + 4$,

$$d_\xi(u,v) = \max_{t\in[0,T]} |u(t) - v(t)|^2,$$

and

$$F(u(t)) = \int_0^T G(t,s)[f(s,u(s)) + \lambda u(s)]ds,\ t \in [0,T]. \tag{41}$$

Clearly, $(d_\xi, C([0,T],\mathbb{R}))$ is a complete extended rectangular b-metric space and F is continuous.

Theorem 6. *If the following conditions hold,*

(i) there exist $\lambda, \mu > 0$ with $\mu < \lambda^2$ and $\psi \in \Psi$ such that

$$0 \leqslant f(t,u) + \lambda u - [f(t,v) + \lambda v],\ \text{for all } u \leqslant v$$

and

$$|f(t,u) + \lambda u - [f(t,v) + \lambda v]|^2 \leqslant \mu\psi(\max_{t\in[0,T]} |u(t) - v(t)|^2),\ \text{for all } u \leqslant v;$$

(ii) (39) *has a lower solution, that is, there exists $u_0(t) \in C([0,T],\mathbb{R})$ such that*

$$\begin{cases} u_0'(t) \leqslant f(t,u_0(t)), & t \in [0,T], \\ u_0(0) \leqslant u_0(T); \text{and} \end{cases}$$

(iii) for u_0 in (ii), we have $\limsup_{n\to\infty} \frac{\psi^{n+1}(t)}{\psi^n(t)} \xi(u_{n+1}, u_p) < 1$, where $p,\ n \in \mathbb{N}$, $u_{n+1} = Fu_n$ and $t \in (0, d_\xi(u_0,u_1)]$ with $u_0 \neq u_1$, then the ordinary differential equation with periodic boundary value (39) *has a solution.*

Proof. First, we define a binary relation $\Re$ by $u\Re v$ if and only if $u(t) \leqslant v(t)$, for all $t \in [0,T]$. Clearly, considering (ii), we have $u_0(t) \leqslant Fu_0(t)$. By $0 \leqslant f(t,u) + \lambda u - [f(t,v) + \lambda v]$, for all $u \leqslant v$, $u_0(t) \leqslant Fu_0(t)$ and the definition of F, we have $F(u_0(t)) \leqslant F^2(u_0(t))$.

We can easily deduce that $u_0(t) \leqslant Fu_0(t)$ and $u_0(t) \leqslant F^2(u_0(t))$. By the definition of $\Re$, there exists $u_0(t)$ such that $u_0(t)\Re F(u_0(t))$ and $u_0(t)\Re F^2(u_0(t))$. We can conclude that $\Re$ is F-closed via $0 \leqslant f(t,u) + \lambda u - [f(t,v) + \lambda v]$, for all $u \leqslant v$, $u_0(t) \leqslant Fu_0(t)$ and the definitions of F and $\Re$. Now, we prove that F satisfies (37). Indeed, for all $u\Re v$, we have

$$\begin{aligned}
|Fu(t) - Fv(t)|^2 &= |\int_0^T G(t,s)[f(s,u(s)) + \lambda u(s)]ds - \int_0^T G(t,s)[f(s,v(s)) + \lambda v(s)]ds|^2 \\
&= |\int_0^T G(t,s)\{[f(s,u(s)) + \lambda u(s)] - [f(s,v(s)) + \lambda v(s)]\}ds|^2 \\
&\leqslant \max_{t\in[0,T]} |\{[f(s,u(s)) + \lambda u(s)] - [f(s,v(s)) + \lambda v(s)]\}|^2 |\int_0^T G(t,s)ds|^2 \\
&\leqslant \mu\psi(\max_{t\in[0,T]} |u(t) - v(t)|^2) | \max_{t\in[0,T]} \int_0^T G(t,s)ds|^2 \\
&\leqslant \mu\psi(M(u,v)) | \max_{t\in[0,T]} \int_0^T G(t,s)ds|^2 \\
&= \mu\psi(M(u,v)) \times \frac{1}{\lambda^2} \\
&= \frac{\mu}{\lambda^2}\psi(M(u,v)),
\end{aligned}$$

that is, $d_\xi(Fu, Fv) \leqslant \frac{\mu}{\lambda^2}\psi(M(u,v))$. Therefore, all conditions of Corollary 1 are satisfied, and thus (39) has a solution. □

4.2. Application to Linear Matrix Equations

In this section, of the paper, Corollary 3 is used to prove the existence of solutions to a class of linear matrix equations. For convenience, we first give the following notations:

We denote M^m is the set of all complex number matrices of order m, H^m is the set of all Hermitian matrices of order m, P^m and H^m_+ represent the set of all $m \times m$ positive matrices and $m \times m$ positive semi-definite matrices, respectively. Clearly, $P^m \subseteq H^m \subseteq M^m$, $H^m_+ \subseteq H^m$. Here, $A_1 \succ O$(O represents null matrix of same order) and $A_1 \succeq O$ mean that $A_1 \in P^m$ and $A_1 \in H^m_+$, respectively; for $A_1 - A_2 \succeq O$ and $A_1 - A_2 \succ O$, we will use $A_1 \succeq A_2$ and $A_1 \succ A_2$, respectively.

In the section, we investigate the existence of the solution to the following linear matrix equations:

$$U = G + \sum_{i-1}^{m} A_i^* U A_i + \sum_{i-1}^{m} B_i^* U B_i, \tag{42}$$

where $G \in P^m$, A_i, B_i are arbitrary $m \times m$ matrices for each i. We use the metric $d(A,B) = \|A - B\|_{tr,X} = \|X^{\frac{1}{2}}(A - B)X^{\frac{1}{2}}\|_{tr}$, which is induced by the norm $\|A\|_{tr} = \sum_{i=1}^{n} \sigma_i(A)$, where $X \in P^m$, A, $B \in H^m$ and $\sigma_i(A)$, $i = 1,2,3,\cdots,n$, are the singular values of $A \in M^m$. Clearly, the set H^m equipped with the metric d is a complete metric space, then (H^m, d) is a complete extended rectangular b-metric space with respect to $\xi = 3$.

Define $\Re$ and mapping $F : H^m \to H^m$ by $A\Re B$ iff $B - A \in H^m$ and

$$F(U) = G + \sum_{i=1}^{m} A_i^* U A_i + \sum_{i=1}^{m} B_i^* U B_i, \text{ for all } A, B \in H^m.$$

Note that the solutions of the matrix Equation (42) are the fixed point of the mapping F, furthermore, the mapping F is continuous in H^m, $\Re$ is F-closed and there exists U_0 such that $U_0\Re F(U_0)$ and $U_0\Re F^2(U_0)$.

To establish the existence result, we introduce the following Lemmas.

Lemma 2 ([24]). *If A, $B \in H^m_+$, then $0 \leqslant tr(AB) \leqslant \|A\|tr(B)$.*

Lemma 3 ([24]). *If $A \in H^m$ such that $A \prec I_n$, then $\|A\| < 1$.*

Theorem 7. *If $X \in P^m$, $\sum_{i=1}^{m} A_i^* X A_i \prec \frac{1}{7}X$ and $\sum_{i=1}^{m} B_i^* X B_i \prec \frac{1}{7}X$, then the mapping F has a fixed point in H^m.*

Proof. Suppose that $U, V \in H^m$ and $U\Re V$. Consider

$$\begin{aligned}
\|F(U) - F(V)\|_{tr,X} &= tr(X^{\frac{1}{2}}(F(U) - F(V))X^{\frac{1}{2}}) \\
&= tr(\sum_{i=1}^{m}\{X^{\frac{1}{2}}(A_i^*(U-V)A_i + B_i^*(U-V)B_i X^{\frac{1}{2}})\}) \\
&= tr(\sum_{i=1}^{m} X^{\frac{1}{2}}A_i^*(U-V)A_i X^{\frac{1}{2}} + \sum_{i=1}^{m} X^{\frac{1}{2}}B_i^*(U-V)B_i X^{\frac{1}{2}}) \\
&= \sum_{i=1}^{m} tr(X^{\frac{1}{2}}A_i^*(U-V)A_i X^{\frac{1}{2}} + X^{\frac{1}{2}}B_i^*(U-V)B_i X^{\frac{1}{2}}) \\
&= \sum_{i=1}^{m} tr(X^{\frac{1}{2}}A_i^*(U-V)A_i X^{\frac{1}{2}}) + \sum_{i=1}^{m} tr(X^{\frac{1}{2}}B_i^*(U-V)B_i X^{\frac{1}{2}}) \\
&= \sum_{i=1}^{m} tr(A_i^* X A_i(U-V)) + \sum_{i=1}^{m} tr(B_i^* X B_i(U-V)) \\
&= \sum_{i=1}^{m} tr(A_i^* X A_i X^{-\frac{1}{2}}X^{\frac{1}{2}}(U-V)X^{-\frac{1}{2}}X^{\frac{1}{2}}) + \sum_{i=1}^{m} tr(B_i^* X B_i X^{-\frac{1}{2}}X^{\frac{1}{2}}(U-V)X^{-\frac{1}{2}}X^{\frac{1}{2}}) \\
&= \sum_{i=1}^{m} tr(X^{-\frac{1}{2}}A_i^* X A_i X^{-\frac{1}{2}}X^{\frac{1}{2}}(U-V)X^{\frac{1}{2}}) + \sum_{i=1}^{m} tr(X^{-\frac{1}{2}}B_i^* X B_i X^{-\frac{1}{2}}X^{\frac{1}{2}}(U-V)X^{\frac{1}{2}}) \\
&= tr(\sum_{i=1}^{m} X^{-\frac{1}{2}}A_i^* X A_i X^{-\frac{1}{2}}X^{\frac{1}{2}}(U-V)X^{\frac{1}{2}}) + tr(\sum_{i=1}^{m} X^{-\frac{1}{2}}B_i^* X B_i X^{-\frac{1}{2}}X^{\frac{1}{2}}(U-V)X^{\frac{1}{2}}) \\
&\leqslant \|\sum_{i=1}^{m} X^{-\frac{1}{2}}A_i^* X A_i X^{-\frac{1}{2}}\| \|(U-V)\|_{tr,X} + \|\sum_{i=1}^{m} X^{-\frac{1}{2}}B_i^* X B_i X^{-\frac{1}{2}}\| \|(U-V)\|_{tr,X} \\
&= (\|\sum_{i=1}^{m} X^{-\frac{1}{2}}A_i^* X A_i X^{-\frac{1}{2}}\| + \|\sum_{i=1}^{m} X^{-\frac{1}{2}}B_i^* X B_i X^{-\frac{1}{2}}\|)\|(U-V)\|_{tr,X} \\
&= k\|(U-V)\|_{tr,X} \\
&\leqslant kM(U,V),
\end{aligned}$$

where $k = \|\sum_{i=1}^{m} X^{-\frac{1}{2}}A_i^* X A_i X^{-\frac{1}{2}}\| + \|\sum_{i=1}^{m} X^{-\frac{1}{2}}B_i^* X B_i X^{-\frac{1}{2}}\|$ and

$$\begin{aligned}
M(U,V) = \max\{&\|(U-V)\|_{tr,X}, \|(U-F(U))\|_{tr,X}, \|(V-F(V))\|_{tr,X}, \\
&\frac{\|(V-F(V))\|_{tr,X}(1+\|(U--F(U))\|_{tr,X})}{1+\|(U-V)\|_{tr,X}}, \frac{\|(U-F(U))\|_{tr,X}(1+\|(V-F(V))\|_{tr,X})}{1+\|(U-V)\|_{tr,X}}\}.
\end{aligned}$$

By Lemma 3, we have $k < \frac{2}{7}$. Mapping F and $\Re$ satisfy the conditions of the Corollary 3; therefore, F has a fixed point, and linear matrix Equation (42) has a solution. □

5. Conclusions

In this paper, some new relation-theoretic coincidence and common fixed point results of for some mappings of F and g are obtained by using hybrid contractions and auxiliary functions in extended rectangular b-metric space. We improve and expand some recent results. Furthermore, we use instances and applications to justify the results. Finally, regarding the main results of this paper, we draw some corollaries. Due to the importance of the fixed point theory, we consider possible future research directions.

These are potential works in the future:

(*i*) replace or weak some conditions in our main theorems;
(*ii*) extend our results to another metric spaces; and
(*iii*) use our contraction to study the problem of fixed-circle and fixed-disc [25–29] in different generalized metric spaces.

Author Contributions: Conceptualization, Y.S. and X.L.; formal analysis, Y.S. and X.L.; investigation, Y.S.; writing—original draft preparation, Y.S. and X.L.; writing—review and editing, Y.S. and X.L. All authors have read and agreed to the published version of the manuscript.

Funding: This research was funded by National Natural Science Foundation of China (Grant No. 11872043), Central Government Funds of Guiding Local Scientific and Technological Development for Sichuan Province (Grant No. 2021ZYD0017), Zigong Science and Technology Program (Grant No. 2020YGJC03), and the 2021 Innovation and Entrepreneurship Training Program for College Students of Sichuan University of Science and Engineering (Grant No. cx2021150).

Data Availability Statement: The data that support the findings of this study are available from the corresponding author upon reasonable request.

Acknowledgments: The authors thanks the anonymous reviewers for their excellent comments, suggestions, and ideas that helped improve this article.

Conflicts of Interest: The authors declare no conflict of interest.

References

1. Czerwik, S. Contraction mappings in *b*-metric spaces. *Acta Math. Inform. Univ. Ostrav.* **1993**, *1*, 5–11.
2. Miculescu, R.; Mihail, A. New fixed point theorems for set-valued contractions in *b*-metric spaces. *J. Fixed Point Theory Appl.* **2017**, *3*, 2153–2163. [CrossRef]
3. Lukács, A.; Kajántó, S. Fixed point theorems for various types of *F*-contraction in complete *b*-metric spaces. *Fixed Point Theory* **2018**, *1*, 321–334. [CrossRef]
4. Chifu, C.; Karapínar, E. Admissible hybrid $\mathcal{Z}$-contractions in *b*-metric spaces. *Axioms* **2019**, *1*, 2. [CrossRef]
5. Branciari, A. A fixed point theorem of Banach-Caccioppoli type on a class of generalized metric spaces. *Publ. Math.* **2000**, *1*, 31–37.
6. George, R.; Radenovic, S.; Reshma, K.P.; Shukla, S. Rectangular *b*-metric space and contraction principles. *J. Nonlinear Sci. Appl.* **2015**, *6*, 1005–1013. [CrossRef]
7. Kamran, T.; Samreen, M.; Ain, O.U. A generalization of *b*-metric space and some fixed point theorems. *Mathematics* **2017**, *5*, 19. [CrossRef]
8. Asim, M.; Mdad, M.I.; Adenovic, S.R. Fixed point resuls in extended rectangular *b*-metric space with an application. *UPB Sci. Bull. Ser. A* **2019**, *81*, 11–20.
9. Abdeljawad, T.; Karapınar, E.; Panda, S.K.; Mlaiki, N. Solutions of boundary value problems on extended Branciari *b*-distance.*J. Inequal. Appl.* **2020**, *1*, 103. [CrossRef]
10. Khojasteh, F.; Shukla, S.; Redenovi, S. A new approach to the study fixed point theorems via simulation functions. *Filomat* **2015**, *6*, 1189–1194. [CrossRef]
11. Argoubi, H.; Samet, B.; Vetro, C. Nonlinear contractions involving simulation functions in a metric space with a partial order. *J. Nonlinear Sci. Appl.* **2015**, *6*, 1082–1094. [CrossRef]
12. Roldán-López-de-Hierro, A.F.; Karapınar, E.; Roldán-López-de-Hierro, C.; Martínez-Moreno, J. Coincidence point theorems on metric spaces via simulation functions. *J. Comput. Appl. Math.* **2015**, *1*, 345–355. [CrossRef]
13. Sawangsup, K.; Sintunavarat, W. On modified $\mathcal{Z}$-contractions and an iterative scheme for solving nonlinear matrix equations. *J. Fixed Point Theory Appl.* **2018**, *2*, 80. [CrossRef]
14. Chifu, C.; Karapinar, E. On contractions via simulation functions on extended *b*-metric spaces. *Miskolc Math. Notes* **2020**, *1*, 127–141. [CrossRef]
15. Al-Sulami, H.H.; Ahmad, J.; Hussain, N.; Latif, A. Relation theoretic $(\theta, \Re)$ contraction results with applications to nonlinear matrix equations. *Symmetry* **2018**, *12*, 767. [CrossRef]
16. Alfaqih, W.M.; Imdad, M.; Gubran, R.; Khan, I.A. Relation-theoretic coincidence and common fixed point results under $(F, \Re)_g$-contractions with an application. *Fixed Point Theory A* **2019**, *12*, 12. [CrossRef]
17. Zadal, M.B.; Sarwar, M. Common fixed point theorems for rational $F_{\Re}$-contractive pairs of mappings with applications. *J. Inequal. Appl.* **2019**, *1*, 11. [CrossRef]
18. Alam, A.; Imdad, M. Relation-theoretic contraction principle. *J. Fixed Point Theory Appl.* **2015**, *4*, 693–702. [CrossRef]
19. Alam, A.; Imdad, M. Relation-theoretic metrical coincidence theorems. *Filomat* **2017**, *14*, 4421–4439. [CrossRef]
20. Hassen, A.; Zoran, D.M.; Stojan, R. On a common jungck type fixed point result in extended rectangular *b*-metric spaces. *Axioms* **2019**, *1*, 4. [CrossRef]
21. Rana, K.; Garg, A.K. Kannan-type fixed piont results in extended rectangular *b*-metric spaces. *Adv. Math.* **2020**, *8*, 5491–5499.

22. Dass, B.K.; Gupta, S. An extension of Banach contraction principle through rational expression. *Indian J. Pure Appl. Math.* **1975**, *12*, 1455–1458.
23. Hossain, A.; Khan, F.A.; Khan, Q.H. A relation-theoretic metrical fixed point theorem for rational type contraction mapping with an application. *Axioms* **2021**, *4*, 316.
24. Ran, A.C.M.; Reurings, M.C.B. A fixed point theorem in partially ordered sets and some applications to matrix equations. *Proc. Am. Math. Soc.* **2003**, *132*, 1435–1443. [CrossRef]
25. Taş, N.; Özgür, N.Y.; Mlaiki, N. New types of F_c-contractions and the fixed-circle problem. *Mathematics* **2018**, *10*, 188. [CrossRef]
26. Mlaiki, N.; Taş, N.; Özgür, N.Y. On the fixed-circle problem and Khan type contractions. *Axioms* **2018**, *4*, 80. [CrossRef]
27. Mlaiki, N.; Çelik, U.; Taş, N.; Özgür, N.Y.; Mukheimer, A. Wardowski type contractions and the fixed-circle problem on S metric spaces. *J. Math.* **2018**, *1*, 9127486. [CrossRef]
28. Mlaiki, N.; Özgür, N.Y.; Taş, N. New fixed-point theorems on an S-metric space via simulation functions. *Mathematics* **2019**, *7*, 583.
29. Ameer, E.; Aydi, H.; Nazam, M.; De la Sen, M. Results on fixed circles and discs for $L(\omega, c)$-contractions and related applications. *Adv. Differ. Equ.* **2021**, *1*, 349. [CrossRef]

symmetry

MDPI

Article

Sufficiency for Weak Minima in Optimal Control Subject to Mixed Constraints

Gerardo Sánchez Licea

Departamento de Matemáticas, Facultad de Ciencias, Universidad Nacional Autónoma de México, Ciudad de México 04510, Mexico; gesl@ciencias.unam.mx

Abstract: For optimal control problems of Bolza involving time-state-control mixed constraints, containing inequalities and equalities, fixed initial end-point, variable final end-point, and nonlinear dynamics, sufficient conditions for weak minima are derived. The proposed algorithm allows us to avoid hypotheses such as the continuity of the second derivatives of the functions delimiting the problems, the continuity of the optimal controls or the parametrization of the final variable end-point. We also present a relaxation relative to some similar works, in the sense that we arrive essentially to the same conclusions but making weaker assumptions.

Keywords: optimal control; mixed constraints; free final end-point; sufficiency; weak minima

MSC: 49K15

1. Introduction

In this paper, we study sufficiency conditions for a weak minimum in two constrained parametric and nonparametric optimal control problems having nonlinear dynamics, a left fixed end-point, a right variable end-point and mixed time-state-control restrictions involving inequalities and equalities. In the parametric problem, we show how the deviation between admissible costs and optimal costs is derived by some functions playing the role of the square of some norms; in particular, the involvement of a functional whose structure is very similar to the square of the classical norm of the Lebesgue measurable functions is a fundamental component. See [1–4], where the authors study sufficient conditions for optimality, and they obtain a similar behaviour with respect to the corresponding deviations between optimal and feasible costs. In the parametric problem, the variable end-point is subject to a parametrization involving a twice continuously differentiable manifold, and, in the nonparametric problem, we make a relaxation of that concept because of the fact that the final end-point is not only variable but also completely free, in the sense that the final end-point may belong to any set which only must be contained in a surface having continuous second derivatives of the independent variable. Another important relaxation of this paper is that we avoid the imposition of two functional restrictions involving the maximum of some crucial integrals, one of them concerning derivatives of admissible and optimal dynamics and the other concerning the admissible and optimal controls, see [5,6]. In contrast, we show how, by fixing the left end-point, we are able to eliminate the integral depending on the admissible dynamics of the problem and only make a weaker hypothesis only involving the integral of admissible and the optimal controls. It is worth emphasizing that the conclusions are very similar and the hypotheses are weaker.

On the other hand, the sufficiency technique employed to prove the main theorem of the paper is self-contained because it is independent of classical approaches used to obtain sufficiency in optimal control such as the Hamilton–Jacobi theory, the incorporation of symmetric solutions of some matrix-valued Riccati equations or the use of fundamental concepts appealing to Jacobi's theory in terms of conjugate points, see [7–9], respectively.

Citation: Licea, G.S. Sufficiency for Weak Minima in Optimal Control Subject to Mixed Constraints. *Symmetry* **2022**, *14*, 1520. https://doi.org/10.3390/sym14081520

Academic Editors: Octav Olteanu and Jan Awrejcewicz

Received: 26 June 2022
Accepted: 20 July 2022
Published: 25 July 2022

In contrast, our approach is direct in nature since it strongly depends upon three fundamental concepts; the first one concerns a similar version of the Legendre–Clebsch necessary condition; the second one is related with the positivity of the second variation over the cone of critical directions, and the third one involves a crucial integral inequality involving a Weierstrass verification excess function and the integral of a mapping whose behavior is very similar to the quadratic function around zero and very analogous to the absolute value function around infinity and minus infinity. As the right end-point is variable in the parametric optimal control problem as well as in the nonparametric optimal control problem, our hypotheses also impose a transversality condition and the properties of the proof of the theorem of the article find out the fulfillment of a second order inequality to be crucial. This second order inequality has its origin in a symmetric inequality presented in hypothesis (ii) of Theorem 1 and Corollary 1 of [5,6]. The absence of the continuity of the proposed optimal controls in the content of this paper is also one of the essential components of this work. See [7–21], where that assumption of continuity in the sufficiency approaches containing a degree of generality very similar to that obtained in this article, is a uniform unfortunate assumption since the admissible controls must only lie in the family of measurable functions. To be more precise, it is an unfortunate issue that, in the works mentioned above, their optimal controls need to be confined to the space of continuous functions; meanwhile, all the feasible controls must only be measurable, see [5,6,22], where we show that this assumption of continuity on the optimal controls is very strong.

The paper is organized as follows: In Section 2, we state the parametric optimal control problem that we shall study, some basic definitions, and we enunciate the main theorem of the article. In Section 3, we pose the nonparametric optimal control problem we are going to study together with a fundamental lemma and a corollary which turns out to be the principal result of the paper. In the same section, we illustrate with two examples how even the non-expert can apply the main corollary of the article. In Section 4, we establish three supplementary lemmas whose proofs can be found in [23] and on which the proof of the theorem is strongly based. In Section 5, we make the proof of the theorem of the paper by means of two lemmas. In Section 6, we present a discussion concerning the relations between necessary and sufficient conditions, we add some comments about an experimental economic model, and we exhibit some relevant references containing the fundamental subject of mixed constraints. Finally, in Section 7, we provide the main conclusions of the article.

2. An Auxiliary Theorem

Suppose that we are given an interval $\mathcal{T} := [t_1, t_2]$ in $\mathbf{R}$, a fixed point $\xi_1 \in \mathbf{R}^n$ and C any nonempty subset of $\mathbf{R}^s$, called the set of *parameters*, that we have functions $\gamma\colon \mathbf{R}^n \to \mathbf{R}$, $\Psi\colon \mathbf{R}^n \to \mathbf{R}^n$, $\Gamma(t,x,u)\colon \mathcal{T} \times \mathbf{R}^n \times \mathbf{R}^m \to \mathbf{R}$, $f(t,x,u)\colon \mathcal{T} \times \mathbf{R}^n \times \mathbf{R}^m \to \mathbf{R}^n$ and $\varphi(t,x,u)\colon \mathcal{T} \times \mathbf{R}^n \times \mathbf{R}^m \to \mathbf{R}^q$. Set

$$R := \{(t,x,u) \in \mathcal{T} \times \mathbf{R}^n \times \mathbf{R}^m \mid \varphi_\sigma(t,x,u) \le 0 \ (\sigma \in P),\ \varphi_\varsigma(t,x,u) = 0 \ (\varsigma \in Q)\}$$

where $P := \{1,\ldots,p\}$ and $Q := \{p+1,\ldots,q\}$ $(p = 0,1,\ldots,q)$. If $p = 0$, then P is empty, and we disregard statements about φ_σ. If $p = q$, then Q is empty, and we disregard statements about φ_ς.

Throughout the paper, we suppose that Γ, f and $\varphi = (\varphi_1,\ldots,\varphi_q)$ have first and second derivatives with respect to x and u. Additionally, if we denote by $G(t,x,u)$ either $\Gamma(t,x,u)$, $f(t,x,u)$, $\varphi(t,x,u)$ or any of their partial derivatives of order ≤ 2 with respect to x and u, we are going to assume that, if $\mathcal{G}$ is any bounded subset of $\mathcal{T} \times \mathbf{R}^n \times \mathbf{R}^m$, then $|G(\mathcal{G})|$ is a bounded subset of $\mathbf{R}$. In addition, we suppose that, if $((h_q, l_q))$ is any sequence in $AC(\mathcal{T};\mathbf{R}^n) \times L^\infty(\mathcal{T};\mathbf{R}^m)$ such that for some $(h,l) \in AC(\mathcal{T};\mathbf{R}^n) \times L^\infty(\mathcal{T};\mathbf{R}^m)$, $(h_q(\cdot), l_q(\cdot)) \xrightarrow{L^\infty} (h(\cdot), l(\cdot))$ on $\mathcal{T}$, then, for all $q \in \mathbf{N}$, $G(\cdot, h_q(\cdot), l_q(\cdot))$ is measurable on $\mathcal{T}$ and

$$G(\cdot, h_q(\cdot), l_q(\cdot)) \xrightarrow{L^\infty} G(\cdot, h(\cdot), l(\cdot)) \text{ on } \mathcal{T}.$$

It is worth observing that conditions given above are satisfied if the functions Γ, f, φ and their first and second derivatives relative to x and u are continuous on $\mathcal{T} \times \mathbf{R}^n \times \mathbf{R}^m$. We are going to suppose that the functions γ and Ψ are of class C^2 on $\mathbf{R}^n$.

Designate by $X := \{x\colon \mathcal{T} \to \mathbf{R}^n \mid x \text{ is absolutely continuous}\}$ and for any positive integer s, set $U_s := L^\infty(\mathcal{T}; \mathbf{R}^s)$. Define $A := X \times U_m \times \mathbf{R}^s$. The notation $z_a := (z, a) = (x, u, a)$ denotes any element $z_a \in A$.

We are going to study a parametric optimal control problem, denoted by $P(\gamma, \Gamma, C, f, \xi_1, \Psi, R, s)$, consisting of minimizing a functional of the form

$$I(z_a) := \gamma(a) + \int_{t_1}^{t_2} \Gamma(t, x(t), u(t))dt$$

over all z_a in A satisfying the constraints

$$\begin{cases} a \in C. \\ \dot{x}(t) = f(t, x(t), u(t)) \text{ (a.e. in } \mathcal{T}). \\ x(t_1) = \xi_1,\ x(t_2) = \Psi(a). \\ (t, x(t), u(t)) \in R \ (t \in \mathcal{T}). \end{cases}$$

Elements $a = (a_1, \ldots, a_s)^*$ in $\mathbf{R}^s$ ($*$ denotes transpose) will be called *parameters,* members z_a in A will be called *processes,* and a process is *admissible* if it verifies the constraints.

- A process $\hat{z}_{\hat{a}}$ solves $P(\gamma, \Gamma, C, f, \xi_1, \Psi, R, s)$ if it is admissible and $I(\hat{z}_{\hat{a}}) \le I(z_a)$ for all admissible processes z_a. An admissible process $\hat{z}_{\hat{a}}$ is a *weak minimum* of $P(\gamma, \Gamma, C, f, \xi_1, \Psi, R, s)$ if it is a minimum of I relative to the norm

$$\|z_a\| := |a| + \|(x, u)\|_\infty,$$

  that is, if, for some $\epsilon > 0$, $I(\hat{z}_{\hat{a}}) \le I(z_a)$ for all admissible processes z_a verifying $\|z_a - \hat{z}_{\hat{a}}\| < \epsilon$.
- For all $(t, x, u, \omega, \nu) \in \mathcal{T} \times \mathbf{R}^n \times \mathbf{R}^m \times \mathbf{R}^n \times \mathbf{R}^q$, define the augmented Hamiltonian by

$$\mathcal{H}(t, x, u, \omega, \nu) := \omega^* f(t, x, u) - \Gamma(t, x, u) - \nu^* \varphi(t, x, u).$$

  If $\omega \in X$ and $\nu \in U_q$ are given, set, for all $(t, x, u) \in \mathcal{T} \times \mathbf{R}^n \times \mathbf{R}^m$,

$$\mathcal{F}(t, x, u) := -\mathcal{H}(t, x, u, \omega(t), \nu(t)) - \dot{\omega}(t)x$$

  and let

$$J(z_a) := \omega^*(t_2)x(t_2) - \omega^*(t_1)x(t_1) + \gamma(a) + \int_{t_1}^{t_2} \mathcal{F}(t, x(t), u(t))dt.$$

- The *second variation* of J with respect to z_a in the direction w_α, is given by

$$J''(z_a; w_\alpha) := \alpha^* \gamma''(a)\alpha + \int_{t_1}^{t_2} 2\Omega(t, x(t), u(t); y(t), v(t))dt,$$

  where, for all $(t, y, v) \in \mathcal{T} \times \mathbf{R}^n \times \mathbf{R}^m$,

$$2\Omega(t, x(t), u(t); y, v) := y^* \mathcal{F}_{xx}(t, x(t), u(t))y + 2y^* \mathcal{F}_{xu}(t, x(t), u(t))v + v^* \mathcal{F}_{uu}(t, x(t), u(t))v,$$

  and the notation w_α means any element $(y, v, \alpha) \in X \times L^2(\mathcal{T}; \mathbf{R}^m) \times \mathbf{R}^s$. In addition, $\gamma''(a)$ is the second derivative of γ evaluated at a.
- Let

$$E(t, x, u, v) := \mathcal{F}(t, x, v) - \mathcal{F}(t, x, u) - \mathcal{F}_u(t, x, u)(v - u).$$

- Define

$$\mathcal{D}(u) := \int_{t_1}^{t_2} L(u(t))dt \quad \text{where} \quad L(c) := (1+|c|^2)^{1/2} - 1 \ (c \in \mathbf{R}^m).$$

Finally, if $(t, x, u) \in \mathcal{T} \times \mathbf{R}^n \times \mathbf{R}^m$ is given, denote by

$$i(t,x,u) := \{\sigma \in P \mid \varphi_\sigma(t,x,u) = 0\},$$

the set of active indices of (t, x, u) relative to the inequality constraints. For all $z_a \in A$, let $Y(z_a)$ be the cone of all $w_\alpha \in X \times L^2(T; \mathbf{R}^m) \times \mathbf{R}^s$ satisfying

$$\begin{cases} \dot{y}(t) = f_x(t,x(t),u(t))y(t) + f_u(t,x(t),u(t))v(t) \text{ (a.e. in } \mathcal{T}). \\ y(t_1) = 0,\ y(t_2) = \Psi'(a)\alpha. \\ \varphi_{\sigma x}(t,x(t),u(t))y(t) + \varphi_{\sigma u}(t,x(t),u(t))v(t) \leq 0 \text{ (a.e. in } \mathcal{T}, \sigma \in i(t,x(t),u(t))). \\ \varphi_{\varsigma x}(t,x(t),u(t))y(t) + \varphi_{\varsigma u}(t,x(t),u(t))v(t) = 0 \text{ (a.e. in } \mathcal{T}, \varsigma \in Q). \end{cases}$$

The set $Y(z_a)$ is the *cone of critical directions* with respect to z_a.

Theorem 1. *Let $\hat{z}_{\hat{a}}$ be an admissible process. Assume that $i(\cdot, \hat{x}(\cdot), \hat{u}(\cdot))$ is piecewise constant on $\mathcal{T}$ that there exist $\omega \in X$, $\nu \in U_q$ with $\nu_\sigma(t) \geq 0$, $\nu_\sigma(t)\varphi_\sigma(t,\hat{x}(t),\hat{u}(t)) = 0$ ($\sigma \in P, t \in \mathcal{T}$) and $\delta, \epsilon > 0$, such that*

$$\dot{\omega}(t) = -\mathcal{H}_x^*(t,\hat{x}(t),\hat{u}(t),\omega(t),\nu(t)) \text{ (a.e. in } \mathcal{T}),$$

$$\mathcal{H}_u^*(t,\hat{x}(t),\hat{u}(t),\omega(t),\nu(t)) = 0 \ (t \in \mathcal{T}),$$

and the following is satisfied:

(i) $\gamma'^*(\hat{a}) + \Psi'^*(\hat{a})\omega(t_2) = 0$.
(ii) $\omega^*(t_2)\Psi''(\hat{a};h) \geq 0$ *for all* $h \in \mathbf{R}^s$.
(iii) $\mathcal{H}_{uu}(t,\hat{x}(t),\hat{u}(t),\omega(t),\nu(t)) \leq 0$ *(a.e. in $\mathcal{T}$).*
(iv) $J''(\hat{z}_{\hat{a}}; w_\alpha) > 0$ *for all* $w_\alpha \in Y(\hat{z}_{\hat{a}})$, $w_\alpha \not\equiv (0,0,0)$.
(v) z_a *admissible with* $\|(x,u) - (\hat{x},\hat{u})\|_\infty < \epsilon$ *implies that* $\int_{t_1}^{t_2} E(t,x(t),\hat{u}(t),u(t)) \geq \delta\mathcal{D}(u-\hat{u})$.

Then, for some $\rho_1, \rho_2 > 0$ and all admissible processes z_a satisfying $\|z_a - \hat{z}_{\hat{a}}\| < \rho_1$,

$$I(z_a) \geq I(\hat{z}_{\hat{a}}) + \rho_2 \min\{|a-\hat{a}|^2, \mathcal{D}(u-\hat{u})\}.$$

In particular, $\hat{z}_{\hat{a}}$ is a weak minimum of $P(\gamma, \Gamma, C, f, \xi_1, \Psi, R, s)$.

3. The Principal Result

Suppose that an interval $\mathcal{T} := [t_1, t_2]$ in $\mathbf{R}$ is given, a fixed point $Y_1 \in \mathbf{R}^n$, a set $B \subset \mathbf{R}^n$ and functions $\ell\colon \mathbf{R}^n \to \mathbf{R}$, $\mathcal{L}(t,x,u)\colon \mathcal{T} \times \mathbf{R}^n \times \mathbf{R}^m \to \mathbf{R}$, $g(t,x,u)\colon \mathcal{T} \times \mathbf{R}^n \times \mathbf{R}^m \to \mathbf{R}^n$ and $\phi(t,x,u)\colon \mathcal{T} \times \mathbf{R}^n \times \mathbf{R}^m \to \mathbf{R}^q$. Set

$$\mathcal{R} := \{(t,x,u) \in \mathcal{T} \times \mathbf{R}^n \times \mathbf{R}^m \mid \phi_\sigma(t,x,u) \leq 0 \ (\sigma \in P),\ \phi_\varsigma(t,x,u) = 0 \ (\varsigma \in Q)\}$$

where $P := \{1, \ldots, p\}$ and $Q := \{p+1, \ldots, q\}$ $(p = 0, 1, \ldots, q)$. If $p = 0$, then P is empty, and we disregard statements about ϕ_σ. If $p = q$, then Q is empty, and we disregard statements about ϕ_ς.

In this section, we shall assume that $\mathcal{L}$, g and $\phi = (\phi_1, \ldots, \phi_q)$ satisfy the regularity hypotheses mentioned in Section 2. In particular, if $\mathcal{L}$, g, and ϕ have first and second continuous partial derivatives with respect to x and u on $\mathcal{T} \times \mathbf{R}^n \times \mathbf{R}^m$, then they verify the previously mentioned regularity hypotheses. Moreover, we shall be assuming that the function ℓ is of class C^2 on $\mathbf{R}^n$.

Set $\mathcal{A} := X \times \mathcal{U}_m$, where usually X is the space of absolutely continuous functions mapping $\mathcal{T}$ to $\mathbf{R}^n$, and $\mathcal{U}_m$ is the space of all essentially bounded measurable functions mapping $\mathcal{T}$ to $\mathbf{R}^m$.

In this section, we are going to study the non-parametric optimal control problem $\mathcal{P}(\ell, \mathcal{L}, g, \Upsilon_1, B, \mathcal{R}, n)$ of finding a minimum value to the functional

$$\mathcal{J}(x,u) := \ell(x(t_2)) + \int_{t_1}^{t_2} \mathcal{L}(t, x(t), u(t))dt$$

over all pairs (x, u) in $\mathcal{A}$ verifying the constraints

$$\begin{cases} \dot{x}(t) = g(t, x(t), u(t)) \text{ (a.e. in } \mathcal{T}). \\ x(t_1) = \Upsilon_1,\ x(t_2) \in B. \\ (t, x(t), u(t)) \in \mathcal{R}\ (t \in \mathcal{T}). \end{cases}$$

The elements (x, u) in $\mathcal{A}$ will be called *processes*. A process is admissible if it satisfies the restrictions.

A process $(\hat{x}, \hat{u})$ is a global solution of $\mathcal{P}(\ell, \mathcal{L}, g, \Upsilon_1, B, \mathcal{R}, n)$ if it is admissible and $\mathcal{J}(\hat{x}, \hat{u}) \leq \mathcal{J}(x, u)$ for all (x, u) admissible. An admissible process $(\hat{x}, \hat{u})$ is a *weak minimum* of $\mathcal{P}(\ell, \mathcal{L}, g, \Upsilon_1, B, \mathcal{R}, n)$ if it is a minimum of $\mathcal{J}$ with respect to the essential supremum norm, that is, $\mathcal{J}(\hat{x}, \hat{u}) \leq \mathcal{J}(x, u)$ for all admissible processes verifying $\|(x, u) - (\hat{x}, \hat{u})\|_\infty < \epsilon$, for some $\epsilon > 0$.

Let $\Psi\colon \mathbf{R}^n \to \mathbf{R}^n$ be any twice continuously differentiable function such that $B \subset \Psi(\mathbf{R}^n)$. Connect the nonparametric optimal control problem $\mathcal{P}(\ell, \mathcal{L}, g, \Upsilon_1, B, \mathcal{R}, n)$ with the parametric optimal control problem stated in Section 2, denoted by $P(\gamma, \Gamma, C, f, \xi_1, \Psi, R, s)$, that is, $P(\gamma, \Gamma, C, f, \xi_1, \Psi, R, s)$ is the parametric problem stated in Section 2, with the next data; $\gamma = \ell \circ \Psi$, $\Gamma = \mathcal{L}$, $C = \Psi^{-1}(B)$, $f = g$, $\xi_1 = \Upsilon_1$, Ψ the function given above, $R = \mathcal{R}$ and $s = n$.

Lemma 1. *The following conditions are satisfied:*

(i) z_a *is an admissible process of* $P(\gamma, \Gamma, C, f, \xi_1, \Psi, R, n)$ *if and only if* (x, u) *is a feasible process of* $\mathcal{P}(\ell, \mathcal{L}, g, \Upsilon_1, B, \mathcal{R}, n)$ *and* $a \in \Psi^{-1}(x(t_2))$.

(ii) If z_a *is an admissible process of* $P(\gamma, \Gamma, C, f, \xi_1, \Psi, R, n)$, *then*

$$\mathcal{J}(x,u) = I(z_a).$$

(iii) If $\hat{z}_{\hat{a}}$ *solves* $P(\gamma, \Gamma, C, f, \xi_1, \Psi, R, n)$, *then* $(\hat{x}, \hat{u})$ *solves* $\mathcal{P}(\ell, \mathcal{L}, g, \Upsilon_1, B, \mathcal{R}, n)$.

Proof. Index (i) follows from the definition of the problems. In order to prove (ii), note that, if z_a is an admissible process of $P(\gamma, \Gamma, C, f, \xi_1, \Psi, R, n)$, then, by (i), (x, u) is an admissible process of $\mathcal{P}(\ell, \mathcal{L}, g, \Upsilon_1, B, \mathcal{R}, n)$ and $x(t_2) = \Psi(a)$. Then,

$$\begin{aligned} \mathcal{J}(x,u) &= \ell(x(t_2)) + \int_{t_1}^{t_2} \mathcal{L}(t, x(t), u(t))dt \\ &= \ell(\Psi(a)) + \int_{t_1}^{t_2} \Gamma(t, x(t), u(t))dt \\ &= \gamma(a) + \int_{t_1}^{t_2} \Gamma(t, x(t), u(t))dt = I(z_a). \end{aligned}$$

Finally, in order to prove (iii), let z_a be an admissible process of $P(\gamma, \Gamma, C, f, \xi_1, \Psi, R, n)$. By (i), $(\hat{x}, \hat{u})$ and (x, u) are admissible of $\mathcal{P}(\ell, \mathcal{L}, g, \Upsilon_1, B, \mathcal{R}, n)$. Then, by (ii) and (iii),

$$\mathcal{J}(\hat{x}, \hat{u}) = I(\hat{z}_{\hat{a}}) \leq I(z_a) = \mathcal{J}(x, u).$$

□

Corollary 1 below is a straightforward implication of Theorem 1 and Lemma 1. It provides sufficient conditions for weak minima of the nonparametric problem $\mathcal{P}(\ell, \mathcal{L}, g, \Upsilon_1, B, \mathcal{R}, n)$. It is worth observing that the proposed optimal control is not necessarily continuous but only measurable as was the case of Theorem 1.

Corollary 1. *Let $\Psi\colon \mathbf{R}^n \to \mathbf{R}^n$ be any twice continuously differentiable function such that $B \subset \Psi(\mathbf{R}^n)$ and let $P(\gamma, \Gamma, C, f, \xi_1, \Psi, R, n)$ be the parametric optimal control problem before pronouncing Lemma 1. Let $\hat{z}_{\hat{a}}$ be an admissible process of $P(\gamma, \Gamma, C, f, \xi_1, \Psi, R, n)$. Suppose that $i(\cdot, \hat{x}(\cdot), \hat{u}(\cdot))$ is piecewise constant on $\mathcal{T}$, there exist $\omega \in X$, $\nu \in \mathcal{U}_q$ satisfying $\nu_\sigma(t) \geq 0$ and $\nu_\sigma(t)\varphi_\sigma(t, \hat{x}(t), \hat{u}(t)) = 0$ $(\sigma \in P, t \in \mathcal{T})$, two positive numbers δ, ϵ such that*

$$\dot{\omega}(t) = -\mathcal{H}_x^*(t, \hat{x}(t), \hat{u}(t), \omega(t), \nu(t)) \text{ (a.e. in } \mathcal{T}),$$

$$\mathcal{H}_u^*(t, \hat{x}(t), \hat{u}(t), \omega(t), \nu(t)) = 0 \ (t \in \mathcal{T}),$$

and the following conditions are satisfied:

(i) $\gamma'^*(\hat{a}) + \Psi'^*(\hat{a})\omega(t_2) = 0.$
(ii) $\omega^*(t_2)\Psi''(\hat{a}; h) \geq 0$ *for all* $h \in \mathbf{R}^n$.
(iii) $\mathcal{H}_{uu}(t, \hat{x}(t), \hat{u}(t), \omega(t), \nu(t)) \leq 0$ *(a.e. in* $\mathcal{T}$*).*
(iv) $J''(\hat{z}_{\hat{a}}; w_\alpha) > 0$ *for all* $w_\alpha \in Y(\hat{z}_{\hat{a}})$, $w_\alpha \not\equiv (0,0,0)$.
(v) z_a *admissible with* $\|(x,u) - (\hat{x}, \hat{u})\|_\infty < \epsilon$ *implies that* $\int_{t_1}^{t_2} E(t, x(t), \hat{u}(t), u(t)) \geq \delta\mathcal{D}(u - \hat{u})$.

Then, $(\hat{x}, \hat{u})$ *is a weak minimum of* $\mathcal{P}(\ell, \mathcal{L}, g, \Upsilon_1, B, \mathcal{R}, n)$.

Examples 1 and 2 below show how even a non-expert can apply Corollary 1. Examples 1 and 2 are concerned with an inequality-equality restrained optimal control problem in which one has to verify that an element $(\hat{x}, \hat{u}, \omega, \nu)$ satisfies the sufficient conditions

$$\dot{\omega}(t) = -\mathcal{H}_x^*(t, \hat{x}(t), \hat{u}(t), \omega(t), \nu(t)) \text{ (a.e. in } \mathcal{T}), \quad \mathcal{H}_u^*(t, \hat{x}(t), \hat{u}(t), \omega(t), \nu(t)) = 0 \ (t \in \mathcal{T}),$$

and that the former also satisfies conditions (i), (ii), (iii), (iv), and (v) of Corollary 1, implying that it is a weak minimum of $\mathcal{P}(\ell, \mathcal{L}, g, \Upsilon_1, B, \mathcal{R}, n)$.

Example 1. *Consider the nonparametric optimal control problem $\mathcal{P}(\ell, \mathcal{L}, g, \Upsilon_1, B, \mathcal{R}, n)$ of finding a minimum value to the functional*

$$\mathcal{J}(x,u) = x^2(1) - x(1) + \int_0^1 \{\exp(tu(t)) + \sinh x(t)\}dt$$

over all (x,u) in $\mathcal{A}$ verifying the constraints

$$\begin{cases} \dot{x}(t) = u(t) \text{ almost everywhere in } [0,1]. \\ x(0) = 0, \ x(1) \in (-\infty, 0]. \\ (t, x(t), u(t)) \in \mathcal{R} \ (t \in [0,1]) \end{cases}$$

where

$$\mathcal{R} := \{(t,x,u) \in [0,1] \times \mathbf{R} \times \mathbf{R} \mid (3/2)u^2 - x^2 - \exp(-x) - x + 1 \leq 0\},$$

$$\mathcal{A} := X \times \mathcal{U}_1,$$

$$X := \{x\colon [0,1] \to \mathbf{R} \mid x \text{ is absolutely continuous on } [0,1]\},$$

$$\mathcal{U}_1 := \{u\colon [0,1] \to \mathbf{R} \mid u \text{ is essentially bounded on } [0,1]\}.$$

For this event, the data of the proposed nonparametric problem are given by $\mathcal{T} = [0,1]$, $m = 1$, $p = 1$, $q = 1$, $\ell(\cdot) = x^2(\cdot) - x(\cdot)$, $\mathcal{L}(t,x,u) = \exp(tu) + \sinh x$, $g(t,x,u) = u$,

$\Upsilon_1 = 0$, $B = (-\infty, 0]$, $\mathcal{R} = \{(t,x,u) \in \mathcal{T} \times \mathbf{R} \times \mathbf{R} \mid (3/2)u^2 - x^2 - \exp(-x) - x + 1 \leq 0\}$ and $n = 1$. Observe that

$$\phi_1(t,x,u) = (3/2)u^2 - x^2 - \exp(-x) - x + 1.$$

We have that the functions $\mathcal{L}$, g, $\phi = \phi_1$, and their first and second derivatives relative to x and u are continuous on $\mathcal{T} \times \mathbf{R} \times \mathbf{R}$. Additionally, the function ℓ is C^2 in $\mathbf{R}$.

Moreover, one can verify that the process $(\hat{x}, \hat{u}) \equiv (0,0)$ is admissible of $\mathcal{P}(\ell, \mathcal{L}, g, \Upsilon_1, B, \mathcal{R}, n)$. Let $\Psi \colon \mathbf{R} \to \mathbf{R}$ be given by $\Psi(b) := b$. Clearly, Ψ is C^2 in $\mathbf{R}$ and $B \subset \Psi(\mathbf{R})$. The connected parametric problem designated by $P(\gamma, \Gamma, C, f, \xi_1, \Psi, R, s)$ has the next data; $\gamma = \ell \circ \Psi$, $\Gamma = \mathcal{L}$, $C = \Psi^{-1}(B)$, $f = g$, $\xi_1 = \Upsilon_1$, Ψ the function given above, $R = \mathcal{R}$ and $s = n$.

Observe that, if we set $\hat{a} := 0$, then $\hat{z}_{\hat{a}} = (\hat{x}, \hat{u}, \hat{a}) \equiv (0,0,0)$ is admissible of $P(\gamma, \Gamma, C, f, \xi_1, \Psi, R, n)$. Moreover, $i(\cdot, \hat{x}(\cdot), \hat{u}(\cdot)) \equiv \{1\}$ is constant on $\mathcal{T}$. Let $\omega \equiv t$, $\nu_1 \equiv 1$ and observe that $(\omega, \nu) \in X \times \mathcal{U}_1$, $\nu_\sigma \geq 0$ and $\nu_\sigma(t)\varphi_\sigma(t, \hat{x}(t), \hat{u}(t)) = 0$ $(t \in \mathcal{T}, \sigma = 1)$. Recall that $\varphi = \phi$.

Now,

$$\mathcal{H}(t,x,u,\omega,\nu) = \omega u - \exp(tu) - \sinh x - \nu_1[(3/2)u^2 - x^2 - \exp(-x) - x + 1],$$

and observe that

$$\mathcal{H}_x(t,x,u,\omega,\nu) = -\cosh x - \nu_1[-2x + \exp(-x) - 1],$$

$$\mathcal{H}_u(t,x,u,\omega,\nu) = \omega - t\exp(tu) - 3\nu_1 u.$$

Then,

$$\dot{\omega}(t) = -\mathcal{H}_x(t, \hat{x}(t), \hat{u}(t), \omega(t), \nu(t)) \text{ (a.e. in } \mathcal{T}) \quad \text{and} \quad \mathcal{H}_u(t, \hat{x}(t), \hat{u}(t), \omega(t), \nu(t)) = 0 \ (t \in \mathcal{T})$$

and hence $(\hat{x}, \hat{u}, \omega, \nu)$ verifies the first order sufficiency conditions of Corollary 1. Since $\Psi(b) = b$ $(b \in \mathbf{R})$, we have that $\gamma(b) = b^2 - b$ $(b \in \mathbf{R})$. Then,

$$\gamma'(\hat{a}) + \Psi'(\hat{a})\omega(1) = 0$$

and hence condition (i) of Corollary 1 is verified. Moreover, one can verify that

$$\omega(1)\Psi''(\hat{a}; h) = 0 \text{ for all } h \in \mathbf{R}$$

and then condition (ii) of Corollary 1 is verified.

Now, for all $(t,x,u) \in \mathcal{T} \times \mathbf{R} \times \mathbf{R}$,

$$\mathcal{H}(t,x,u,\omega(t),\nu(t)) = tu - \exp(tu) - \sinh x - [(3/2)u^2 - x^2 - \exp(-x) - x + 1]$$

and hence, for all $t \in \mathcal{T}$,

$$\mathcal{H}_{uu}(t, \hat{x}(t), \hat{u}(t), \omega(t), \nu(t)) = -t^2 - 3 \leq 0$$

implying that $(\hat{x}, \hat{u}, \omega, \nu)$ satisfies condition (iii) of Corollary 1.

Additionally, note that, for all $t \in \mathcal{T}$,

$$f_x(t, \hat{x}(t), \hat{u}(t)) = 0 \quad \text{and} \quad f_u(t, \hat{x}(t), \hat{u}(t)) = 1,$$

$$\varphi_x(t, \hat{x}(t), \hat{u}(t)) = 0 \quad \text{and} \quad \varphi_u(t, \hat{x}(t), \hat{u}(t)) = 0.$$

Consequently, $Y(\hat{z}_{\hat{a}})$ is given by all $w_\alpha \in X \times L^2(\mathcal{T}; \mathbf{R}) \times \mathbf{R}$ verifying

$$\begin{cases} \dot{y}(t) = v(t) \text{ (a.e. in } \mathcal{T}). \\ y(0) = 0,\ y(1) = \alpha. \end{cases}$$

In addition, observe that, for all $(t, x, u) \in \mathcal{T} \times \mathbf{R} \times \mathbf{R}$,

$$\mathcal{F}(t, x, u) = -tu + \exp(tu) + (3/2)u^2 + \sinh x - x^2 - \exp(-x) - 2x + 1$$

and, for all $t \in \mathcal{T}$,

$$\mathcal{F}_{xx}(t, \hat{x}(t), \hat{u}(t)) = -3, \quad \mathcal{F}_{xu}(t, \hat{x}(t), \hat{u}(t)) = 0, \quad \mathcal{F}_{uu}(t, \hat{x}(t), \hat{u}(t)) = t^2 + 3.$$

Thus, for all $w_\alpha \in Y(\hat{z}_{\hat{a}})$,

$$J''(\hat{z}_{\hat{a}}; w_\alpha) = 2\alpha^2 + \int_0^1 3\{v^2(t) - y^2(t)\}dt + \int_0^1 3t^2 v^2(t)dt \geq 2\alpha^2 + \int_0^1 3\{\dot{y}^2(t) - y^2(t)\}dt.$$

Hence,

$$J''(\hat{z}_{\hat{a}}; w_\alpha) > 0$$

for all $w_\alpha \in Y(\hat{z}_{\hat{a}})$, $w_\alpha \not\equiv (0, 0, 0)$, and hence condition (iv) of Corollary 1 is fulfilled.

Now, note that, if z_a is admissible, for all $t \in \mathcal{T}$,

$$E(t, x(t), \hat{u}(t), u(t)) = -tu(t) + \exp(tu(t)) + (3/2)u^2(t) - 1.$$

Thus, if z_a is admissible,

$$\begin{aligned} \int_0^1 E(t, x(t), \hat{u}(t), u(t))dt &= \int_0^1 \{-tu(t) + \exp(tu(t)) + (3/2)u^2(t) - 1\}dt \geq \int_0^1 (1/2)u^2(t)dt \\ &\geq \int_0^1 L(u(t) - \hat{u}(t))dt = \mathcal{D}(u - \hat{u}). \end{aligned}$$

Therefore, condition (v) of Corollary 1 is satisfied for any $\epsilon > 0$ and $\delta = 1$. By Corollary 1, $(\hat{x}, \hat{u})$ is a weak minimum of $\mathcal{P}(\ell, \mathcal{L}, g, \Upsilon_1, B, \mathcal{R}, n)$.

Example 2. *Let us study the nonparametric optimal control problem $\mathcal{P}(\ell, \mathcal{L}, g, \Upsilon_1, B, \mathcal{R}, n)$ of minimizing the functional*

$$\mathcal{J}(x, u) = x^2(1) + \int_0^1 \{\tfrac{1}{2}(u_1(t) + u_2(t))^2 + u_1(t)\}dt$$

over all (x, u) in $\mathcal{A}$ satisfying the constraints

$$\begin{cases} \dot{x}(t) = u_1(t) + u_2(t) + x^3(t) \text{ almost everywhere in } [0,1]. \\ x(0) = 0,\ x(1) \in \mathbf{R}. \\ (t, x(t), u(t)) \in \mathcal{R}\ (t \in [0,1]) \end{cases}$$

where

$$\mathcal{R} := \{(t, x, u) \in [0,1] \times \mathbf{R} \times \mathbf{R}^2 \mid -\tfrac{1}{2}x^2 - u_1 \leq 0,\ \sin u_2 = 0\},$$

$$\mathcal{A} := X \times \mathcal{U}_2,$$

$$X := \{x\colon [0,1] \to \mathbf{R} \mid x \text{ is absolutely continuous on } [0,1]\},$$

$$\mathcal{U}_2 := \{u\colon [0,1] \to \mathbf{R}^2 \mid u \text{ is essentially bounded on } [0,1]\}.$$

For this event, the data of the nonparametric problem are given by $\mathcal{T} = [0,1]$, $m = 2$, $p = 1$, $q = 2$, $\ell(\cdot) = x^2(\cdot)$, $\mathcal{L}(t, x, u) = \frac{1}{2}(u_1 + u_2)^2 + u_1$, $g(t, x, u) = u_1 + u_2 + x^3$, $\Upsilon_1 = 0$, $B = \mathbf{R}$, $\mathcal{R} = \{(t, x, u) \in \mathcal{T} \times \mathbf{R} \times \mathbf{R}^2 \mid -\frac{1}{2}x^2 - u_1 \leq 0,\ \sin u_2 = 0\}$ and $n = 1$. Observe that

$$\phi_1(t, x, u) = -\tfrac{1}{2}x^2 - u_1 \quad \text{and} \quad \phi_2(t, x, u) = \sin u_2.$$

We have that the functions $\mathcal{L}$, g, $\phi = (\phi_1, \phi_2)$ and their first and second derivatives with respect to x and u are continuous on $\mathcal{T} \times \mathbf{R} \times \mathbf{R}^2$. Additionally, the function ℓ is C^2 in $\mathbf{R}$.

Moreover, as one readily verifies, the process $(\hat{x}, \hat{u}) \equiv (0,0,0)$ is admissible of $\mathcal{P}(\ell, \mathcal{L}, g, \Upsilon_1, B, \mathcal{R}, n)$. Let $\Psi\colon \mathbf{R} \to \mathbf{R}$ be defined by $\Psi(b) := b$. Clearly, Ψ is C^2 in $\mathbf{R}$ and $B \subset \Psi(\mathbf{R})$. The connected parametric problem designated by $P(\gamma, \Gamma, C, f, \xi_1, \Psi, R, s)$ has the next data; $\gamma = \ell \circ \Psi$, $\Gamma = \mathcal{L}$, $C = \Psi^{-1}(B)$, $f = g$, $\xi_1 = \Upsilon_1$, Ψ the function given above, $R = \mathcal{R}$ and $s = n$.

Observe that, if we set $\hat{a} := 0$, then $\hat{z}_{\hat{a}} = (\hat{x}, \hat{u}, \hat{a}) \equiv (0,0,0,0)$ is admissible of $P(\gamma, \Gamma, C, f, \xi_1, \Psi, R, n)$. Moreover, $i(\cdot, \hat{x}(\cdot), \hat{u}(\cdot)) \equiv \{1\}$ is constant on $\mathcal{T}$. Let $\omega \equiv 0$, $\nu_1 \equiv 1$, $\nu_2 \equiv 0$ and observe that $(\omega, \nu) \in X \times \mathcal{U}_2$, $\nu_\sigma \geq 0$ and $\nu_\sigma(t)\varphi_\sigma(t, \hat{x}(t), \hat{u}(t)) = 0$ $(t \in \mathcal{T}, \sigma = 1)$. Recall that $\varphi = \phi$.

Now,

$$\mathcal{H}(t,x,u,\omega,\nu) = \omega u_1 + \omega u_2 + \omega x^3 - \tfrac{1}{2}(u_1+u_2)^2 - u_1 + \tfrac{1}{2}\nu_1 x^2 + \nu_1 u_1 - \nu_2 \sin u_2,$$

and observe that

$$\mathcal{H}_x(t,x,u,\omega,\nu) = 3\omega x^2 + \nu_1 x,$$

$$\mathcal{H}_u(t,x,u,\omega,\nu) = (\omega - u_1 - u_2 - 1 + \nu_1, \omega - u_1 - u_2 - \nu_2 \cos u_2).$$

Consequently,

$$\dot{\omega}(t) = -\mathcal{H}_x(t,\hat{x}(t),\hat{u}(t),\omega(t),\nu(t)) \text{ (a.e. in } \mathcal{T}) \quad \text{and} \quad \mathcal{H}_u(t,\hat{x}(t),\hat{u}(t),\omega(t),\nu(t)) = (0,0) \ (t \in \mathcal{T})$$

and hence $(\hat{x}, \hat{u}, \omega, \nu)$ satisfies the first order sufficiency conditions of Corollary 1. Since $\Psi(b) = b$ $(b \in \mathbf{R})$, we have that $\gamma(b) = b^2$ $(b \in \mathbf{R})$. Then,

$$\gamma'(\hat{a}) + \Psi'(\hat{a})\omega(1) = 0$$

and then condition (i) of Corollary 1 is satisfied. Moreover, one can verify that

$$\omega(1)\Psi''(\hat{a}; h) = 0 \text{ for all } h \in \mathbf{R}$$

and hence condition (ii) of Corollary 1 is fulfilled.

Now, for all $(t, x, u) \in \mathcal{T} \times \mathbf{R} \times \mathbf{R}^2$,

$$\mathcal{H}(t,x,u,\omega(t),\nu(t)) = -\tfrac{1}{2}(u_1+u_2)^2 + \tfrac{1}{2}x^2$$

and hence, for all $t \in \mathcal{T}$,

$$\mathcal{H}_{uu}(t,\hat{x}(t),\hat{u}(t),\omega(t),\nu(t)) = \begin{pmatrix} -1 & -1 \\ -1 & -1 \end{pmatrix} \leq 0$$

implying that $(\hat{x}, \hat{u}, \omega, \nu)$ verifies condition (iii) of Corollary 1.

Additionally, note that, for all $t \in \mathcal{T}$,

$$f_x(t,\hat{x}(t),\hat{u}(t)) = 0 \quad \text{and} \quad f_u(t,\hat{x}(t),\hat{u}(t)) = (1,1),$$

$$\varphi_x(t,\hat{x}(t),\hat{u}(t)) = \begin{pmatrix} 0 \\ 0 \end{pmatrix} \quad \text{and} \quad \varphi_u(t,\hat{x}(t),\hat{u}(t)) = \begin{pmatrix} -1 & 0 \\ 0 & 1 \end{pmatrix}.$$

Therefore, $Y(\hat{z}_{\hat{a}})$ is given by all $w_\alpha \in X \times L^2(\mathcal{T}; \mathbf{R}^2) \times \mathbf{R}$ verifying

$$\begin{cases} \dot{y}(t) = v_1(t) + v_2(t) \text{ (a.e. in } \mathcal{T}). \\ y(0) = 0,\ y(1) = \alpha. \\ -v_1(t) \leq 0,\ v_2(t) = 0 \text{ (a.e. in } \mathcal{T}). \end{cases}$$

In addition, observe that, for all $(t,x,u) \in \mathcal{T} \times \mathbf{R} \times \mathbf{R}^2$,

$$\mathcal{F}(t,x,u) = \tfrac{1}{2}(u_1+u_2)^2 - \tfrac{1}{2}x^2$$

and, for all $t \in \mathcal{T}$,

$$\mathcal{F}_{xx}(t,\hat{x}(t),\hat{u}(t)) = -1, \quad \mathcal{F}_{xu}(t,\hat{x}(t),\hat{u}(t)) = (0,0), \quad \mathcal{F}_{uu}(t,\hat{x}(t),\hat{u}(t)) = \begin{pmatrix} 1 & 1 \\ 1 & 1 \end{pmatrix}.$$

Thus, for all $w_\alpha \in Y(\hat{z}_{\hat{a}})$,

$$J''(\hat{z}_{\hat{a}}; w_\alpha) = 2\alpha^2 + \int_0^1 \{(v_1(t)+v_2(t))^2 - y^2(t)\}dt = 2\alpha^2 + \int_0^1 \{\dot{y}^2(t) - y^2(t)\}dt.$$

Hence,

$$J''(\hat{z}_{\hat{a}}; w_\alpha) > 0$$

for all $w_\alpha \in Y(\hat{z}_{\hat{a}})$, $w_\alpha \not\equiv (0,0,0,0)$, and then condition (iv) of Corollary 1 is verified.

Now, note that, if z_a is admissible, for all $t \in \mathcal{T}$,

$$E(t,x(t),\hat{u}(t),u(t)) = \tfrac{1}{2}(u_1(t)+u_2(t))^2.$$

Therefore, if z_a is admissible,

$$\int_0^1 E(t,x(t),\hat{u}(t),u(t))dt = \int_0^1 \tfrac{1}{2}(u_1(t)+u_2(t))^2 dt \geq \int_0^1 L(u(t)-\hat{u}(t))dt = \mathcal{D}(u-\hat{u}).$$

Thus, condition (v) of Corollary 1 is verified for any $\epsilon > 0$ and $\delta = 1$. By Corollary 1, $(\hat{x},\hat{u})$ is a weak minimum of $\mathcal{P}(\ell,\mathcal{L},g,\Upsilon_1,B,\mathcal{R},n)$.

4. Supplementary Lemmas

Now, we enunciate three supplementary lemmas which are going to be fundamental in proving Theorem 1. These lemmas are direct consequences of Lemmas 3.1–3.3 of [23].

If (Σ_n) is a sequence of measurable functions and Σ is a measurable function, we shall designate uniform convergence of (Σ_n) to Σ by $\Sigma_n \xrightarrow{\text{u}} \Sigma$. Similarly, strong convergence in L^p by $\Sigma_n \xrightarrow{L^p} \Sigma$ and weak convergence by $\Sigma_n \xrightarrow{L^p} \Sigma$.

In the next three lemmas, we suppose that $\hat{u} \in L^1(\mathcal{T};\mathbf{R}^m)$ is given and a sequence (u_q) in $L^1(T;\mathbf{R}^m)$ such that

$$\lim_{q\to\infty} \mathcal{D}(u_q - \hat{u}) = 0 \quad \text{and} \quad d_q := [2\mathcal{D}(u_q-\hat{u})]^{1/2} > 0 \quad (q \in \mathbf{N}).$$

For all $q \in \mathbf{N}$, define

$$v_q := \frac{u_q - \hat{u}}{d_q}.$$

Lemma 2. *For some $\hat{v} \in L^2(\mathcal{T};\mathbf{R}^m)$ and some subsequence of (u_q) (without relabeling), $v_q \xrightarrow{L^1} \hat{v}$ on $\mathcal{T}$.*

Lemma 3. *Let $A_q \in L^\infty(\mathcal{T};\mathbf{R}^{n\times n})$ and $B_q \in L^\infty(\mathcal{T};\mathbf{R}^{n\times m})$ be matrix-valued functions for which we have the existence of some constants $m_0, m_1 > 0$ such that $\|A_q\|_\infty \leq m_0$, $\|B_q\|_\infty \leq m_1$ $(q \in \mathbf{N})$, and for all $q \in \mathbf{N}$ indicate by y_q the solution of the initial value problem*

$$\dot{y}(t) = A_q(t)y(t) + B_q(t)v_q(t) \text{ (a.e. in } \mathcal{T}), \quad y(t_1) = 0.$$

Then, there exist $\zeta \in L^2(\mathcal{T};\mathbf{R}^n)$ and a subsequence (without relabeling), such that $\dot{y}_q \xrightarrow{L^1} \zeta$ on $\mathcal{T}$, and hence, if $\hat{y}(t) := \int_{t_1}^t \zeta(\tau)d\tau$ $(t \in \mathcal{T})$, then $y_q \xrightarrow{u} \hat{y}$ on $\mathcal{T}$.

Lemma 4. *Suppose $u_q \xrightarrow{L^\infty} \hat{u}$ on $\mathcal{T}$, let $\Phi_q, \Phi \in L^\infty(\mathcal{T};\mathbf{R}^{m\times m})$; suppose that $\Phi_q \xrightarrow{L^\infty} \Phi$ on $\mathcal{T}$, $\Phi(t) \geq 0$ (a.e. in $\mathcal{T}$) and let $\hat{v}$ be the function given in Lemma 2. Then,*

$$\liminf_{q\to\infty} \int_{t_1}^{t_2} v_q^*(t)\Phi_q(t)v_q(t)dt \geq \int_{t_1}^{t_2} \hat{v}^*(t)\Phi(t)\hat{v}(t)dt.$$

5. Proof of Theorem 1

The proof of Theorem 1 will be divided into two Lemmas. In Lemmas 5 and 6 below, we shall suppose that all the hypotheses of Theorem 1 are verified. Before stating the lemmas, let us present some definitions.

Note first that, given $x = (x_1, \ldots, x_n)^*$ in $\mathbf{R}^n$ and $a = (a_1, \ldots, a_s)^*$ in $\mathbf{R}^s$, if we set $x\mathbf{i}$, $a\mathbf{j}$ in $\mathbf{R}^{n+s}$ by $x\mathbf{i} := (x_1, \ldots, x_n, 0, \ldots, 0)^*$ and $a\mathbf{j} := (0, \ldots, 0, a_1, \ldots, a_s)^*$, then

$$x\mathbf{i} + a\mathbf{j} = (x_1, \ldots, x_n, a_1, \ldots, a_s)^* = \begin{pmatrix} x \\ a \end{pmatrix} \in \mathbf{R}^{n+s}.$$

Define $\tilde{\mathcal{F}} \colon \mathcal{T} \times \mathbf{R}^{n+s} \times \mathbf{R}^m \to \mathbf{R}$ by

$$\tilde{\mathcal{F}}(t,\xi,u) := \frac{\gamma(\xi_{n+1}, \ldots, \xi_{n+s})}{t_2 - t_1} + \mathcal{F}(t, \xi_1, \ldots, \xi_n, u).$$

Observe that the Weierstrass function $\tilde{E} \colon \mathcal{T} \times \mathbf{R}^{n+s} \times \mathbf{R}^m \times \mathbf{R}^m \to \mathbf{R}$ of $\tilde{\mathcal{F}}$ is given by

$$\tilde{E}(t,\xi,u,v) := \tilde{\mathcal{F}}(t,\xi,v) - \tilde{\mathcal{F}}(t,\xi,u) - \tilde{\mathcal{F}}_u(t,\xi,u)(v-u).$$

It is not difficult to see that, for all $(t,x,u,v) \in \mathcal{T} \times \mathbf{R}^n \times \mathbf{R}^m \times \mathbf{R}^m$ and all a in $\mathbf{R}^s$,

$$\tilde{E}(t, x\mathbf{i} + a\mathbf{j}, u, v) = E(t,x,u,v).$$

Set

$$\tilde{J}(z_a) := \omega^*(t_2)x(t_2) - \omega^*(t_1)x(t_1) + \int_{t_1}^{t_2} \tilde{\mathcal{F}}(t, x(t)\mathbf{i} + a\mathbf{j}, u(t))dt.$$

As one readily verifies, $J(z_a) = \tilde{J}(z_a)$ for all z_a in A, and

$$\tilde{J}(z_a) = \tilde{J}(\hat{z}_{\hat{a}}) + \tilde{J}'(\hat{z}_{\hat{a}}; z_a - \hat{z}_{\hat{a}}) + \tilde{\mathcal{K}}(\hat{z}_{\hat{a}}; z_a) + \tilde{\mathcal{E}}(\hat{z}_{\hat{a}}; z_a) \quad (1)$$

where

$$\tilde{\mathcal{E}}(\hat{z}_{\hat{a}}; z_a) := \int_{t_1}^{t_2} \tilde{E}(t, x(t)\mathbf{i} + a\mathbf{j}, \hat{u}(t), u(t))dt,$$

$$\tilde{\mathcal{K}}(\hat{z}_{\hat{a}}; z_a) := \int_{t_1}^{t_2} \{\tilde{\mathcal{M}}(t, x(t)\mathbf{i} + a\mathbf{j}) + [u^*(t) - \hat{u}^*(t)]\tilde{\mathcal{N}}(t, x(t)\mathbf{i} + a\mathbf{j})\}dt,$$

$$\begin{aligned} \tilde{J}'(\hat{z}_{\hat{a}}; z_a - \hat{z}_{\hat{a}}) \;:=\; & \omega^*(t_2)[x(t_2) - \hat{x}(t_2)] - \omega^*(t_1)[x(t_1) - \hat{x}(t_1)] \\ & + \int_{t_1}^{t_2} \{\tilde{\mathcal{F}}_\xi(t, \hat{x}(t)\mathbf{i} + \hat{a}\mathbf{j}, \hat{u}(t))([x(t) - \hat{x}(t)]\mathbf{i} + [a - \hat{a}]\mathbf{j}) \\ & \qquad + \tilde{\mathcal{F}}_u(t, \hat{x}(t)\mathbf{i} + \hat{a}\mathbf{j}, \hat{u}(t))(u(t) - \hat{u}(t))\}dt, \end{aligned}$$

and $\tilde{\mathcal{M}}, \tilde{\mathcal{N}}$ are defined by

$$\begin{aligned} \tilde{\mathcal{M}}(t, x\mathbf{i} + a\mathbf{j}) \;:=\; & \tilde{\mathcal{F}}(t, x\mathbf{i} + a\mathbf{j}, \hat{u}(t)) - \tilde{\mathcal{F}}(t, \hat{x}(t)\mathbf{i} + \hat{a}\mathbf{j}, \hat{u}(t)) \\ & - \tilde{\mathcal{F}}_\xi(t, \hat{x}(t)\mathbf{i} + \hat{a}\mathbf{j}, \hat{u}(t))([x - \hat{x}(t)]\mathbf{i} + [a - \hat{a}]\mathbf{j}), \end{aligned}$$

$$\tilde{\mathcal{N}}(t, x\mathbf{i} + a\mathbf{j}) := \tilde{\mathcal{F}}_u^*(t, x\mathbf{i} + a\mathbf{j}, \hat{u}(t)) - \tilde{\mathcal{F}}_u^*(t, \hat{x}(t)\mathbf{i} + \hat{a}\mathbf{j}, \hat{u}(t)).$$

By Taylor's theorem,

$$\tilde{\mathcal{M}}(t, x\mathbf{i} + a\mathbf{j}) = \tfrac{1}{2}([x^* - \hat{x}^*(t)]\mathbf{i} + [a^* - \hat{a}^*]\mathbf{j})\tilde{\mathcal{P}}(t, x\mathbf{i} + a\mathbf{j})([x - \hat{x}(t)]\mathbf{i} + [a - \hat{a}]\mathbf{j}), \quad \text{(2a)}$$

$$\tilde{\mathcal{N}}(t, x\mathbf{i} + a\mathbf{j}) = \tilde{\mathcal{Q}}(t, x\mathbf{i} + a\mathbf{j})([x - \hat{x}(t)]\mathbf{i} + [a - \hat{a}]\mathbf{j}), \quad \text{(2b)},$$

where

$$\tilde{\mathcal{P}}(t, x\mathbf{i} + a\mathbf{j}) := 2\int_0^1 (1-\theta)\tilde{\mathcal{F}}_{\xi\xi}(t, [\hat{x}(t) + \theta(x - \hat{x}(t))]\mathbf{i} + [\hat{a} + \theta(a - \hat{a})]\mathbf{j}, \hat{u}(t))d\theta,$$

$$\tilde{\mathcal{Q}}(t, x\mathbf{i} + a\mathbf{j}) := \int_0^1 \tilde{\mathcal{F}}_{u\xi}(t, [\hat{x}(t) + \theta(x - \hat{x}(t))]\mathbf{i} + [\hat{a} + \theta(a - \hat{a})]\mathbf{j}, \hat{u}(t))d\theta.$$

Lemma 5. *If the deduction of Theorem 1 is false, then we have the existence of a subsequence* $(z_{a_q}^q)$ *of admissible processes such that*

$$\lim_{q\to\infty} \mathcal{D}(u_q - \hat{u}) = 0 \quad \textit{and} \quad d_q := [2\mathcal{D}(u_q - \hat{u})]^{1/2} > 0 \quad (q \in \mathbf{N}).$$

Proof. If the deduction of Theorem 1 is false, then, for all $\rho_1, \rho_2 > 0$, there exists an admissible process z_a such that

$$\|z_a - \hat{z}_{\hat{a}}\| < \rho_1 \quad \text{and} \quad I(z_a) < I(\hat{z}_{\hat{a}}) + \rho_2 \min\{|a - \hat{a}|^2, \mathcal{D}(u - \hat{u})\}. \quad (3)$$

Since

$$\nu_\sigma(t) \geq 0 \; (\sigma \in P, \text{ a.e. in } \mathcal{T}),$$

if z_a is admissible, then $I(z_a) \geq J(z_a)$. Additionally, as

$$\nu_\sigma(t)\varphi_\sigma(t, \hat{x}(t), \hat{u}(t)) = 0 \; (\sigma \in P, \text{ a.e. in } \mathcal{T})$$

then $I(\hat{z}_{\hat{a}}) = J(\hat{z}_{\hat{a}})$. Thus, (3) implies that, for $\rho_1, \rho_2 > 0$, we have the existence of z_a admissible such that

$$\|z_a - \hat{z}_{\hat{a}}\| < \rho_1 \quad \text{and} \quad J(z_a) < J(\hat{z}_{\hat{a}}) + \rho_2 \min\{|a - \hat{a}|^2, \mathcal{D}(u - \hat{u})\}.$$

Therefore, if the deduction of Theorem 1 is false, then, for all $q \in \mathbf{N}$, we have the existence of a sequence of admissible processes $(z_{a_q}^q)$ such that

$$\|z_{a_q}^q - \hat{z}_{\hat{a}}\| < \min\{\epsilon, 1/q\}, \quad J(z_{a_q}^q) - J(\hat{z}_{\hat{a}}) < \min\left\{\frac{|a_q - \hat{a}|^2}{q}, \frac{\mathcal{D}(u_q - \hat{u})}{q}\right\}. \quad (4)$$

The first relation in (4) assures that

$$\lim_{q\to\infty} \mathcal{D}(u_q - \hat{u}) = 0.$$

Moreover, as $(z_{a_q}^q)$ is a sequence of admissible processes, we see that $\mathcal{D}(u_q - \hat{u}) = 0$ if and only if $z^q = \hat{z}$. Hence, the second relation of (4) implies that

$$\mathcal{D}(u_q - \hat{u}) = 0 \Longrightarrow a_q \neq \hat{a}.$$

Assume that $\mathcal{D}(u_q - \hat{u}) = 0$ for infinitely many q's. We have

$$0 = x_q(t_2) - \hat{x}(t_2) = \Psi(a_q) - \Psi(\hat{a}) = \int_0^1 \Psi'(\hat{a} + \theta[a_q - \hat{a}])(a_q - \hat{a})d\theta, \quad (5)$$

$$0 = \Psi(a_q) - \Psi(\hat{a}) = \Psi'(\hat{a})(a_q - \hat{a}) + \int_0^1 (1-\theta)\Psi''(\hat{a} + \theta[a_q - \hat{a}]; a_q - \hat{a})d\theta. \quad (6)$$

If we designate by $(a_q, \hat{a})$ the line segment in $\mathbf{R}^s$ joining the points a_q and $\hat{a}$, by the second relation of (4), by hypothesis (i) of Theorem (1), by (6), and the mean value theorem, we have the existence of $\Theta_q \in (a_q, \hat{a})$ such that

$$\begin{aligned}
0 &> J(\hat{z}_{a_q}) - J(\hat{z}_{\hat{a}}) \\
&= \gamma(a_q) - \gamma(\hat{a}) \\
&= \gamma'(\hat{a})(a_q - \hat{a}) + \tfrac{1}{2}(a_q - \hat{a})^*\gamma''(\Theta_q)(a_q - \hat{a}) \\
&= -\omega^*(t_2)\Psi'(\hat{a})(a_q - \hat{a}) + \tfrac{1}{2}(a_q - \hat{a})^*\gamma''(\Theta_q)(a_q - \hat{a}) \\
&= \int_0^1 (1-\theta)\omega^*(t_2)\Psi''(\hat{a} + \theta[a_q - \hat{a}]; a_q - \hat{a})d\theta + \tfrac{1}{2}(a_q - \hat{a})^*\gamma''(\Theta_q)(a_q - \hat{a}).
\end{aligned} \tag{7}$$

Select an adequately subsequence of $((a_q - \hat{a})/|a_q - \hat{a}|)$, such that

$$\lim_{q\to\infty} \frac{a_q - \hat{a}}{|a_q - \hat{a}|} = \hat{\alpha} \tag{8}$$

for some $\hat{\alpha} \in \mathbf{R}^s$ satisfying $|\hat{\alpha}| = 1$. By (5),

$$\Psi'(\hat{a})\hat{\alpha} = 0.$$

By (7) and (8) and hypothesis (ii) of Theorem 1, we see that

$$0 \geq \tfrac{1}{2}\omega^*(t_2)\Psi''(\hat{a}; \hat{\alpha}) + \tfrac{1}{2}\hat{\alpha}^*\gamma''(\hat{a})\hat{\alpha} \geq \tfrac{1}{2}\hat{\alpha}^*\gamma''(\hat{a})\hat{\alpha} = \tfrac{1}{2}J''(\hat{z}_{\hat{a}}; 0_{\hat{\alpha}})$$

contradicting (iv) of Theorem 1. Consequently, we may suppose that, for all $q \in \mathbf{N}$,

$$d_q = [2\mathcal{D}(u_q - \hat{u})]^{1/2} > 0.$$

□

Lemma 6. *If the deduction of Theorem 1 is false, then condition (iv) of Theorem 1 is false.*

Proof. Let $(z^q_{a_q})$ be the sequence of admissible processes provided in Lemma 5. Hence,

$$\lim_{q\to\infty} \mathcal{D}(u_q - \hat{u}) = 0 \quad \text{and} \quad d_q = [2\mathcal{D}(u_q - \hat{u})]^{1/q} > 0 \quad (q \in \mathbf{N}).$$

Case(1): First, assume that the sequence $((a_q - \hat{a})/d_q)$ is bounded in $\mathbf{R}^s$. For all $q \in \mathbf{N}$, set

$$y_q := \frac{x_q - \hat{x}}{d_q}, \quad v_q := \frac{u_q - \hat{u}}{d_q}, \quad \varpi_q := y_q\mathbf{i} + \frac{a_q - \hat{a}}{d_q}\mathbf{j}.$$

By Lemma 2, there exist $\hat{v} \in L^2(\mathcal{T}; \mathbf{R}^m)$ and a subsequence of $(z^q_{a_q})$ (without relabeling) such that $v_q \xrightarrow{L^1} \hat{v}$ on $\mathcal{T}$. We have, for all $q \in \mathbf{N}$, that

$$\dot{y}_q(t) = A_q(t)y_q(t) + B_q(t)v_q(t) \text{ (a.e. in } \mathcal{T}), \quad y_q(t_1) = 0,$$

where

$$A_q(t) := \int_0^1 f_x(t, \hat{x}(t) + \theta[x_q(t) - \hat{x}(t)], \hat{u}(t) + \theta[u_q(t) - \hat{u}(t)])d\theta,$$

$$B_q(t) := \int_0^1 f_u(t, \hat{x}(t) + \theta[x_q(t) - \hat{x}(t)], \hat{u}(t) + \theta[u_q(t) - \hat{u}(t)])d\theta.$$

We obtain the existence of $m_0, m_1 > 0$ such that $\|A_q\|_\infty \leq m_0$, $\|B_q\|_\infty \leq m_1$ $(q \in \mathbf{N})$. By Lemma 3, there exist $\zeta \in L^2(\mathcal{T}; \mathbf{R}^n)$ and some subsequence of $(z^q_{a_q})$ (we do not relabel) such that, if for all $t \in \mathcal{T}$, $\hat{y}(t) := \int_{t_1}^t \zeta(\tau)d\tau$, then

$$y_q \xrightarrow{\text{u}} \hat{y} \text{ on } \mathcal{T}. \tag{9}$$

As the sequence $((a_q - \hat{a})/d_q)$ is bounded in $\mathbf{R}^s$, then we can suppose that there exists some $\hat{\alpha} \in \mathbf{R}^s$ such that

$$\lim_{q\to\infty} \frac{a_q - \hat{a}}{d_q} = \hat{\alpha}. \tag{10}$$

First, we shall show that

$$\hat{y}(t_2) = \Psi'(\hat{a})\hat{\alpha}. \tag{11}$$

Note that, we have, for all $q \in \mathbf{N}$, that

$$y_q(t_2) = \int_0^1 \Psi'(\hat{a} + \theta[a_q - \hat{a}])\frac{(a_q - \hat{a})}{d_q} d\theta. \tag{12}$$

By (9), (10), and (12), as one readily verifies, (11) holds. Now, we claim that

$$J''(\hat{z}_{\hat{a}}; \hat{w}_{\hat{\alpha}}) \leq 0 \quad \text{and} \quad \hat{w}_{\hat{\alpha}} = (\hat{y}, \hat{v}, \hat{\alpha}) \not\equiv (0,0,0). \tag{13}$$

In order to prove it, note that, by (2), (9), and (10),

$$\begin{aligned} \frac{\tilde{\mathcal{M}}(\cdot, x_q(\cdot)\mathbf{i} + a_q\mathbf{j})}{d_q^2} &= \tfrac{1}{2}\varpi_q^*(\cdot)\tilde{\mathcal{P}}(\cdot, x_q(\cdot)\mathbf{i} + a_q\mathbf{j})\varpi_q(\cdot) \xrightarrow{L^\infty} \\ &\tfrac{1}{2}[\hat{y}^*(\cdot)\mathbf{i} + \hat{\alpha}^*\mathbf{j}]\tilde{\mathcal{F}}_{\xi\xi}(\cdot, \hat{x}(\cdot)\mathbf{i} + \hat{a}\mathbf{j}, \hat{u}(\cdot))[\hat{y}(\cdot)\mathbf{i} + \hat{\alpha}\mathbf{j}], \end{aligned}$$

$$\frac{\tilde{\mathcal{N}}(\cdot, x_q(\cdot)\mathbf{i} + a_q\mathbf{j})}{d_q} = \tilde{\mathcal{Q}}(\cdot, x_q(\cdot)\mathbf{i} + a_q\mathbf{j})\varpi_q(\cdot) \xrightarrow{L^\infty} \tilde{\mathcal{F}}_{u\xi}(\cdot, \hat{x}(\cdot)\mathbf{i} + \hat{a}\mathbf{j}, \hat{u}(\cdot))[\hat{y}(\cdot)\mathbf{i} + \hat{\alpha}\mathbf{j}]$$

both on $\mathcal{T}$. This fact together with Lemma 2 implies that

$$\begin{aligned} \lim_{q\to\infty} \frac{\tilde{\mathcal{K}}(\hat{z}_{\hat{a}}; z_{a_q}^q)}{d_q^2} &= \frac{1}{2}\int_{t_1}^{t_2} \{[\hat{y}^*(t)\mathbf{i} + \hat{\alpha}^*\mathbf{j}]\tilde{\mathcal{F}}_{\xi\xi}(t, \hat{x}(t)\mathbf{i} + \hat{a}\mathbf{j}, \hat{u}(t))[\hat{y}(t)\mathbf{i} + \hat{\alpha}\mathbf{j}] \\ &+ 2\hat{v}^*(t)\tilde{\mathcal{F}}_{u\xi}(t, \hat{x}(t)\mathbf{i} + \hat{a}\mathbf{j}, \hat{u}(t))[\hat{y}(t)\mathbf{i} + \hat{\alpha}\mathbf{j}]\}dt. \end{aligned} \tag{14}$$

As $(\hat{x}, \hat{u}, \omega, \nu)$ satisfies the first order sufficient conditions

$$\dot{\omega}(t) = -\mathcal{H}_x^*(t, \hat{x}(t), \hat{u}(t), \omega(t), \nu(t)) \text{ (a.e. in } \mathcal{T}), \quad \mathcal{H}_u^*(t, \hat{x}(t), \hat{u}(t), \omega(t), \nu(t)) = 0 \ (t \in \mathcal{T}),$$

and, by condition (i) of Theorem 1, we obtain

$$\begin{aligned} \lim_{q\to\infty} \frac{\tilde{J}'(\hat{z}_{\hat{a}}; z_{a_q}^q - \hat{z}_{\hat{a}})}{d_q^2} &= \lim_{q\to\infty} \frac{1}{d_q^2}[\omega^*(t_2)(x_q(t_2) - \hat{x}(t_2)) + \gamma'(\hat{a})(a_q - \hat{a})] \\ &= \lim_{q\to\infty} \frac{1}{d_q^2}[\omega^*(t_2)(\Psi(a_q) - \Psi(\hat{a})) - \omega^*(t_2)\Psi'(\hat{a})(a_q - \hat{a})] \\ &= \lim_{q\to\infty} \frac{1}{d_q^2}\omega^*(t_2)(\Psi(a_q) - \Psi(\hat{a}) - \Psi'(\hat{a})(a_q - \hat{a})) \\ &= \lim_{q\to\infty} \frac{1}{d_q^2}\int_0^1 \omega^*(t_2)(1-\theta)\Psi''(\hat{a} + \theta[a_q - \hat{a}]; a_q - \hat{a})d\theta \\ &= \tfrac{1}{2}\omega^*(t_2)\Psi''(\hat{a}; \hat{\alpha}). \end{aligned} \tag{15}$$

Then, by (1), the fact that

$$J(z_{a_q}^q) - J(\hat{z}_{\hat{a}}) < \min\left\{ \frac{|a_q - \hat{a}|^2}{q}, \frac{\mathcal{D}(u_q - \hat{u})}{q} \right\},$$

Equation (15) and hypothesis (ii) of Theorem 1,

$$0 \geq \lim_{q\to\infty} \frac{\tilde{\mathcal{K}}(\hat{z}_{\hat{a}}; z_{a_q}^q)}{d_q^2} + \liminf_{q\to\infty} \frac{\tilde{\mathcal{E}}(\hat{z}_{\hat{a}}; z_{a_q}^q)}{d_q^2}. \quad (16)$$

Now, we have, for all $t \in \mathcal{T}$ and $q \in \mathbf{N}$, that

$$\frac{1}{d_q^2} \tilde{E}(t, x_q(t)\mathbf{i} + a_q\mathbf{j}, \hat{u}(t), u_q(t)) = \tfrac{1}{2} v_q^*(t)\Phi_q(t)v_q(t),$$

where

$$\Phi_q(t) := 2\int_0^1 (1-\theta)\tilde{\mathcal{F}}_{uu}(t, x_q(t)\mathbf{i} + a_q\mathbf{j}, \hat{u}(t) + \theta[u_q(t) - \hat{u}(t)])d\theta.$$

We have

$$\Phi_q(\cdot) \xrightarrow{L^\infty} \Phi(\cdot) := \tilde{\mathcal{F}}_{uu}(\cdot, \hat{x}(\cdot)\mathbf{i} + \hat{a}\mathbf{j}, \hat{u}(\cdot)) \text{ on } \mathcal{T}.$$

By condition (iii) of Theorem 1, we have

$$\tilde{\mathcal{F}}_{uu}(t, \hat{x}(t)\mathbf{i} + \hat{a}\mathbf{j}, \hat{u}(t)) = \Phi(t) \geq 0 \text{ (a.e. in } \mathcal{T}). \quad (17)$$

By the fact that

$$\|z_{a_q}^q - \hat{z}_{\hat{a}}\| < \frac{1}{q},$$

$u_q \xrightarrow{L^\infty} \hat{u}$ on $\mathcal{T}$. Keeping this in mind, by (17) and Lemma 4,

$$\begin{aligned} \liminf_{q\to\infty} \frac{\tilde{\mathcal{E}}(\hat{z}_{\hat{a}}; z_{a_q}^q)}{d_q^2} &= \liminf_{q\to\infty} \frac{1}{d_q^2}\int_{t_1}^{t_2} \tilde{E}(t, x_q(t)\mathbf{i} + a_q\mathbf{j}, \hat{u}(t), u_q(t))dt \\ &= \frac{1}{2}\liminf_{q\to\infty}\int_{t_1}^{t_2} v_q^*(t)\Phi_q(t)v_q(t)dt \geq \frac{1}{2}\int_{t_1}^{t_2} \hat{v}^*(t)\Phi(t)\hat{v}(t)dt. \end{aligned} \quad (18)$$

By (16) and (18), we have

$$\begin{aligned} 0 &\geq \int_{t_1}^{t_2} \{\hat{v}^*(t)\tilde{\mathcal{F}}_{uu}(t, \hat{x}(t)\mathbf{i} + \hat{a}\mathbf{j}, \hat{u}(t))\hat{v}(t) + 2\hat{v}^*(t)\tilde{\mathcal{F}}_{u\xi}(t, \hat{x}(t)\mathbf{i} + \hat{a}\mathbf{j}, \hat{u}(t))[\hat{y}(t)\mathbf{i} + \hat{\alpha}\mathbf{j}] \\ &\qquad + [\hat{y}^*(t)\mathbf{i} + \hat{\alpha}^*\mathbf{j}]\tilde{\mathcal{F}}_{\xi\xi}(t, \hat{x}(t)\mathbf{i} + \hat{a}\mathbf{j}, \hat{u}(t))[\hat{y}(t)\mathbf{i} + \hat{\alpha}\mathbf{j}]\}dt \\ &= \hat{\alpha}^*\gamma''(\hat{a})\hat{\alpha} + \int_{t_1}^{t_2} \{\hat{v}^*(t)\mathcal{F}_{uu}(t, \hat{x}(t), \hat{u}(t))\hat{v}(t) + 2\hat{v}^*(t)\mathcal{F}_{ux}(t, \hat{x}(t), \hat{u}(t))\hat{y}(t) \\ &\qquad + \hat{y}^*(t)\mathcal{F}_{xx}(t, \hat{x}(t), \hat{u}(t))\hat{y}(t)\}dt \\ &= \hat{\alpha}^*\gamma''(\hat{a})\hat{\alpha} + \int_{t_1}^{t_2} 2\Omega(t, \hat{x}(t), \hat{u}(t); \hat{y}(t), \hat{v}(t))dt = J''(\hat{z}_{\hat{a}}; \hat{w}_{\hat{\alpha}}). \end{aligned}$$

Now, let us prove that $\hat{w}_{\hat{\alpha}} \not\equiv (0,0,0)$. By (16) and hypothesis (v) of Theorem 1, we have

$$0 \geq \lim_{q\to\infty} \frac{\tilde{\mathcal{K}}(\hat{z}_{\hat{a}}; z_{a_q}^q)}{d_q^2} + \liminf_{q\to\infty} \frac{\delta}{d_q^2}\mathcal{D}(u_q - \hat{u}) = \lim_{q\to\infty} \frac{\tilde{\mathcal{K}}(\hat{z}_{\hat{a}}; z_{a_q}^q)}{d_q^2} + \frac{\delta}{2}.$$

Keeping this in mind together with (14), if we assume that $\hat{w}_{\hat{\alpha}} \equiv (0,0,0)$, then δ would be nonpositive, which is a contradiction, and this proves (13). Now, let us show that

$$\frac{d}{dt}\hat{y}(t) = f_x(t, \hat{x}(t), \hat{u}(t))\hat{y}(t) + f_u(t, \hat{x}(t), \hat{u}(t))\hat{v}(t) \text{ (a.e. in } \mathcal{T}). \tag{19}$$

In fact, since

$$A_q(\cdot) \xrightarrow{L^\infty} f_x(\cdot, \hat{x}(\cdot), \hat{u}(\cdot)), \quad B_q(\cdot) \xrightarrow{L^\infty} f_u(\cdot, \hat{x}(\cdot), \hat{u}(\cdot)), \quad y_q \xrightarrow{\mathrm{u}} \hat{y}, \quad v_q \xrightarrow{L^1} \hat{v}$$

all on $\mathcal{T}$, we see that

$$\dot{y}_q(\cdot) \xrightarrow{L^1} f_x(\cdot, \hat{x}(\cdot), \hat{u}(\cdot))\hat{y}(\cdot) + f_u(\cdot, \hat{x}(\cdot), \hat{u}(\cdot))\hat{v}(\cdot) \text{ on } \mathcal{T}.$$

By Lemma 3, $\dot{y}_q \xrightarrow{L^1} \zeta = \frac{d\hat{y}}{dt}$ on $\mathcal{T}$. Consequently, (19) is fulfilled. Additionally, we claim that

i. $\varphi_{\sigma x}(t, \hat{x}(t), \hat{u}(t))\hat{y}(t) + \varphi_{\sigma u}(t, \hat{x}(t), \hat{u}(t))\hat{v}(t) \leq 0$ (a.e. in $\mathcal{T}$, $\sigma \in i(t, \hat{x}(t), \hat{u}(t))$).
ii. $\varphi_{\varsigma x}(t, \hat{x}(t), \hat{u}(t))\hat{y}(t) + \varphi_{\varsigma u}(t, \hat{x}(t), \hat{u}(t))\hat{v}(t) = 0$ (a.e. in $\mathcal{T}$, $\varsigma \in Q$).

As one readily verifies, (i) and (ii) above follows if one copies the proofs from (13) to (15) of [24].

Hence, from (11), (19), (i) and (ii), above, we see that $\hat{\omega}_{\tilde{\alpha}} \in Y(\hat{z}_{\hat{a}})$. This fact combined with (13) contradict condition (iv) of Theorem 1.

Case (2): Now, suppose that the sequence $((a_q - \hat{a})/d_q)$ is not bounded. Then,

$$\lim_{q\to\infty} \left| \frac{a_q - \hat{a}}{d_q} \right| = +\infty. \tag{20}$$

Select an adequately subsequence of $((a_q - \hat{a})/|a_q - \hat{a}|)$ (without relabeling), and $\tilde{\alpha} \in \mathbf{R}^s$ satisfying $|\tilde{\alpha}| = 1$, such that

$$\lim_{q\to\infty} \frac{a_q - \hat{a}}{|a_q - \hat{a}|} = \tilde{\alpha}. \tag{21}$$

For all $q \in \mathbf{N}$ and $t \in \mathcal{T}$, set

$$\tilde{\omega}(t) := \frac{x_q(t) - \hat{x}(t)}{|a_q - \hat{a}|}\mathbf{i} + \frac{a_q - \hat{a}}{|a_q - \hat{a}|}\mathbf{j}.$$

By Lemma 2 and (20),

$$\frac{x_q(\cdot) - \hat{x}(\cdot)}{|a_q - \hat{a}|} = y_q(\cdot) \cdot \frac{d_q}{|a_q - \hat{a}|} \xrightarrow{\mathrm{u}} \hat{y}(\cdot) \cdot 0 = 0 \text{ on } \mathcal{T}. \tag{22}$$

For all $q \in \mathbf{N}$, we have

$$\frac{x_q(t_2) - \hat{x}(t_2)}{|a_q - \hat{a}|} = \int_0^1 \Psi'(\hat{a} + \theta[a_q - \hat{a}])\left(\frac{a_q - \hat{a}}{|a_q - \hat{a}|}\right) d\theta. \tag{23}$$

By (21)–(23),

$$\Psi'(\hat{a})\tilde{\alpha} = 0. \tag{24}$$

Now, by (2), (21), and (22),

$$\begin{aligned} \frac{\tilde{\mathcal{M}}(\cdot, x_q(\cdot)\mathbf{i} + a_q\mathbf{j})}{|a_q - \hat{a}|^2} &= \tfrac{1}{2}\tilde{\omega}_q^*(\cdot)\tilde{\mathcal{P}}(\cdot, x_q(\cdot)\mathbf{i} + a_q\mathbf{j})\tilde{\omega}_q(\cdot) \\ &\xrightarrow{L^\infty} \tfrac{1}{2}0_{\tilde{\alpha}}^*\tilde{\mathcal{F}}_{\xi\xi}(\cdot, \hat{x}(\cdot)\mathbf{i} + \hat{a}\mathbf{j}, \hat{u}(\cdot))0_{\tilde{\alpha}} = \frac{\tilde{\alpha}^*\gamma''(\hat{a})\tilde{\alpha}}{2(t_2 - t_1)}, \end{aligned}$$

$$\begin{aligned}\frac{\tilde{\mathcal{N}}(\cdot, x_q(\cdot)\mathbf{i} + a_q\mathbf{j})}{|a_q - \hat{a}|} &= \tilde{\mathcal{Q}}(\cdot, x_q(\cdot)\mathbf{i} + a_q\mathbf{j})\tilde{\omega}_q(\cdot) \\ &\xrightarrow{L^\infty} \tilde{\mathcal{F}}_{u\xi}(\cdot, \hat{x}(\cdot)\mathbf{i} + \hat{a}\mathbf{j}, \hat{u}(\cdot))0_{\tilde{\alpha}} = 0\end{aligned}$$

both on $\mathcal{T}$. Combined this fact with Lemma 2, this implies that

$$\begin{aligned}\lim_{q\to\infty} \frac{\tilde{\mathcal{K}}(\hat{z}_{\hat{a}}; z^q_{a_q})}{|a_q - \hat{a}|^2} &= \tfrac{1}{2}\tilde{\alpha}^*\gamma''(\hat{a})\tilde{\alpha} + \lim_{q\to\infty}\int_{t_1}^{t_2} \frac{d_q}{|a_q - \hat{a}|}\cdot v_q^*(t)\frac{\tilde{\mathcal{N}}(t, x_q(t)\mathbf{i} + a_q\mathbf{j})}{|a_q - \hat{a}|}dt \\ &= \tfrac{1}{2}\tilde{\alpha}^*\gamma''(\hat{a})\tilde{\alpha}.\end{aligned} \tag{25}$$

As in (15), we have

$$\lim_{q\to\infty} \frac{\tilde{J}'(\hat{z}_{\hat{a}}; z^q_{a_q} - \hat{z}_{\hat{a}})}{|a_q - \hat{a}|^2} = \tfrac{1}{2}\omega^*(t_2)\Psi''(\hat{a}; \tilde{\alpha}). \tag{26}$$

In addition, by (1), (4), and (26) and condition (ii) of Theorem 1,

$$0 \geq \lim_{q\to\infty} \frac{\tilde{\mathcal{K}}(\hat{z}_{\hat{a}}; z^q_{a_q})}{|a_q - \hat{a}|^2} + \liminf_{q\to\infty} \frac{\tilde{\mathcal{E}}(\hat{z}_{\hat{a}}; z^q_{a_q})}{|a_q - \hat{a}|^2}. \tag{27}$$

Hence, as $\tilde{\mathcal{E}}(\hat{z}_{\hat{a}}; z^q_{a_q}) \geq 0$ ($q \in \mathbf{N}$), by (25) and (27),

$$0 \geq \tfrac{1}{2}\tilde{\alpha}^*\gamma''(\hat{a})\tilde{\alpha} = \tfrac{1}{2}J''(\hat{z}_{\hat{a}}; 0_{\tilde{\alpha}}). \tag{28}$$

Accordingly, (24) and (28) contradict condition (iv) of Theorem 1. □

6. Discussion Part

Let us point out that our hypotheses try to respect the property that the first and second order sufficient conditions are closely related to the necessary conditions for optimality. For instance, the sufficient conditions

$$\dot{\omega}(t) = -\mathcal{H}_x^*(t, \hat{x}(t), \hat{u}(t), \omega(t), \nu(t)) \text{ (a.e. in } \mathcal{T}), \quad \mathcal{H}_u^*(t, \hat{x}(t), \hat{u}(t), \omega(t), \nu(t)) = 0 \ (t \in \mathcal{T}),$$

are the Pontryagin maximum principle in normal form. On the other hand, a cone of critical directions that we strengthen in the article is the following:

$$\mathcal{Y}(\hat{z}_{\hat{a}}) := \begin{cases} \dot{y}(t) = f_x(t, x(t), u(t))y(t) + f_u(t, x(t), u(t))v(t) \text{ (a.e. in } \mathcal{T}). \\ y(t_1) = 0,\ y(t_2) = \Psi'(a)\alpha. \\ \varphi_{\sigma x}(t, x(t), u(t))y(t) + \varphi_{\sigma u}(t, x(t), u(t))v(t) \leq 0 \text{ a.e. in } \mathcal{T}, \sigma \in i(t, x(t), u(t))) \text{ with } \nu_\sigma(t) = 0. \\ \varphi_{\varsigma x}(t, x(t), u(t))y(t) + \varphi_{\varsigma u}(t, x(t), u(t))v(t) = 0 \text{ a.e. in } \mathcal{T}, \varsigma \in P \text{ with } \nu_\varsigma(t) > 0 \text{ or } \varsigma \in Q. \end{cases}$$

Here, condition (iv) of Theorem 1 and Corollary 1 asks for

$$J''(\hat{z}_{\hat{a}}; w_\alpha) > 0 \text{ for all } w_\alpha \in Y(\hat{z}_{\hat{a}}),\ w_\alpha \not\equiv (0,0,0),$$

that is, the positivity of the second variation on $Y(\hat{z}_{\hat{a}})$, which can be considered as a strengthening of the second order necessary condition

$$J''(\hat{z}_{\hat{a}}; w_\alpha) \geq 0 \text{ for all } w_\alpha \in \mathcal{Y}(\hat{z}_{\hat{a}}).$$

Additionally, condition (i),

$$\gamma'^*(\hat{a}) + \Psi'^*(\hat{a})\omega(t_2) = 0,$$

is the classical transversality condition. It is well-known that the transversality condition is a necessary condition for a weak minimum of problem $P(\gamma, \Gamma, C, f, \xi_1, \Psi, R, s)$. As explained in the article, condition (iii),

$$\mathcal{H}_{uu}(t, \hat{x}(t), \hat{u}(t), \omega(t), \nu(t)) \leq 0 \text{ (a.e. in } \mathcal{T}),$$

is a similar version of the Legendre–Clebsch necessary condition. It is not the necessary condition of Legendre–Clebsch because the former is less restrictive, that is,

$$\mathcal{H}_{uu}(t, \hat{x}(t), \hat{u}(t), \omega(t), \nu(t))$$

must be less or equal than zero almost everywhere on $\mathcal{T}$, but only in a subset related with the kernel of the linear transformation $\varphi_u(t, \hat{x}(t), \hat{u}(t))$. In the fixed-endpoints problem of calculus of variations, it is well-known that, if $\hat{x}$ is a smooth nonsingular extremal satisfying Legendre necessary condition, then, for some $\epsilon > 0$,

$$E(t, x, \dot{x}, u) > 0 \text{ for } (t, x, \dot{x}, u) \in T(\hat{x}, \epsilon), u \neq \dot{x},$$

is a sufficient condition for a weak minimum. Here,

$$T(\hat{x}, \epsilon) := \{(t, x, \dot{x}, u) \in \mathcal{T} \times \mathbf{R}^n \times \mathbf{R}^n \times \mathbf{R}^n \mid |x - \hat{x}(t)| < \epsilon, \ |\dot{x} - (d/dt)\hat{x}(t)| < \epsilon\}.$$

In fact, as one can be seen in [10], the above condition implies that

$$E(t, x, \dot{x}, u) \geq \delta L(u - \dot{x}) \text{ for } (t, x, \dot{x}, u) \in T(\hat{x}, \epsilon) \tag{29}$$

for some $\delta, \epsilon > 0$. Then, (29) implies that for some $\delta, \epsilon > 0$,

$$\int_{t_1}^{t_2} E(t, x(t), (d/dt)\hat{x}(t), \dot{x}(t))dt \geq \delta \int_{t_1}^{t_2} L(\dot{x}(t) - (d/dt)\hat{x}(t))dt = \delta \mathcal{D}(\dot{x} - (d/dt)\hat{x}), \tag{30}$$

whenever x is such that $\|x - \hat{x}\|_1 < \epsilon$, where

$$\|x\|_1 := \|x\|_\infty + \|\dot{x}\|_\infty.$$

It is worth to say that (30) gave us the inspiration to obtain the sufficient condition (v) of Theorem 1 and Corollary 1. Condition (ii) arises from the properties of the algorithm established to prove Theorem 1. In summary, our goal consists of providing an alternate model of sufficiency. Even though we do not necessarily obtain no gap hypotheses between necessary and sufficient conditions for optimality, we follow a classical way of obtaining sufficient conditions by strengthening the necessary ones. Finally, in [25], one could find an experimental application involving an economic model of population growth. More precisely, in [25], an application concerning a model for a one sector economy taking into consideration population growth is presented. In the proposed economic model, it is shown that the only factor decreasing the capital per worker is the inclusion of additional workers to the economy, and the only factor increasing the economy is the rate of production. The presence of nonlinear time-state-control mixed constraints plays a crucial role in that model, see [25], for details. For comparison reasons, it is worthwhile mentioning some of the bibliography studying necessary and sufficient conditions involving mixed constraints. Some relevant works we found convenient for that issue are the following [26–36].

7. Conclusions

In this article, we derive sufficiency conditions for weak minima in optimal control problems of Bolza in the parametric as well as in the nonparametric forms. These problems include nonlinear dynamics, a fixed initial end-point, a variable final end-point, and nonlinear mixed time-state-control constraints involving inequalities and equalities. In the nonparametric optimal control problem, the final end-point is not only variable, but also completely free, in the sense that it must not be confined to a parametrization, but it only must be contained in the image of a twice continuously differentiable manifold. Due to the fact that the left end-point is fixed, we were able to make a relaxation, in the sense that we arrived essentially to the same conclusions, but we made weaker assumptions. This relaxation is relative to some recently published works whose initial left end-point is not necessarily fixed. The algorithm used to prove the main theorem of the paper is independent of some classical concepts such as the Hamilton–Jacobi theory, the verification of bounded solutions of certain matrix Riccati equations, or extended notions of the conjugate points theory. Finally, in the parametric problem, we were able to present how the deviation between optimal costs and admissible costs is estimated by quadratic functions, in particular, the square of the norm of the classical Banach space of integrable functions in the deviation mentioned above, is a fundamental component.

Funding: This research was financially supported by Dirección General de Asuntos del Personal Académico, DGAPA-UNAM, by the project PAPIIT-IN102220.

Institutional Review Board Statement: Not applicable.

Informed Consent Statement: Not applicable.

Data Availability Statement: Not applicable.

Acknowledgments: The authors are incredibly grateful to Dirección General de Asuntos del Personal Académico, Universidad Nacional Autónoma de México, for the management of funds granted by the project PAPIIT-IN102220. The author also appreciates the encouragement suggestions made by the three referees in their reports.

Conflicts of Interest: The author declares no conflict of interest.

References

1. Dmitruk, A.V. Quadratic conditions for the Pontryagin minimum in an optimal control problem linear with respect to the control. I. Decoding theorem. *Math. USSR Izv.* **1987**, *28*, 275–303. [CrossRef]
2. Tröltzsch, F. *Optimal Control of Partial Differential Equations. Theory, Methods and Applications*; Translated from the 2005 German Original by Jürgen Sprekels; Graduate Studies in Mathematics, 112; American Mathematical Society: Providence, RI, USA, 2010.
3. Alt, W.; Felgenhauer, U.; Seydenschwanz, M. Euler discretization for a class of nonlinear optimal control problems with control appearing linearly. *Comput. Optim. Appl.* **2018**, *69*, 825–856. [CrossRef]
4. Osmolovskii, N.P.; Veliov, V.M. Metric sub-regularity in optimal control of affine problems with free end state. *ESAIM Control. Optim. Calc. Var.* **2020**, *26*, 47. [CrossRef]
5. Sánchez Licea, G. Sufficiency for purely essentially bounded optimal controls. *Symmetry* **2020**, *12*, 238. [CrossRef]
6. Sánchez Licea, G. Weak measurable optimal controls for the problems of Bolza. *Mathematics* **2021**, *9*, 191. [CrossRef]
7. Maurer, H.; Oberle, H.J. Second order sufficient conditions for optimal control problems with free final time: The Riccati approach. *SIAM J. Control Optim.* **2002**, *41*, 380–403. [CrossRef]
8. Maurer, H.; Pickenhain, S. Second order sufficient conditions for control problems with mixed control-state constraints. *J. Optim. Theory Appl.* **1995**, *86*, 649–667. [CrossRef]
9. Rosenblueth, J.F. Variational conditions and conjugate points for the fixed-endpoint control problem. *IMA J. Math. Control. Inf.* **1999**, *16*, 147–163. [CrossRef]
10. Hestenes, M.R. *Calculus of Variations and Optimal Control Theory*; John Wiley: New York, NY, USA, 1966.
11. Loewen, P.D. Second-order sufficiency criteria and local convexity for equivalent problems in the calculus of variations. *J. Math. Anal. Appl.* **1990**, *146*, 512–522. [CrossRef]
12. Malanowski, K. Sufficient optimality conditions for optimal control subject to state constraints. *SIAM J. Control. Optim.* **1997**, *35*, 205–227. [CrossRef]
13. Malanowski, K.; Maurer, H.; Pickenhain, S. Second order sufficient conditions for state-constrained optimal control problems. *J. Optim. Theory Appl.* **2004**, *123*, 595–617. [CrossRef]
14. Maurer, H. First and second order sufficient optimality conditions in mathematical programming and optimal control. In *Mathematical Programming at Oberwolffach*; Springer: Berlin/Heidelberg, Germany, 1981; Volume 14, pp. 163–177.
15. Maurer, H.; Pickenhain, S. Sufficient conditions and sensitivity analysis for economic control problems. *Ann. Oper. Res.* **1999**, *88*, 3–14. [CrossRef]
16. McShane, E.J. Sufficient conditions for a weak relative minimum in the problem of Bolza. *Trans. Am. Math. Soc.* **1942**, *52*, 344–379. [CrossRef]

17. Milyutin, A.A.; Osmolovskii, N.P. *Calculus of Variations and Optimal Control*; American Mathematical Society: Providence, RI, USA, 1998.
18. Osmolovskii, N.P. Second order sufficient conditions for an extremum in optimal control. *Control Cybern.* **2002**, *31*, 803–831.
19. Osmolovskii, N.P. Second-order sufficient optimality conditions for control problems with linearly independent gradients of control constraints. *ESAIM Control. Optim. Calc. Var.* **2012**, *18*, 452–482. [CrossRef]
20. Rosenblueth, J.F. Systems with time delays in the calculus of variations: A variational approach. *IMA J. Math. Control Inf.* **1988**, *5*, 125–145. [CrossRef]
21. Rosenblueth, J.F.; Sánchez Licea, G. A direct sufficiency proof for a weak minimum in optimal control. *Appl. Math. Sci.* **2010**, *4*, 253–269.
22. Sánchez Licea, G. Sufficiency for essentially bounded controls which do not satisfy the strengthened Legendre Clebsch-condition. *Appl. Math. Sci.* **2018**, *12*, 1297–1315.
23. Sánchez Licea, G. Relaxing strengthened Legendre-Clebsch condition. *SIAM J. Control Optim.* **2013**, *51*, 3886–3902. [CrossRef]
24. Sánchez Licea, G. A straightforward sufficiency proof for a nonparametric problem of Bolza in the calculus of variations. *Axioms* **2022**, *11*, 55. [CrossRef]
25. Sánchez Licea, G. A singular solution in an economic model of population growth. *Int. J. Math. Anal.* **2016**, *10*, 1189–1196. [CrossRef]
26. Aquino, P.G.P.; de Pinho, M.D.R.; Silva, G.N. Necessary optimality conditions for minimax optimal control problems with mixed constraints. *ESAIM COCV* **2021**, *10*, 1189–1196. [CrossRef]
27. Becerril, J.A.; de Pinho, M.D.R. Optimal control problems with nonregular mixed constraints: An optimization approach. *SIAM J. Control Optim.* **2021**, *59*, 2093–2120. [CrossRef]
28. Boccia, A.; de Pinho, M.D.R.; Vinter, R.B. Optimal control problems with mixed and pure state constraints. *SIAM J. Control. Optim.* **2016**, *54*, 3061–3083. [CrossRef]
29. Biswas, M.H.A.; de Pinho, M.D.R. A maximum principle for optimal control problems with state and mixed constraints. *ESAIM COCV* **2015**, *72*, 939–957. [CrossRef]
30. Clarke, F.H. *Functional Analysis, Calculus of Variations and Optimal Control*; Springer: London, UK, 2013.
31. de Pinho, M.D.R.; Loewen, P.D.; Silva, G.N. A weak maximum principle for optimal control problems with nonsmooth mixed constraints. *Set Valued Anal.* **2009**, *17*, 203–221. [CrossRef]
32. Rosenblueth, J.F. *Equality-Inequality mixed constraints in optimal control. Int. J. Math. Anal.* **2009**, *3*, 1369–1387.
33. de Pinho, M.D.R.; Rosenblueth, J.F. Mixed constraints in optimal control: An implicit function theorem approach. *IMA J. Math. Control Inf.* **2007**, *24*, 197–218. [CrossRef]
34. Rosenblueth, J.F. A direct approach to second order conditions for mixed equality constraints. *J. Math. Anal. Appl.* **2007**, *333*, 770–779. [CrossRef]
35. Rosenblueth, J.F. Admissible variations for optimal control problems with mixed constraints. *WSEAS Trans. Syst.* **2005**, 2204–2211.
36. Zeidan, V.M. The Riccati equation for optimal control problems with mixed state-control constraints: Necessity and Sufficiency. *SIAM J. Control Optim.* **1994**, *32*, 5. [CrossRef]

symmetry

MDPI

Article

Abstraction of Interpolative Reich-Rus-Ćirić-Type Contractions and Simplest Proof Technique

Monairah Alansari [1,†] and Muhammad Usman Ali [2,*,†]

1 Department of Mathematics, King Abdulaziz University, P.O. Box 80203, Jeddah 21589, Saudi Arabia; malansari@kau.edu.sa
2 Department of Mathematics, COMSATS University Islamabad, Attock Campus, Attock 43600, Pakistan
* Correspondence: musman.ali@cuiatk.edu.pk or muh_usman_ali@yahoo.com
† These authors contributed equally to this work.

Abstract: The concept of symmetry is a very vast topic that is involved in the studies of several phenomena. This concept enables us to discuss the phenomenon in some systematic pattern depending upon the type of phenomenon. Each phenomenon has its own type of symmetry. The phenomenon that is used in the discussion of this article is a symmetric distance-measuring function. This article presents the notions of abstract interpolative Reich-Rus-Ćirić-type contractions with a shrink map and examines the existence of ϕ-fixed points for such maps in complete metric space. These notions are defined through special types of simulation functions. The proof technique of the results presented in this article is easy to understand compared with the existing literature on interpolative Reich-Rus-Ćirić-type contractions.

Keywords: ϕ-fixed points; interpolative Kannan contraction; abstract interpolative Reich-Rus-Ćirić-type contractions with a shrink map

Citation: Alansari, M.; Ali, M.U. Abstraction of Interpolative Reich-Rus-Ćirić-Type Contractions and Simplest Proof Technique. *Symmetry* **2022**, *14*, 1504. https://doi.org/10.3390/sym14081504

Academic Editor: Savin Treanta

Received: 4 July 2022
Accepted: 17 July 2022
Published: 22 July 2022

Publisher's Note: MDPI stays neutral with regard to jurisdictional claims in published maps and institutional affiliations.

1. Introduction and Preliminaries

Metric fixed point theory has a significant contribution to nonlinear analysis with its applications. This branch of fixed point theory is based on the work of the famous mathematician Banach. He proved that [1], on a complete metric space, every contraction map possesses a unique fixed point. Later on, Kannan [2] and Chatterjea [3] modified the contraction inequality to study the existence of fixed points of discontinuous self-maps on a complete metric space. Afterward, this field has flourished with several interesting results. A few results have been obtained for the following aspects:

(1) Modifying contraction inequality,
(2) Modifying distance measuring function.

Recently, Karapınar [4] derived the interpolative Kannan contraction, which can be considered a modified form of the Kannan contraction. Inspiration from this work led several researchers to extend the existing contraction type inequalities in the pattern of interpolative Kannan contraction.

A few generalizations of contraction inequality have been obtained using some special types of simulation functions, for example [5,6].

Symmetry is a very vast topic that is involved in the studies of several phenomena. Each phenomenon has its own definition of symmetry, which helps to discuss the phenomenon in a systematic pattern. Metric space is a symmetric distance measuring function, which is used in the discussion of this article. In the literature related to interpolative Kannan contractions, we have seen several results based on the symmetric distance measuring function, for example, [7,8], and the asymmetric distance measuring function, for example, [9,10].

In this article, we use special types of simulation functions to extend interpolative Reich-Rus-Ćirić-type contraction inequalities. The proof technique of the fixed point results involving interpolative contraction type inequalities is more complicated than the proof technique of the fixed point results involving contraction type inequalities. With the help of a simulation function, we have tried minimizing these complications of the proof technique, and now the presented proofs are easier to understand.

Before moving on to the next section, we will recall some basic concepts such as interpolative Kannan contraction, a few generalizations of the interpolative Kannan contraction, well-known simulation functions and some other notions that are required for the next section.

Let (V, d_V) be a metric space and let $Q : V \to V$ be a self map. Then, we have the following notions.

- A map $Q : V \to V$ is said to be an interpolative Kannan contraction [4], if
$$d_V(Qk, Ql) \leq \eta d_V(k, Qk)^{\omega_1} d_V(l, Ql)^{1-\omega_1}$$
for all $k, l \in V$ with $k \neq Qk$, where $\eta \in [0, 1)$ and $\omega_1 \in (0, 1)$.
Later on, it was observed by Karapinar et al. [11] that the above inequality does not ensure the existence of a unique fixed point of a map in complete metric space. Hence, to discuss the uniqueness of a fixed point, the above inequality was redefined in the following way.
- A map $Q : V \to V$ is said to be an improved interpolative Kannan contraction [11], if
$$d_V(Qk, Ql) \leq \eta d_V(k, Qk)^{\omega_1} d_V(l, Ql)^{1-\omega_1}$$
for all $k, l \in V \backslash Fix(Q)$, where $\eta \in [0, 1)$, $\omega_1 \in (0, 1)$ and $Fix(Q) = \{k \in V : Qk = k\}$.
- A map $Q : V \to V$ is said to be an interpolative Reich-Rus-Ćirić-type contraction [12], if
$$d_V(Qk, Ql) \quad \leq \quad \eta d_V(k, l)^{\omega_1} d_V(k, Qk)^{\omega_2} d_V(l, Ql)^{1-\omega_1-\omega_2}$$
for each $k, l \in V \setminus Fix(Q)$, where $\eta \in [0, 1)$ and $\omega_1, \omega_2 \in (0, 1)$ with $\omega_1 + \omega_2 < 1$.

In the literature, $CB(V)$ represents the collection of all nonvoid closed and bounded subsets of V and the Pompeiu–Hausdorff distance is a map $H_V : CB(V) \times CB(V) \to [0, \infty)$ defined by
$$H_V(E, F) = \max\{\sup_{e \in E} d_V(e, F), \sup_{f \in F} d_V(f, E)\}$$
where $d_V(f, E) = \inf\{d_V(f, e) : e \in E\}$.

A set-valued generalization of interpolative Reich-Rus-Ćirić-type contraction is defined in the way: A map $Q : V \to CB(V)$ is said to be a set-valued interpolative Reich-Rus-Ćirić-type contraction [13], if
$$H_V(Qk, Ql) \quad \leq \quad \eta d_V(k, l)^{\omega_1} d_V(k, Qk)^{\omega_2} d_V(l, Ql)^{1-\omega_1-\omega_2}$$
for each $k, l \in V \setminus Fix(Q)$, where $\eta \in [0, 1)$ and $\omega_1, \omega_2 \in (0, 1)$ with $\omega_1 + \omega_2 < 1$.

In the literature, we have seen many auxiliary type functions from $[0, \infty) \times [0, \infty)$ into $\mathbb{R}$, for example, simulation functions, R-functions and C-class functions. Recently, Karapinar [14] used the simulation function $\zeta : [0, \infty) \times [0, \infty) \to \mathbb{R}$ given by Khojasteh et al. [15] to define the following notion.

A map $Q : V \to V$ is said to be an interpolative Hardy–Rogers type Z-contraction, if
$$\zeta(d_V(Qk, Ql), C(k, l)) \geq 0,$$
for each $k, l \in V \setminus Fix(Q)$, where $\omega_1, \omega_2, \omega_3 \in (0, 1)$ with $\omega_1 + \omega_2 + \omega_3 < 1$, and
$$C(k, l) = d_V(k, l)^{\omega_1} d_V(k, Qk)^{\omega_2} d_V(l, Ql)^{\omega_3} \left[\frac{d_V(k, Ql) + d_V(l, Qk)}{2}\right]^{1-\omega_1-\omega_2-\omega_3}.$$

A few more studies related to interpolative type contractions are available in [16–18].

In the next section, we use the following family of functions defined in [19]:

Θ_F is the collection of functions $\theta_f : [0,\infty)^4 \to [0,\infty)$ with the given properties

θ_1: $\theta_f(d,b,c,0) = 0\ \forall d,b,c \in [0,\infty)$;

θ_2: continuous and nondecreasing.

It is well-known that for a self-map $Q : V \to V$, a point $v \in V$ with $v = Qv$ is called a fixed point of Q. If v is a fixed point of Q with $\phi(v) = 0$ for a map $\phi : V \to [0,\infty)$, then v is called a ϕ-fixed point of Q. This notion is presented in [20].

2. Results

In this section, we denote Ξ_F by the collection of functions $\xi_f : [0,\infty)^3 \to [0,\infty)$ such that

(f1) ξ_f is nondecreasing in each coordinate;

(f2) $\xi_f(g^{\omega_1}, g^{\omega_2}, g^{\omega_3}) \le g$ for each $g \in (0,\infty)$ and for each $\omega_1,\omega_2,\omega_3 \in [0,1]$ with $\omega_1 + \omega_2 + \omega_3 = 1$.

Example 1. *The following functions belong to* Ξ_F.

(E1) $\xi_f(a,b,c) = abc$;

(E2) $\xi_f(a,b,c) = \left(\frac{ac}{1+b}\right)\left(\frac{ab}{1+c}\right)\left(\frac{bc}{1+a}\right)$.

Throughout this article, ξ_f belongs to Ξ_f, θ_f belongs to Θ_F, ϕ represents a map from V into $[0,\infty)$, and (V,d_V) is a metric space.

The following definition is the first form of abstract interpolative Reich-Rus-Ćirić type contraction with a shrink map.

Definition 1. *A self-map $Q : V \to V$ is called an abstract interpolative Reich-Rus-Ćirić type-I contraction with ϕ shrink, if the below-stated inequalities hold:*

$$\begin{aligned} d_V(Qk,Ql) \le\ & \eta\xi_f(d_V(k,l)^{\omega_1}, d_V(k,Qk)^{\omega_2}, d_V(l,Ql)^{\omega_3}) \\ & + L\theta_f(d_V(k,l)^{\omega_1}, d_V(k,Qk)^{\omega_2}, d_V(l,Ql)^{\omega_3}, d_V(l,Qk)^{\omega_4}) \end{aligned} \tag{1}$$

for each $k,l \in V \setminus Fix(Q)$ with $l \ne k$, where $\omega_1,\omega_2,\omega_3 \in [0,1]$ with $\omega_1+\omega_2+\omega_3 = 1$, $\omega_4 > 0$, and $L \ge 0$;

for every $l \in V$, we have

$$\phi(Ql) \le \eta\phi(l), \tag{2}$$

where $\eta \in [0,1)$ and $Fix(Q) = \{v \in V : v = Qv\}$.

The following theorem ensures the existence of ϕ-fixed points of the map Q satisfying the above definition.

Theorem 1. *Let $Q : V \to V$ be an abstract interpolative Reich-Rus-Ćirić type-I contraction with ϕ shrink on a complete metric space (V,d_V). Then at least one ϕ-fixed point of Q exists in V.*

Proof. Take an arbitrary point $l_0 \in V$, and define an iterative sequence $l_n = Ql_{n-1} \forall n \in \mathbb{N}$. If $l_{n_0} = l_{n_0+1}$ for some n_0, then l_{n_0} is a fixed point of Q. Moreover, by (2) we get $\phi(l_{n_0}) = \phi(Ql_{n_0}) \le \lambda\phi(l_{n_0})$. This gives $\phi(l_{n_0}) = 0$. Hence, l_{n_0} is a ϕ-fixed point of Q. Now, consider $l_{n-1} \ne l_n\ \forall n \in \mathbb{N}$. By (1), for each $n \in \mathbb{N}$, we get

$$\begin{aligned} d_V(Ql_{n-1},Ql_n) \le\ & \eta\xi_f(d_V(l_{n-1},l_n)^{\omega_1}, d_V(l_{n-1},Ql_{n-1})^{\omega_2}, d_V(l_n,Ql_n)^{\omega_3}) \\ & + L\theta_f(d_V(l_{n-1},l_n)^{\omega_1}, d_V(l_{n-1},Ql_{n-1})^{\omega_2}, d_V(l_n,Ql_n)^{\omega_3}, d_V(l_n,Ql_{n-1})^{\omega_4}). \end{aligned} \tag{3}$$

That is,

$$d_V(l_n, l_{n+1}) \leq \eta\xi_f(d_V(l_{n-1}, l_n)^{\omega_1}, d_V(l_{n-1}, l_n)^{\omega_2}, d_V(l_n, l_{n+1})^{\omega_3}) \; \forall n \in \mathbb{N}. \quad (4)$$

Now, claim that $d_V(l_n, l_{n+1}) < d_V(l_{n-1}, l_n) \; \forall n \in \mathbb{N}$. If it is wrong, then we have $m_0 \in N$ with $d_V(l_{m_0}, l_{m_0+1}) \geq d_V(l_{m_0-1}, l_{m_0})$. By (4) we get

$$\begin{aligned} d_V(l_{m_0}, l_{m_0+1}) &\leq \eta\xi_f(d_V(l_{m_0-1}, l_{m_0})^{\omega_1}, d_V(l_{m_0-1}, l_{m_0})^{\omega_2}, d_V(l_{m_0}, l_{m_0+1})^{\omega_3}) \\ &\leq \eta\xi_f(d_V(l_{m_0}, l_{m_0+1})^{\omega_1}, d_V(l_{m_0}, l_{m_0+1})^{\omega_2}, d_V(l_{m_0}, l_{m_0+1})^{\omega_3}) \\ &\leq \eta d_V(l_{m_0}, l_{m_0+1}) \end{aligned}$$

which is only possible when $d_V(l_{m_0}, l_{m_0+1}) = 0$, and it contradicts our assumption. Thus, the claim is true. Since $d_V(l_n, l_{n+1}) < d_V(l_{n-1}, l_n) \; \forall n \in \mathbb{N}$, then (4) we get

$$\begin{aligned} d_V(l_n, l_{n+1}) &\leq \eta\xi_f(d_V(l_{n-1}, l_n)^{\omega_1}, d_V(l_{n-1}, l_n)^{\omega_2}, d_V(l_n, l_{n+1})^{\omega_3}) \\ &\leq \eta\xi_f(d_V(l_{n-1}, l_n)^{\omega_1}, d_V(l_{n-1}, l_n)^{\omega_2}, d_V(l_{n-1}, l_n)^{\omega_3}) \\ &\leq \eta d_V(l_{n-1}, l_n) \; \forall n \in \mathbb{N}. \end{aligned} \quad (5)$$

The above inequality implies that

$$d_V(l_n, l_{n+1}) \leq \eta^n d_V(l_0, l_1) \; \forall n \in \mathbb{N}. \quad (6)$$

To verify that the sequence $\{l_n\}$ is Cauchy. Consider $m, n \in \mathbb{N}$ with $n > m$. By triangle inequality and (6) we obtain

$$d_V(l_m, l_n) \leq \sum_{j=m}^{n-1} d_V(l_j, l_{j+1}) \leq \sum_{j=m}^{n-1} \eta^j d_V(l_0, l_1).$$

Since $\sum_{j=1}^{\infty} \eta^j$ is a convergent series, thus, by the above inequality, we get $\lim_{n,m\to\infty} d_V(l_m, l_n) = 0$. As (V, d_V) is complete and $\{l_n\}$ is Cauchy in V, then there exists an element $l^* \in V$ with $l_n \to l^*$. Now, claim that $l^* = Ql^*$. If it is wrong, then $d_V(l^*, Ql^*) > 0$. Since $\{l_n\}$ is an iterative sequence with $l_n \to l^*$, thus, we get

$$\max\{d_V(l_n, l^*), d_V(l_n, l_{n+1}), d_V(l^*, Ql^*)\} = d_V(l^*, Ql^*) \; \forall n \geq N_0 \quad (7)$$

for some $N_0 \in \mathbb{N}$. By (1), for each $n \in \mathbb{N}$, we obtain

$$\begin{aligned} d_V(Ql_n, Ql^*) &\leq \eta\xi_f(d_V(l_n, l^*)^{\omega_1}, d_V(l_n, Ql_n)^{\omega_2}, d_V(l^*, Ql^*)^{\omega_3}) \\ &\quad + L\theta_f(d_V(l_n, l^*)^{\omega_1}, d_V(l_n, Ql_n)^{\omega_2}, d_V(l^*, Ql^*)^{\omega_3}, d_V(l^*, Ql_n)^{\omega_4}). \end{aligned} \quad (8)$$

From (7) and (8), for each $n \geq N_0$, we get

$$\begin{aligned} d_V(l_{n+1}, Ql^*) &\leq \eta\xi_f(d_V(l_n, l^*)^{\omega_1}, d_V(l_n, l_{n+1})^{\omega_2}, d_V(l^*, Ql^*)^{\omega_3}) \\ &\quad + L\theta_f(d_V(l_n, l^*)^{\omega_1}, d_V(l_n, Ql_n)^{\omega_2}, d_V(l^*, Ql^*)^{\omega_3}, d_V(l^*, l_{n+1})^{\omega_4}) \\ &\leq \eta\xi_f(d_V(l^*, Ql^*)^{\omega_1}, d_V(l^*, Ql^*)^{\omega_2}, d_V(l^*, Ql^*)^{\omega_3}) \\ &\quad + L\theta_f(d_V(l_n, l^*)^{\omega_1}, d_V(l_n, Ql_n)^{\omega_2}, d_V(l^*, Ql^*)^{\omega_3}, d_V(l^*, l_{n+1})^{\omega_4}) \\ &\leq \eta d_V(l^*, Ql^*) \\ &\quad + L\theta_f(d_V(l_n, l^*)^{\omega_1}, d_V(l_n, Ql_n)^{\omega_2}, d_V(l^*, Ql^*)^{\omega_3}, d_V(l^*, l_{n+1})^{\omega_4}). \end{aligned} \quad (9)$$

By applying the limit $n \to \infty$ in (9), we get

$$d_V(l^*, Ql^*) \leq \eta d_V(l^*, Ql^*).$$

As $\eta < 1$, thus, the above inequality, only exists when $d_V(l^*, Ql^*) = 0$. Hence, the claim is correct. Since $l^* = Ql^*$, then by (2) we get

$$\phi(l^*) = \phi(Ql^*) \leq \lambda\phi(l^*).$$

This implies that $\phi(l^*) = 0$. Hence, l^* is ϕ-fixed point of Q. □

By letting $\xi_f(a,b,c) = abc$ and $\theta_f(a,b,c,d) = abcd$ in Theorem 1, we get the following result.

Corollary 1. *Let (V, d_V) be a complete metric space. Let $Q : V \to V$ and $\phi : V \to [0, \infty)$ be two maps such that*

$$\begin{aligned} d_V(Qk, Ql) &\leq \eta d_V(k,l)^{\omega_1} d_V(k, Qk)^{\omega_2} d_V(l, Ql)^{\omega_3} \\ &\quad + L d_V(k,l)^{\omega_1} d_V(k, Qk)^{\omega_2} d_V(l, Ql)^{\omega_3} d_V(l, Qk)^{\omega_4} \end{aligned}$$

for each $k, l \in V \setminus Fix(Q)$ with $l \neq k$, where $\omega_1, \omega_2, \omega_3 \in [0,1]$ with $\omega_1 + \omega_2 + \omega_3 = 1$ and $\omega_4 > 0$; further, for every $l \in V$, we have

$$\phi(Ql) \leq \eta\phi(l),$$

where $\eta \in [0,1)$ and $L \geq 0$. Then at least one ϕ-fixed point of Q exists in V.

By taking $\omega_1 = \omega_4 = 1$ and $\omega_2 = \omega_3 = 0$ in the above mentioned corollary, we obtain the following result.

Corollary 2. *Let (V, d_V) be a complete metric space. Let $Q : V \to V$ and $\phi : V \to [0, \infty)$ be two maps such that*

$$d_V(Qk, Ql) \leq \eta d_V(k,l) + L d_V(k,l) d_V(l, Qk)$$

for each $k, l \in V \setminus Fix(Q)$ with $l \neq k$; further, for every $l \in V$, we have

$$\phi(Ql) \leq \eta\phi(l),$$

where $\eta \in [0,1)$ and $L \geq 0$. Then at least one ϕ-fixed point of Q exists in V.

Corollary 3. *Let (V, d_V) be a complete metric space. Let $Q : V \to V$ be a map such that*

$$d_V(Qk, Ql) \leq \eta d_V(k,l)^{\omega_1} d_V(k, Qk)^{\omega_2} d_V(l, Ql)^{\omega_3} \tag{10}$$

for each $k, l \in V \setminus Fix(Q)$ with $l \neq k$, where $\omega_1, \omega_2, \omega_3 \in [0,1]$ with $\omega_1 + \omega_2 + \omega_3 = 1$, and $\eta \in [0,1)$. Then a fixed point of Q exists in V.

The conclusion of the above result can be concluded from Corollary 1 by considering $L = 0$ and $\phi(k) = 0\ \forall k \in V$.

The following corollary follows from Corollary 3 by defining $\omega_1 = \tau_1$, $\omega_2 = \tau_2$ and $\omega_3 = 1 - \tau_1 - \tau_2$.

Corollary 4. *Let (V, d_V) be a complete metric space. Let $Q : V \to V$ be a map such that*

$$d_V(Qk, Ql) \leq \eta d_V(k,l)^{\tau_1} d_V(k, Qk)^{\tau_2} d_V(l, Ql)^{1-\tau_1-\tau_2} \tag{11}$$

for each $k, l \in V \setminus Fix(Q)$ with $l \neq k$, where $\tau_1, \tau_2 \in (0,1)$ with $\tau_1 + \tau_2 < 1$, and $\eta \in [0,1)$. Then fixed point of Q exists in V.

Inequality (12) can be considered as a rational type interpolative contraction inequality obtained through (1) by taking $\xi_f(a,b,c) = \left(\frac{ac}{1+b}\right)\left(\frac{ab}{1+c}\right)\left(\frac{bc}{1+a}\right)$ and $L = 0$. Some interesting results related to rational type contraction conditions are given in [21].

Corollary 5. *Let (V, d_V) be a complete metric space. Let $Q : V \to V$ and $\phi : V \to [0,\infty)$ be two maps such that*

$$d_V(Qk, Ql) \leq \eta\Big(\frac{d_V(k,l)^{\omega_1} d_V(l,Ql)^{\omega_3}}{1 + d_V(k,Qk)^{\omega_2}}\Big)\Big(\frac{d_V(k,l)^{\omega_1} d_V(k,Qk)^{\omega_2}}{1 + d_V(l,Ql)^{\omega_3}}\Big)\Big(\frac{d_V(k,Qk)^{\omega_2} d_V(l,Ql)^{\omega_3}}{1 + d_V(k,l)^{\omega_1}}\Big) \tag{12}$$

for each $k, l \in V \setminus Fix(Q)$ with $k \neq l$, where $\omega_1, \omega_2, \omega_3 \in [0,1]$ with $\omega_1 + \omega_2 + \omega_3 = 1$; further, for every $l \in V$, we have

$$\phi(Ql) \leq \eta\phi(l)$$

where $\eta \in [0,1)$. Then at least one ϕ-fixed point of Q exists in V.

Consider a simulation function $\beta_\psi : [0,\infty)^2 \to \mathbb{R}$ with the properties:

(b1) $\beta_\psi(0,0) = 0$;

(b2) $\beta_\psi(t,s) \leq \psi(s) - t$;

where $\psi : [0,\infty) \to [0,\infty)$ is a nondecreasing function that fulfills that $\sum_{j=1}^{\infty} \psi^j(s)$ is convergent for each $s > 0$, moreover, $\psi(0) = 0$ and $\psi(s) < s$ if $s > 0$.

Example 2. *A function $\beta_\psi : [0,\infty) \times [0,\infty) \to \mathbb{R}$ defined by $\beta_\psi(k,l) = \alpha l - k$ for each $k, l \in [0,\infty)$, where $\psi(l) = \alpha l$ and $\alpha \in (0,1)$, is the simplest example of the above-defined simulation function.*

Throughout the article, β_ψ represents the above simulation function. Now, we define an abstract interpolative Reich-Rus-Ćirić type-II contraction with ϕ shrink by using the simulation function β_ψ.

Definition 2. *A self-map $Q : V \to V$ is called an abstract interpolative Reich-Rus-Ćirić type-II contraction with ϕ shrink, if the below-stated inequalities hold:*

$$\begin{aligned}\beta_\psi\Big(d_V(Qk,Ql), \xi_f\big(d_V(k,l)^{\omega_1}, d_V(k,Qk)^{\omega_2}, d_V(l,Ql)^{\omega_3}\big)\Big)\\ + L\theta_f\big(d_V(k,l)^{\omega_1}, d_V(k,Qk)^{\omega_2}, d_V(l,Ql)^{\omega_3}, d_V(l,Qk)^{\omega_4}\big) \geq 0\end{aligned} \tag{13}$$

for each $k, l \in V \setminus Fix(Q)$ with $l \neq k$, where $\omega_1, \omega_2, \omega_3 \in [0,1]$ with $\omega_1 + \omega_2 + \omega_3 = 1$, $\omega_4 > 0$, and $L \geq 0$;

for every $l \in V$, we have

$$\beta_\psi(\phi(Ql), \phi(l)) \geq 0. \tag{14}$$

Now, we discuss the following ϕ-fixed point result for self-maps satisfying the above definition.

Theorem 2. *Let $Q : V \to V$ be an abstract interpolative Reich-Rus-Ćirić type-II contraction with ϕ shrink on a complete metric space (V, d_V). Then at least one ϕ-fixed point of Q exists in V.*

Proof. Define an iterative sequence $\{l_n\}$, that is $l_n = Ql_{n-1} \forall n \in \mathbb{N}$, for an arbitrary point $l_0 \in V$. If $l_{n_0} = l_{n_0+1}$ for some n_0, then l_{n_0} is a fixed point of Q. Moreover, from (14) we obtain $0 \leq \beta_\psi(\phi(Ql_{n_0}), \phi(l_{n_0})) \leq \psi(\phi(l_{n_0})) - \phi(Ql_{n_0})$; that is $\phi(l_{n_0}) = \phi(Ql_{n_0}) \leq \psi(\phi(l_{n_0}))$. This gives $\phi(l_{n_0}) = 0$. Hence, l_{n_0} is a ϕ-fixed point of Q. To work with the proof, we consider $l_{n-1} \neq l_n \; \forall n \in \mathbb{N}$. By (13), for each $n \in \mathbb{N}$, we get

$$\beta_\psi\Big(d_V(Ql_{n-1}, Ql_n), \xi_f(d_V(l_{n-1}, l_n)^{\omega_1}, d_V(l_{n-1}, Ql_{n-1})^{\omega_2}, d_V(l_n, Ql_n)^{\omega_3})\Big) \quad (15)$$
$$+ L\theta_f(d_V(l_{n-1}, l_n)^{\omega_1}, d_V(l_{n-1}, Ql_{n-1})^{\omega_2}, d_V(l_n, Ql_n)^{\omega_3}, d_V(l_n, Ql_{n-1})^{\omega_4}) \geq 0.$$

Using (b2) and (15), we get

$$\begin{aligned}&\psi(\xi_f(d_V(l_{n-1}, l_n)^{\omega_1}, d_V(l_{n-1}, Ql_{n-1})^{\omega_2}, d_V(l_n, Ql_n)^{\omega_3})) - d_V(Ql_{n-1}, Ql_n)\\ &\quad + L\theta_f(d_V(l_{n-1}, l_n)^{\omega_1}, d_V(l_{n-1}, Ql_{n-1})^{\omega_2}, d_V(l_n, Ql_n)^{\omega_3}, d_V(l_n, Ql_{n-1})^{\omega_4})\\ &\geq \beta_\psi\Big(d_V(Ql_{n-1}, Ql_n), \xi_f(d_V(l_{n-1}, l_n)^{\omega_1}, d_V(l_{n-1}, Ql_{n-1})^{\omega_2}, d_V(l_n, Ql_n)^{\omega_3})\Big)\\ &\quad + L\theta_f(d_V(l_{n-1}, l_n)^{\omega_1}, d_V(l_{n-1}, Ql_{n-1})^{\omega_2}, d_V(l_n, Ql_n)^{\omega_3}, d_V(l_n, Ql_{n-1})^{\omega_4}) \geq 0.\end{aligned}$$

This implies

$$\begin{aligned}d_V(Ql_{n-1}, Ql_n) \;\leq\; &\psi(\xi_f(d_V(l_{n-1}, l_n)^{\omega_1}, d_V(l_{n-1}, Ql_{n-1})^{\omega_2}, d_V(l_n, Ql_n)^{\omega_3})) \quad (16)\\ &+ L\theta_f(d_V(l_{n-1}, l_n)^{\omega_1}, d_V(l_{n-1}, Ql_{n-1})^{\omega_2}, d_V(l_n, Ql_n)^{\omega_3}, d_V(l_n, Ql_{n-1})^{\omega_4}).\end{aligned}$$

That is,

$$d_V(l_n, l_{n+1}) \;\leq\; \psi(\xi_f(d_V(l_{n-1}, l_n)^{\omega_1}, d_V(l_{n-1}, Ql_{n-1})^{\omega_2}, d_V(l_n, Ql_n)^{\omega_3})) \; \forall n \in \mathbb{N}. \quad (17)$$

Now, let us claim that $d_V(l_n, l_{n+1}) < d_V(l_{n-1}, l_n) \; \forall n \in \mathbb{N}$. Assume that the claim is wrong, then we have $m_0 \in N$ with $d_V(l_{m_0}, l_{m_0+1}) \geq d_V(l_{m_0-1}, l_{m_0})$. By (17) we get

$$\begin{aligned}d_V(l_{m_0}, l_{m_0+1}) &\leq \psi(\xi_f(d_V(l_{m_0-1}, l_{m_0})^{\omega_1}, d_V(l_{m_0-1}, l_{m_0})^{\omega_2}, d_V(l_{m_0}, l_{m_0+1})^{\omega_3}))\\ &\leq \psi(\xi_f(d_V(l_{m_0}, l_{m_0+1})^{\omega_1}, d_V(l_{m_0}, l_{m_0+1})^{\omega_2}, d_V(l_{m_0}, l_{m_0+1})^{\omega_3}))\\ &\leq \psi(d_V(l_{m_0}, l_{m_0+1}))\end{aligned}$$

which is impossible, since $l_{m_0} \neq l_{m_0+1}$. Hence, the claim holds. As $d_V(l_n, l_{n+1}) < d_V(l_{n-1}, l_n) \; \forall n \in \mathbb{N}$, then (17) we get

$$\begin{aligned}d_V(l_n, l_{n+1}) &\leq \psi(\xi_f(d_V(l_{n-1}, l_n)^{\omega_1}, d_V(l_{n-1}, l_n)^{\omega_2}, d_V(l_n, l_{n+1})^{\omega_3}))\\ &\leq \psi(\xi_f(d_V(l_{n-1}, l_n)^{\omega_1}, d_V(l_{n-1}, l_n)^{\omega_2}, d_V(l_{n-1}, l_n)^{\omega_3}))\\ &\leq \psi(d_V(l_{n-1}, l_n)) \; \forall n \in \mathbb{N}. \quad (18)\end{aligned}$$

This yields

$$d_V(l_n, l_{n+1}) \leq \psi^n(d_V(l_0, l_1)) \; \forall n \in \mathbb{N}. \quad (19)$$

Consider $m, n \in \mathbb{N}$ with $n > m$. By triangle inequality and (19) we obtain

$$d_V(l_m, l_n) \;\leq\; \sum_{j=m}^{n-1} d_V(l_j, l_{j+1}) \leq \sum_{j=m}^{n-1} \psi^j(d_V(l_0, l_1)).$$

Since $\sum_{j=1}^{\infty} \psi^j(s)$ is a convergent series for each $s > 0$, hence, by the above inequality we get $\lim_{n,m\to\infty} d_V(l_m, l_n) = 0$. The completeness of (V, d_V) confirms the existence of an element $l^* \in V$ with $l_n \to l^*$. Now, let us claim that $l^* = Ql^*$. Let us suppose that the claim is wrong, then $d_V(l^*, Ql^*) > 0$. Since $\{l_n\}$ is an iterative sequence with $l_n \to l^*$, thus, we get

$$\max\{d_V(l_n, l^*), d_V(l_n, l_{n+1}), d_V(l^*, Ql^*)\} = d_V(l^*, Ql^*) \; \forall n \geq N_0 \quad (20)$$

for some $N_0 \in \mathbb{N}$. By (13), for each $n \in \mathbb{N}$, we obtain

$$\begin{aligned} &\beta_\psi(d_V(Ql_n, Ql^*), \xi_f(d_V(l_n, l^*)^{\omega_1}, d_V(l_n, Ql_n)^{\omega_2}, d_V(l^*, Ql^*)^{\omega_3})) \\ &+L\theta_f(d_V(l_n, l^*)^{\omega_1}, d_V(l_n, Ql_n)^{\omega_2}, d_V(l^*, Ql^*)^{\omega_3}, d_V(l^*, Ql_n)^{\omega_4}) \geq 0. \end{aligned} \tag{21}$$

This gives

$$\begin{aligned} d_V(Ql_n, Ql^*) \leq\ &\psi(\xi_f(d_V(l_n, l^*)^{\omega_1}, d_V(l_n, Ql_n)^{\omega_2}, d_V(l^*, Ql^*)^{\omega_3})) \\ &+L\theta_f(d_V(l_n, l^*)^{\omega_1}, d_V(l_n, Ql_n)^{\omega_2}, d_V(l^*, Ql^*)^{\omega_3}, d_V(l^*, Ql_n)^{\omega_4}). \end{aligned} \tag{22}$$

By (20) and (22), for each $n \geq N_0$, we get

$$\begin{aligned} d_V(l_{n+1}, Ql^*) \leq\ &\psi(\xi_f(d_V(l_n, l^*)^{\omega_1}, d_V(l_n, l_{n+1})^{\omega_2}, d_V(l^*, Ql^*)^{\omega_3})) \\ &+L\theta_f(d_V(l_n, l^*)^{\omega_1}, d_V(l_n, Ql_n)^{\omega_2}, d_V(l^*, Ql^*)^{\omega_3}, d_V(l^*, l_{n+1})^{\omega_4}) \\ \leq\ &\psi(\xi_f(d_V(l^*, Ql^*)^{\omega_1}, d_V(l^*, Ql^*)^{\omega_2}, d_V(l^*, Ql^*)^{\omega_3})) \\ &+L\theta_f(d_V(l_n, l^*)^{\omega_1}, d_V(l_n, Ql_n)^{\omega_2}, d_V(l^*, Ql^*)^{\omega_3}, d_V(l^*, l_{n+1})^{\omega_4}) \\ \leq\ &\psi(d_V(l^*, Ql^*)) \\ &+L\theta_f(d_V(l_n, l^*)^{\omega_1}, d_V(l_n, Ql_n)^{\omega_2}, d_V(l^*, Ql^*)^{\omega_3}, d_V(l^*, l_{n+1})^{\omega_4}). \end{aligned} \tag{23}$$

Letting $n \to \infty$ in (23), we get

$$d_V(l^*, Ql^*) \leq \psi(d_V(l^*, Ql^*)).$$

The above inequality, only holds when $d_V(l^*, Ql^*) = 0$. Hence, the claim is correct, $l^* = Ql^*$. By (14) we get $0 \leq \beta_\psi(\phi(Ql^*), \phi(l^*)) \leq \psi(\phi(l^*)) - \phi(Ql^*)$; that is $\phi(l^*) = \phi(Ql^*) \leq \psi(\phi(l^*))$. This implies that $\phi(l^*) = 0$. Hence, l^* is a ϕ-fixed point of Q. □

We will extend the above results by considering Q as a set-valued map. In the following, $CB(V)$ represents the collection of all nonvoid closed and bounded subsets of V and $CL(V)$ represents the collection of all nonvoid closed subsets of V.

Definition 3. *A set-valued map $Q : V \to CB(V)$ is called an abstract interpolative Reich-Rus-Ćirić type-I set-valued contraction with ϕ shrink, if the below-stated inequalities hold:*

$$\begin{aligned} H_V(Qk, Ql) \leq\ &\eta\xi_f(d_V(k, l)^{\omega_1}, d_V(k, Qk)^{\omega_2}, d_V(l, Ql)^{\omega_3}) \\ &+L\theta_f(d_V(k, l)^{\omega_1}, d_V(k, Qk)^{\omega_2}, d_V(l, Ql)^{\omega_3}, d_V(l, Qk)^{\omega_4}) \end{aligned} \tag{24}$$

for each $k, l \in V \setminus Fix(Q)$ with $l \neq k$, where $\omega_1, \omega_2, \omega_3 \in [0,1]$ with $\omega_1 + \omega_2 + \omega_3 = 1$, $\omega_4 > 0$, and $L \geq 0$;

for every $k \in V$, we have

$$\sup_{l \in Qk} \phi(l) \leq \eta\phi(k), \tag{25}$$

where $\eta \in (0,1)$ and $Fix(Q) = \{v \in V : v \in Qv\}$.

The following theorem can be used to validate the existence of ϕ-fixed points for a map satisfying the above definition.

Theorem 3. *Let $Q : V \to CB(V)$ be an abstract interpolative Reich-Rus-Ćirić type-I set-valued contraction with ϕ shrink on a complete metric space (V, d_V). Then at least one ϕ-fixed point of Q exists in V; that is, there exists a point v^* in V with $v^* \in Qv^*$ and $\phi(v^*) = 0$.*

Proof. For an arbitrary point $l_0 \in V$, we get some $l_1 \in Ql_0$. If $l_0 = l_1$, then l_0 is a fixed point of Q. Moreover, by (25) we get $\phi(l_0) \leq \sup_{l \in Ql_0} \phi(l) \leq \eta\phi(l_0)$; that is $\phi(l_0) = 0$. Hence, l_0 is a ϕ-fixed point of Q. Suppose that neither l_0 nor l_1 is a fixed point of Q, then by (24) we get

$$\begin{aligned} d_V(l_1, Ql_1) &\leq H_V(Ql_0, Ql_1) \\ &\leq \eta\xi_f\big(d_V(l_0, l_1)^{\omega_1}, d_V(l_0, Ql_0)^{\omega_2}, d_V(l_1, Ql_1)^{\omega_3}\big) \\ &\quad + L\theta_f\big(d_V(l_0, l_1)^{\omega_1}, d_V(l_0, Ql_0)^{\omega_2}, d_V(l_1, Ql_1)^{\omega_3}, d_V(l_1, Ql_0)^{\omega_4}\big). \end{aligned} \tag{26}$$

That is,

$$d_V(l_1, Ql_1) \leq \eta\xi_f\big(d_V(l_0, l_1)^{\omega_1}, d_V(l_0, Ql_0)^{\omega_2}, d_V(l_1, Ql_1)^{\omega_3}\big). \tag{27}$$

Since $\eta \in (0,1)$, thus, for $\frac{1}{\sqrt{\eta}} > 1$ we have $l_2 \in Ql_1$ satisfying the given inequality

$$d_V(l_1, l_2) \leq \frac{1}{\sqrt{\eta}} d_V(l_1, Ql_1). \tag{28}$$

To proceed with the proof, we assume that $l_1 \neq l_2$, otherwise l_2 is a ϕ-fixed point. From (27) and (28), we get

$$d_V(l_1, l_2) \leq \sqrt{\eta}\xi_f\big(d_V(l_0, l_1)^{\omega_1}, d_V(l_0, Ql_0)^{\omega_2}, d_V(l_1, Ql_1)^{\omega_3}\big). \tag{29}$$

From the facts that $l_1 \in Ql_0$, $l_2 \in Ql_1$, and nondecreasing property of ξ_f, by (29), we get

$$d_V(l_1, l_2) \leq \sqrt{\eta}\xi_f\big(d_V(l_0, l_1)^{\omega_1}, d_V(l_0, l_1)^{\omega_2}, d_V(l_1, l_2)^{\omega_3}\big). \tag{30}$$

If $d_V(l_0, l_1) \leq d_V(l_1, l_2)$, then from the above inequality we get $d_V(l_1, l_2) = 0$, which is impossible. Thus, $d_V(l_1, l_2) < d_V(l_0, l_1)$. Now, by (30), we get

$$\begin{aligned} d_V(l_1, l_2) &\leq \sqrt{\eta}\xi_f\big(d_V(l_0, l_1)^{\omega_1}, d_V(l_0, l_1)^{\omega_2}, d_V(l_1, l_2)^{\omega_3}\big) \\ &\leq \sqrt{\eta}\xi_f\big(d_V(l_0, l_1)^{\omega_1}, d_V(l_0, l_1)^{\omega_2}, d_V(l_0, l_1)^{\omega_3}\big) \\ &\leq \sqrt{\eta} d_V(l_0, l_1). \end{aligned} \tag{31}$$

Continuing the proof on the above lines we can obtain a sequence $\{l_n\}$ with $l_n \in Ql_{n-1}$ $\forall n \in \mathbb{N}$, $l_{n-1} \neq l_n$ $\forall n \in \mathbb{N}$, and

$$d_V(l_n, l_{n+1}) \leq (\sqrt{\eta})^n d_V(l_0, l_1) \ \forall n \in \mathbb{N}.$$

Moreover, it is trivial to conclude that $\{l_n\}$ is a Cauchy sequence in a complete metric space (V, d_V), thus, there is a point $l^* \in V$ with $l_n \to l^*$. Now, we claim that $l^* \in Ql^*$. If it is wrong, then $d_V(l^*, Ql^*) > 0$. Thus, we can obtain $N_0 \in \mathbb{N}$ such that

$$\max\{d_V(l_n, l^*), d_V(l_n, l_{n+1}), d_V(l^*, Ql^*)\} = d_V(l^*, Ql^*) \ \forall n \geq N_0. \tag{32}$$

By (24), for $k = l_n$ and $l = l^*$, we obtain

$$\begin{aligned} d_V(l_{n+1}, Ql^*) &\leq H_V(Ql_n, Ql^*) \\ &\leq \eta\xi_f\big(d_V(l_n, l^*)^{\omega_1}, d_V(l_n, Ql_n)^{\omega_2}, d_V(l^*, Ql^*)^{\omega_3}\big) \\ &\quad + L\theta_f\big(d_V(l_n, l^*)^{\omega_1}, d_V(l_n, Ql_n)^{\omega_2}, d_V(l^*, Ql^*)^{\omega_3}, d_V(l^*, Ql_n)^{\omega_4}\big) \ \forall n \in \mathbb{N}. \end{aligned} \tag{33}$$

From (32) and (33), for each $n \geq N_0$, we get

$$\begin{aligned} d_V(l_{n+1}, Ql^*) &\leq \eta\xi_f\big(d_V(l_n, l^*)^{\omega_1}, d_V(l_n, l_{n+1})^{\omega_2}, d_V(l^*, Ql^*)^{\omega_3}\big) \\ &\quad + L\theta_f\big(d_V(l_n, l^*)^{\omega_1}, d_V(l_n, Ql_n)^{\omega_2}, d_V(l^*, Ql^*)^{\omega_3}, d_V(l^*, l_{n+1})^{\omega_4}\big) \\ &\leq \eta\xi_f\big(d_V(l^*, Ql^*)^{\omega_1}, d_V(l^*, Ql^*)^{\omega_2}, d_V(l^*, Ql^*)^{\omega_3}\big) \\ &\quad + L\theta_f\big(d_V(l_n, l^*)^{\omega_1}, d_V(l_n, Ql_n)^{\omega_2}, d_V(l^*, Ql^*)^{\omega_3}, d_V(l^*, l_{n+1})^{\omega_4}\big) \\ &\leq \eta d_V(l^*, Ql^*) \\ &\quad + L\theta_f\big(d_V(l_n, l^*)^{\omega_1}, d_V(l_n, Ql_n)^{\omega_2}, d_V(l^*, Ql^*)^{\omega_3}, d_V(l^*, l_{n+1})^{\omega_4}\big). \end{aligned} \tag{34}$$

By applying the limit $n \to \infty$ in (34), we get

$$d_V(l^*, Ql^*) \leq \eta d_V(l^*, Ql^*).$$

The existence of the above inequality is impossible when $d_V(l^*, Ql^*) > 0$. Hence, the claim is correct, $l^* \in Ql^*$. By (25) we get

$$\phi(l^*) \leq \sup_{l \in Ql^*} \phi(l) \leq \lambda\phi(l^*).$$

This implies that $\phi(l^*) = 0$. Hence, l^* is a ϕ-fixed point of Q. □

The following result examines the existence of ϕ-fixed points for a set-valued map $Q : V \to CL(V)$.

Theorem 4. *Let (V, d_V) be a complete metric space and let $Q : V \to CL(V)$ be a set-valued map and $\phi : V \to [0, \infty)$ be another map fulfilling the following inequalities:*

$$d_V(l, Ql) \leq \eta\xi_f\big(d_V(k, l)^{\omega_1}, d_V(k, Qk)^{\omega_2}, d_V(l, Ql)^{\omega_3}\big) \tag{35}$$

for each $k, l \in V \setminus Fix(Q)$ with $l \in Qk$, where $\omega_1, \omega_2, \omega_3 \in [0, 1]$ with $\omega_1 + \omega_2 + \omega_3 = 1$, and $\omega_3 \neq 1$; further, for every $k \in V$, we have

$$\sup_{l \in Qk} \phi(l) \leq \eta\phi(k), \tag{36}$$

where $\eta \in (0, 1)$. Moreover, assume that $Graph(Q) = \{(k, l) : k \in V, l \in Qk\}$ is closed. Then at least one ϕ-fixed point of Q exists in V.

Proof. Following the proof of Theorem 3, here, one can easily obtain a Cauchy sequence $\{l_n\}$ in a complete metric space (V, d_V) with $l_n \in Ql_{n-1}$ $\forall n \in \mathbb{N}$, $l_{n-1} \neq l_n$ $\forall n \in \mathbb{N}$, and

$$d_V(l_n, l_{n+1}) \leq (\sqrt{\eta})^n d_V(l_0, l_1) \ \forall n \in \mathbb{N}.$$

Furthermore, there exists a point $l^* \in V$ with $l_n \to l^*$. Since $l_n \in Ql_{n-1}$ $\forall n \in \mathbb{N}$, thus, $(l_{n-1}, l_n) \in Graph(Q)$ $\forall n \in \mathbb{N}$. As given that $Graph(Q)$ is closed, thus, $(l^*, l^*) \in Graph(Q)$, that is $l^* \in Ql^*$. Hence, l^* is a fixed point of Q. By considering (36), we conclude that l^* is a ϕ-fixed point of Q. □

Now we present the definition of the abstract interpolative Reich-Rus-Ćirić type-II set-valued contraction with ϕ shrink.

Definition 4. *A set-valued map $Q : V \to CB(V)$ is called an abstract interpolative Reich-Rus-Ćirić type-II set-valued contraction with ϕ shrink, if the below-stated inequalities are fulfilled:*

$$\begin{aligned} &\beta_\psi\Big(H_V(Qk, Ql), \xi_f\big(d_V(k, l)^{\omega_1}, d_V(k, Qk)^{\omega_2}, d_V(l, Ql)^{\omega_3}\big)\Big) \\ &\quad + L\theta_f\big(d_V(k, l)^{\omega_1}, d_V(k, Qk)^{\omega_2}, d_V(l, Ql)^{\omega_3}, d_V(l, Qk)^{\omega_4}\big) \geq 0 \end{aligned} \tag{37}$$

for each $k, l \in V \setminus Fix(Q)$ *with* $l \neq k$, *where* $\omega_1, \omega_2, \omega_3 \in [0,1]$ *with* $\omega_1 + \omega_2 + \omega_3 = 1, \omega_3 \neq 0$, $\omega_4 > 0$, *and* $L \geq 0$;

for every $k \in V$, *we have*

$$\beta_\psi\big(\sup_{l \in Qk} \phi(l), \phi(k)\big) \geq 0. \tag{38}$$

In the following theorems, we assume that ξ_f and ψ are strictly increasing instead of nondecreasing.

Theorem 5. *Let* $Q : V \to CB(V)$ *be an abstract interpolative Reich-Rus-Ćirić type-II set-valued contraction with* ϕ *shrink on a complete metric space* (V, d_V). *Then at least one* ϕ*-fixed point of* Q *exists in* V.

Proof. For an arbitrary point $l_0 \in V$, we get a point $l_1 \in Ql_0$. If $l_0 = l_1$, then l_0 is a fixed point of Q. Moreover, by (38), we get $0 \leq \beta_\psi(\sup_{l \in Ql_0} \phi(l), \phi(l_0)) \leq \psi(\phi(l_0)) - \sup_{l \in Ql_0} \phi(l)$, this implies $\phi(l_0) \leq \psi(\phi(l_0))$, hence, l_0 is a ϕ-fixed point of Q. Suppose that neither l_0 nor l_1 is a fixed point of Q, then by (37) we get

$$\begin{aligned} &\beta_\psi\Big(H_V(Ql_0, Ql_1), \xi_f(d_V(l_0, l_1)^{\omega_1}, d_V(l_0, Ql_0)^{\omega_2}, d_V(l_1, Ql_1)^{\omega_3}) \\ &+L\theta_f(d_V(l_0, l_1)^{\omega_1}, d_V(l_0, Ql_0)^{\omega_2}, d_V(l_1, Ql_1)^{\omega_3}, d_V(l_1, Ql_0)^{\omega_4}\Big) \geq 0. \end{aligned} \tag{39}$$

This implies that

$$\begin{aligned} H_V(Ql_0, Ql_1) \leq\ & \psi(\xi_f(d_V(l_0, l_1)^{\omega_1}, d_V(l_0, Ql_0)^{\omega_2}, d_V(l_1, Ql_1)^{\omega_3})) \\ &+L\theta_f(d_V(l_0, l_1)^{\omega_1}, d_V(l_0, Ql_0)^{\omega_2}, d_V(l_1, Ql_1)^{\omega_3}, d_V(l_1, Ql_0)^{\omega_4}). \end{aligned} \tag{40}$$

Since $l_1 \in Ql_0$, thus, by the above inequality we get

$$d_V(l_1, Ql_1) \leq \psi(\xi_f(d_V(l_0, l_1)^{\omega_1}, d_V(l_0, l_1)^{\omega_2}, d_V(l_1, Ql_1)^{\omega_3})). \tag{41}$$

If $d_V(l_0, l_1) \leq d_V(l_1, Ql_1)$, then by (41) we get $d_V(l_1, Ql_1) \leq \psi(d_V(l_1, Ql_1)) < d_V(l_1, Ql_1)$, which is impossible. Thus, we conclude $d_V(l_0, l_1) > d_V(l_1, Ql_1)$. By considering strictly increasing behavior of ψ, ξ_f, and using (41) we get

$$\begin{aligned} d_V(l_1, Ql_1) &\leq \psi(\xi_f(d_V(l_0, l_1)^{\omega_1}, d_V(l_0, l_1)^{\omega_2}, d_V(l_1, Ql_1)^{\omega_3})) \\ &< \psi(\xi_f(d_V(l_0, l_1)^{\omega_1}, d_V(l_0, l_1)^{\omega_2}, d_V(l_0, l_1)^{\omega_3})) \\ &\leq \psi(d_V(l_0, l_1)). \end{aligned} \tag{42}$$

As $d_V(l_1, Ql_1) < \psi(d_V(l_0, l_1))$, there exists some real number $\epsilon_1 > 0$ such that $d_V(l_1, Ql_1) + \epsilon_1 = \psi(d_V(l_0, l_1))$. Thus, we get $l_2 \in Ql_1$ such that $d_V(l_1, l_2) \leq d_V(l_1, Ql_1) + \epsilon_1$. Hence, we conclude that

$$d_V(l_1, l_2) \leq \psi(d_V(l_0, l_1)). \tag{43}$$

Continuing the proof on the above lines we can obtain a sequence $\{l_n\}$ with $l_n \in Ql_{n-1}\ \forall n \in \mathbb{N}$, $l_{n-1} \neq l_n\ \forall n \in \mathbb{N}$, and

$$d_V(l_n, l_{n+1}) \leq \psi^n(d_V(l_0, l_1))\ \forall n \in \mathbb{N}.$$

Further, it can be seen that $\{l_n\}$ is a Cauchy sequence in a complete metric space (V, d_V) and there exists $l^* \in V$ with $l_n \to l^*$. Now, we claim that $l^* \in Ql^*$. If it is wrong then $d_V(l^*, Ql^*) > 0$. Thus, we can obtain $N_0 \in \mathbb{N}$ such that

$$\max\{d_V(l_n, l^*), d_V(l_n, l_{n+1}), d_V(l^*, Ql^*)\} = d_V(l^*, Ql^*)\ \forall n \geq N_0. \tag{44}$$

By (37), for $k = l_n$ and $l = l^*$, we get

$$\beta_\psi(H_V(Ql_n, Ql^*), \xi_f(d_V(l_n, l^*)^{\omega_1}, d_V(l_n, Ql_n)^{\omega_2}, d_V(l^*, Ql^*)^{\omega_3})) \\ +L\theta_f(d_V(l_n, l^*)^{\omega_1}, d_V(l_n, Ql_n)^{\omega_2}, d_V(l^*, Ql^*)^{\omega_3}, d_V(l^*, Ql_n)^{\omega_4})\ \forall n \in \mathbb{N}. \quad (45)$$

From the above inequality, we obtain

$$\begin{aligned} d_V(l_{n+1}, Ql^*) &\leq H_V(Ql_n, Ql^*) \\ &\leq \psi(\xi_f(d_V(l_n, l^*)^{\omega_1}, d_V(l_n, Ql_n)^{\omega_2}, d_V(l^*, Ql^*)^{\omega_3})) \\ &\quad +L\theta_f(d_V(l_n, l^*)^{\omega_1}, d_V(l_n, Ql_n)^{\omega_2}, d_V(l^*, Ql^*)^{\omega_3}, d_V(l^*, Ql_n)^{\omega_4})\ \forall n \in \mathbb{N}. \end{aligned} \quad (46)$$

From (44) and (46), for each $n \geq N_0$, we get

$$\begin{aligned} d_V(l_{n+1}, Ql^*) &\leq \psi(\xi_f(d_V(l_n, l^*)^{\omega_1}, d_V(l_n, l_{n+1})^{\omega_2}, d_V(l^*, Ql^*)^{\omega_3})) \\ &\quad +L\theta_f(d_V(l_n, l^*)^{\omega_1}, d_V(l_n, Ql_n)^{\omega_2}, d_V(l^*, Ql^*)^{\omega_3}, d_V(l^*, l_{n+1})^{\omega_4}) \\ &\leq \psi(\xi_f(d_V(l^*, Ql^*)^{\omega_1}, d_V(l^*, Ql^*)^{\omega_2}, d_V(l^*, Ql^*)^{\omega_3})) \\ &\quad +L\theta_f(d_V(l_n, l^*)^{\omega_1}, d_V(l_n, Ql_n)^{\omega_2}, d_V(l^*, Ql^*)^{\omega_3}, d_V(l^*, l_{n+1})^{\omega_4}) \\ &\leq \psi(d_V(l^*, Ql^*)) \\ &\quad +L\theta_f(d_V(l_n, l^*)^{\omega_1}, d_V(l_n, Ql_n)^{\omega_2}, d_V(l^*, Ql^*)^{\omega_3}, d_V(l^*, l_{n+1})^{\omega_4}). \end{aligned} \quad (47)$$

By letting $n \to \infty$ in (47), we get

$$d_V(l^*, Ql^*) \leq \psi(d_V(l^*, Ql^*))$$

which is impossible for $d_V(l^*, Ql^*) > 0$. Hence, the claim is correct, $l^* \in Ql^*$. Moreover, by (38) we get $0 \leq \beta_\psi(\sup_{l \in Ql^*} \phi(l), \phi(l^*)) \leq \psi(\phi(l^*)) - \sup_{l \in Ql^*} \phi(l)$. As $l^* \in Ql^*$, thus, $\phi(l^*) \leq \sup_{l \in Ql^*} \phi(l) \leq \psi(\phi(l^*))$. This implies that $\phi(l^*) = 0$. Hence, l^* is a ϕ-fixed point of Q. □

The following theorem can examine ϕ-fixed points of set-valued map $Q : V \to CL(V)$.

Theorem 6. *Let (V, d_V) be a complete metric space and let $Q : V \to CL(V)$ be a set-valued map and $\phi : V \to [0, \infty)$ be another map fulfilling the following inequalities:*

$$\beta_\psi\Big(d_V(l, Ql), \xi_f(d_V(k, l)^{\omega_1}, d_V(k, Qk)^{\omega_2}, d_V(l, Ql)^{\omega_3})\Big) \geq 0 \quad (48)$$

for each $k, l \in V \setminus Fix(Q)$ with $l \in Qk$, where $\omega_1, \omega_2 \in [0, 1]$ and $\omega_3 \in (0, 1)$ with $\omega_1 + \omega_2 + \omega_3 = 1$; further, for every $k \in V$, we have

$$\beta_\psi(\sup_{l \in Qk} \phi(l), \phi(k)) \geq 0. \quad (49)$$

Furthermore, assume that $Graph(Q) = \{(k, l) : k \in V, l \in Qk\}$ is closed. Then at least one ϕ-fixed point of Q exists in V.

3. Application

A suitable application of the work can be seen as an existence theorem for the following type of fractional-order integral equation:

$$k(t) = q(t) + \frac{\mu}{[\Gamma(\alpha)]^2} \int_0^{p(t)} (p(t) - s)^{\alpha - 1} w(s, k(s)) ds, \quad \alpha \in (0, 1), \quad t \in J = [a, b] \quad (50)$$

where $q : J \to \mathbb{R}$, $p : J \to \mathbb{R}^+ = [0, \infty)$, and $w : J \times \mathbb{R} \to \mathbb{R}$ are continuous functions, μ is constant real number, and Γ is the Euler gamma function; that is $\Gamma(\alpha) = \int_0^\infty t^{\alpha - 1} e^{-t} dt$.

Consider $V = (C[a,b], \mathbb{R})$ is the space of all continuous and bounded real-valued functions defined on $J = [a,b]$. Define a metric on V by

$$d_V(k,l) = \|k - l\| = \max_{t \in J} |k(t) - l(t)| \; \forall k,l \in V.$$

Clearly, (V, d_V) is a complete metric space.

Now, we move towards the existence theorem of (50).

Theorem 7. *Consider $V = (C[a,b], \mathbb{R})$ and consider the operator*

$$Q\colon V \to V, \quad Qk(t) = q(t) + \frac{\mu}{[\Gamma(\alpha)]^2} \int_0^{p(t)} (p(t) - s)^{\alpha-1} w(s, k(s)) ds, \quad \alpha \in (0,1), \quad t \in J$$

where $q\colon J \to \mathbb{R}$, $p\colon J \to \mathbb{R}^+ = [0, \infty)$, and $w\colon J \times \mathbb{R} \to \mathbb{R}$ are continuous functions, μ is constant, and Γ is the Euler gamma function; that is $\Gamma(\alpha) = \int_0^\infty t^{\alpha-1} e^{-t} dt$. Moreover, consider that there are $\omega_1, \omega_2, \omega_3 \in [0,1]$ with $\omega_1 + \omega_2 + \omega_3 = 1$ satisfying

$$\frac{|w(s,k(s)) - w(s,l(s))|}{\|k - Qk\|^{\omega_2} \|l - Ql\|^{\omega_3}} \le [\Gamma(\alpha+1)]^2 |k(s) - l(s)|^{\omega_1} \tag{51}$$

for all $s \in J$ and for each $k, l \in V$ with $\min\{\|k - l\|, \|k - Qk\|, \|l - Ql\|\} > 0$, moreover,

$$\sup_{t \in J} \left| \mu (p(t))^\alpha \right| \le 1.$$

Then, (50) possesses at least one solution.

Proof. For each $k, l \in V$ with $\min\{\|k - l\|, \|k - Qk\|, \|l - Ql\|\} > 0$, we obtain

$$\begin{aligned} |Qk(t) - Ql(t)| &= \left| \frac{\mu}{[\Gamma(\alpha)]^2} \int_0^{p(t)} (p(t) - s)^{\alpha-1} [w(s,k(s)) - w(s,l(s))] ds \right| \\ &\le \left| \frac{\mu}{[\Gamma(\alpha)]^2} \int_0^{p(t)} (p(t) - s)^{\alpha-1} ds \right| [\Gamma(\alpha+1)]^2 \|k - l\|^{\omega_1} \|k - Qk\|^{\omega_2} \|l - Ql\|^{\omega_3} \\ &= \left| \frac{\mu}{[\Gamma(\alpha)]^2} \frac{(p(t))^\alpha}{\alpha} \right| [\alpha \Gamma(\alpha)]^2 \|k - l\|^{\omega_1} \|k - Qk\|^{\omega_2} \|l - Ql\|^{\omega_3} \\ &= \alpha \left| \mu (p(t))^\alpha \right| \|k - l\|^{\omega_1} \|k - Qk\|^{\omega_2} \|l - Ql\|^{\omega_3} \; \forall t \in J. \end{aligned}$$

Thus, we get

$$\|Qk - Ql\| \le \alpha \|k - l\|^{\omega_1} \|k - Qk\|^{\omega_2} \|l - Ql\|^{\omega_3}$$

for each $k, l \in V \setminus Fix(Q)$ with $k \ne l$. Thus, by Corollary 3, a fixed point of Q occurs; that is, the integral Equation (50) possesses at least one solution. □

Example 3. *Consider $V = \{0, 1, 2 \cdots, 20\}$ and define*

$$d_V(k,l) = \begin{cases} 0, & k = l \\ \max\{k, l\}, & k \ne l. \end{cases}$$

Define $Q : V \to V$ and $\phi : V \to [0, \infty)$ by

$$Q(k) = \begin{cases} 0, & k = 0 \\ k - 1, & \textit{otherwise} \end{cases}$$

and

$$\phi(k) = \frac{k}{2}.$$

Then, it is easy to verify that the axioms of Theorem 1 are valid, by taking $\xi_f(a,b,c) = abc$, $\omega_1 = 0.99$, $\omega_2 = 0.005$, $\omega_3 = 0.005$, $L = 0$ *and* $\eta = \frac{99}{100}$. *Thus, there is an element* $k \in V$ *with* $Qk = k$ *and* $\phi(k) = 0$.

Example 4. *Consider* $V = \mathbb{W}$ *the set of all whole numbers and define*

$$d_V(k,l) = \begin{cases} 0, & k = l \\ \max\{k,l\}, & k \neq l. \end{cases}$$

Define $Q : V \to CB(V)$ *and* $\phi : V \to [0,\infty)$ *by*

$$Q(k) = \begin{cases} \{0\}, & k \in \{0,1\} \\ \{0, k-1\}, & k \in \{2,3,\cdots,10\} \\ \{0,k\}, & \text{otherwise} \end{cases}$$

and

$$\phi(k) = \begin{cases} k/2, & k \in \{1,2,\cdots,10\} \\ 0, & \text{otherwise.} \end{cases}$$

Then, it is easy to check that the axioms of Theorem 6 are valid, by taking $\xi_f(a,b,c) = abc$, $\beta_\psi(k,l) = (49/50)l - k$, $\omega_1 = 0.99$, $\omega_2 = 0.005$, *and* $\omega_3 = 0.005$. *Since*

$$(k-1)^{0.995} \leq (49/50)k^{0.995} \text{ for each } k \in \{1,2,\cdots,10\}.$$

Hence, there is an element $k \in V$ *with* $k \in Qk$ *and* $\phi(k) = 0$.

4. Conclusions

In this article, we have studied the existence of ϕ-fixed points for the mappings satisfying abstract interpolative Reich-Rus-Ćirić-type contractions with a shrink map on a complete metric space. Abstract interpolative Reich-Rus-Ćirić-type contraction with a shrink map has the following characteristics:

- It is an extended form of interpolative Reich-Rus-Ćirić-type contraction.
- It provides an easier proof of the results, ensuring ϕ-fixed points.

Finally, we have studied the existence of a solution for a fractional-order integral equation using our results.

Author Contributions: Both authors contributed equally to this article and approved the final manuscript. All authors have read and agreed to the published version of the manuscript.

Funding: The Deanship of Scientific Research (DSR) at King Abdulaziz University, Jeddah, Saudi Arabia has funded this project, under grant number FP-083-43.

Institutional Review Board Statement: Not applicable.

Informed Consent Statement: Not applicable.

Data Availability Statement: Not applicable.

Acknowledgments: The authors are grateful to the Deanship of Scientific Research (DSR) at King Abdulaziz University, Jeddah, Saudi Arabia for funding this project, under grant number FP-083-43.

Conflicts of Interest: The authors declare no conflict of interest.

References

1. Banach, S. Sur les operations dans les ensembles abstraits et leur application aux equations integrales. *Fund. Math.* **1922**, *3*, 133–181. [CrossRef]
2. Kannan, R. Some results on fixed point. *Bull. Cal. Math. Soc.* **1968**, *60*, 71–76.
3. Chatterjea, S.K. Fixed point theorem. *C. R. Acad. Bulg. Sci.***1972**, *25*, 727–730. [CrossRef]
4. Karapınar, E. Revisiting the Kannan type contractions via interpolation. *Adv. Theory Nonlinear Anal. Appl.* **2018**, *2*, 85–87. [CrossRef]
5. Argoubi, H.; Samet, B.; Vetro, C. Nonlinear contractions involving simulation functions in a metric space with a partial order. *J. Nonlinear Sci. Appl.* **2015**, *8*, 1082–1094. [CrossRef]
6. Alqahtani, B.; Alzaid, S.S.; Fulga, A.; Yesilkaya, S.S. Common fixed point theorem on Proinov type mappings via simulation function. *Adv. Diff. Equ.* **2021**, *2021*, 328. [CrossRef]
7. Debnath, P.; de La Sen, M. Fixed-Points of Interpolative Ćirić-Reich-Rus-Type Contractions in b-Metric Spaces. *Symmetry* **2020**, *12*, 12. [CrossRef]
8. Errai, Y.; Marhrani, E.M.; Aamri, M. Fixed Points of g-Interpolative Ćirić-Reich-Rus-Type Contractions in b-Metric Spaces. *Axioms* **2020**, *9*, 132. [CrossRef]
9. Gautam, P.; Sánchez Ruiz, L.M.; Verma, S. Fixed Point of Interpolative Rus-Reich-Ćirić Contraction Mapping on Rectangular Quasi-Partial b-Metric Space. *Symmetry* **2021**, *13*, 32. [CrossRef]
10. Mishra, V.N.; Sánchez Ruiz, L.M.; Gautam, P.; Verma, S. Interpolative Reich-Rus-Ćirić and Hardy–Rogers Contraction on Quasi-Partial b-Metric Space and Related Fixed Point Results. *Mathematics* **2020**, *8*, 1598. [CrossRef]
11. Karapınar, E.; Agarwal, R.P.; Aydi, H. Interpolative Reich-Rus-Ćirić type contractions on partial metric spaces. *Mathematics* **2018**, *6*, 256. [CrossRef]
12. Aydi, H.; Chen, C.M.; Karapınar, E. Interpolative Ćirić-Reich-Rus type contractions via the Branciari distance. *Mathematics* **2019**, *7*, 84. [CrossRef]
13. Debnath, P.; de La Sen, M. Set-valued interpolative Hardy–Rogers and set-valued Reich–Rus–Ćirić-type contractions in b-metric spaces. *Mathematics* **2019**, *7*, 849. [CrossRef]
14. Karapınar, E. Revisiting simulation functions via interpolative contractions. *Appl. Anal. Discrete Math.* **2019**, *13*, 859–870. [CrossRef]
15. Khojasteh, F.; Shukla, S.; Radenovic, S. A new approach to the study of fixed point theorems via simulation functions. *Filomat* **2015**, *29*, 1189–1194. [CrossRef]
16. Gaba, Y.U.; Karapınar, E. A new approach to the interpolative contractions. *Axioms* **2019**, *8*, 110. [CrossRef]
17. Karapınar, E.; Algahtani, O.; Aydi, H. On interpolative Hardy–Rogers type contractions. *Symmetry* **2018**, *11*, 8. [CrossRef]
18. Alansari, M.; Ali, M.U. Unified multivalued interpolative Reich-Rus-Ćirić-type contractions. *Adv. Diff. Equ.* **2021**, *2021*, 311. [CrossRef]
19. Samet, B. Some results on best proximity points. *J. Optim. Theory Appl.* **2013**, *159*, 281–291. [CrossRef]
20. Jleli, M.; Samet, B.; Vetro, C. Fixed point theory in partial metric spaces via ϕ-fixed point's concept in metric spaces. *J. Inequal. Appl.* **2014**, *2014*, 426. [CrossRef]
21. Fulga, A. On interpolative contractions that involve rational forms. *Adv. Diff. Equ.* **2021**, *2021*, 448. [CrossRef]

symmetry

MDPI

Article

Solving a System of Differential Equations with Infinite Delay by Using Tripled Fixed Point Techniques on Graphs

Hasanen A. Hammad [1,2,*,†] and Mohra Zayed [3,†]

1 Department of Mathematics, Unaizah College of Sciences and Arts, Qassim University, Buraydah 52571, Saudi Arabia
2 Department of Mathematics, Faculty of Science, Sohag University, Sohag 82524, Egypt
3 Mathematics Department, College of Science, King Khalid University, Abha 61413, Saudi Arabia; mzayed@kku.edu.sa
* Correspondence: hassanein_hamad@science.sohag.edu.eg or h.abdelwareth@qu.edu.sa
† These authors contributed equally to this work.

Abstract: In this manuscript, some similar tripled fixed point results under certain restrictions on a $b-$metric space endowed with graphs are established. Furthermore, an example is provided to support our results. The obtained results extend, generalize, and unify several similar significant contributions in the literature. Finally, to further extend our results, the existence of a solution to a system of ordinary differential equations with infinite delay is derived.

Keywords: tripled fixed point; edge-preserving; directed graph; b-metric space; differential equation with infinite delay

Citation: Hammad, H.A.; Zayed, M. Solving a System of Differential Equations with Infinite Delay by Using Tripled Fixed Point Techniques on Graphs. *Symmetry* **2022**, *14*, 1388. https://doi.org/10.3390/sym14071388

Academic Editor: Ioan Rașa

Received: 8 June 2022
Accepted: 4 July 2022
Published: 6 July 2022

1. Introduction and Basic Concepts

One of the most crucial methods for comprehending the world around us is mathematics. With the help of the various fields of mathematics, other sciences can be analyzed. The use of integral and differential equations is crucial for creating patterns for better understanding. Integral and differential equations likewise heavily rely on the fixed point theory.

In 2011, Berinde and Borcut [1] defined the notion of a tripled fixed point (TFP) for self-mappings and established some interesting consequences in partially ordered metric spaces. The (TFP) theory has a large number of significant applications that have been successfully employed to address a wide variety of issues. Researchers have focused on these issues to examine possible solutions, as seen in [2–7].

In 2008, Jachymski [8] proposed considering partial order sets as graphs in metric spaces. He obtained novel contraction mappings using this concept, which generalized many of the prior contractions. Moreover, in a metric space endowed with a graph, some results of the fixed points under these contractions were successfully deduced. Several authors have used this contribution in various applications. See the series of papers [9–12].

As a continuation of this approach, the results of coupled fixed points and TFPs for edge-preserving mappings with applications in abstract spaces have been investigated. For more details, see [13–17].

Czerwik [18] introduced the concept of $b-$metric spaces as a generalization of ordinary metric spaces as follows:

Definition 1. *Let $\chi \neq \emptyset$ be a set and $s \geq 1$ be a real number. A function $\varpi : \chi \times \chi \to \mathbb{R}^+$ is said to be a $b-$metric on χ, if for each $z, d, r \in \chi$, the hypotheses below hold:*

- $\varpi(z,d) = 0 \Leftrightarrow z = d;$
- $\varpi(z,d) = \varpi(d,z) \Leftrightarrow z = d;$
- $\varpi(z,d) \leq s[\varpi(z,r) + \varpi(r,d)].$

The pair (χ, ϖ) *is known as* $b-$*metric space.*

In the context of a metric space (χ, ϖ), let $\nabla = \{(z,z) : z \in \chi\}$ be the set of self loops and $\mho = (\vee(\mho), \Xi(\mho))$ be a directed graph where $\vee(\mho)$ represents the set of vertices and $\Xi(\mho)$ refers to the set of edges, so $\Xi(\mho) \supseteq \nabla$ and $\mho$ has no parallel edges.

Consider $z, d \in \vee(\mho)$, a path from z to d is a finite sequence $\{z_t\}_{t=0}^{N} \subseteq \mho$, where $z_0 = z$, $z_t = d$, and $(z_t, z_{t-1}) \in \Xi(\mho)$, $t = 1, 2, \ldots, N$. For simplicity, we write

$$[z]_{\mho} = \{d \in \chi \text{ there is a path from } z \text{ to } d\}.$$

If $\vee(\mho) = [z]_{\mho}$, then $\mho$ is said to be connected for all $l \in \chi$.

By reversing the directions of the edges on a directed graph $\mho$, we may obtain the directed graph $\mho^{-1}$, i.e., $\vee(\mho^{-1}) = \vee(\mho)$ and

$$\Xi\left(\mho^{-1}\right) = \{(d,z) : (z,d) \in \Xi(\mho)\}.$$

Moreover, by neglecting the direction of edges, we have the indirect graph $\widetilde{\mho}$, i.e., $\vee(\widetilde{\mho}) = \vee(\mho)$ and

$$\Xi\left(\widetilde{\mho}\right) = \Xi(\mho) \cup \Xi\left(\mho^{-1}\right).$$

Herein, we assume that (χ, ϖ) is a $b-$metric space, and $\mho$ is a directed graph, so $\vee(\mho) = \chi$ and $\Xi(\mho) \supseteq \nabla$. Further, we define another graph $\mho$ on the product $\chi \times \chi \times \chi$ as follows:

$$\left((z,d,r), \left(\overline{z}, \overline{d}, \overline{r}\right)\right) \in \Xi(\mho) \Leftrightarrow (z, \overline{z}) \in \Xi(\mho),\ \left(\overline{d}, d\right) \in \Xi(\mho) \text{ and } (r, \overline{r}) \in \Xi(\mho),$$

for all $(z,d,r), \left(\overline{z}, \overline{d}, \overline{r}\right) \in \chi^3$.

Definition 2 ([1])**.** *A trio* $(z,d,r) \in \chi^3$ *is called a TFP of the mapping* $\Omega : \chi^3 \to \chi$ *if*

$$z = \Omega(z,d,r),\ d = \Omega(d,r,z),\ \text{and } r = \Omega(r,z,d).$$

Definition 3 ([15])**.** *Let* $\Omega : \chi \times \chi \to \chi$ *be a given mapping defined on a complete metric space* (χ, ϖ) *equipped with a directed graph* $\mho$*. We say that* Ω *has the mixed* $\mho-$*monotone property if for all* $z, z_1, z_2, d, d_1, d_2 \in \chi$,

$$(z_1, z_2) \in \Xi(\mho) \text{ implies } (\Omega(z_1, d), \Omega(z_2, d)) \in \Xi(\mho),$$

and

$$(d_1, d_2) \in \Xi(\mho) \text{ implies } (\Omega(z, d_2), \Omega(z, d_1)) \in \Xi(\mho).$$

In a similar vein, our work seeks to create a new generalization of TFP results in the context of a $b-$metric space with a graph. Our results extend and unify the results of Alfuraidan and Khamsi [15], Luong and Thuan [19], and Işik and Türkoğlu [20] in partially ordered metric spaces. Our theoretical findings have been used to show that a system of ordinary differential equations with infinite delay has a solution.

2. Main Results

This section starts with a generalization of Definition 3 as follows:

Definition 4. *Let $\Omega : \chi^3 \to \chi$ be a function defined on a complete metric space (χ, ϖ) with a directed graph. We say that Ω has the mixed $\mho$-monotone property if for all $z, z_1, z_2, d, d_1, d_2, r, r_1, r_2 \in \chi$,*

$$\begin{aligned}(z_1, z_2) &\in \Xi(\mho) \text{ implies } (\Omega(z_1, d, r), \Omega(z_2, d, r)) \in \Xi(\mho),\\ (d_1, d_2) &\in \Xi(\mho) \text{ implies } (\Omega(z, d_1, r), \Omega(z, d_2, r)) \in \Xi(\mho),\end{aligned}$$

and

$$(r_1, r_2) \in \Xi(\mho) \text{ implies } (\Omega(z, d, r_1), \Omega(z, d, r_2)) \in \Xi(\mho).$$

In order to facilitate our study, we denote by Γ the set of pairs of functions (θ, ϑ), where $\theta, \vartheta : [0, \infty) \to [0, \infty)$ fulfilling the constraints below:

(c_1) θ is non-decreasing and continuous;
(c_2) $\theta(a) = 0$, if and only if $a = 0$;
(c_3) ϑ is continuous;
(c_4) for all $a > 0$, $\theta(a) > \vartheta(a)$.

The lemma below is useful for our main results.

Lemma 1. *Assume that (χ, ϖ) is a $b-$metric space with $s \geq 1$. Suppose that $\{\ell_k\}$, $\{\delta_k\}$, and $\{\lambda_k\}$ are three sequences in χ, and there is $\sigma \in [0, \frac{1}{s})$, justifying*

$$\varpi(\ell_k, \ell_{k+1}) + \varpi(\delta_k, \delta_{k+1}) + \varpi(\lambda_k, \lambda_{k+1}) \leq \sigma(\varpi(\ell_{k-1}, \ell_k) + \varpi(\delta_{k-1}, \delta_k) + \varpi(\lambda_{k-1}, \lambda_k)), \tag{1}$$

for any $k \in \mathbb{N}$. Then, $\{\ell_k\}$, $\{\delta_k\}$, and $\{\lambda_k\}$ are Cauchy sequences.

Proof. Let $j, k \in \mathbb{N}$, and $j < k$. Then,

$$\begin{aligned}
\varpi(\ell_j, \ell_k) + \varpi(\delta_j, \delta_k) + \varpi(\lambda_j, \lambda_k) \leq\; & s(\varpi(\ell_j, \ell_{j+1}) + \varpi(\ell_{j+1}, \ell_k)) + s(\varpi(\delta_j, \delta_{j+1}) + \varpi(\delta_{j+1}, \delta_k)) \\
& + s(\varpi(\lambda_j, \lambda_{j+1}) + \varpi(\lambda_{j+1}, \lambda_k)) \\
\leq\; & s(\varpi(\ell_j, \ell_{j+1}) + \varpi(\delta_j, \delta_{j+1}) + \varpi(\lambda_j, \lambda_{j+1})) \\
& + s^2(\varpi(\ell_{j+1}, \ell_{j+2}) + \varpi(\delta_{j+1}, \delta_{j+2}) + \varpi(\lambda_{j+1}, \lambda_{j+2})) \\
& + s^2(\varpi(\ell_{j+2}, \ell_k) + \varpi(\delta_{j+2}, \delta_k) + \varpi(\lambda_{j+2}, \lambda_k)) \\
\leq\; & \cdots \\
\leq\; & s(\varpi(\ell_j, \ell_{j+1}) + \varpi(\delta_j, \delta_{j+1}) + \varpi(\lambda_j, \lambda_{j+1})) \\
& + s^2(\varpi(\ell_{j+1}, \ell_{j+2}) + \varpi(\delta_{j+1}, \delta_{j+2}) + \varpi(\lambda_{j+1}, \lambda_{j+2})) + \cdots \\
& + s^{k-j-1}(\varpi(\ell_{k-2}, \ell_{k-1}) + \varpi(\ell_{k-1}, \ell_k) + \varpi(\delta_{k-2}, \delta_{k-1}) + \varpi(\delta_{k-1}, \delta_k)) \\
& + s^{k-j-1}(\varpi(\lambda_{k-2}, \lambda_{k-1}) + \varpi(\lambda_{k-1}, \lambda_k)) \\
\leq\; & s(\varpi(\ell_j, \ell_{j+1}) + \varpi(\delta_j, \delta_{j+1}) + \varpi(\lambda_j, \lambda_{j+1})) \\
& + s^2(\varpi(\ell_{j+1}, \ell_{j+2}) + \varpi(\delta_{j+1}, \delta_{j+2}) + \varpi(\lambda_{j+1}, \lambda_{j+2})) \\
& + s^{k-j-1}(\varpi(\ell_{k-2}, \ell_{k-1}) + \varpi(\delta_{k-2}, \delta_{k-1}) + \varpi(\lambda_{k-2}, \lambda_{k-1})) \\
& + s^{k-j}(\varpi(\ell_{k-1}, \ell_k) + \varpi(\delta_{k-1}, \delta_k) + \varpi(\lambda_{k-1}, \lambda_k)).
\end{aligned}$$

From the fact that $s\sigma < 1$, and using (1), we have

$$
\begin{aligned}
& \varpi(\ell_j,\ell_k)+\varpi(\delta_j,\delta_k)+\varpi(\lambda_j,\lambda_k) \\
\leq\ & \left(s\sigma^j+s^2\sigma^{j+1}+\cdots+s^{k-j-1}\sigma^{k-2}+s^{k-j}\sigma^{k-1}\right)(\varpi(\ell_0,\ell_1)+\varpi(\delta_0,\delta_1)+\varpi(\lambda_0,\lambda_1)) \\
=\ & s\sigma^j\left(1+s\sigma+\cdots+s^{k-j-2}\sigma^{k--j-2}+s^{k-j-1}\sigma^{k-j-1}\right)(\varpi(\ell_0,\ell_1)+\varpi(\delta_0,\delta_1)+\varpi(\lambda_0,\lambda_1)) \\
=\ & \frac{s\sigma^j}{1+s\sigma}(\varpi(\ell_0,\ell_1)+\varpi(\delta_0,\delta_1)+\varpi(\lambda_0,\lambda_1)).
\end{aligned}
$$

It follows that

$$\lim_{j\to\infty}(\varpi(\ell_j,\ell_k)+\varpi(\delta_j,\delta_k)+\varpi(\lambda_j,\lambda_k))=0.$$

Hence, $\{\ell_k\}$, $\{\delta_k\}$, and $\{\lambda_k\}$ are Cauchy sequences. □

Now, we formulate and prove the first main result.

Theorem 1. *On (χ,Ξ,ϖ), let (χ,ϖ) be a complete $b-$metric space with $s\geq 1$ and $\Omega:\chi^3\to\chi$ be a continuous mapping that has the mixed $\mho-$monotone property on χ for which there is a pair $(\theta,\vartheta)\in\Gamma$, so that*

$$\theta\left(s^2\varpi(\Omega(z,d,r),\Omega(z^*,d^*,r^*))\right)\leq\frac{1}{3}\vartheta(\varpi(z,z^*)+\varpi(d,d^*)+\varpi(r,r^*)), \tag{2}$$

for all $(z,d,r),(z^*,d^*,r^*)\in\chi^3$, where $((z,d,r),(z^*,d^*,r^*))\in\Xi(\mho)$. If there are $z_0,d_0,r_0\in\chi$ so that

$$((z_0,d_0,r_0),(\Omega(z_0,d_0,r_0),\Omega(d_0,r_0,z_0),\Omega(r_0,z_0,d_0)))\in\Xi(\mho);$$

then, Ω owns a TFP $\left(\widehat{z},\widehat{d},\widehat{r}\right)\in\chi^3$.

Proof. Put $z_{k+1}=\Omega(z_k,d_k,r_k)$, $d_{k+1}=\Omega(d_k,r_k,z_k)$, and $r_{k+1}=\Omega(r_k,z_k,d_k)$. Based on our assumption, we have

$$((z_0,d_0,r_0),(z_1,d_1,r_1))\in\Xi(\mho),$$

which leads to

$$
\begin{aligned}
\theta\left(s^2\varpi(z_2,z_1)\right) &= \theta\left(s^2\varpi(\Omega(z_1,d_1,r_1),\Omega(z_0,d_0,r_0))\right) \\
&\leq \frac{1}{3}\vartheta(\varpi(z_1,z_0)+\varpi(d_1,d_0)+\varpi(r_1,r_0)).
\end{aligned}
$$

Analogously, since $((d_0,r_0,z_0),(d_1,r_1,z_1))\in\Xi(\mho)$, one can obtain

$$\theta\left(s^2\varpi(d_2,d_1)\right)\leq\frac{1}{3}\vartheta(\varpi(d_1,d_0)+\varpi(r_1,r_0)+\varpi(z_1,z_0)).$$

Similarly, since $((r_0,z_0,d_0),(r_1,z_1,d_1))\in\Xi(\mho)$, we can write

$$\theta\left(s^2\varpi(r_2,r_1)\right)\leq\frac{1}{3}\vartheta(\varpi(r_1,r_0)+\varpi(z_1,z_0)+\varpi(d_1,d_0)).$$

Because Ω has the mixed $\mho-$monotone property, we have for $k\geq 1$,

$$
\begin{aligned}
((z_k,d_k,r_k),(z_{k+1},d_{k+1},r_{k+1})) &\in \Xi(\mho), \\
((d_k,r_k,z_k),(d_{k+1},r_{k+1},z_{k+1})) &\in \Xi(\mho),
\end{aligned}
$$

and

$$((r_k,z_k,d_k),(r_{k+1},z_{k+1},d_{k+1}))\in\Xi(\mho).$$

Then,

$$\theta\left(s^2\varpi(z_{k+1},z_k)\right) \leq \frac{1}{3}\vartheta(\varpi(z_k,z_{k-1}) + \varpi(d_k,d_{k-1}) + \varpi(r_k,r_{k-1})), \quad (3)$$

$$\theta\left(s^2\varpi(d_{k+1},d_k)\right) \leq \frac{1}{3}\vartheta(\varpi(d_k,d_{k-1}) + \varpi(r_k,r_{k-1}) + \varpi(z_k,z_{k-1})), \quad (4)$$

and

$$\theta\left(s^2\varpi(r_{k+1},r_k)\right) \leq \frac{1}{3}\vartheta(\varpi(r_k,r_{k-1}) + \varpi(z_k,z_{k-1}) + \varpi(d_k,d_{k-1})). \quad (5)$$

Adding (3)–(5), we obtain

$$\theta\left(s^2\varpi(z_{k+1},z_k)\right) + \theta\left(s^2\varpi(d_{k+1},d_k)\right) + \theta\left(s^2\varpi(r_{k+1},r_k)\right) \leq \vartheta(\varpi(z_k,z_{k-1}) + \varpi(d_k,d_{k-1}) + \varpi(r_k,r_{k-1})).$$

It follows from the properties of (θ,ϑ) that

$$\theta\left(s^2(\varpi(z_{k+1},z_k) + \varpi(d_{k+1},d_k) + \varpi(r_{k+1},r_k))\right) \leq \vartheta(\varpi(z_k,z_{k-1}) + \varpi(d_k,d_{k-1}) + \varpi(r_k,r_{k-1}));$$

again, from the properties of (θ,ϑ), we have

$$\theta\left(s^2(\varpi(z_{k+1},z_k) + \varpi(d_{k+1},d_k) + \varpi(r_{k+1},r_k))\right) \leq \theta(\varpi(z_k,z_{k-1}) + \varpi(d_k,d_{k-1}) + \varpi(r_k,r_{k-1}));$$

since θ is non-decreasing, we obtain

$$s^2(\varpi(z_{k+1},z_k) + \varpi(d_{k+1},d_k) + \varpi(r_{k+1},r_k)) \leq \varpi(z_k,z_{k-1}) + \varpi(d_k,d_{k-1}) + \varpi(r_k,r_{k-1}),$$

which leads to

$$\varpi(z_{k+1},z_k) + \varpi(d_{k+1},d_k) + \varpi(r_{k+1},r_k) \leq \frac{1}{s^2}(\varpi(z_k,z_{k-1}) + \varpi(d_k,d_{k-1}) + \varpi(r_k,r_{k-1})).$$

Because $0 \leq \frac{1}{s^2} < \frac{1}{s}$, then by Lemma 1, we observe that $\{z_k\}$, $\{d_k\}$, and $\{r_k\}$ are Cauchy sequences. The completeness of χ implies that there are $\widehat{z},\widehat{d},\widehat{r} \in \chi$, so that

$$\lim_{k\to\infty} z_k = \widehat{z},\ \lim_{k\to\infty} d_k = \widehat{d}m \text{ and } \lim_{k\to\infty} r_k = \widehat{r}.$$

Since Ω is continuous, we obtain

$$\begin{aligned}
\widehat{z} &= \lim_{k\to\infty} z_k = \lim_{k\to\infty} \Omega(z_{k-1},d_{k-1},r_{k-1}) = \Omega\left(\lim_{k\to\infty} z_{k-1}, \lim_{k\to\infty} d_{k-1}, \lim_{k\to\infty} r_{k-1}\right) = \Omega\left(\widehat{z},\widehat{d},\widehat{r}\right), \\
\widehat{d} &= \lim_{k\to\infty} d_k = \lim_{k\to\infty} \Omega(d_{k-1},r_{k-1},z_{k-1}) = \Omega\left(\lim_{k\to\infty} d_{k-1}, \lim_{k\to\infty} r_{k-1}, \lim_{k\to\infty} z_{k-1}\right) = \Omega\left(\widehat{d},\widehat{r},\widehat{z}\right), \\
\widehat{r} &= \lim_{k\to\infty} r_k = \lim_{k\to\infty} \Omega(r_{k-1},z_{k-1},d_{k-1}) = \Omega\left(\lim_{k\to\infty} r_{k-1}, \lim_{k\to\infty} z_{k-1}, \lim_{k\to\infty} d_{k-1}\right) = \Omega\left(\widehat{r},\widehat{z},\widehat{d}\right).
\end{aligned}$$

This proves that $\left(\widehat{z},\widehat{d},\widehat{r}\right)$ is a TFP of Ω. □

In the case of the non continuity of Ω, we can state another sufficient condition for the existence of TFP by giving the following postulate on the trio (χ,Ξ,ϖ) :

(p) for any sequence $\{z_k\}_{k\in\mathbb{N}}$ in χ, so that $(z_k,z_{k+1}) \in \Xi(\mho)$, $(z_{k+1},z_k) \in \Xi(\mho)$, and $\lim_{k\to\infty} z_k = z$, we have $(z_k,z,) \in \Xi(\mho)$ and $(z,z_k) \in \Xi(\mho)$.

Now, our second theoretical result is as follows:

Theorem 2. *On (χ,Ξ,ϖ), suppose that (χ,ϖ) is a complete $b-$ms with $s \geq 1$, and (χ,Ξ,ϖ) satisfies Postulate (p). Suppose also the mapping $\Omega : \chi^3 \to \chi$ has the mixed $\mho-$monotone property* *on χ. Assume that $(\theta, \vartheta) \in \Gamma$, so that the contractive condition (2) holds. If there are $z_0, d_0, r_0 \in \chi$ so that*

$$((z_0, d_0, r_0), (\Omega(z_0, d_0, r_0), \Omega(d_0, r_0, z_0), \Omega(r_0, z_0, d_0))) \in \Xi(\mho),$$

then Ω possesses a TFP $\left(\widehat{z}, \widehat{d}, \widehat{r}\right) \in \chi^3$.

Proof. By the same line proof of Theorem 1 and since

$$\begin{aligned} \lim_{k\to\infty} z_{k+1} &= \lim_{k\to\infty} \Omega(z_k, d_k, r_k) = \widehat{z}, \\ \lim_{k\to\infty} d_{k+1} &= \lim_{k\to\infty} \Omega(d_k, r_k, z_k) = \widehat{d}, \\ \lim_{k\to\infty} r_{k+1} &= \lim_{k\to\infty} \Omega(r_k, z_k, d_k) = \widehat{r}, \end{aligned}$$

and

$$(z_k, z_{k+1}) \in \Xi(\mho),\ (d_k, d_{k+1}) \in \Xi(\mho) \text{ and } (r_k, r_{k+1}) \in \Xi(\mho),$$

then, by Postulate (p), one can write

$$(z_k, \widehat{z}) \in \Xi(\mho),\ \left(d_k, \widehat{d}\right) \in \Xi(\mho) \text{ and } (r_k, \widehat{r}) \in \Xi(\mho).$$

Then,

$$\left((z_k, d_k, r_k), \left(\widehat{z}, \widehat{d}, \widehat{r}\right)\right) \in \Xi(\mho).$$

Hence, we obtain

$$\theta\left(s^2\varpi\left(\Omega(z_k, d_k, r_k), \Omega\left(\widehat{z}, \widehat{d}, \widehat{r}\right)\right)\right) \le \frac{1}{3}\vartheta\left(\varpi(z_k, \widehat{z}) + \varpi\left(d_k, \widehat{d}\right) + \varpi(r_k, \widehat{r})\right). \tag{6}$$

Analogously, we obtain

$$\theta\left(s^2\varpi\left(\Omega(d_k, r_k, z_k), \Omega\left(\widehat{d}, \widehat{r}, \widehat{z}\right)\right)\right) \le \frac{1}{3}\vartheta\left(\varpi\left(d_k, \widehat{d}\right) + \varpi(r_k, \widehat{r}) + \varpi(z_k, \widehat{z})\right), \tag{7}$$

and

$$\theta\left(s^2\varpi\left(\Omega(d_k, r_k, z_k), \Omega\left(\widehat{d}, \widehat{r}, \widehat{z}\right)\right)\right) \le \frac{1}{3}\vartheta\left(\varpi\left(d_k, \widehat{d}\right) + \varpi(r_k, \widehat{r}) + \varpi(z_k, \widehat{z})\right). \tag{8}$$

Taking the limit as $k \to \infty$ in (6)–(8), we have

$$\begin{aligned} \lim_{k\to\infty} \varpi\left(\Omega(z_k, d_k, r_k), \Omega\left(\widehat{z}, \widehat{d}, \widehat{r}\right)\right) &= 0,\ \lim_{k\to\infty} \varpi\left(\Omega(d_k, r_k, z_k), \Omega\left(\widehat{d}, \widehat{r}, \widehat{z}\right)\right) = 0 \\ \text{and } \lim_{k\to\infty} \varpi\left(\Omega(d_k, r_k, z_k), \Omega\left(\widehat{d}, \widehat{r}, \widehat{z}\right)\right) &= 0. \end{aligned}$$

This implies that

$$\lim_{k\to\infty} z_{k+1} = \Omega\left(\widehat{z}, \widehat{d}, \widehat{r}\right),\ \lim_{k\to\infty} d_{k+1} = \Omega\left(\widehat{d}, \widehat{r}, \widehat{z}\right) \text{ and } \lim_{k\to\infty} r_{k+1} = \Omega\left(\widehat{r}, \widehat{z}, \widehat{d}\right),$$

which yields that

$$\widehat{z} = \Omega\left(\widehat{z}, \widehat{d}, \widehat{r}\right),\ \widehat{d} = \Omega\left(\widehat{d}, \widehat{r}, \widehat{z}\right) \text{ and } \widehat{r} = \Omega\left(\widehat{r}, \widehat{z}, \widehat{d}\right);$$

that is, $\left(\widehat{z}, \widehat{d}, \widehat{r}\right)$ is a TFP of Ω on χ. □

Next, we shall state some contributions of Theorems 1 and 2 in the literature.

The results of Alfuraidan and Khamsi [15] can be generalized if we let $\theta(a) = a$ and $\vartheta(a) = \ell a$ in Theorems 1 and 2 with $b = 1$ as follows:

Corollary 1. *Let (χ, ϖ) be a complete metric space with a direct graph Ξ and the mapping $\Omega : \chi^3 \to \chi$ has the mixed $\mho-$monotone property on χ for which there exists $\ell \in [0,1)$ such that*

$$\theta(\varpi(\Omega(z,d,r),\Omega(z^*,d^*,r^*))) \leq \frac{\ell}{3}\theta(\varpi(z,z^*) + \varpi(d,d^*) + \varpi(r,r^*)),$$

for all $(z,d,r),(z^*,d^*,r^*) \in \chi^3$ with $((z,d,r),(z^*,d^*,r^*)) \in \Xi(\mho)$. Assume that either Ω is a continuous mapping or the triple (χ, Ξ, ϖ) has the property (p). If there are $z_0, d_0, r_0 \in \chi$ so that

$$((z_0,d_0,r_0),(\Omega(z_0,d_0,r_0),\Omega(d_0,r_0,z_0),\Omega(r_0,z_0,d_0))) \in \Xi(\mho),$$

then, Ω has a TFP $\left(\widehat{z},\widehat{d},\widehat{r}\right) \in \chi^3$.

It should be noted that if $(\theta, \vartheta) \in \Gamma$ and $\vartheta_1(a) = \theta(a) - 3\vartheta\left(\frac{a}{3}\right)$, then $(\theta, \vartheta_1) \in \Gamma$. Based on this notion, the results of Luong and Thuan [19] in a metric space endowed with a graph can be re-formulated as follows:

Corollary 2. *Let (χ, ϖ) be a complete metric space with a direct graph Ξ, and the mapping $\Omega : \chi^3 \to \chi$ has the mixed $\mho-$monotone property. Let $(\theta, \vartheta) \in \Gamma$, so that*

$$\begin{aligned}\theta(\varpi(\Omega(z,d,r),\Omega(z^*,d^*,r^*))) \leq\ & \frac{1}{3}\theta(\varpi(z,z^*) + \varpi(d,d^*) + \varpi(r,r^*)) \\ & -\vartheta\left(\frac{\varpi(z,z^*) + \varpi(d,d^*) + \varpi(r,r^*)}{3}\right)\end{aligned}$$

for all $(z,d,r),(z^*,d^*,r^*) \in \chi^3$ with $((z,d,r),(z^*,d^*,r^*)) \in \Xi(\mho)$. Assume either the mapping Ω is continuous or a trio (χ, Ξ, ϖ) satisfies the postulate (p). If there are $z_0, d_0, r_0 \in \chi$, so that

$$((z_0,d_0,r_0),(\Omega(z_0,d_0,r_0),\Omega(d_0,r_0,z_0),\Omega(r_0,z_0,d_0))) \in \Xi(\mho),$$

then, Ω has a TFP $\left(\widehat{z},\widehat{d},\widehat{r}\right) \in \chi^3$.

In the following, we discuss the uniqueness of a TFP of the mapping Ω.

Theorem 3. *In addition to the assumptions of Theorems 1 and 2, assume that for any (z,d,r), $(z^*,d^*,r^*) \in \chi^3$, there is $\left(\widehat{\ell},\widetilde{\ell},\overline{\ell}\right) \in \chi^3$, so that*

$$\left((z,d,r),\left(\widehat{\ell},\widetilde{\ell},\overline{\ell}\right)\right) \in \Xi(\mho) \text{ and } \left((z^*,d^*,r^*),\left(\widehat{\ell},\widetilde{\ell},\overline{\ell}\right)\right) \in \Xi(\mho).$$

Then, Ω has a unique TFP.

Proof. Assume that there are two TFPs (z,d,r) and (z^*,d^*,r^*) of Ω. By our hypothesis, there is $(\varkappa,\eta,\zeta) \in \chi^3$, so that $((z,d,r),(\varkappa,\eta,\zeta)) \in \Xi(\mho)$, and $((z^*,d^*,r^*),(\varkappa,\eta,\zeta)) \in \Xi(\mho)$. Define three sequences $\{\varkappa_k\}$, $\{\eta_k\}$, and $\{\zeta_k\}$ by

$$\varkappa = \varkappa_0,\ \eta = \eta_0,\ \zeta = \zeta_0,\ \varkappa_{k+1} = \Omega(\varkappa_k,\eta_k,\zeta_k),\ \eta_{k+1} = \Omega(\eta_k,\zeta_k,\varkappa_k) \text{ and } \zeta_{k+1} = \Omega(\zeta_k,\varkappa_k,\eta_k), \text{ for all } n.$$

Since $((z,d,r),(\varkappa,\eta,\zeta)) \in \Xi(\mho)$ and Ω has a mixed $\mho-$monotone property, we can show that $((z,d,r),(\varkappa_k,\eta_k,\zeta_k)) \in \Xi(\mho)$. Then,

$$\theta\left(s^2\varpi(z,\varkappa_{k+1})\right) = \theta\left(s^2\varpi(\Omega(z,d,r),\Omega(\varkappa_k,\eta_k,\zeta_k))\right) \leq \frac{1}{3}\vartheta(\varpi(z,\varkappa_k) + \varpi(d,\eta_k) + \varpi(r,\zeta_k)). \tag{9}$$

Similarly, we can write

$$\theta\left(s^2\varpi(d,\eta_{k+1})\right) = \theta\left(s^2\varpi(\Omega(d,r,z),\Omega(\eta_k,\zeta_k,\varkappa_k))\right) \leq \frac{1}{3}\vartheta(\varpi(d,\eta_k) + \varpi(r,\zeta_k) + \varpi(z,\varkappa_k)), \tag{10}$$

and

$$\theta\left(s^2\varpi(r,\zeta_{k+1})\right) = \theta\left(s^2\varpi(\Omega(r,z,d),\Omega(\zeta_k,\varkappa_k,\eta_k))\right) \leq \frac{1}{3}\vartheta(\varpi(r,\zeta_k)+\varpi(z,\varkappa_k)+\varpi(d,\eta_k)). \tag{11}$$

Combining (9)–(11) and using the properties of θ and ϑ, we have

$$\theta\left(s^2(\varpi(z,\varkappa_{k+1})+\varpi(d,\eta_{k+1})+\varpi(r,\zeta_{k+1}))\right) \leq \vartheta(\varpi(z,\varkappa_k)+\varpi(d,\eta_k)+\varpi(r,\zeta_k)). \tag{12}$$

Because θ is non-decreasing function, and $\theta(a) > \vartheta(a)$ for $a > 0$, we have

$$s^2(\varpi(z,\varkappa_{k+1})+\varpi(d,\eta_{k+1})+\varpi(r,\zeta_{k+1})) \leq \varpi(z,\varkappa_k)+\varpi(d,\eta_k)+\varpi(r,\zeta_k).$$

Since $s \geq 1$, we obtain

$$\varpi(z,\varkappa_{k+1})+\varpi(d,\eta_{k+1})+\varpi(r,\zeta_{k+1}) \leq \varpi(z,\varkappa_k)+\varpi(d,\eta_k)+\varpi(r,\zeta_k).$$

This leads to $\{\varpi(z,\varkappa_k)+\varpi(d,\eta_k)+\varpi(r,\zeta_k)\}$ being a nonnegative decreasing sequence; consequently, there is $\rho \geq 0$, so that

$$\lim_{k\to\infty}(\varpi(z,\varkappa_k)+\varpi(d,\eta_k)+\varpi(r,\zeta_k)) = \rho.$$

As the functions θ and ϑ are continuous, and by taking $k \to \infty$ in (12), one can write

$$\theta\left(s^2\rho\right) \leq \vartheta(\rho).$$

It follows from the properties of θ and ϑ that $\rho = 0$. Hence,

$$\lim_{k\to\infty}(\varpi(z,\varkappa_k)+\varpi(d,\eta_k)+\varpi(r,\zeta_k)) = 0;$$

that is,

$$\lim_{k\to\infty}\varpi(z,\varkappa_k) = 0, \lim_{k\to\infty}\varpi(d,\eta_k) = 0, \text{ and } \lim_{k\to\infty}\varpi(r,\zeta_k) = 0.$$

Following the same scenario, we have

$$\lim_{k\to\infty}\varpi(z^*,\varkappa_k) = 0, \lim_{k\to\infty}\varpi(d^*,\eta_k) = 0 \text{ and } \lim_{k\to\infty}\varpi(r^*,\zeta_k) = 0.$$

Let $k \to \infty$ in the following inequalities

$$\begin{aligned}
\varpi(z,z^*) &\leq s(\varpi(z,\varkappa_k)+\varpi(\varkappa_k,z^*)),\\
\varpi(d,d^*) &\leq s(\varpi(d,\varkappa_k)+\varpi(\varkappa_k,d^*)),\\
\varpi(r,r^*) &\leq s(\varpi(r,\varkappa_k)+\varpi(\varkappa_k,r^*)).
\end{aligned}$$

Thus, $\varpi(z,z^*) = 0$, $\varpi(d,d^*) = 0$, and $\varpi(r,r^*) = 0$. Hence, $z = z^*$, $d = d^*$, and $r = r^*$. □

Theorem 4. *Assume that* $\left(\left(\widehat{z},\widehat{d}\right),\left(\widehat{d},\widehat{r}\right),(\widehat{r},\widehat{z})\right) \in \Xi(\mho)$ *and the assumptions of Theorems 1 and 2 are true. If* $\left(\widehat{z},\widehat{d},\widehat{r}\right)$ *is a TFP of* Ω, *then* $\widehat{z} = \widehat{d} = \widehat{r}$.

Proof. Because $\left(\left(\widehat{z},\widehat{d}\right),\left(\widehat{d},\widehat{r}\right),(\widehat{r},\widehat{z})\right) \in \Xi(\mho)$, we have

$$\begin{aligned}
\theta\left(s^2\varpi\left(\widehat{z},\widehat{d}\right)\right) &= \theta\left(s^2\varpi\left(\Omega\left(\widehat{z},\widehat{d},\widehat{r}\right),\Omega\left(\widehat{d},\widehat{r},\widehat{z}\right)\right)\right)\\
&\leq \frac{1}{3}\vartheta\left(\varpi\left(\widehat{z},\widehat{d}\right)+\varpi\left(\widehat{d},\widehat{r}\right)+\varpi(\widehat{r},\widehat{z})\right).
\end{aligned}$$

Similarly, we can write

$$\theta\left(s^2\varpi\left(\widehat{d},\widehat{r}\right)\right) \leq \frac{1}{3}\vartheta\left(\varpi\left(\widehat{d},\widehat{r}\right)+\varpi(\widehat{r},\widehat{z})+\varpi\left(\widehat{z},\widehat{d}\right)\right),$$

and

$$\theta\left(s^2\varpi(\widehat{r},\widehat{z})\right) \leq \frac{1}{3}\vartheta\left(\varpi(\widehat{r},\widehat{z})+\varpi\left(\widehat{z},\widehat{d}\right)+\varpi\left(\widehat{d},\widehat{r}\right)\right).$$

Combining the above three inequalities, we have

$$\begin{aligned}\theta\left(s^2\left[\varpi\left(\widehat{z},\widehat{d}\right)+\varpi\left(\widehat{d},\widehat{r}\right)+\varpi(\widehat{r},\widehat{z})\right]\right) &\leq \vartheta\left(\varpi\left(\widehat{z},\widehat{d}\right)+\varpi\left(\widehat{d},\widehat{r}\right)+\varpi(\widehat{r},\widehat{z})\right)\\ &< \theta\left(\varpi\left(\widehat{z},\widehat{d}\right)+\varpi\left(\widehat{d},\widehat{r}\right)+\varpi(\widehat{r},\widehat{z})\right).\end{aligned}$$

Since the function θ is non-decreasing, we obtain

$$s^2\left(\varpi\left(\widehat{z},\widehat{d}\right)+\varpi\left(\widehat{d},\widehat{r}\right)+\varpi(\widehat{r},\widehat{z})\right) < \varpi\left(\widehat{z},\widehat{d}\right)+\varpi\left(\widehat{d},\widehat{r}\right)+\varpi(\widehat{r},\widehat{z}).$$

Hence, $\varpi\left(\widehat{z},\widehat{d}\right)+\varpi\left(\widehat{d},\widehat{r}\right)+\varpi(\widehat{r},\widehat{z}) = 0$; that is, $\varpi\left(\widehat{z},\widehat{d}\right) = 0$, $\varpi\left(\widehat{d},\widehat{r}\right) = 0$, and $\varpi(\widehat{r},\widehat{z}) = 0$. So, $\widehat{z} = \widehat{d} = \widehat{r}$. This completes the proof. □

In the end of this part, we present the following example to support our theoretical results.

Example 1. *Assume that $\chi = \mathbb{R}$, $\varpi(z,d) = |z-d|^2$ is a $b-$metric space with $s = 2$. Define a directed graph $\mho$ on χ by*

$$((z,d,r),(z^*,d^*,r^*)) \in \Xi(\mho), \textit{ if and only if } z \leq z^*,\ d^* \leq d \textit{ and } r \leq r^*.$$

Describe the mapping $\Omega : \chi^3 \to \chi$ as $\Omega(z,d,r) = \frac{1}{6}(z+d+r)$, $(z^*,d^*,r^*) \in \chi^3$. It is clear that Ω has a $\mho-$monotone property. For any $(z,d,r),(z^*,d^*,r^*) \in \chi^3$ with $((z,d,r),(z^*,d^*,r^*)) \in \Xi(\mho)$, we have

$$\begin{aligned}\theta\left(s^2\varpi(\Omega(z,d,r),\Omega(z^*,d^*,r^*))\right) &= \frac{1}{4}\left(2^2\left(\frac{z+d+r}{6}-\frac{z^*+d^*+r^*}{6}\right)^2\right)\\ &= \frac{1}{36}((z-z^*)+(d-d^*)+(r-r^*))^2\\ &\leq \frac{1}{9}\left((z-z^*)^2+(d-d^*)^2+(r-r^*)^2\right)\\ &= \frac{1}{3}\vartheta(\varpi(z,z^*)+\varpi(d,d^*)+\varpi(r,r^*)).\end{aligned}$$

Hence, the condition (2) is satisfied with $\theta(a) = \frac{1}{4}a$ and $\vartheta(a) = \frac{1}{3}a$. Clearly, $(\theta,\vartheta) \in \Gamma$. Therefore, all requirements of Theorem 1 are fulfilled. Moreover, $((0,0,0),(0,0,0)) \in \Xi(\mho)$ So, by Theorems 1 and 3, the point $(0,0,0)$ is a unique TFP of the mapping Ω.

3. Solving a System of Ordinary Differential Equations

This section is the mainstay of our paper in which the existence and uniqueness of the solution to a system of ordinary differential equations is investigated. This system is given as follows:

$$\begin{cases} z'(\nu) = \wp(\nu, z_\nu, u_\nu, r_\nu), \\ u'(\nu) = \wp(\nu, u_\nu, r_\nu, z_\nu), \quad \nu \in \chi, \\ r'(\nu) = \wp(\nu, r_\nu, z_\nu, u_\nu), \end{cases} \tag{13}$$

under the conditions

$$z(\nu) = \varpi_1(\nu),\ u(\nu) = \varpi_2(\nu) \text{ and } r(\nu) = \varpi_3(\nu),\ \nu \in (-\infty, 0], \tag{14}$$

where $\chi = [0, b]$, $\wp : \chi \times \eth^3 \to \mathbb{R}^k$, (where $\eth^3 = \eth \times \eth \times \eth$) $\varpi_1, \varpi_2, \varpi_3 \in \eth$, and z_ν, u_ν, r_ν are the history of the state from $-\infty$ to the time ν. Let the histories $z_\nu, u_\nu, r_\nu \in \eth$, where $(\eth, \|.\|_\eth)$ is a seminormed linear space of functions mapping $z : (-\infty, 0] \to \mathbb{R}^k$, $k \in \mathbb{N}$ and satisfying the hypotheses below that were presented by Hale and Kato [21] for the ODE.

(i) If $z : (-\infty, b] \to \mathbb{R}^k$, $b > 0$ is continuous on χ and $z_0 \in \eth$, then there are constant $\tau, \xi > 0$; so, for each $a \in [0, b)$, the following assumptions are satisfied:
   (1) $z_a \in \eth$;
   (2) $\|z\| \leq \|z_a\|_\eth$;
   (3) $\|z_a\|_\eth \leq \tau \sup\{\|z(c)\| : 0 \leq c \leq a\} + \xi \|z_0\|_\eth$.
(ii) The function z_a is a $\eth-$valued continuous function on $[0, b)$, where $z(.)$ is the function defined in (i).
(iii) The space $\eth$ is complete.

Now, we consider the following space to define a solution for Problems (13) and (14):

$$\Theta = \left\{z,\ z : (-\infty, 0] \to \mathbb{R}^k,\ z \in C\left(\chi, \mathbb{R}^k\right),\ k \in \mathbb{N},\ z(\nu) = \varpi_1(\nu),\ \nu \in (-\infty, 0],\ \varpi_1 \in \eth\right\},$$

equipped with the following seminorm

$$\|z\|_\Theta = \|z_0\|_\eth + \sup_{0 \leq c \leq b} \|z(c)\|.$$

It should be noted that the function $(z, u, r) \in \Theta^3$ (where $\Theta^3 = \Theta \times \Theta \times \Theta$) is a solution of (13) and (14), if (z, u, r) fulfills (13) and (14).

Describe the operator $\Upsilon : \Theta^3 \to \Theta$ as

$$\Upsilon(z, u, r) = \begin{cases} \varpi_1(\nu) & \text{if } \nu \in (-\infty, 0) \\ \varpi_1(\nu) + \int\limits_0^\nu \wp(\hbar, z_\hbar, u_\hbar, r_\hbar) d\hbar & \text{if } \nu \in \chi \end{cases},$$

$$\Upsilon(u, r, z) = \begin{cases} \varpi_2(\nu) & \text{if } \nu \in (-\infty, 0) \\ \varpi_2(\nu) + \int\limits_0^\nu \wp(\hbar, u_\hbar, r_\hbar, z_\hbar) d\hbar & \text{if } \nu \in \chi \end{cases},$$

and

$$\Upsilon(r, z, u) = \begin{cases} \varpi_3(\nu) & \text{if } \nu \in (-\infty, 0) \\ \varpi_3(\nu) + \int\limits_0^\nu \wp(\hbar, r_\hbar, z_\hbar, u_\hbar) d\hbar & \text{if } \nu \in \chi \end{cases}.$$

Assume that $\widetilde{\varpi}_1, \widetilde{\varpi}_2, \widetilde{\varpi}_3 : (-\infty, b) \to \mathbb{R}^k$ are functions defined by

$$\widetilde{\varpi}_1(\nu) = \begin{cases} \varpi_1(\nu) & \text{if } \nu \in (-\infty, 0) \\ \varpi_1(0) & \text{if } \nu \in \chi \end{cases},\quad \widetilde{\varpi}_2(\nu) = \begin{cases} \varpi_2(\nu) & \text{if } \nu \in (-\infty, 0) \\ \varpi_2(0) & \text{if } \nu \in \chi \end{cases},$$

and

$$\widetilde{\varpi}_3(\nu) = \begin{cases} \varpi_3(\nu) & \text{if } \nu \in (-\infty, 0) \\ \varpi_3(0) & \text{if } \nu \in \chi \end{cases}.$$

Then, $\widetilde{\varpi}_1^0 = \varpi_1$, $\widetilde{\varpi}_2^0 = \varpi_2$, and $\widetilde{\varpi}_3^0 = \varpi_3$. For each $\delta_1, \delta_2, \delta_3 \in C\left([0,b], \mathbb{R}^k\right)$ with $\delta_1(0) = 0$, $\delta_2(0) = 0$, and $\delta_3(0) = 0$. Describe the functions $\widehat{\delta}_1$, $\widehat{\delta}_2$, and $\widehat{\delta}_3$ as

$$\widehat{\delta}_1(\nu) = \begin{cases} 0 & \text{if } \nu \in (-\infty, 0) \\ \delta_1(\nu) & \text{if } \nu \in \chi \end{cases}, \quad \widehat{\delta}_2(\nu) = \begin{cases} 0 & \text{if } \nu \in (-\infty, 0) \\ \delta_2(\nu) & \text{if } \nu \in \chi \end{cases},$$

and

$$\widehat{\delta}_3(\nu) = \begin{cases} 0 & \text{if } \nu \in (-\infty, 0) \\ \delta_3(\nu) & \text{if } \nu \in \chi \end{cases}.$$

If $z(.)$, $u(.)$, and $r(.)$ satisfy the integral equations

$$\begin{aligned} z(\nu) &= \varpi_1(\nu) + \int_0^\nu \wp(\hbar, z_\hbar, u_\hbar, r_\hbar) d\hbar, \\ u(\nu) &= \varpi_2(\nu) + \int_0^\nu \wp(\hbar, u_\hbar, r_\hbar, z_\hbar) d\hbar, \end{aligned}$$

and

$$r(\nu) = \varpi_3(\nu) + \int_0^\nu \wp(\hbar, r_\hbar, z_\hbar, u_\hbar) d\hbar,$$

we can decompose $z(.)$, $u(.)$, and $r(.)$ as $z(\nu) = \widehat{\delta}_1(\nu) + \widetilde{\varpi}_1(\nu)$, $u(\nu) = \widehat{\delta}_2(\nu) + \widetilde{\varpi}_2(\nu)$, and $r(\nu) = \widehat{\delta}_3(\nu) + \widetilde{\varpi}_3(\nu)$ for every $0 \le \nu \le b$. In addition, the functions δ_1, δ_2, and δ_3 satisfy

$$\begin{aligned} \delta_1(\nu) &= \int_0^\nu \wp\left(\hbar, \widehat{\delta}_1(\hbar) + \widetilde{\varpi}_1(\hbar), \widehat{\delta}_2(\hbar) + \widetilde{\varpi}_2(\hbar), \widehat{\delta}_3(\hbar) + \widetilde{\varpi}_3(\hbar)\right) d\hbar, \\ \delta_2(\nu) &= \int_0^\nu \wp\left(\hbar, \widehat{\delta}_2(\hbar) + \widetilde{\varpi}_2(\hbar), \widehat{\delta}_3(\hbar) + \widetilde{\varpi}_3(\hbar), \widehat{\delta}_1(\hbar) + \widetilde{\varpi}_1(\hbar)\right) d\hbar, \end{aligned}$$

and

$$\delta_3(\nu) = \int_0^\nu \wp\left(\hbar, \widehat{\delta}_3(\hbar) + \widetilde{\varpi}_3(v), \widehat{\delta}_1(\hbar) + \widetilde{\varpi}_1(\hbar), \widehat{\delta}_2(\hbar) + \widetilde{\varpi}_2(\hbar)\right) d\hbar.$$

Put $C_0 = \left\{\delta \in C\left([0,b], \mathbb{R}^k\right) : \delta(0) = 0\right\}$ equipped with a $b-$metric $\varpi(z,u) = \left(\sup_{\nu \in \chi} \|z(\nu) - u(\nu)\|\right)^2$ with $s = 2$.

Consider the following partial order relation on C_0^3 (where $C_0^3 = C_0 \times C_0 \times C_0$) :

$$(z_1, u_1, r_1) \le (z_2, u_2, r_2) \Leftrightarrow z_1(a) \le z_2(a),\ u_1(a) \ge u_2(a), \text{ and } r_1(a) \le r_2(a),\ a \in \chi.$$

Now, Problems (13) and (14) will be considered under the following hypotheses:

Hypothesis 1 (H1). *The function $\wp : \chi \times \eth^3 \to \mathbb{R}^k$, $k \in \mathbb{N}$ is continuous.*

Hypothesis 2 (H2). *For all $z, u, r, z_1, u_1, r_1 \in \mathbb{R}^k$ with $z \le z_1$, $u_1 \le u$ and $r \le r_1$,*

$$\wp(\nu, z, u, r) \le \wp(\nu, z_1, u_1, r_1).$$

Hypothesis 3 (H3). *For each $\nu \in [0,b]$, $z, u, r, z_1, u_1, r_1 \in \mathbb{R}^k$, $z \le z_1$, $u_1 \le u$, and $r \le r_1$, we have*

$$\|\wp(\nu, z, u, r) - (\nu, z_1, u_1, r_1)\|^2 \le \frac{1}{12b^2} \ln\left(1 + \frac{1}{\tau}\|z - z_1\|_\eth^2 + \|u - u_1\|_\eth^2 + \|r - r_1\|_\eth^2\right).$$

Theorem 5. *Consider Problems (13) and (14) under the hypotheses* (H_1)–(H_3). *If there are* $(e, f, g) \in C_0^3$, *so that*

$$e(\nu) \geq \int_0^\nu \wp\Big(\hbar, \widehat{e}(\hbar) + \widetilde{\omega}_1(\hbar), \widehat{f}(\hbar) + \widetilde{\omega}_2(\hbar), \widehat{g}(\hbar) + \widetilde{\omega}_3(\hbar)\Big) d\hbar,$$

$$f(\nu) \leq \int_0^\nu \wp\Big(\hbar, \widehat{f}(\hbar) + \widetilde{\omega}_1(\hbar), \widehat{g}(\hbar) + \widetilde{\omega}_2(\hbar), \widehat{e}(\hbar) + \widetilde{\omega}_3(\hbar)\Big) d\hbar,$$

and

$$g(\nu) \geq \int_0^\nu \wp\Big(\hbar, g(\hbar) + \widetilde{\omega}_1(\hbar), \widehat{e}(\hbar) + \widetilde{\omega}_2(\hbar), \widehat{f}(\hbar) + \widetilde{\omega}_3(\hbar)\Big) d\hbar.$$

Then, there is at least one solution to the problem (13) and (14).

Proof. Let $\aleph : C_0^3 \to C_0$ be an operator defined by

$$\aleph(\delta_1, \delta_2, \delta_3) = \int_0^\nu \wp\Big(\hbar, \widehat{\delta}_1(\nu) + \widetilde{\omega}_1(\nu), \widehat{\delta}_2(\nu) + \widetilde{\omega}_2(\nu), \widehat{\delta}_3(\nu) + \widetilde{\omega}_3(\nu)\Big) d\hbar.$$

It is clear that if Y has a TFP, then $\aleph$ has a TFP and vice versa. So the existence solution of Problems (13) and (14) is equivalent to finding a TFP of the mapping $\aleph$. To achieve this, we demonstrate that $\aleph$ fulfills the requirements of Theorems 1 or 2.

Define the graph $\mho$ with $\vee(\mho) = C_0^3$ and

$$\Xi(\mho) = \Big\{((z, u, r), (z^*, u^*, r^*)) \in C_0^3 \times C_0^3 : z \leq z^*, u^* \geq u \text{ and } r \leq r^*\Big\}.$$

It follows that

$$((z, u, r), (z^*, u^*, r^*)) \in \Xi(\mho) \Leftrightarrow (z, z^*) \in \Xi(\mho), (u^*, u) \in \Xi(\mho) \text{ and } (r, r^*) \in \Xi(\mho),$$

for all $((z, u, r), (z^*, u^*, r^*)) \in C_0^3$.

Consider $z, u, r, z_1, u_1, r_1, z_2, u_2, r_2 \in C_0$. If $(z_1, z_2) \in \Xi(\mho)$, then, from (H_2), we can write

$$\aleph(z_1, u, r) = \int_0^\nu \wp(\hbar, \widehat{z}_1(\hbar) + \widetilde{\omega}_1(\hbar), \widehat{u}(\hbar) + \widetilde{\omega}_2(\hbar), \widehat{r}(\hbar) + \widetilde{\omega}_3(\hbar)) d\hbar$$

$$\leq \int_0^\nu \wp(\hbar, \widehat{z}_2(\hbar) + \widetilde{\omega}_1(\hbar), \widehat{u}(\hbar) + \widetilde{\omega}_2(\hbar), \widehat{r}(\hbar) + \widetilde{\omega}_3(\hbar)) d\hbar$$

$$= \aleph(z_2, u, r),$$

which implies that $(\aleph(z_1, u, r), \aleph(z_2, u, r)) \in \Xi(\mho)$. Moreover, if $(u_1, u_2) \in \Xi(\mho)$, we can write

$$\aleph(z, u_2, r) = \int_0^\nu \wp(\hbar, \widehat{z}_1(\hbar) + \widetilde{\omega}_1(\hbar), \widehat{u}_2(\hbar) + \widetilde{\omega}_2(\hbar), \widehat{r}(\hbar) + \widetilde{\omega}_3(\hbar)) d\hbar$$

$$\leq \int_0^\nu \wp(\hbar, \widehat{z}_2(\hbar) + \widetilde{\omega}_1(\hbar), \widehat{u}_1(\hbar) + \widetilde{\omega}_2(\hbar), \widehat{r}(\hbar) + \widetilde{\omega}_3(\hbar)) d\hbar$$

$$= \aleph(z, u_1, r),$$

which leads to $(\aleph(z,u_2,r),\aleph(y,u_1,r)) \in \Xi(\mho)$. Analogously, we obtain $(\aleph(z,u,r_1),\aleph(y,u,r_2)) \in \Xi(\mho)$. Hence, $\aleph$ has the mixed $\mho$-monotone property. In order to prove the contractive condition of Theorem 1, assume that $((z,u,r),(z^*,u^*,r^*)) \in C_0^3$, so that

$$((z,u,r),(z_1,u_1,r_1)) \in \Xi(\mho) \Leftrightarrow (z,z_1) \in \Xi(\mho),\ (u_1,u) \in \Xi(\mho), \text{ and } (r,r_1) \in \Xi(\mho);$$

then, by using the assumptions (H_1), (H_1), and (H_3), we have

$$\begin{aligned}
&\|\aleph((z,u,r)) - \aleph(z_1,u_1,r_1)\|^2 \\
= &\left\| \int_0^{v} \wp(\hbar,\widehat{z}(\hbar)+\widetilde{\omega}_1(\hbar),\widehat{u}(\hbar)+\widetilde{\omega}_2(\hbar),\widehat{r}(\hbar)+\widetilde{\omega}_3(\hbar))d\hbar \right. \\
&\left. - \int_0^{v} \wp(\hbar,\widehat{z}_1(\hbar)+\widetilde{\omega}_1(\hbar),\widehat{u}_1(\hbar)+\widetilde{\omega}_2(\hbar),\widehat{r}_1(\hbar)+\widetilde{\omega}_3(\hbar))d\hbar \right\|^2 \\
\leq\ & b\int_0^{v} \|\wp(\hbar,\widehat{z}(\hbar)+\widetilde{\omega}_1(\hbar),\widehat{u}(\hbar)+\widetilde{\omega}_2(\hbar),\widehat{r}(\hbar)+\widetilde{\omega}_3(\hbar)) \\
&- \wp(\hbar,\widehat{z}_1(\hbar)+\widetilde{\omega}_1(\hbar),\widehat{u}_1(\hbar)+\widetilde{\omega}_2(\hbar),\widehat{r}_1(\hbar)+\widetilde{\omega}_3(\hbar))\|^2 d\hbar \\
\leq\ & \frac{1}{12b}\int_0^{v} \ln\left(1+\frac{1}{\tau}\|\widehat{z}(d\hbar)-\widehat{z}_1(\hbar)\|_{\eth}^2+\frac{1}{\tau}\|\widehat{u}(\hbar)-\widehat{u}_1(\hbar)\|_{\eth}^2+\frac{1}{\tau}\|\widehat{r}(\hbar)-\widehat{r}_1(\hbar)\|_{\eth}^2\right)d\hbar \\
\leq\ & \frac{1}{12}\ln\left(\sup_{\hbar\in\chi}\|\widehat{z}(\hbar)-\widehat{z}_1(\hbar)\|_{\eth}^2+\sup_{\hbar\in\chi}\|\widehat{u}(\hbar)-\widehat{u}_1(\hbar)\|_{\eth}^2+\sup_{\hbar\in\chi}\|\widehat{r}(\hbar)-\widehat{r}_1(\hbar)\|_{\eth}^2\right),
\end{aligned}$$

which yields

$$\theta\left(s^2\varpi(\aleph((z,u,r))-\aleph(z_1,u_1,r_1))\right) \leq \frac{1}{3}\vartheta(\varpi(z,z_1),\varpi(u,u_1),\varpi(r,r_1)),$$

where $\theta(a) = a$, and $\vartheta(a) = \ln(1+a)$. Obviously, the pair $(\theta,\vartheta) \in \Gamma$. Hence, by our assumptions, we conclude that

$$((z,u,r),(\Omega(z,u,r),\Omega(u,r,z),\Omega(r,z,u))) \in \Xi(\mho).$$

The operator $\aleph$ is continuous, and the triple (C_0,Ξ,ϖ) satisfy the property (p). Hence, all requirements of Theorems 1 and 3 are fulfilled. Hence, there is a TFP of the mapping Ω in C_0^3, which represents a solution to the problem (13) and (14). □

4. Conclusions

There has been much development of the theory of delay differential equations. This was connected to a variety of practical issues whose study required the resolution of delay equations. Equations of this kind are necessary to describe processes whose rate depends on their prior states. Such processes are commonly described as "delay processes" or "processes with aftereffects". The present paper was dedicated to the study of the existence and uniqueness of tripled fixed points in a $b-$metric space with a directed graph. Common tripled fixed point results were also provided. Moreover, some applications of the main results in solving different types of tripled equation systems were presented. Then, using our main results, we studied the existence and uniqueness of a solution to a system of ordinary differential equations with infinite delay. Our results help to improve some results from the related literature and provide new directions in the study of economic phenomena, using the tripled fixed point technique.

Author Contributions: All authors contributed equally and significantly in writing this article. All authors have read and agreed to the published version of the manuscript.

Funding: This work was funded through research groups program under grant R.G.P.2/207/43 provided by the Deanship of Scientific Research at King Khalid University, Saudi Arabia.

Institutional Review Board Statement: Not applicable.

Informed Consent Statement: Not applicable.

Data Availability Statement: No data were associated with this study.

Acknowledgments: The authors thank the anonymous referees for their constructive reviews that greatly improved the paper. M. Zayed appreciates the support by the Deanship of Scientific Research at King Khalid University, Saudi Arabia through the research groups program under grant R.G.P.2/207/43.

Conflicts of Interest: The authors declare that they have no conflict of interest.

References

1. Berinde, V.; Borcut, M. Tripled fixed point theorems for contractive type mappings in partially ordered metric spaces. *Nonlin. Anal. Theory Methods Appl.* **2011**, *74*, 4889–4897. [CrossRef]
2. Berinde, V.; Borcut, M. Tripled coincidence theorems for contractive type mappings in partially ordered metric spaces. *Appl. Math. Comput.* **2012**, *218*, 5929–5936.
3. Amini-Harandi, A. Coupled and tripled fixed point theory in partially ordered metric spaces with application to initial value problem. *Math. Comput. Model.* **2013**, *57*, 2343–2348. [CrossRef]
4. Kadelburg, Z.; Radenović, S. Fixed point and tripled fixed point theorems under Pata-type conditions in ordered metric spaces. *Int. J. Anal. Appl.* **2014**, *6*, 113–122.
5. Vats, R.; Tas, K.; Sihag, V.; Kumar, A. Triple fixed point theorems via α-series in partially ordered metric spaces. *J. Inequal. Appl.* **2014**, *2014*, 176. [CrossRef]
6. Hammad, H.A; Aydi, H.; De la Sen, M. New contributions for tripled fixed point methodologies via a generalized variational principle with applications. *Alex. Eng. J.* **2022**, *61*, 2687–2696. [CrossRef]
7. Hammad, H.A; De la Sen, M. Fixed-point results for a generalized almost $(s,q)-$Jaggi $F-$contraction-type on $b-$metric-like spaces. *Mathematics* **2020**, *8*, 63. [CrossRef]
8. Jachymski, J. The contraction principle for mappings on a metric space with a graph. *Proc. Am. Math. Soc.* **2008**, *136*, 1359–1373. [CrossRef]
9. Bojor, F. Fixed point of $\varphi-$contraction in metric spaces endowed with a graph. *Ann. Univ. Craiova, Math. Comput. Sci. Ser.* **2010**, *37*, 85–92.
10. Boonsri, N.; Saejung, S. Fixed point theorems for contractions of Reich type on a metric space with a graph. *J. Fixed Point Theory Appl.* **2018**, *20*, 84. [CrossRef]
11. Chifu, C.; Petruşel, G. Generalized contractions in metric spaces endowed with a graph. *Fixed Point Theory Appl.* **2012**, *2012*, 161. [CrossRef]
12. Beg, I.; Butt, A.R. Fixed point of set-valued graph contractive mappings. *J. Inequal. Appl.* **2013**, *2013*, 252. [CrossRef]
13. Chifu, C.; Petruşel, G. New results on coupled fixed point theory in metric spaces endowed with a directed graph. *Fixed Point Theory Appl.* **2014**, *2014*, 151. [CrossRef]
14. Chifu, I.; Petrusel, G. Coupled fixed point results for (ϕ, g)-contractions of type (b) in b-metric spaces endowed with a graph. *J. Nonlinear Sci. Appl.* **2017**, *10*, 671–683. [CrossRef]
15. Alfuraidan, M.R.; Khamsi, M.A. Coupled fixed points of monotone mappings in a metric space with a graph. *arXiv* **2018**, arXiv:1801.07675.
16. Hammad, H.A.; Buta, M.; Guran, L. Wardowski's, Contraction and fixed point technique for solving systems of functional and integral equations. *J. Funct. Spaces* **2021**, *2021*, 7017046. [CrossRef]
17. Hammad, H.A.; Aydi, H.; De la Sen, M. Solutions of fractional differential type equations by fixed point techniques for multivalued contractions. *Complexity* **2021**, *2021*, 5730853. [CrossRef]
18. Czerwik, S. Nonlinear set-valued contraction mappings in $b-$ metric spaces. *Atti Del Semin. Mat. Fis. Dell'Universita Modena Reggio Emilia* **1998**, *46*, 263–276.
19. Luong, N.V.; Thuan, N.X. Coupled fixed points in partially ordered metric spaces and application. *Nonlinear Anal. Theory Methods Appl.* **2011**, *74*, 983–992. [CrossRef]
20. Işik, H.; Türkoğlu, D. Coupled fixed point theorems for new contractive mixed monotone mappings and applications to integral equations. *Filomat* **2014**, *28*, 1253–1264. [CrossRef]
21. Hale, J.K.; Kato, J. Phase space for retarded equations with infinite delay. *Funkc. Ekvacioj* **1978**, *21*, 11–41.

symmetry

Review

On Special Properties for Continuous Convex Operators and Related Linear Operators

Octav Olteanu

Department Mathematics-Informatics, University Politehnica of Bucharest, Splaiul Independenţei, 313, 060042 Bucharest, Romania; octav.olteanu50@gmail.com

Abstract: This paper provides a uniform boundedness theorem for a class of convex operators, such as Banach–Steinhaus theorem for families of continuous linear operators. The case of continuous symmetric sublinear operators is outlined. Second, a general theorem characterizing the existence of the solution of the Markov moment problem is reviewed, and a related minimization problem is solved. Convexity is the common point of the two aims of the paper mentioned above.

Keywords: convex operator; uniform boundedness; symmetric operators; Hahn–Banach type theorems; Markov moment problems; constrained minimization

Citation: Olteanu, O. On Special Properties for Continuous Convex Operators and Related Linear Operators. *Symmetry* **2022**, *14*, 1390. https://doi.org/10.3390/sym14071390

Academic Editor: Palle E. T. Jorgensen

Received: 6 June 2022
Accepted: 4 July 2022
Published: 6 July 2022

1. Introduction

This paper provides an overview on a few basic topics in functional analysis, joined together by the notion of convexity and its applications. The references partially illustrate old and recent research in this area and relationships between them. The motivation of this paper consists of pointing out two different main aspects of convexity: convex operators and their properties, and Hahn–Banach type theorems applied to the Moment Problem. Concerning the second aspect, a related optimization problem with infinitely many linear constraints is solved. For basic notions in analysis and functional analysis related to this work, see references [1–9]. First, we prove a uniform boundedness theorem for a class of convex continuous operators. The corresponding result for classes of bounded linear operators is the well-known Banach–Steinhaus theorem, whose proof is based on Baire's theorem. We assume that the domain space, which is a topological vector space, cannot be written as a union of a sequence of closed subsets, each of them having an empty interior. Similar results to our Theorem 1 proved below concerning classes of continuous convex operators were published in [9–11]. Notably, in [9], the case of sublinear operators is under attention. Following the idea of [10], we prove the existence of a common convex neighborhood of the origin W_0 in the domain space, for all involved convex operators, without assuming that the domain space is locally convex. The convexity of W_0 is a consequence of the properties of the codomain and of the convex continuous operators in the given class. The important case of classes of continuous sublinear operators is under attention. We study the classes of sublinear operators P satisfying the symmetry condition $P(x) = P(-x)$ for all x in the domain space X. We point out an example related to this first part. The relevance consists not only in reviewing the result from [10] but also completing it with some consequences and remarks, discussed in the end of Section 3.1. Such theorems and their consequences are published in [11]. From the point of view of uniform boundedness, references [12,13] discuss the collections of linear operators more. In the papers [14–17], the interested reader could find similar properties formulated in the physics setting and possible interactions, especially concerning new results in the Jensen-type inequalities.

The second part of the results section is first motivated by solving the existence problems related to the moment problem. Basic results on this subject are outlined in [1–4]

and [18]. Second, we continue with results on the extension of linear functionals and linear operators, most of them being related to the moment problem. The classical moment problem is formulated as follows: given a sequence $(y_n)_{n\in\mathbb{N}^n}$ of real numbers, and a non-empty closed subset $F \subseteq \mathbb{R}^n$, find a positive regular Borel measure ν on F such that the interpolation moment conditions hold.

$$\int_F \varphi_j(t)\mathrm{d}\nu = \int_F t^j \mathrm{d}\nu = y_j,\ j \in \mathbb{N}^n, \tag{1}$$

Here, we use the notations:

$$\begin{gathered}\mathbb{N} = \{0,1,2,\ldots\}, \varphi_j(t) = t^j = t_1^{j_1}\cdots t_n^{j_n}, j = (j_1,\ldots,j_n) \in \mathbb{N}^n, \\ t = (t_1,\ldots,t_n) \in F \subseteq \mathbb{R}^n, \mathcal{P} = \mathbb{R}[t_1,\ldots,t_n], n \in \mathbb{N}, n \geq 1.\end{gathered} \tag{2}$$

If $n = 1$, we have a one-dimensional moment problem, while for $n \geq 2$, the corresponding moment problem is called a multidimensional moment problem. From the scalar moment problem (1), many authors studied the vector valued (or operator valued, or matrix valued) moment problems, when the $y_j,\ j \in \mathbb{N}^n$ are elements of an ordered vector space Y with additional properties, whose elements are vectors, functions, self-adjoint operators or symmetric matrices with real entries. The moment problem is an inverse problem, since we are looking for an unknown positive measure ν which satisfies the moment conditions (1), knowing only his known (given) moments $\int_F t^j d\nu,\ j \in \mathbb{N}^n$. Finding the measure means studying its existence, uniqueness, and construction. In case of the vector-valued moment problem, the codomain Y is assumed to be an order complete vector space. This condition is required since we need to extend the linear operator

$$T_0 : \mathcal{P} \to Y, T_0\left(\sum_{j\in J_0} \alpha_j\varphi_j\right) = \sum_{j\in J_0} \alpha_j y_j. \tag{3}$$

from the vector space of all polynomials with real coefficients to an ordered Banach function space X which contains $\mathcal{P}$ and the vector space $C_c(F)$ of all real valued continuous compactly supported functions defined on F. In Equation (3), $J_0 \subset \mathbb{N}^n$ is a finite subset, $\alpha_j \in \mathbb{R}$. To ensure the existence of a linear positive extension $T : X \to Y$ of T_0, we need a Hahn–Banach type extension result, which requires the order completeness of Y. From (3), it results

$$T(\varphi_j) = T_0(\varphi_j) = y_j,\ j \in \mathbb{N}^n,$$

which is the vector-valued variant of (1). There are moment problems when, besides the positivity of the solution T, we naturally obtain, from the proof of its existence, the property

$$T(x) \leq P(x), \tag{4}$$

for all $x \in X$, where X, Y are Banach lattices, Y is order complete, and $P : X \to Y$ is a continuous convex or sublinear operator. Such problems are Markov moment problems. Sometimes, the constraints on the solution T are $T_1 \leq T \leq T_2$ on the positive cone of the domain space X, where $T_i,\ i = 1,2$ are two given bounded linear operators from X to Y.

The moment problems mentioned up to now are called full moment problems, because they involve the moment conditions $T(\varphi_j) = y_j$ for all $j \in \mathbb{N}^n$. The reduced (or truncated) moment problem requires the conditions $T(\varphi_j) = y_j$ only for

$$j = (j_1,\ldots,j_n),\ j_k \in \{0,1,\ldots,d\},\ k = 1,\ldots,n,$$

where d is a fixed natural number. For a basic result on the extension of linear positive operators, see [19]. Other extension results of linear operators, with two constraints, were published in [20–22]. Such old theorems found new applications in characterizing the isotonicity of continuous convex operators on a convex cone, recently published in [23]. We recall that an operator $P : X_+ \to Y$ defined on the positive cone X_+ of the ordered vector space X, to the ordered vector space Y is called isotone (monotone increasing) if:

$$\mathbf{0} \leq x_1 \leq x_2 \text{ in } X \text{ implies } P(x_1) \leq P(x_2).$$

Various aspects of the full and reduced moment problem are discussed in [24–34]. These results include the existence, the uniqueness, and the construction of the solution. Obviously, the uniqueness of the solution makes sense only for the full moment problem. In the end of the article [34], a minimization problem related to a Markov moment problem is discussed. Here, we start from an idea appearing in the PhD thesis [28], also using some other methods. This is the second purpose of the paper. Optimization problems are studied in the articles [35–39], from which the last three are providing corresponding iterative methods and algorithms. As is well known, in any reflexive Banach space, for a non-empty closed convex subset not containing the origin, there exists at least one element of minimum norm in that subset. The point of this work is to discuss the case when the convex subset under attention appears from natural constraints related to a Markov moment problem.

Thus, the points of the first part of this paper are recalling and mainly completing the uniformly boundedness of some classes of convex operators, a subject which is not very well covered in the literature, except the references cited here. The significance of the second part consists in pointing out a necessary and sufficient condition for the existence of a solution of a Markov moment problem (an interpolation problem with two constraints), accompanied by a related minimization problem with infinitely many constraints. One characterizes the non-emptiness of the set of feasible solutions, and the existence of at least one minimum point is also proved (see Theorem 4). The uniqueness of such a point is briefly discussed (see Remark 7). The reader can find details and completions to the second part of this work by means of our references.

The rest of the paper is organized as follows. In Section 2, the main methods used in the sequel are pointed out. Section 3 contains the results on the subjects briefly mentioned above and is divided into two subsections. The common point is the notion of convexity for operators and for real valued functions, and its relationships with linear operators. Section 4 discusses the relevant results and concludes the paper.

2. Methods

The main methods used in what follows are:

(1) The general notions and results in algebra and topology, Baire categories, Baire spaces, Banach spaces, Banach lattices, and the Banach–Steinhaus theorem (see [5,9–11]).
(2) General knowledge on convex functions and convex operators (see [7,10,11,13,19–26,28–30,34–39]).
(3) A Hahn–Banach-type theorem formulated in terms of a Markov moment problem, recalled in the second subsection of Section 3 (see [11,22,24,26]).
(4) Weak compactness and a related property of weakly lower semi-continuous real function on a weak compact subset (see [5,34,36]).
(5) Giving supporting examples for the theoretical results (see [5,11,23]).

3. Results

3.1. *Uniform Boundedness for Families of Convex Operators and Related Consequences*

In the sequel, X will be a (not necessarily locally convex) topological vector space which cannot be expressible as the countable union of closed subsets having empty interiors, and Y will be a locally convex vector lattice (on which the lattice operations are continuous and there exists a fundamental system $\mathcal{V}$ of neighborhoods V of 0_Y which are convex, closed, and solid subsets, i.e.,

$$|y_1| \leq |y_2|,\ y_2 \in V \Rightarrow y_1 \in V.$$

Both spaces X, Y are vector spaces over the real field. Consider a class $\mathcal{C}$ of convex continuous operators $P : X \to Y, P(\mathbf{0}) = \mathbf{0}$. Recall that we can always reduce the problem of proving the equicontinuity of a family of convex operators at a point $x_0 \in X$ to the equicontinuity of a corresponding family of convex operators at $\mathbf{0}$, where each element P of the latter family satisfies the condition $P(\mathbf{0}) = \mathbf{0}$ (cf. [10], the proof of Theorem 3.1). The next result was published in [11].

Theorem 1. *Additionally assume that for each $V \in \mathcal{V}$, and any $x \in X$, there exists a small enough positive number r such that*

$$rP(x) \in V \ \forall P \in \mathcal{C}.$$

Then, for any $V_0 \in \mathcal{V}$, there exists a closed convex neighborhood W_0 of 0_X such that

$$\bigcup_{P \in \mathcal{C}} P(\ W_0) \subset V_0.$$

One writes $\lim_{x \to 0_X} P(x) = \mathbf{0}_Y$ uniformly in $P \in \mathcal{C}$.

Proof. For any $V_0 \in \mathcal{V}$ and any $P \in \mathcal{C}$, define $P_1 : X \to Y,\ P_1(x) := sup\{P(x), P(-x)\}$, $x \in X$. The operator P_1 is obviously convex. An additional property of P_1 is $P_1(x) = P_1(-x), x \in X$. Consequently, the codomain of P_1 is Y_+, since $\mathbf{0}_Y = P_1(\mathbf{0}_X) = P_1\left(\frac{1}{2}x + \frac{1}{2}(-x)\right) \leq \frac{1}{2}2P_1(x) = P_1(x), x \in X$. The operator P_1 is also continuous, as the least upper bound of two continuous operators, thanks to the continuity of "sup" operation from $Y \times Y$ to Y. The subset $P_1^{-1}(V_0)$ is closed, due to the continuity of P_1. Now, we prove that it is also convex. Indeed, for $x_1, x_2 \in P_1^{-1}(V_0), t \in [0,1]$, the following relations hold:

$$P_1((1-t)x_1 + tx_2) \leq (1-t)P_1(x_1) + tP_1(x_2) \in V_0,$$

since V_0 is convex and P_1 is convex too. Now, using the assumption on V_0 of being solid, it results

$$P_1((1-t)x_1 + tx_2) \in V_0\left(\Leftrightarrow ((1-t)x_1 + tx_2) \in P_1^{-1}(V_0)\right).$$

We define

$$W_0 := \bigcap\nolimits_{P \in \mathcal{C}} P_1^{-1}(V_0).$$

The subset W_0 is closed and convex, as an intersection of such subsets. Clearly, $\bigcup_{P \in \mathcal{C}} P_1(\ W_0) \subset V_0$. For any $x \in\ W_0$ and any $P \in \mathcal{P}$, it results

$$|P(x)| \leq sup\{P(x), P(-x)\} = P_1(x) \in V_0,$$

because of $-P(x) \leq P(-x),\ x \in X$. Indeed, $0_Y = P(0_X) \leq \frac{1}{2}(P(x) + P(-x)),\ x \in X$. Having in mind the property of V_0, we infer that $P(x) \in V_0,\ \forall x \in W_0,\ \forall P \in \mathcal{C}$. The first conclusion is $\bigcup_{P \in \mathcal{C}} P(\ W_0) \subset V_0$. To finish the proof, we have to show that W_0 is a neighborhood of $\mathbf{0}_X$. For any $x \in X$ and for any $V_0 \in \mathcal{V}$, there exists a sufficiently small $r_0 > 0$ such that $\alpha P_1(x) \in V_0\ \forall \alpha \in \mathbb{R},\ |\alpha| \leq r_0,\ \forall P \in \mathcal{C}$. We can suppose that $r_0 \leq 1$. From the preceding considerations, it results

$$\alpha \in [0, r_0] \subset [0,1] \Rightarrow P_1(\alpha x) = P_1((1-\alpha)\mathbf{0}_X + \alpha x) \leq$$

$$\alpha P_1(x) \in V_0 \Rightarrow P_1(\alpha x) \in V_0,$$

$$\alpha \in [-r_0, 0] \Rightarrow P_1(\alpha x) = P_1((-\alpha)(-x)) \leq (-\alpha)P_1(-x) \leq r_0 P_1(x) \in V_0,\ P \in \mathcal{C}.$$

These relations lead to $x \in X,\ |\alpha| \leq r_0 \Rightarrow \alpha x \in W_0 \Rightarrow x \in \frac{1}{|\alpha|}W_0 \subset nW_0$ for a sufficiently large $n \in \mathbb{N}$. Consequently, the following basic relation holds true: $X = \bigcup_{n \in \mathbb{N}} nW_0$. Now, recall that W_0 is closed, convex, and our assumption on X yields $int(W_0) \neq \varnothing$, so that there exists $x_0 \in int(W_0) \Rightarrow \mathbf{0}_X = \frac{1}{2}(x_0 + (-x_0)) \in int(W_0)$. This concludes the proof. □

Corollary 1. *Let X be a Banach space, Y a Banach lattice, C a collection of continuous convex operators* $P : X \to Y, P(\mathbf{0}) = \mathbf{0}$, *such that for any* $x \in X$, *we have* $\sup_{P \in C} ||P(x)||_Y < \infty$. *Then the following relation holds:* $\sup_{P \in C, \, ||x|| \le 1} ||P(x)||_Y < \infty$.

In the sequel, X will be an (F) space, i.e., a metrizable complete (not necessarily locally convex) topological vector space, Y will be a normed vector lattice (in particular, its norm is monotone on $Y_+ :$ $(\mathbf{0}_Y \le y_1 \le y_2 \Rightarrow ||y_1||_Y \le ||y_2||_Y)$ and the multiplication with scalars is continuous). Recall that a normed vector lattice Y is a vector lattice endowed with a solid norm $(|y_1| \le |y_2| \Rightarrow ||y_1|| \le ||y_2||)$, so the lattice operations are continuous. Consider a class $\mathcal{S}$ of sublinear operators $\Phi : X \to Y_+$ such that $\Phi(x) = \Phi(-x) \ \forall x \in X, \ \forall \Phi \in \mathcal{S}$.

Corollary 2. *Let* $X, Y, \mathcal{S}$ *be as above. Assume that* Φ *is continuous* $\forall \Phi \in \mathcal{S}$ *and* $\sup_{\Phi \in \mathcal{S}} ||\Phi(x)||_Y < \infty \ \forall x \in X$. *Then there exists a convex closed neighborhood* U *of* 0_X *such that* $\bigcup_{\Phi \in \mathcal{S}} \Phi(U) \subset B_{1,Y} := B_1(\mathbf{0}_Y)$, *where* $B_1(\mathbf{0}_Y)$ *is the closed unit ball centered at the origin of the space* Y.

The poof follows the ideas from that of Theorem 1, also applying Baire's theorem.

Remark 1. *Under previous conditions, assuming that Y is a normed vector lattice (the norm on Y is solid and the lattice operations are continuous), Corollary 2 says that*

$$x_1 - x_2 \in U \Rightarrow |\Phi(x_1) - \Phi(x_2)| \le \Phi(x_1 - x_2) \in B_{1,Y} \Rightarrow$$

$$\Phi(x_1) - \Phi(x_2) \in B_{1,Y} \ \ \forall \Phi \in \mathcal{S}.$$

It results that $\mathcal{S}$ *is equicontinuous.*

Example 1. *Using the above notations, let* $\mathcal{L}$ *be a family of linear continuous operators from X to Y such that* $\sup_{T \in \mathcal{L}} ||T(x)||_Y < \infty \ \forall x \in X$. *Define* $\Phi(x) = \Phi_T(x) := |T(x)|, \ x \in X, \ T \in \mathcal{L}$. *Then, the family* $\mathcal{S} = \{\Phi_T\}_{T \in \mathcal{L}}$ *verifies the condition* $\sup_{T \in \mathcal{L}} ||\Phi_T(x)||_Y < \infty \ \forall x \in X$.

Remark 2. *Theorem 1 holds true when X is a Banach space, Y is a normed vector lattice, and the other conditions of Theorem 1 are accomplished. It is possible that a similar result be true for more general spaces X (involving the notion of a barreled TVS). However, only for a few spaces can it be easily proved that they are barreled spaces, without using Baire's theorem. On the other side, for applications, the most important spaces are Banach spaces, especially Banach lattices.*

Theorem 2. *Let X be a Banach space and Y an order complete normed vector lattice with strong order unit* u_0, *such that* $B_{1,Y} = [-u_0, u_0]$. *Let* $\mathcal{S}$ *be a class of sublinear operators with the properties mentioned in Corollary 2. Additionally, assume that* $\Phi(x) = \Phi(-x) \ \forall x \in X, \ \forall \Phi \in \mathcal{S}$. *Then, the relation*

$$\widetilde{\Phi}(x) = \sup_{\Phi \in \mathcal{S}} \Phi(x) \quad \forall x \in X,$$

defines a sublinear Lipschitz operator $\widetilde{\Phi}$, *such that* $\widetilde{\Phi}(x) = \widetilde{\Phi}(-x) \in Y_+ \ \forall x \in X$.

Proof. Application of Corollary 2 leads to the existence of a closed ball of sufficiently small radius $r > 0$ such that

$$||x||_X \le r \Rightarrow \Phi(x) \in B_{1,Y} = [-u_0, u_0] \ \ \forall \Phi \in \mathcal{S}.$$

It results

$$\Phi\left(r\frac{x}{||x||_X}\right) \le u_0 \ \Leftrightarrow \ \Phi(x) \le \frac{||x||_X}{r} u_0 \ \forall x \in X \backslash \{0_X\}, \ \forall \Phi \in \mathcal{S}. \tag{5}$$

Thus, according to (5), for any fixed $x \in X$, the set $\{\Phi(x); \Phi \in \mathcal{S}\}$ is bounded from above in Y. Thanks to the hypothesis on order completeness of Y, there exists

$$\widetilde{\Phi}(x) := \sup_{\Phi \in \mathcal{S}} \Phi(x) \leq \frac{||x||_X}{r} u_0 \quad \forall x \in X. \tag{6}$$

It is easy to see that $\widetilde{\Phi}$ is sublinear and has the property $\widetilde{\Phi}(x) = \widetilde{\Phi}(-x) \in Y_+ \ \forall x \in X$. Next, we prove the Lipschitz property of $\widetilde{\Phi}$. To do this, one uses the subadditivity property of $\widetilde{\Phi}$, the fact that the norm of Y is monotone on Y_+, and relation (6). Namely, the following implications hold:

$$x_1,\ x_2 \in X,\ |\widetilde{\Phi}(x_1) - \widetilde{\Phi}(x_2)| \leq \widetilde{\Phi}(x_1 - x_2) \Rightarrow$$

$$||\widetilde{\Phi}(x_1) - \widetilde{\Phi}(x_2)||_Y \leq ||\widetilde{\Phi}(x_1 - x_2)||_Y \leq \left|\left|\frac{||x_1 - x_2||_X}{r} u_0\right|\right|_Y = \frac{||x_1 - x_2||_X}{r}.$$

Hence, $\widetilde{\Phi}$ is a Lipschitz mapping from X to Y_+. This concludes the proof. □

Remark 3. *Under the hypothesis of Theorem 2, each element of $\Phi \in \mathcal{S}$ is a Lipschitz operator, with the same Lipschitz constant $1/r$.*

Remark 4. *It seems that topological completeness of Y is not necessary for the above results. However, the usual concrete spaces verifying the hypothesis of Theorem 2 are Banach spaces.*

Remark 5. *The set C of all continuous sublinear operators Φ from X to Y_+, such that $\Phi(x) = \Phi(-x)\ \forall x \in X,\ \forall \Phi \in C,\ \sup_{\varphi \in C} ||\varphi(x)||_Y < \infty\ \forall x \in X$, is a convex cone. With the notations and under the assumptions of Theorem 2, the subset of all $\Phi \in C$ formed by all elements of C with the property $\varphi(B_{1,X}) \subset B_{1,Y}$ is convex, and its elements are the non-expansive operators from C. If r of the proof of Theorem 2 is strictly greater than 1, then the elements of $\mathcal{S}$ (as well as the operator $\widetilde{\Phi}$) are contractions.*

Remark 6. *An arbitrary sublinear operator $\varphi : X \to Y_+$ is a Lipschitz operator if and only if Φ is continuous at $\mathbf{0}_X$.*

Corollary 3. *Let X and Y be as in Theorem 2, $\mathcal{S} = \{\Phi_n; n \in N\}$ a countable set of sublinear continuous operators from X to Y, such that $\Phi_n(x) = \Phi_n(-x)\ \forall x \in X,\ \forall n \in \mathbb{N}$, and $\sup_{n \in \mathbb{N}} ||\Phi_n(x)||_Y < \infty\ \forall x \in X$. Then, the relation*

$$\widetilde{\Phi}(x) = \sup_{n \in \mathbb{N}} \Phi_n(x) \quad \forall x \in X$$

defines a sublinear Lipschitz operator $\widetilde{\Phi} : X \to Y_+$, such that $\widetilde{\Phi}(x) = \widetilde{\Phi}(-x)\ \forall x \in X$.

Corollary 4. *Let X, Y be as in Theorem 2, $\mathcal{T} = \{\Phi_n; n \in N,\ n \geq 1\}$ a countable set of sublinear continuous operators from X to Y_+, such that $\Phi_n(x) = \Phi_n(-x)\ \forall x \in X,\ \forall n \in \{1,2,\ldots\}$, and*

$$\sup_{n \in \mathbb{N},\ n \geq 1} ||\sum_{k=1}^{n} \Phi_k(x)||_Y < \infty \quad \forall x \in X.$$

Then, the relation

$$\widetilde{\Phi}(x) = \sup_{n \in \mathbb{N},\ n \geq 1} \left(\sum_{k=1}^{n} \Phi_k(x)\right) \quad \forall x \in X,$$

defines a sublinear Lipschitz operator $\widetilde{\Phi}: X \to Y_+$, *such that* $\widetilde{\Phi}(x) = \widetilde{\Phi}(-x)\ \forall x \in X$.

Example 2. *Let K be a Hausdorff compact topological space, endowed with a regular Borel probability measure* μ, $X := C(K)$ *the Banach lattice of all real valued, continuous functions on K,* $Y := l_\infty$ *the space of all bounded sequences of real numbers. The norm* $||\cdot||_{sup}$ *on the space X is the sup-norm and the norm on* $||\cdot||_Y$ *is the usual norm* $||\cdot||_Y = ||\cdot||_\infty$, $||(x_n)_{n\geq 1}||_\infty = \sup_{n\geq 1}|x_n|$. *The space* $Y = l_\infty$ *verifies the hypothesis of Theorem 2, since it is an order complete normed vector lattice, the appropriate strong order unit being the sequence* u_0, *which has all the terms equal to 1. Define the scalar valued norms on X*

$$N_k(f) := \left(\int_K |f|^k d\mu \right)^{1/k}, \ f \in X,\ k \in \mathbb{N},\ k \geq 1,$$

and the finite dimensional vector-valued norms on X

$$S_n(f) := ||f||_n : X \to Y,$$

$$||f||_n := \left(N_1(f),\ 2^{1/2}N_2(f), \ldots, n^{1/n}N_n(f),\ 0, \ldots, 0, \ldots \right),\ n \in \mathbb{N},\ n \geq 1,\ f \in X,$$

$$N_k(f) \leq ||f||_{sup}(\mu(K))^{1/k} = ||f||_{sup},\ N_k(f) = 1 \Rightarrow \sup_{||f||_{sup}=1} N_k(f) = 1,$$

$$k \in \{1, 2, \ldots\}, f \in X.$$

Consider the elementary function $t \to g(t) := ln(t)/t,\ t \in [1, \infty)$, *which is increasing on* $[1, e]$ *and decreasing on the interval* $[e, \infty)$. *This function has a global maximum point at* $t_0 = e \in (2, 3)$. *It results that the function*

$$h : (1, \infty) \to (0, \infty),\ h(t) := t^{1/t} = e^{ln(t)/t}$$

has the same monotonicity properties; hence,

$$\max_{1\leq k\leq n} k^{1/k} \leq \max\left\{ 2^{1/2}, 3^{1/3} \right\} = 3^{1/3}\ \forall n \in \{1, 2, \ldots\}$$

Thus, we obtain

$$f \in X \Rightarrow S_n(f) = ||f||_n \leq \max_{1\leq k\leq n} k^{1/k} ||f||_{sup} u_0 \leq 3^{1/3}\ ||f||_{sup} u_0\ \forall n \in \{1, 2, \ldots\} \Rightarrow$$

$$\widetilde{\Phi}(f) = \sup_{n\in\mathbb{N}} S_n(f) = \left(n^{1/n} N_n(f) \right)_{n\geq 1} \leq 3^{1/3} := ||f||_{sup} u_0,$$

$$u_0 = (1, \ldots, 1, \ldots),\ f \in X,$$

where $\widetilde{\Phi}$ *is the sublinear operator from Corollary 4. Observe that* $\widetilde{\Phi}$ *has as Lipschitz constant* $3^{1/3} > 1$. *Next, we apply the same method, replacing* $n^{1/n}$ *by*

$$n^{-1/n} = exp(-ln(n)/n) \leq 1\ \forall n \in \{1, 2, \ldots\}.$$

In this case, the above estimations turn into the following ones:

$$\widetilde{\Phi}(f) = \sup_{n\in\mathbb{N}} S_n(f) = \left(n^{-1/n} N_n(f) \right)_{n\geq 1} \leq ||f||_{sup} u_0\ \forall f \in X \Rightarrow$$

$$|\widetilde{\Phi}(f) - \widetilde{\Phi}(g)| \leq \widetilde{\Phi}(f - g) \leq ||f - g||_{sup} u_0 \Rightarrow$$

$$||\widetilde{\Phi}(f) - \widetilde{\Phi}(g)||_Y \leq ||\widetilde{\Phi}(f - g)|| \leq ||f - g||_{sup}\ \forall f, g \in X.$$

To conclude, in this case, $\widetilde{\Phi}$ is a nonexpansive vector valued norm from X to Y. To obtain contractions $\widetilde{\Phi}$, consider

$$(c_n)_{n\geq 1} \in Y = l_\infty,\ 0 \leq c_n \leq q < 1\ \forall n \geq 1,$$

$$S_n(f) = (c_1 N_1(f), \ldots, c_n N_n(f), 0, \ldots, 0, \ldots),$$

$$\widetilde{\Phi}(f) = \sup_{n\geq 1} S_n(f) = (c_n N_n(f))_{n\geq 1} \leq q||f||_{sup} u_0\ \forall f \in X \Rightarrow$$

$$|\widetilde{\Phi}(f) - \widetilde{\Phi}(g)|_Y \leq \widetilde{\Phi}(f-g) \leq q||f-g||_{sup} u_0 \Rightarrow$$

$$||\widetilde{\Phi}(f) - \widetilde{\Phi}(g)||_Y \leq q||f-g||_{sup}||u_0||_Y = q||f-g||_{sup}\quad \forall f.g \in X.$$

Thus $\widetilde{\Phi} : X \to Y_+$ is a contraction vector-valued norm, of contraction constant q, and the best value for q is $q = \sup_{n\geq 1} c_n$. In particular, if $0 \leq \inf_{n\geq 1} c_n \leq \sup_{n\geq 1} c_n = 1/2\ \forall n \geq 1$, then $\widetilde{\Phi}$ is a contraction operator, of contraction constant $q = 1/2$. In this example, the operators Φ_n mentioned in Corollary 4 stand for $(0, \ldots, 0, c_n N_n(f), 0, 0, \ldots)$, and $c_n N_n(f)$ is the $n-th$ coordinate of the vector $S_n(f) \in Y_+$.

3.2. A Constrained Minimization Problem Related to a Markov Moment Problem

The present subsection has as a motivation proving similar results to some of those of [28]. One proves a result in a general setting, obtained by means of Theorem 3 stated below. A constrained related optimization problem in infinite dimensional spaces is solved too. The results presented in the sequel were published in [34]. In particular, using the latter theorem, one obtains a necessary and sufficient condition for the existence of a feasible solution (see theorem 4 from below). Under such a condition, the existence of an optimal feasible solution follows too. On the other hand, the uniqueness and the construction of the optimal solution does not seem to be obtained easily by such general methods. Therefore, we focus mainly on the existence problem. For other aspects of such problems on an optimal solution (uniqueness or non-uniqueness, construction of a unique solution, etc.), see [28]. In the latter work, one considers the following primal problem (P): study the constrained minimization problem:

$$\nu = \inf\left\{ ||\varphi||_\infty; \varphi \in L^\infty_\mu(Z),\ \int_X \varphi f_j d\mu = b_j,\ j = 1, \ldots, n,\ 0 \leq \alpha \leq \varphi \leq \beta \right\},$$

where α, β are in $L^\infty_\mu(Z)$, $(f_j)_{j=1}^n$ is a subset of $L^1_\mu(Z)$, and $b = (b_1, \ldots, b_n)^t \in \mathbb{R}^n$. The function φ is unknown, and in general, it is not determined by a finite number of moments. The next theorem discusses some of the above existence type results for a feasible solution. Here, $(Z, \mathcal{M})$ is a measure space endowed with a $\sigma-$finite positive measure μ, and $\mathcal{M}$ is the $\sigma-$algebra of all measurable subsets of Z.

Theorem 3. See [22]. *Let X be an ordered vector space, Y an order complete vector lattice, $\{\varphi_j\}_{j\in J} \subset X$, $\{y_j\}_{j\in J} \subset Y$ given arbitrary families, $T_1, T_2 \in L(X,Y)$ two linear operators. The following statements are equivalent:*

(a) there is a linear operator $T \in L(X,Y)$, such that

$$T_1(x) \leq T(x) \leq T_2(x)\ \forall x \in X_+,\ T(\varphi_j) = y_j\ \forall j \in J;$$

(b) for any finite subset $J_0 \subset J$ and any $\{\lambda_j; j \in J_0\} \subset \mathbb{R}$, the following implication holds true:

$$\left(\sum_{j\in J_0} \lambda_j \varphi_j = \psi_2 - \psi_1, \psi_1, \psi_2 \in X_+ \right) := \sum_{j\in J_0} \lambda_j y_j \leq T_2(\psi_2) - T_1(\psi_1);$$

If X is a vector lattice, then assertions (a) and (b) are equivalent to (c), where (c) is formulated as follows:

(c) $T_1(w) \le T_2(w)$ *for all* $w \in X_+$ *and for any finite subset* $J_0 \subset J$ *and* $\forall\{\lambda_j; j \in J_0\} \subset \mathbb{R}$, *we have*

$$\sum_{j\in J_0} \lambda_j y_j \le T_2\left(\left(\sum_{j\in J_0} \lambda_j \varphi_j\right)^+\right) - T_1\left(\left(\sum_{j\in J_0} \lambda_j \varphi_j\right)^-\right).$$

The next result is an application of Theorem 3 stated above, also using a constrained minimization argument.

Theorem 4. *Let* $p \in (1,\infty)$ *and let* q *be the conjugate of* p. *Let* $(f_j)_{j\in J}$ *be an arbitrary family of functions in* $L^p_\mu(Z)$, *where the measure* μ *is* σ*–finite, and* $(b_j)_{j\in J}$ *a family of real numbers. Assume that* $\alpha, \beta \in L^q_\mu(Z)$ *are such that* $\mathbf{0} \le \alpha \le \beta$. *The following statements are equivalent:*

(a) *there exists* $\varphi \in L^q_\mu(Z)$ *such that* $\int_Z \varphi f_j d\mu = b_j, \forall\, j \in J,\ \mathbf{0} \le \alpha \le \varphi \le \beta$;

(b) *for any finite subset* $J_0 \subseteq J$ *and any* $\{\lambda_j\}_{j\in J_0} \subset \mathbb{R}$, *the following implication holds:*

$$\sum_{j\in J_0} \lambda_j f_j = \psi_2 - \psi_1,\ \ \psi_1, \psi_2 \in \left(L^p_\mu(Z)\right)_+ \Longrightarrow \sum_{j\in J_0} \lambda_j b_j \le \int_Z \beta\psi_2\, d\mu - \int_Z \alpha\psi_1\, d\mu;$$

Moreover, the set of all feasible solutions φ *(satisfying the conditions (a)) is weakly compact with respect the dual pair* (L^p, L^q) *and the inferior*

$$v = inf\left\{ ||\varphi||_q; \varphi \in L^q_\mu(Z),\ \int_Z \varphi f_j d\mu = b_j,\ j \in J,\ \mathbf{0} \le \alpha \le \varphi \le \beta \right\} \ge ||\alpha||_q,$$

is attained for at least one optimal feasible solution φ_0.

Proof. Since the implication $(\mathrm{a}) \Longrightarrow (\mathrm{b})$ is obvious, the next step consists in proving that $(\mathrm{b}) \Longrightarrow (\mathrm{a})$. We define the linear positive (continuous) forms $T_1,\ T_2$ on $X = L^p_\mu(Z)$, by

$$T_1(f) = \int_Z \alpha f d\mu,\ T_2(\varphi) = \int_Z \beta f d\mu,\ \ f \in X.$$

Then, condition (b) of the present theorem coincides with condition (b) of Theorem 3. A straightforward application of the latter theorem leads to the existence of a linear form T on X, such that the interpolation conditions $T(\varphi_j) = b_j,\ j \in J$ are verified and

$$\int_Z \alpha\psi d\mu \le T(\psi) \le \int_Z \beta\psi d\mu,\ \psi \in X_+.$$

In particular, the linear form T is positive on $X = L^p_\mu(Z)$, and this space is a Banach lattice. It is known that on such spaces, any linear positive functional is continuous (see [5], or [8], or [23]). The conclusion is that T can be represented by means of a nonnegative function $\varphi \in L^q_\mu(Z)$. From the previous relations, we infer that

$$\int_Z \alpha\psi d\mu \le \int_Z \varphi\psi d\mu \le \int_Z \beta\psi d\mu,\ \psi \in X_+.$$

Writing these relations for $\psi = \chi_B$, where B is an arbitrary measurable set of positive measure $\mu(B)$, one deduces

$$\int_B (\varphi - \alpha) d\mu \ge 0,\ \int_B (\beta - \varphi) d\mu \ge 0,\ \ B \in \mathcal{M},\ \mu(B) > 0.$$

Now, a standard measure theory argument shows that $\alpha \leq \varphi \leq \beta$ almost everywhere in Z. This finishes the proof of (b) $\Longrightarrow$ (a). To prove the last assertion of the theorem, observe that the set of all feasible solutions is weakly compact in $L^q_\mu(Z)$, by Alaoglu's theorem; it is a weakly closed subset of the closed ball centered at the origin, of radius $||\beta||_q$, and $L^q_\mu(Z)$ is reflexive. On the other hand, the norm of any normed linear space is lower weakly semi-continuous, as the supremum of continuous linear forms, which are also weak continuous with respect to the dual pair $\left(L^q_\mu(Z), L^p_\mu(Z)\right)$, $1 < p < \infty$, $1/p + 1/q = 1$. Since $L^q_\mu(Z)$ is reflexive for $1 < q < \infty$, we conclude that the norm $||\cdot||_q$ is weakly lower semi-continuous on the weakly (convex) and compact set described at point (a), so that it attains its minimum at a function φ_0 of this set. Hence, there exists at least one optimal feasible solution. This concludes the proof. □

Remark 7. *If the set* $\{f_j\}_{j \in J}$ *is total in the space* $L^p_\mu(Z)$, *then the set of all feasible solutions is a singleton, so that there exists a unique solution.*

Remark 8. *In the proof of Theorem 4, we claimed that any positive linear function on* $L^p_\mu(Z)$, $1 < p < \infty$ *is continuous. Actually, there is a much more general result on this subject. Namely, any positive linear operator acting between two ordered Banach spaces is continuous (see* [8] *and/or* [23]*). In particular, this result holds for positive linear operators acting between Banach lattices.*

4. Discussion

In the first part of Section 3, this paper brings a few new elements and completions with respect to the basic results previously published on this subject. The main completions are formulated as Corollaries, Remarks, and two examples. The second subsection of Section 3 reviews the main Theorem 3 and gives one of its applications, stated as Theorem 4. The latter theorem can be applied to the existence of at least one feasible solution for the constrained minimization problem formulated in the same theorem. The problem under attention is solved on a concrete function space. The index set J appearing in Theorems 3 and 4 is arbitrary, finite, countable, or uncountable. In the case of the full moment problem on a closed subset of $\mathbb{R}^n$, we have $J = \mathbb{N}^n$, $n \in \mathbb{N}$, $n \geq 1$, so in this case, J is a countable infinite set of indexes. Theorem 4 provides a necessary and sufficient condition for the feasible set of a minimization problem with many countable constraints being non-empty. The common point of the two subsections of Section 3 is the notion of convexity, applied to real-valued functions and to operators. The connection of convex functions (respectively, convex operators) with the linear functionals (respectively, linear operators) is emphasized in both subsections. As a direction for future work, we recall the importance of Markov linear operators. Many such operators arise as solutions of Markov moment problems. They are dominated by a given continuous sublinear operator and apply the strong order unit of the domain space to the strong order unit of the codomain space (assuming that both the domain and the codomain are endowed with a strong order unit).

Funding: This research received no external funding.

Institutional Review Board Statement: Not applicable.

Informed Consent Statement: Not applicable.

Data Availability Statement: Not applicable.

Acknowledgments: The author would like to thank the reviewers for their comments and suggestions, leading to the improvement of the presentation of this paper.

Conflicts of Interest: The author declares no conflict of interest.

References

1. Akhiezer, N.I. *The Classical Moment Problem and Some Related Questions in Analysis;* Oliver and Boyd: Edinburgh, UK, 1965.
2. Berg, C.; Christensen, J.P.R.; Ressel, P. *Harmonic Analysis on Semigroups: Theory of Positive Definite and Related Functions;* Springer: New York, NY, USA, 1984.
3. Krein, M.G.; Nudelman, A.A. *Markov Moment Problem and Extremal Problems;* American Mathematical Society: Providence, RI, USA, 1977.
4. Schmüdgen, K. The Moment Problem. In *Graduate Texts in Mathematics;* Springer International Publishing AG: Cham, Switzerland, 2017.
5. Schaefer, H.H.; Wolff, M.P. *Topological Vector Spaces,* 2nd ed.; Springer: New York, NY, USA, 1999.
6. Cristescu, R. *Ordered Vector Spaces and Linear Operators;* Academiei: Bucharest, Romania; Abacus Press: Tunbridge Wells, UK, 1976.
7. Niculescu, C.P.; Persson, L.-E. *Convex Functions and Their Applications. A Contemporary Approach,* 2nd ed.; CMS Books in Mathematics; Springer: New York, NY, USA, 2018; Volume 23.
8. Niculescu, C.; Popa, N. *Elements of Theory of Banach Spaces;* Academiei: Bucharest, Romania, 1981. (In Romanian)
9. Yosida, K. *Functional Analysis,* 6th ed.; Springer: Berlin/Heidelberg, Germany; New York, NY, USA, 1980.
10. Neumann, M.M. Uniform boundedness and closed graph theorems for convex operators. *Mat. Nachr.* **1985,** *120,* 113–125. [CrossRef]
11. Olteanu, O. *Recent Results on Markov Moment Problem, Polynomial Approximation and Related Fields in Analysis;* Generis Publishing: Chişinău, Republic of Moldova, 2020.
12. Estrada, R.; Vindas, J. A Generalization of the Banach-Steinhaus Theorem for Finite Part Limits. *Bull. Malays. Math. Sci. Soc.* **2017,** *40,* 907–918. [CrossRef]
13. Drábek, P. Properties of Linear and Nonlinear Operators. In *Methods of Nonlinear Analysis;* Birkhäuser Advanced Texts/Basler Lehrbücher; Birkhäuser Basel: Basel, Switzerland, 2007. [CrossRef]
14. Liang, Z.X.; Zhang, Z.D.; Liu, W.M. Dynamics of a Bright Soliton in Bose-Einstein Condensates with Time-Dependent Atomic Scattering Length in an Expulsive Parabolic Potential. *Phys. Rev. Lett.* **2005,** *94,* 050402. [CrossRef] [PubMed]
15. Ji, A.-C.; Liu, W.M.; Song, J.L.; Zhou, F. Dynamical Creation of Fractionalized Vortices and Vortex Lattices. *Phys. Rev. Lett.* **2008,** *101,* 010402. [CrossRef]
16. Li, L.; Li, Z.; Malomed, B.A.; Mihalache, D.; Liu, W.M. Exact soliton solutions and nonlinear modulation instability in spinor Bose-Einstein condensates. *Phys. Rev.* **2005,** *A72,* 033611. [CrossRef]
17. Wang, D.-S.; Hu, X.-H.; Hu, J.; Liu, W.M. Quantized quasi-two-dimensional Bose-Einstein condensates with spatially modulated nonlinearity. *Phys. Rev.* **2010,** *A81,* 025604. [CrossRef]
18. Haviland, E.K. On the momentum problem for distributions in more than one dimension. *Am. J. Math.* **1936,** *58,* 164–168. [CrossRef]
19. Kutateladze, S.S. Convex operators. *Russ. Math. Surv.* **1979,** *34,* 181–214. [CrossRef]
20. Olteanu, O. Convexité et prolongement d'opérateurs linéaires (Convexity and extension of linear operators). *C. R. Acad. Sci. Paris A* **1978,** *286,* 511–514.
21. Olteanu, O. Théorèmes de prolongement d'opérateurs linéaires (Theorems of extension of linear operators). *Rev. Roumaine Math. Pures Appl.* **1983,** *28,* 953–983.
22. Olteanu, O. Application de théorèmes de prolongement d'opérateurs linéaires au problème des moments e à une generalization d'un théorème de Mazur-Orlicz, (Applications of theorems on extension of linear operators to the moment problem and to a generalization of Mazur-Orlicz theorem). *C. R. Acad. Sci. Paris* **1991,** *313,* 739–742.
23. Niculescu, C.P.; Olteanu, O. From the Hahn-Banach extension theorem to the isotonicity of convex functions and the majorization theory. *Rev. R. Acad. Cienc. Exactas Fis. Nat.* **2020,** *114,* 171. [CrossRef]
24. Olteanu, O. From Hahn-Banach type theorems to the Markov moment problem, sandwich theorems and further applications. *Mathematics* **2020,** *8,* 1328. [CrossRef]
25. Olteanu, O. On Markov moment problem and related results. *Symmetry* **2021,** *13,* 986. [CrossRef]
26. Olteanu, O. On Hahn-Banach theorem and some of its applications. *Open Math.* **2022,** *20,* 366–390. [CrossRef]
27. Stoyanov, J.M.; Lin, G.D.; Kopanov, P. New checkable conditions for moment determinacy of probability distributions. *SIAM Theory Probab. Appl.* **2020,** *65,* 497–509. [CrossRef]
28. Norris, D.T. Optimal Solutions to the L_∞ Moment Problem with Lattice Bounds. Ph.D. Thesis, Department of Mathematics, College of Arts and Sciences, University Colorado Boulder, Boulder, CO, USA, 2002.
29. Tagliani, A. Maximum entropy solutions and moment problem in unbounded domains. *Appl. Math. Lett.* **2003,** *16,* 519–524. [CrossRef]
30. Inverardi, P.L.N.; Tagliani, A. Stieltjies and Hamburger reduced moment problem when MaxEnt solution does not exist. *Mathematics* **2021,** *9,* 309. [CrossRef]
31. Gosse, L.; Runborg, O. Resolution of the finite Markov moment problem. *C. R. Acad. Sci. Paris* **2005,** *341,* 775–780. [CrossRef]
32. Gosse, L.; Runborg, O. Existence, uniqueness, and a constructive solution algorithm for a class of finite Markov moment problems. *SIAM J. Appl. Math.* **2008,** *68,* 16181640. [CrossRef]
33. Stochel, J. Solving the truncated moment problem solves the full moment problem. *Glasg. Math. J.* **2001,** *43,* 335–341. [CrossRef]

34. Olteanu, O.; Mihăilă, J.M. Extension and decomposition of linear operators dominated by continuous increasing sublinear operators. *U.P.B. Sci. Bull. Ser. A* **2018**, *80*, 133–144.
35. Cobzaş, Ş. Geometric properties of Banach spaces and the existence of nearest and farthest points. *Abstr. Appl. Anal.* **2005**, *2005*, 259–285. [CrossRef]
36. Cobzaş, Ş. Ekeland variational principle and its equivalents in T_1 quasi-uniform spaces. *Optimization* **2022**, 1–32. [CrossRef]
37. Pakkaranang, N.; Kumam, P.; Cho, Y.J. Proximal point algorithms for solving convex minimization problem and common fixed points of asymptotically quasi-nonexpansive mappings in in CAT(0) spaces with convergenece analysis. *Numer. Algorithms* **2018**, *78*, 827–845. [CrossRef]
38. Dong, Q.-L.; Cho, Y.J.; Rassias, T.M. The projection and contraction methods for finding common solutions for variational inequalitiy problems. *Optim. Lett.* **2018**, *12*, 1871–1896. [CrossRef]
39. Sahu, D.R.; Cho, Y.J.; Dong, Q.L.; Kashyap, M.R.; Li, X.H. Inertial relaxed CQ algorithms for solving a split feasibility problem in Hilbert spaces. *Numer. Algorithms* **2021**, *87*, 1075–1095. [CrossRef]

symmetry

MDPI

Article

Sharp Bounds for Trigonometric and Hyperbolic Functions with Application to Fractional Calculus

Vuk Stojiljković [1,*,†], Slobodan Radojević [2,†], Eyüp Çetin [3,4,†], Vesna Šešum Čavić [5,†] and Stojan Radenović [2,†]

1 Faculty of Science, University of Novi Sad, Trg Dositeja Obradovića 3, 21000 Novi Sad, Serbia
2 Faculty of Mechanical Engineering, University of Belgrade, Kraljice Marije 16, 11120 Belgrade , Serbia; s.radojevic@mas.bg.ac.rs (S.R.); radens@beotel.rs (S.R.)
3 Laboratory for Industrial and Applied Mathematics, York University, Toronto, ON M3J 1P3, Canada; eyupc@yorku.ca
4 New York Business Global, 9591 Baltimore Avenue 703, College Park, MD 20741, USA
5 Građevinski Fakultet, University of Belgrade, Bulevar kralja Aleksandra 73, 11000 Belgrade , Serbia; vsesumcavic@grf.bg.ac.rs
* Correspondence: vuk.stojiljkovic999@gmail.com
† These authors contributed equally to this work.

Abstract: Sharp bounds for $\frac{\cosh(x)}{x}$, $\frac{\sinh(x)}{x}$, and $\frac{\sin(x)}{x}$ were obtained, as well as one new bound for $\frac{e^x+\arctan(x)}{\sqrt{x}}$. A new situation to note about the obtained boundaries is the symmetry in the upper and lower boundary, where the upper boundary differs by a constant from the lower boundary. New consequences of the inequalities were obtained in terms of the Riemann–Liovuille fractional integral and in terms of the standard integral.

Keywords: polynomial bounds; L'Hôpital's rule of monotonicity; Jordan's inequality; trigonometric functions

MSC: 26D05; 26D07; 26D20

Citation: Stojiljković, V.; Radojević, S.; Çetin, E.; Čavić, V.Š.; Radenović, S. Sharp Bounds for Trigonometric and Hyperbolic Functions with Application to Fractional Calculus. *Symmetry* **2022**, *14*, 1260. https://doi.org/10.3390/sym14061260

Academic Editor: Savin Treanta

Received: 26 May 2022
Accepted: 15 June 2022
Published: 18 June 2022

1. Introduction and Preliminaries

Inequalities have been an ongoing topic of research since their discovery. As the proof of how interesting they are, many books were written in that field; for example, refer to the famous book [1]. The $\frac{\sin(x)}{x}$ inequality in this paper will be improved; thus, we must mention the first inequality of that nature known as Jordan's inequality.

$$\frac{2}{\pi} < \frac{\sin(x)}{x} < 1; 0 < x < \frac{\pi}{2}.$$

Multiple proofs of the Jordans inequality exist, and we refer the reader to the following papers for more detail [2–4]. Jordan's inequality was improved on the left-hand side by Mitrinović-Adamović, while the right-hand side is the known Cusa inequality. We state it here for educational purposes.

$$(\cos(x))^{\frac{1}{3}} < \frac{\sin(x)}{x} < \frac{2+\cos(x)}{3}.$$

Recently, the authors [5] sharpened Jordan's inequality further.

$$\left(1-\frac{x^2}{\pi^2}\right)e^{-\frac{\ln(2)}{\pi^2}x^2} < \frac{\sin(x)}{x} < \left(1-\frac{x^2}{\pi^2}\right)e^{\left(\frac{1}{\pi^2}-\frac{1}{6}\right)x^2}; 0 < x < \pi.$$

They also provided other interesting bounds in another paper [6].

$$\left(1-\frac{x^2}{\pi^2}\right)^{\frac{\pi^4}{90}} e^{\left(\frac{\pi^2}{90}-\frac{1}{6}\right)x^2} < \frac{\sin(x)}{x}; 0<x<\pi$$

$$\frac{\sin(x)}{x} < \frac{2}{3}+\frac{1}{3}\left(1-\frac{4x^2}{\pi^2}\right)^{\frac{\pi^4}{96}} e^{\left(\frac{\pi^2}{24}-\frac{1}{2}\right)x^2}; 0<x<\frac{\pi}{2}.$$

In this paper, we will sharpen these bounds in a simple and efficient manner. More about such inequalities can be found in the following papers [7–11].

We provide our first definition of a fractional integral that will be used in the corollaries of the results.

Definition 1. *The generalized hypergeometric function* ${}_qF_q(a;b;x)$ *is defined as follows [12]:*

$${}_pF_q(a;b;x) = \sum_{k=0}^{+\infty} \frac{(a_1)_k \ldots (a_p)_k}{(b_1)_k \ldots (b_q)_k} \frac{x^k}{k!}$$

where $(a)_k$ *is the Pochhammer symbol defined as follows [12].*

$$(a)_k = \frac{\Gamma(a+k)}{\Gamma(a)} = a(a+1)\ldots(a+k-1).$$

Definition 2. *The Riemann–Liouville fractional integral is defined by [13–15] where* $\Re(\alpha) > 0$ *and* f *is locally integrable.*

$${}_aI_t^{\alpha} f(t) = \frac{1}{\Gamma(\alpha)} \int_a^t (t-x)^{\alpha-1} f(x)dx.$$

The functions on which we apply the Riemann–Liouville fractional integral are well defined in terms of the integral formula. We will require the following Lemma. Lemma 1 ([16], p. 10) taken below is known as L'Hôpital's rule of monotonicity. It is a very useful tool in the theory of inequalities.

Lemma 1. *Let* $f, g : [m,n] \to \mathbb{R}$ *be two continuous functions which are differentiable on* (m,n) *and* $g' \neq 0$ *in* (m,n). *If* $\frac{f'}{g'}$ *is increasing (or decreasing) on* (m,n), *then the functions* $\frac{f(x)-f(m)}{g(x)-g(m)}$ *and* $\frac{f(x)-f(n)}{g(x)-g(n)}$ *are also increasing (or decreasing) on* (m,n). *If* $\frac{f'}{g'}$ *is strictly monotone, then the monotonicity in the relationship is also strict.*

2. Main Results

We provide our first Theorem in the paper.

Theorem 1. *The following bounds hold for* $x \in (0,1)$.

$$\frac{1}{\sqrt{x}} + \frac{x^{\frac{3}{2}}}{2} + \sqrt{x} < \frac{e^x + \arctan(x)}{\sqrt{x}} < e + \frac{1}{4}(\pi - 10) + \frac{1}{\sqrt{x}} + \frac{x^{\frac{3}{2}}}{2} + \sqrt{x}.$$

Proof. Set the following:

$$g(x) = \frac{e^x - 1 + \arctan(x) - \frac{x^2}{2} - x}{\sqrt{x}} = \frac{h_1(x)}{h_2(x)}$$

where $h_1(x) = e^x - 1 + \arctan(x) - \frac{x^2}{2} - x$ and $h_2(x) = \sqrt{x}$ with $h_1(0) = 0$ and $h_2(0) = 0$.

After differentiating, we obtain the following.

$$\frac{h_1'(x)}{h_2'(x)} = \left(-1 + e^x - x + \frac{1}{1+x^2}\right) \cdot 2\sqrt{x}.$$

Taking the following:

$$f(x) = \left(-1 + e^x - x + \frac{1}{1+x^2}\right) \cdot 2\sqrt{x}$$

and by differentiating it, we obtain the following.

$$f'(x) = \frac{(2e^x-3)x^5 + (e^x-1)x^4 + 2(2e^x-3)x^3 + (2e^x-5)x^2 + (2e^x-3)x + e^x}{\sqrt{x}(x^2+1)^2}$$

The denominator is positive for all $x \in (0,1)$. We need to show that $q(x) > 0$ where $q(x)$ denotes the numerator. Using the simple estimates $e^x \geq 1+x, 1 > x^2$ where $x \in (0,1)$, we obtain the following.

$$q(x) > 2x^6 + 4x^4 > 0.$$

Therefore $f'(x) > 0$, which implies $f(x)$ is increasing; therefore, $\frac{h_1'(x)}{h_2'(x)}$ is increasing, which by Lemma 1 means $\frac{h_1(x)-h_1(0)}{h_2(x)-h_2(0)}$ is increasing. However, since we chose functions $h_1(x), h_2(x)$ such that $h_1(0) = 0$ and $h_2(0) = 0$, we obtain the fact that the following:

$$g(x) = \frac{e^x - 1 + \arctan(x) - x - \frac{x^2}{2}}{\sqrt{x}} = \frac{h_1(x)}{h_2(x)}$$

is increasing. Therefore, the following inequality holds:

$$g(0_+) < g(x) < g(1).$$

which provides us with the following inequality.

$$0 < \frac{e^x - 1 + \arctan(x) - x - \frac{x^2}{2}}{\sqrt{x}} < e + \frac{1}{4}(\pi - 10)$$

This is rearranged and provides us with the desired inequality.

$$\frac{1}{\sqrt{x}} + \frac{x^{\frac{3}{2}}}{2} + \sqrt{x} < \frac{e^x + \arctan(x)}{\sqrt{x}} < e + \frac{1}{4}(\pi - 10) + \frac{1}{\sqrt{x}} + \frac{x^{\frac{3}{2}}}{2} + \sqrt{x}$$

□

We provide a corollary in which we provide an estimate of the fractional inequality using the previous theorem.

Corollary 1. *The following inequality holds for $0 < a < t, \alpha > t > 0$ and $t \in (0,1)$:*

$$\frac{1}{\Gamma(\alpha)}\left(\frac{\sqrt{\pi}\Gamma(\alpha)t^{\alpha-\frac{1}{2}}}{\Gamma\left(\alpha+\frac{1}{2}\right)} - 2\sqrt{a}t^{\alpha-1}\,{}_2F_1\left(\frac{1}{2}, 1-\alpha; \frac{3}{2}; \frac{a}{t}\right) + \psi(a,t,\alpha)\right.$$

$$\left. + \frac{t^{\alpha}\left(\frac{4\left(1-\frac{a}{t}\right)^{\alpha}(2\alpha a - a + t) - 4t\,{}_2F_1\left(-\frac{1}{2}, 1-\alpha; \frac{1}{2}; \frac{a}{t}\right)}{4\alpha^2-1} + \frac{\sqrt{\pi}\left((at)^{3/2} - \sqrt{at^5}\right)\Gamma(\alpha)}{t(a-t)\Gamma\left(\alpha+\frac{3}{2}\right)}\right)}{2\sqrt{a}}\right)$$

$$
< {}_aI_t^\alpha\left(\frac{e^x+\arctan(x)}{\sqrt{x}}\right) < \frac{1}{\Gamma(\alpha)}\left(\frac{(-10+4e+\pi)(t-a)^\alpha}{4\alpha}\right.
$$

$$
+\frac{\sqrt{\pi}\Gamma(\alpha)t^{\alpha-\frac{1}{2}}}{\Gamma\left(\alpha+\frac{1}{2}\right)} - 2\sqrt{a}t^{\alpha-1}\,{}_2F_1\left(\frac{1}{2},1-\alpha;\frac{3}{2};\frac{a}{t}\right) + \psi(a,t,\alpha)
$$

$$
\left. + \frac{t^\alpha\left(\frac{4\left(1-\frac{a}{t}\right)^\alpha(2\alpha a-a+t)-4t\,{}_2F_1\left(-\frac{1}{2},1-\alpha;\frac{1}{2};\frac{a}{t}\right)}{4\alpha^2-1} + \frac{\sqrt{\pi}\left((at)^{3/2}-\sqrt{at^5}\right)\Gamma(\alpha)}{t(a-t)\Gamma\left(\alpha+\frac{3}{2}\right)}\right)}{2\sqrt{a}}\right)
$$

where $\psi(a,t,\alpha) = {}_aI_t^\alpha\left(\frac{x^{\frac{3}{2}}}{2}\right)\Gamma(\alpha)$.

Proof. Let us first consider the convergence of the integral for the sake of completeness.

$$
{}_aI_t^\alpha\left(\frac{e^x+\arctan(x)}{\sqrt{x}}\right) = \int_a^t (t-x)^{\alpha-1}\frac{\arctan(x)+e^x}{\sqrt{x}}dx.
$$

As we can see, the quantity that can induce a problem is $(t-x)^{\alpha-1}$ when $x \to t$. The thing to note here is that $\alpha > 0$, which means that the degree of the expression $(t-x)^{\alpha-1}$ will be between $(0,1)$, which when integrated will not proceed to the denominator; therefore, there is no division by zero. Another situation to note is that when $a = 0$, the quantity in the denominator $\sqrt{x}$ can be integrated around zero.

Similar discussions in the other corollaries lead to the same conclusion; therefore, they are omitted.

Now we are certain about applying the formula. By pplying the Riemann–Liouville integral transform:

$$
{}_aI_t^\alpha f(t) = \frac{1}{\Gamma(\alpha)}\int_a^t (t-x)^{\alpha-1}f(x)dx
$$

on both sides of the inequality, we derived in the last theorem:

$$
\frac{1}{\sqrt{x}} + \frac{x^{\frac{3}{2}}}{2} + \sqrt{x} < \frac{e^x+\arctan(x)}{\sqrt{x}} < e + \frac{1}{4}(\pi-10) + \frac{1}{\sqrt{x}} + \frac{x^{\frac{3}{2}}}{2} + \sqrt{x}
$$

and we obtain the following inequality. □

Corollary 2. *The derived inequality can be used to approximate the solution to a first-order nonlinear ordinary differential equation. Consider differential equation* $y = f(x)$ *such that* $f : (0,1) \to (0,1)$ *and* $y(t_0)$ *are defined.*

$$
y' = \frac{\sqrt{y}x}{e^y+\arctan(y)}.
$$

Separating the variables and integrating from t_0 *to* t*, we obtain the following.*

$$
\int_{t_0}^t \frac{e^y+\arctan(y)}{\sqrt{y}}dy = \int_{t_0}^t xdx.
$$

Using the inequality and solving the integral, which is then in terms of polynomials, we obtain the following solution.

The following inequality provides an estimate for $\frac{\cosh(x)}{x}$.

Theorem 2. *The following bounds hold for* $x \in (0,1)$,

$$\frac{1}{x}+\frac{x}{2}+\frac{x^3}{24}+\frac{x^5}{720}<\frac{\cosh(x)}{x}<\cosh(1)-\frac{1111}{720}+\frac{1}{x}+\frac{x}{2}+\frac{x^3}{24}+\frac{x^5}{720}.$$

Proof. Let us consider the following function.

$$g(x)=\frac{\cosh(x)-1-\frac{x^2}{2}-\frac{x^4}{24}-\frac{x^6}{720}}{x}=\frac{h_1(x)}{h_2(x)}$$

where $h_1(x)=\cosh(x)-1-\frac{x^2}{2}-\frac{x^4}{24}-\frac{x^6}{720}$ and $h_2(x)=x$.

Taking its derivative, we obtain the following.

$$\frac{h_1'(x)}{h_2'(x)}=\sinh(x)-x-\frac{x^3}{6}-\frac{x^5}{120}$$

Now we realize that the terms with a negative sign are exactly the terms in the $\sinh(x)$ Taylor expansion

$$\sinh(x)=\sum_{n=0}^{+\infty}\frac{x^{2n+1}}{(2n+1)!}.$$

$$\frac{h_1'(x)}{h_2'(x)}=\sum_{n=3}^{+\infty}\frac{x^{2n+1}}{(2n+1)!}$$

This is obviously positive. Now, we need its increasing form. We take the following.

$$G(x)=\frac{h_1'(x)}{h_2'(x)}=\sum_{n=3}^{+\infty}\frac{x^{2n+1}}{(2n+1)!}$$

Taking a derivative, we obtain the following:

$$G'(x)=\left(\frac{h_1'(x)}{h_2'(x)}\right)'=\sum_{n=3}^{+\infty}(2n+1)\frac{x^{2n}}{(2n+1)!}>0$$

which means that $G(x)$ is increasing. Therefore, according to the Lemma 1, we obtain an increasing function $g(x)=\frac{h_1(x)-h_1(0)}{h_2(x)-h_2(0)}$. However, since we chose h_1,h_2 to be zero at $x=0$, we obtain an increasing function $g(x)$. Therefore, the following inequality holds.

$$g(0)<\frac{\cosh(x)-1-\frac{x^2}{2}-\frac{x^4}{24}-\frac{x^6}{720}}{x}<g(1)$$

This provides us with the following:

$$0<\frac{\cosh(x)-1-\frac{x^2}{2}-\frac{x^4}{24}-\frac{x^6}{720}}{x}<\cosh(1)-\frac{1111}{720}$$

which when rearranged provides us with the desired inequality. □

The following Corollary shows how our inequality can be paired up with the fractional integral to produce an effective inequality for ${}_aI_t^{\alpha}(\frac{\cosh(x)}{x})$.

Corollary 3. *The following inequality holds for* $0<a<t$ *and* $\Re(\alpha)>0$, $t\in(0,1)$:

$$\frac{1}{\Gamma(\alpha)}\Big(\psi(a,t,\alpha)+\zeta(a,t,\alpha)\Big)<{}_aI_t^{\alpha}\left(\frac{\cosh(x)}{x}\right)<$$

$$\frac{1}{\Gamma(\alpha)}\left(\frac{(720\cosh(1)-1111)(t-a)^{\alpha}}{720\alpha}+\psi(a,t,\alpha)+\zeta(a,t,\alpha)\right)$$

where

$$\psi(a,t,\alpha)=\frac{(t-a)^{\alpha}(a\alpha+t)}{2\alpha(\alpha+1)}$$

$$+\frac{(t-a)^{\alpha}\left(\alpha(\alpha+1)(\alpha+2)a^{3}+3\alpha(\alpha+1)a^{2}t+6\alpha a t^{2}+6t^{3}\right)}{24\alpha(\alpha+1)(\alpha+2)(\alpha+3)}+{}_aI_t^{\alpha}\left(\frac{x^{5}}{720}\right)\Gamma(\alpha)$$

$$\zeta(a,t,\alpha)=t^{\alpha-2}\left(a(\alpha-1)\,{}_3F_2\left(1,1,2-\alpha;2,2;\frac{a}{t}\right)-t(\log(a)+\psi^{(0)}(\alpha)-\log(t)+\gamma)\right)$$

Proof. Applying the Riemann–Liouville integral transform on both sides of the inequality we derived in the last Theorem and evaluating the left and right hand side, we arrive at the following inequality. □

Corollary 4. *Using similar reasoning to the Corollary 2, we can form the following differential equation, $y=f(x)$, such that $f:(0,1)\to(0,1)$ and $y(t_0)$ are defined.*

$$y'=\frac{yx}{\cosh(y)}.$$

Separating the variables and using the inequality, we can find the following solution. We omit the calculations for obvious reasons.

A similar construction of Corollaries for other Theorems can be performed, and we omit them due to obvious reasons.
The following Theorem sharpens Jordan's inequality.

Theorem 3. *The following bounds hold for $x\in(0,\frac{\pi}{2})$.*

$$1-\frac{x^2}{3!}+\frac{x^4}{5!}-\frac{x^6}{7!}+\frac{x^8}{9!}-\frac{x^{10}}{11!}<\frac{\sin(x)}{x}<$$

$$1-\frac{x^2}{3!}+\frac{x^4}{5!}-\frac{x^6}{7!}+\frac{x^8}{9!}-\frac{x^{10}}{11!}-1+\frac{2}{\pi}+\frac{\pi^2}{24}-\frac{\pi^4}{1920}+\frac{\pi^6}{322560}-\frac{\pi^8}{92897280}+\frac{\pi^{10}}{40874803200}.$$

Proof. Let us consider the following function.

$$g(x)=\frac{\sin(x)-x+\frac{x^3}{3!}-\frac{x^5}{5!}+\frac{x^7}{7!}-\frac{x^9}{9!}+\frac{x^{11}}{11!}}{x}=\frac{h_1(x)}{h_2(x)}$$

Differentiating h_1 and h_2, respectively, we obtain the following.

$$\frac{h_1'(x)}{h_2'(x)}=\cos(x)-1+\frac{x^2}{2!}-\frac{x^4}{4!}+\frac{x^6}{6!}-\frac{x^8}{8!}+\frac{x^{10}}{10!}$$

Expanding $\cos(x)$ into a Taylor series:

$$\cos(x)=\sum_{k=0}^{+\infty}\frac{(-1)^k x^{2k}}{(2k)!}$$

we realize that the terms outside of summation are exactly the coefficients of the $\cos(x)$ expansion and, to be precise, the terms are exactly the first five terms of the $\cos(x)$ expansion, which leaves us with the following:

$$\frac{h_1'(x)}{h_2'(x)}=\sum_{k=6}^{+\infty}\frac{(-1)^k x^{2k}}{(2k)!}.$$

which is obviously positive since it is a remainder of the positive Taylor expansion.

Now, we need an increasing form. Taking the following:

$$G(x) = \frac{h_1'(x)}{h_2'(x)} = \sum_{k=6}^{+\infty} \frac{(-1)^k x^{2k}}{(2k)!}.$$

and differentiating $G(x)$, we obtain the following:

$$G'(x) = \left(\frac{h_1'(x)}{h_2'(x)}\right)' = \sum_{k=6}^{+\infty} 2k\frac{(-1)^k x^{2k-1}}{(2k)!} > 0.$$

which means that $G(x)$ is increasing. Therefore, we obtain the fact that $\frac{h_1'(x)}{h_2'(x)}$ is increasing in both cases; therefore, $\frac{h_1(x)-h_1(0)}{h_2(x)-h_2(0)}$ is increasing, but we chose $h_1(x), h_2(x)$ such that the following holds $h_{1,2}(0) = 0$. Therefore since $g(x)$ is an increasing function, the following relation holds:

$$g(0) < g(x) < g\left(\frac{\pi}{2}\right).$$

which is evaluated at the following.

$$0 < \frac{\sin(x) - x + \frac{x^3}{3!} - \frac{x^5}{5!} + \frac{x^7}{7!} - \frac{x^9}{9!} + \frac{x^{11}}{11!}}{x} <$$

$$-1 + \frac{2}{\pi} + \frac{\pi^2}{24} - \frac{\pi^4}{1920} + \frac{\pi^6}{322560} - \frac{\pi^8}{92897280} + \frac{\pi^{10}}{40874803200}$$

When rearranged, it provides us with the desired inequality. □

In the following, we provide a corollary of the previously improved inequality.

Corollary 5. *The following inequality holds.*

$$1.37076216382 < \int_0^{\frac{\pi}{2}} \frac{\sin(x)}{x} dx < 1.37076222008$$

Proof. Integrating the inequality derived in the last Theorem from 0 to $\frac{\pi}{2}$ and integrating term by term, we obtain the following inequality. □

The next Theorem provides an estimate on the $\frac{\sinh(x)}{x}$ inequality.

Theorem 4. *The following bounds hold for $x \in (0,1)$.*

$$1 + \frac{x^2}{3!} + \frac{x^4}{5!} + \frac{x^6}{7!} < \frac{\sinh(x)}{x} < 1 + \frac{x^2}{3!} + \frac{x^4}{5!} + \frac{x^6}{7!} + \sinh(1) - \frac{5923}{5040}.$$

Proof. Let us consider the following function.

$$g(x) = \frac{\sinh(x) - x - \frac{x^3}{3!} - \frac{x^5}{5!} - \frac{x^7}{7!}}{x} = \frac{h_1(x)}{h_2(x)}$$

Taking derivative of $h_1(x)$ and $h_2(x)$, we obtain the following.

$$\frac{h_1'(x)}{h_2'(x)} = \cosh(x) - 1 - \frac{x^2}{2!} - \frac{x^4}{4!} - \frac{x^6}{6!}$$

Now we expand the cosh into its Taylor series and realize that the terms outside of the sum are exactly the first four terms in the summation. Therefore, we obtain the following:

$$\frac{h_1'(x)}{h_2'(x)} = \sum_{n=4}^{+\infty} \frac{x^{2n}}{(2n)!}.$$

which is positive. We also it in increasing form. Taking the following:

$$G(x) = \frac{h_1'(x)}{h_2'(x)} = \sum_{n=4}^{+\infty} \frac{x^{2n}}{(2n)!}$$

and taking a derivative, we obtain the following:

$$G'(x) = \left(\frac{h_1'(x)}{h_2'(x)}\right)' = \sum_{n=4}^{+\infty} 2n\frac{x^{2n-1}}{(2n)!}.$$

which is positive; therefore, $G(x)$ is increasing. From the Lemma, we obtain that function $\frac{h_1(x)-h_1(0)}{h_2(x)-h_2(0)}$ is increasing too. However, since we chose functions h_1, h_2 to be zero when $x = 0$, we obtain an increasing $g(x)$. Therefore, the following inequality follows.

$$g(0) < g(x) < g(1).$$

When the expression is solved for $\frac{\sinh(x)}{x}$, we obtained the desired inequality. □

The following Corollary illustrates how the improved bounds can be used in estimating the integral.

Corollary 6. *The following bounds for the integral hold.*

$$1.05725056689 < \int_0^1 \frac{\sinh(x)}{x} dx < 1.05725334784.$$

Proof. Integrating the inequality in the previously derived Theorem from 0 to 1, we obtain the desired bounds. □

3. Conclusions

1. Sharper upper and lower bounds were obtained in terms of polynomials. New consequences of such sharper bounds are provided in the corollaries in terms of the integral estimate of $\int_0^{\frac{\pi}{2}} \frac{\sin(x)}{x} dx$ and in terms of the fractional integral estimates of ${}_aI_t^\alpha\left(\frac{e^x+\arctan(x)}{\sqrt{x}}\right)$ and ${}_aI_t^\alpha\left(\frac{\cosh(x)}{x}\right)$.
2. Question arises with respect to which would be the lowest upper and biggest lower bound for obtained inequalities, which leaves room for further research.
3. Each of Theorem 2–4 can be easily generalized to arbitrary n as they rely on the remainder of Taylor expansion.

Author Contributions: Conceptualization V.S.Č. and S.R. (Stojan Radenović); methodology, V.S.Č., S.R. (Stojan Radenović) and E.Ç.; formal analysis, V.S.Č. and S.R. (Stojan Radenović); writing—original draft preparation, V.S.Č. and S.R. (Stojan Radenović); supervision, S.R. (Stojan Radenović), S.R. (Slobodan Radojević), V.Š.Č. and E.Ç. All authors have read and agreed to the published version of the manuscript.

Funding: This research received no external funding.

Data Availability Statement: Not applicable.

Conflicts of Interest: The authors declare no conflict of interest.

References

1. Mitrinović, D.S. *Analytic Inequalities;* Springer: Berlin/Heidelberg, Germany, 1970.
2. Bullen, P.S. A Dictionary of Inequalities. In *Pitman Monographs and Surveys in Pure and Applied Mathematics;* Addison Wesley Longman Limited: Harlow, UK, 1998; Volume 97.
3. Kober, H. Approximation by integral functions in the complex domain. *Trans. Am. Math. Soc.* **1944**, *56*, 7–31. [CrossRef]
4. Sándor, J. On the concavity of sin x/x. *Octogon Math. Mag.* **2005**, *13*, 406–407.
5. Bagul, Y.J.; Dhaigude, R.M.; Kostić, M.; Chesneau, C. Polynomial-Exponential Bounds for Some Trigonometric and Hyperbolic Functions. *Axioms* **2021**, *10*, 308. [CrossRef]
6. Chouikla, R.A.; Chesneau, C.; Yogesh, J.B. Some refinements of well-known inequalities involving trigonometric functions. *J. Ramanujan Math. Soc.* **2021**, *36*, 193–202.
7. Bagul, J.Y.; Chesneau, C. Generalized bounds for sine and cosine functions. *Asian-Eur. J. Math.* **2022**, *15*, 2250012. [CrossRef]
8. Dhaigude, M.R.; Yogesh, J.B. Simple efficient bounds for arcsine and arctangent functions. *Punjab Univ. J. Math.* **2021**. [CrossRef]
9. Neuman, E. Refinements and generalizations of certain inequalities involving trigonometric and hyperbolic functions. *Adv. Inequal. Appl.* **2012**, *1*, 1–11.
10. Rodić, M. On the Converse Jensen-Type Inequality for Generalized f-Divergences and Zipf–Mandelbrot Law. *Mathematics* **2022**, *10*, 947. [CrossRef]
11. Rodić, M. Some Generalizations of the Jensen-Type Inequalities with Applications. *Axioms* **2022**, *11*, 227. [CrossRef]
12. Abramowitz, M.; Stegun, I.A. *Handbook of Mathematical Functions: With Formulas, Graphs, and Mathematical Tables;* Dover Publications: New York, NY, USA, 1992.
13. Hermann, R. *Fractional Calculus An Introduction For Physicists;* World Scientific Publishing Co. Pte. Ltd.: Singapore, 2011.
14. Oldham, K.B.; Spanier, J. *The Fractional Calculus Theory and Applications of Differentation and Integration to Arbitrary Order;* Academic Press, Inc.: London, UK, 1974.
15. Yang, X.J. *General Fractional Derivatives Theory, Methods and Applications;* Taylor and Francis Group: London, UK, 2019.
16. Anderson, G.D.; Vamanamurthy, M.K.; Vuorinen, M. *Conformal Invariants, Inequalities and Quasiconformal Maps;* John Wiley and Sons: New York, NY, USA, 1997.

symmetry

MDPI

Article

Hermite–Hadamard Type Inclusions for Interval-Valued Coordinated Preinvex Functions

Kin Keung Lai [1,*], Shashi Kant Mishra [2], Jaya Bisht [2] and Mohd Hassan [2]

[1] International Business School, Shaanxi Normal University, Xi'an 710119, China
[2] Department of Mathematics, Institute of Science, Banaras Hindu University, Varanasi 221005, India; shashikant.mishra@bhu.ac.in (S.K.M.); jaya.bisht10@bhu.ac.in (J.B.); mohd.hassan10@bhu.ac.in (M.H.)
* Correspondence: mskklai@outlook.com

Abstract: The connection between generalized convexity and symmetry has been studied by many authors in recent years. Due to this strong connection, generalized convexity and symmetry have arisen as a new topic in the subject of inequalities. In this paper, we introduce the concept of interval-valued preinvex functions on the coordinates in a rectangle from the plane and prove Hermite–Hadamard type inclusions for interval-valued preinvex functions on coordinates. Further, we establish Hermite–Hadamard type inclusions for the product of two interval-valued coordinated preinvex functions. These results are motivated by the symmetric results obtained in the recent article by Kara et al. in 2021 on weighted Hermite–Hadamard type inclusions for products of coordinated convex interval-valued functions. Our established results generalize and extend some recent results obtained in the existing literature. Moreover, we provide suitable examples in the support of our theoretical results.

Keywords: invex set; coordinated preinvex functions; Hermite–Hadamard inequalities; interval-valued functions

Citation: Lai, K.K.; Mishra, S.K.; Bisht, J.; Hassan, M. Hermite–Hadamard Type Inclusions for Interval-Valued Coordinated Preinvex Functions. *Symmetry* **2022**, *14*, 771. https://doi.org/10.3390/sym14040771

Academic Editors: Octav Olteanu and Savin Treanta

Received: 18 March 2022
Accepted: 2 April 2022
Published: 8 April 2022

1. Introduction

In recent years, many researchers have made efforts to generalize and extend the classical convexity in different directions and discovered new integral inequalities for this generalized and extended convexity; see, for instance, [1–6]. In 1981, Hanson [7] introduced a useful generalization of convex functions known as invex functions. Craven and Glover [8] showed that the class of invex functions is equivalent to the class of functions whose stationary points are global minima. The concept of preinvex functions was introduced by Ben-Israel and Mond [9]. It is well known that preinvex functions are nonconvex functions. This concept inspired a large number of research papers dealing with the analysis and applications of this newly defined nonconvex function in optimization theory and related fields; see [10–12].

Noor [13] obtained Hermite–Hadamard (H-H) inequality for the preinvex functions, which is a generalization of the classical H-H inequality. Dragomir [14] defined the concept of classical convex functions on coordinates and demonstrated H-H type inequalities for these functions. Further, Latif and Dragomir [15] defined preinvex functions on the coordinates and established some H-H type inequalities for functions whose second-order partial derivatives in absolute value are preinvex on the coordinates. Matłoka [16] introduced the class of (h_1, h_2)-preinvex functions on the coordinates and proved H-H and Fejér type inequalities using the symmetricity of the positive function. For more details on preinvex functions and related inequalities, see [17–21].

The concept of interval analysis was first considered by Moore [22]. In 1979, Moore [23] studied the integration of interval-valued functions and investigated interval methods for computing upper and lower bounds on exact values of integrals of interval-valued functions. Bhurjee and Panda [24] presented a general multi-objective fractional programming problem whose parameters in the objective functions and constraints are intervals and developed a methodology to determine its efficient solutions. Zhang et al. [25] extended the concepts of invexity and preinvexity to interval-valued functions and derived KKT optimality conditions for LU-prinvex and invex optimization problems with an interval-valued objective function. Zhao et al. [26] introduced the interval double integral for interval-valued functions and gave Chebyshev type inequalities for interval-valued functions. Practical applications of interval analysis include areas of economics, chemical engineering, beam physics, control circuitry design, global optimization, robotics, error analysis, signal processing, and computer graphics (see [27–31]).

Budak et al. [32] defined interval-valued right-sided Riemann–Liouville fractional integral and derived H-H type inequalities for interval-valued Riemann–Liouville fractional integrals. Sharma et al. [33] introduced interval-valued preinvex function and established fractional H-H type inequalities for these functions. Recently, Zhao et al. [34,35] proposed the notion of interval-valued convex functions on coordinates and established H-H type inequalities for these interval-valued coordinated convex functions. Further, Budak et al. [36] described a new concept of interval-valued fractional integrals on coordinates and investigated H-H type inequalities for interval-valued coordinated convex functions using these fractional integrals. Kara et al. [37] proved H–H–Fejér type inclusions for the product of two interval-valued convex functions on coordinates. For more details of the relationships between the different forms of interval-valued functions and integral inequalities, we refer to [38–43] and references therein.

The work in this research paper is mainly motivated by Zhao et al. [34] and Sharma et al. [33]. We propose the notion of interval-valued preinvex functions on coordinates, which is a generalization of interval-valued convex functions on coordinates, and prove new H-H type inclusions for these interval-valued coordinated preinvex functions. We also present H-H type inclusions for the product of two interval-valued preinvex functions on coordinates. Moreover, we illustrate our results with the help of some suitable examples. The results established in this paper include the previously known results for interval-valued convex functions on coordinates as a special case. For future directions, we can investigate H-H type inclusions for interval-valued coordinated preinvex functions using interval-valued fractional integrals on coordinates.

The organization of this paper is as follows: In Section 2, we present some necessary preliminaries. In Section 3, we define preinvex interval-valued functions on coordinates and investigate H-H type inclusions for coordinated preinvex interval-valued functions. Further, we present H-H type inclusions for the product of two interval-valued preinvex functions on coordinates. Some special cases of these results are also investigated in Section 3. In Section 4, we discuss the conclusions and future directions of this study.

2. Preliminaries

In this section, we recall some notations, basic definitions, and related results that are necessary for this paper.

Let $\mathbb{R}_I$, $\mathbb{R}_I^+$, $\mathbb{R}_I^-$ be the set of all closed intervals of $\mathbb{R}$, set of all positive closed intervals of $\mathbb{R}$, and set of all negative closed intervals of $\mathbb{R}$, respectively. If $\Lambda \in \mathbb{R}_I$, then interval Λ is defined by:

$$\Lambda = [\underline{\Lambda}, \overline{\Lambda}] = \{u \in \mathbb{R} : \underline{\Lambda} \leq u \leq \overline{\Lambda}\}, \ \underline{\Lambda}, \overline{\Lambda} \in \mathbb{R}.$$

The interval $\Lambda = [\underline{\Lambda}, \overline{\Lambda}]$ is called degenerated if $\underline{\Lambda} = \overline{\Lambda}$; positive if $\underline{\Lambda} > 0$; and negative if $\overline{\Lambda} < 0$.

Let $\Lambda_1 = [\underline{\Lambda}_1, \overline{\Lambda}_1], \Lambda_2 = [\underline{\Lambda}_2, \overline{\Lambda}_2] \in \mathbb{R}_I$. We say $\Lambda_1 \subseteq \Lambda_2$ (or $\Lambda_2 \supseteq \Lambda_1$) if and only if $\underline{\Lambda}_2 \leq \underline{\Lambda}_1$ and $\overline{\Lambda}_1 \leq \overline{\Lambda}_2$.

The Hausdorff distance between $\Lambda_1 = [\underline{\Lambda}_1, \overline{\Lambda}_1]$ and $\Lambda_2 = [\underline{\Lambda}_2, \overline{\Lambda}_2]$ is defined as

$$d(\Lambda_1, \Lambda_2) = d([\underline{\Lambda}_1, \overline{\Lambda}_1], [\underline{\Lambda}_2, \overline{\Lambda}_2]) = max\{| \underline{\Lambda}_1 - \underline{\Lambda}_2 |, | \overline{\Lambda}_1 - \overline{\Lambda}_2 |\}.$$

For more properties and notations of intervals, we refer to [23,28].

Definition 1 ([23]). *A function Ω is called an interval-valued function on $[p,q]$ if it assigns a nonempty interval to each $u \in [p,q]$ and*

$$\Omega(u) = [\underline{\Omega}(u), \overline{\Omega}(u)],$$

where $\underline{\Omega}$ and $\overline{\Omega}$ are real-valued functions.

A partition P_1 of $[p,q]$ is a set of numbers $\{\omega_{i-1}, \nu_i, \omega_i\}_{i=1}^m$ such that

$$P_1 : p = \omega_0 < \omega_1 < \ldots < \omega_m = q$$

with $\omega_{i-1} \leq \nu_i \leq \omega_i$ for all $i = 1, 2, 3 \ldots m$. Partition P_1 is said to be δ-fine if $\Delta \omega_i < \delta$ for all i, where $\Delta \omega_i = \omega_i - \omega_{i-1}$. Let the set of all δ-fine partitions of $[p,q]$ be denoted by $\mathcal{P}(\delta, [p,q])$. If $\{\omega_{i-1}, \nu_i, \omega_i\}_{i=1}^m$ is a δ-fine P_1 of $[p,q]$ and $\{\sigma_{j-1}, \mu_j, \sigma_j\}_{j=1}^n$ is a δ-fine P_2 of $[r,s]$, then the rectangles

$$\Delta_{i,j} = [\omega_{i-1}, \omega_i] \times [\sigma_{j-1}, \sigma_j]$$

partition rectangle $\Delta = [p,q] \times [r,s]$ with the points (ν_i, μ_j) are inside the rectangles $[\omega_{i-1}, \omega_i] \times [\sigma_{j-1}, \sigma_j]$. Furthermore, we denote the set of all δ-fine partitions of Δ with $P_1 \times P_2$ by $\mathcal{P}(\delta, \Delta)$, where $P_1 \in \mathcal{P}(\delta, [p,q])$ and $P_2 \in \mathcal{P}(\delta, [r,s])$. Let $\Delta A_{i,j}$ be the area of the rectangle $\Delta_{i,j}$. Choose an arbitrary (ν_i, μ_j) from each rectangle $\Delta_{i,j}$, where $1 \leq i \leq m$, $1 \leq j \leq n$, and we get

$$S(\Omega, P, \delta, \Delta) = \sum_{i=1}^{m} \sum_{j=1}^{n} \Omega(\nu_i, \mu_j) \Delta A_{i,j},$$

where $\Omega : \Delta \to \mathbb{R}_I$. $S(\Omega, P, \delta, \Delta)$ denotes integral sum of Ω corresponding to the $P \in \mathcal{P}(\delta, \Delta)$.

Definition 2 ([26]). *A function $\Omega : [p,q] \to \mathbb{R}_I$ is called interval Riemann integrable (IR-integrable) on $[p,q]$ with (IR)-integral $I = (IR) \int_p^q \Omega(\lambda) d\lambda$ if for each $\epsilon > 0$, there exists $\delta > 0$ such that*

$$d(S(\Omega, P, \delta, [p,q]), I) < \epsilon$$

for each $P \in \mathcal{P}(\delta, [p,q])$.

The collection of all (IR)-integrable functions on $[p,q]$ denoted by $IR_{([p,q])}$.

Definition 3 ([26]). *A function $\Omega : \Delta \to \mathbb{R}_I$ is called interval double integrable (ID-integrable) on Δ with (ID)-integral $I = (ID) \int \int_\Delta \Omega(u, v) dA$ if for each $\epsilon > 0$, there exists $\delta > 0$ such that*

$$d(S(\Omega, P, \delta, \Delta), I) < \epsilon$$

for each $P \in \mathcal{P}(\delta, \Delta)$.

The collection of all (ID)-integrable functions on Δ denoted by $ID_{(\Delta)}$.

Theorem 1 ([28]). *Let $\Omega : [p,q] \to R_I$ be an interval-valued function such that $\Omega = [\underline{\Omega}, \overline{\Omega}]$. Then, ψ is (IR)-integrable on $[p,q]$ if and only if $\underline{\Omega}$ and $\overline{\Omega}$ are R-integrable on $[p,q]$ and*

$$(IR) \int_p^q \Omega(u) du = \left[(R) \int_p^q \underline{\Omega}(u) du, (R) \int_p^q \overline{\Omega}(u) du \right].$$

Theorem 2 ([26]). *Let $\Delta = [p,q] \times [r,s]$. If $\Omega : \Delta \to R_I$ be an interval-valued function such that $\Omega = [\underline{\Omega}, \overline{\Omega}]$ and $\Omega \in ID_{(\Delta)}$, then we have*

$$(ID) \int \int_\Delta \Omega(u,v) dA = (ID) \int_p^q (ID) \int_r^s \Omega(u,v) dv du.$$

Definition 4 ([12]). *The set* $X \subseteq \mathbb{R}^n$ *is said to be invex with respect to vector function* $\eta : \mathbb{R}^n \times \mathbb{R}^n \to \mathbb{R}^n$, *if*

$$v + \lambda\eta(u,v) \in X, \quad \textit{for all } u,v \in X, \ \lambda \in [0,1].$$

Remark 1. *Every convex set is invex with respect to* $\eta(u,v) = u - v$ *but not conversely.*

Definition 5 ([12]). *The function* Ω *on the invex set* X *is said to be preinvex with respect to* η, *if*

$$\Omega(v + \lambda\eta(u,v)) \leq (1-\lambda)\Omega(v) + \lambda\Omega(u), \quad \textit{for all } u,v \in X, \ \lambda \in [0,1].$$

Remark 2. *Every convex function is preinvex with respect to* $\eta(u,v) = u - v$ *but not conversely.*

Condition C [10] Let $X \subseteq \mathbb{R}$ be an invex set with respect to $\eta(.,.)$. Then, function η satisfies Condition C if for any $\lambda \in [0,1]$ and any $u,v \in X$,

$$\eta(v, v + \lambda\eta(u,v)) = -\lambda\eta(u,v),$$

$$\eta(u, v + \lambda\eta(u,v)) = (1-\lambda)\eta(u,v).$$

For all $\lambda_1, \lambda_2 \in [0,1]$, $u,v \in X$ and from Condition C, we have

$$\eta(v + \lambda_2\eta(u,v), v + \lambda_1\eta(u,v)) = (\lambda_2 - \lambda_1)\eta(u,v).$$

Theorem 3 ([13]). *Let* $\Omega : [p, p+\eta(q,p)] \to (0,\infty)$ *be a preinvex function on the interval of the real numbers* X^o *(the interior of X) and* $p,q \in X^o$ *with* $p < p + \eta(q,p)$. *Then the following inequality holds:*

$$\Omega\left(\frac{2p+\eta(q,p)}{2}\right) \leq \frac{1}{\eta(q,p)} \int_p^{p+\eta(q,p)} \Omega(u)du \leq \frac{\Omega(p)+\Omega(q)}{2}.$$

Definition 6 ([33]). *If* $X \subseteq \mathbb{R}$ *is an invex set with respect to* $\eta(.,.)$, $\Omega(u) = [\underline{\psi}(u), \overline{\psi}(u)]$ *is an interval-valued function on X. Then* Ω *is preinvex interval-valued function on* $\overline{X}$ *with respect to* $\eta(.,.)$ *if*

$$\Omega(v + \lambda\eta(u,v)) \supseteq \lambda\Omega(u) + (1-\lambda)\Omega(v), \quad \textit{for all } u,v \in X, \ \lambda \in [0,1].$$

Let X_1 and X_2 be two nonempty subsets of $\mathbb{R}^n$, $\eta_1 : X_1 \times X_1 \to \mathbb{R}^n$ and $\eta_2 : X_2 \times X_2 \to \mathbb{R}^n$.

Definition 7 ([16]). *Let* $(u,v) \in X_1 \times X_2$. *The set* $X_1 \times X_2$ *is said to be invex at* (u,v) *with respect to* η_1 *and* η_2, *if for each* $(w,z) \in X_1 \times X_2$ *and* $\lambda_1, \lambda_2 \in [0,1]$,

$$(u + \lambda_1\eta_1(w,u), v + \lambda_2\eta_2(z,v)) \in X_1 \times X_2.$$

$X_1 \times X_2$ is said to be invex set with respect to η_1 and η_2 if $X_1 \times X_2$ is invex at each $(w,z) \in X_1 \times X_2$.

Theorem 4 ([33]). *Let* $X \subseteq \mathbb{R}$ *be an open invex subset with respect to* $\eta : X \times X \to \mathbb{R}$ *and* $p,q \in X$ *with* $p < p + \eta(q,p)$. *If* $\Omega : [p, p+\eta(q,p)] \to \mathbb{R}_I^+$ *is a preinvex interval-valued function such that* $\Omega(\lambda) = [\underline{\Omega}(\lambda), \overline{\Omega}(\lambda)]$; $\Omega \in L[p, p+\eta(q,p)]$ *and* η *satisfies Condition C and* $\alpha > 0$, *then*

$$\Omega\left(p + \frac{\eta(q,p)}{2}\right) \supseteq \frac{\Gamma(\alpha+1)}{2\eta^\alpha(q,p)}[J^\alpha_{p^+}\Omega(p+\eta(q,p)) + J^\alpha_{(p+\eta(q,p))^-}\Omega(p)]$$
$$\supseteq \frac{\Omega(p) + \Omega(p+\eta(q,p))}{2} \supseteq \frac{\Omega(p)+\Omega(q)}{2}.$$

Corollary 1. *If $\alpha = 1$, then Theorem 4 reduces to the following result:*

$$\Omega\left(p+\frac{\eta(q,p)}{2}\right) \supseteq \frac{1}{\eta(q,p)}\int_{p}^{p+\eta(q,p)} \Omega(\lambda)d\lambda$$
$$\supseteq \frac{\Omega(p)+\Omega(p+\eta(q,p))}{2} \supseteq \frac{\Omega(p)+\Omega(q)}{2}.$$

Theorem 5 ([33]). *Let $X \subseteq \mathbb{R}$ be an open invex subset with respect to $\eta : X \times X \to \mathbb{R}$ and $p,q \in X$ with $p < p+\eta(q,p)$. If $\Omega, Y : [p, p+\eta(q,p)] \to \mathbb{R}_I^+$ is a preinvex interval-valued function such that $\Omega(\lambda) = [\underline{\Omega}(\lambda), \overline{\Omega}(\lambda)]$ and $Y(\lambda) = [\underline{Y}(\lambda), \overline{Y}(\lambda)]$; $\Omega, Y \in L[p, p+\eta(q,p)]$ and η satisfies Condition C and $\alpha > 0$, then*

$$\frac{\Gamma(\alpha+1)}{2\eta^{\alpha}(q,p)}[J_{p^+}^{\alpha}\Omega(p+\eta(q,p))Y(p+\eta(q,p)) + J_{(p+\eta(q,p))^-}^{\alpha}\Omega(p)Y(p)]$$
$$\supseteq \left(\frac{1}{2}-\frac{\alpha}{(\alpha+1)(\alpha+2)}\right)F(p,p+\eta(q,p)) + \frac{\alpha}{(\alpha+1)(\alpha+2)}G(p,p+\eta(q,p)) \quad (1)$$

and

$$2\Omega\left(p+\frac{1}{2}\eta(q,p)\right)Y\left(p+\frac{1}{2}\eta(q,p)\right)$$
$$\supseteq \frac{\Gamma(\alpha+1)}{2\eta^{\alpha}(q,p)}[J_{p^+}^{\alpha}\Omega(p+\eta(q,p))Y(p+\eta(q,p)) + J_{(p+\eta(q,p))^-}^{\alpha}\Omega(p)Y(p)]$$
$$+ \left(\frac{1}{2}-\frac{\alpha}{(\alpha+1)(\alpha+2)}\right)G(p,p+\eta(q,p)) + \frac{\alpha}{(\alpha+1)(\alpha+2)}F(p,p+\eta(q,p)), \quad (2)$$

where $F(p,p+\eta(q,p)) = \Omega(p)Y(p) + \Omega(p+\eta(q,p))Y(p+\eta(q,p))$ and $G(p,p+\eta(q,p)) = \Omega(p)Y(p+\eta(q,p)) + \Omega(p+\eta(q,p))Y(p)$.

Corollary 2. *If $\alpha = 1$, then (1) reduces to the following result:*

$$\frac{1}{\eta(q,p)}\int_{p}^{p+\eta(q,p)} \Omega(\lambda)Y(\lambda)d\lambda \supseteq \frac{1}{3}F(p,p+\eta(q,p)) + \frac{1}{6}G(p,p+\eta(q,p)).$$

Corollary 3. *If $\alpha = 1$, then (2) reduces to the following result:*

$$2\Omega\left(p+\frac{1}{2}\eta(q,p)\right)Y\left(p+\frac{1}{2}\eta(q,p)\right)$$
$$\supseteq \frac{1}{\eta(q,p)}\int_{p}^{p+\eta(q,p)} \Omega(\lambda)Y(\lambda)d\lambda + \frac{1}{3}G(p,p+\eta(q,p)) + \frac{1}{6}F(p,p+\eta(q,p)).$$

3. Main Results

In this section, first, we give the definition of interval-valued coordinated preinvex function.

Definition 8. *Let $X_1 \times X_2$ be an invex set with respect to η_1 and η_2, $\Omega = [\underline{\Omega}, \overline{\Omega}]$ be an interval valued function defined on $X_1 \times X_2$. The function Ω is said to be interval-valued coordinated preinvex function with respect to η_1 and η_2 if the partial mappings $\Omega_v : X_1 \to \mathbb{R}_I^+$, $\Omega_v(w) = (w,v)$ and $\Omega_u : X_2 \to \mathbb{R}_I^+$, $\Omega_u(z) = (u,z)$ are interval-valued preinvex functions with respect to η_1 and η_2, respectively, for all $u \in X_1$ and $v \in X_2$.*

Remark 3. *From the definition of interval-valued coordinated preinvex functions, it follows that if* Ω *is an interval-valued coordinated preinvex function, then*

$$\Omega(u+\lambda_1\eta_1(w,u),v+\lambda_2\eta_2(z,v)) \supseteq (1-\lambda_1)(1-\lambda_2)\Omega(u,v)+(1-\lambda_1)\lambda_2\Omega(u,z) \\ +\lambda_1(1-\lambda_2)\Omega(w,v)+\lambda_1\lambda_2\Omega(w,z),$$

for all $(u,v),(u,z),(w,v),(w,z) \in X_1 \times X_2$ *and* $\lambda_1,\lambda_2 \in [0,1]$.

If $\eta_1(w,u) = w-u$ and $\eta_2(z,v) = z-v$, then the definition of interval-valued coordinated preinvex function reduces to the definition of interval-valued coordinated convex function proposed by Zhao et al. [34].

Example 1. *An interval-valued function* $\Omega : [0,1] \times [\frac{1}{2},1] \to \mathbb{R}_I^+$ *defined as* $\Omega(u,v) = [u+v,(2-u)(2-v)]$ *is an interval-valued coordinated preinvex function with respect to* $\eta_1(w,u) = w-u-1$ *and* $\eta_2(z,v) = z-2v$ *for all* $u,w \in [0,1]$ *and* $v,z \in [\frac{1}{2},1]$.

Now, we establish H-H type inclusions for interval-valued preinvex functions on coordinates. In what follows, without any confusion, we will not include the symbol (R), (IR), or (ID) before the integral sign.

Theorem 6. *Let* $X_1 \times X_2$ *be an invex set with respect to* η_1 *and* η_2. *If* $\Omega : X_1 \times X_2 \to \mathbb{R}_I^+$ *is an interval-valued coordinated preinvex function with respect to* η_1 *and* η_2 *such that* $\Omega = [\underline{\Omega},\overline{\Omega}]$ *and* $p < p+\eta_1(q,p)$, $r < r+\eta_2(s,r)$, *where* $p,q \in X_1$ *and* $r,s \in X_2$. *If* η_1,η_2 *satisfy Condition C, then we have*

$$\Omega\left(p+\frac{1}{2}\eta_1(q,p),r+\frac{1}{2}\eta_2(s,r)\right) \supseteq \frac{1}{\eta_1(q,p)\eta_2(s,r)}\int_p^{p+\eta_1(q,p)}\int_r^{r+\eta_2(s,r)}\Omega(u,v)dvdu \\ \supseteq \frac{1}{4}[\Omega(p,r)+\Omega(q,r)+\Omega(p,s)+\Omega(q,s)].$$

Proof. Since Ω is an interval-valued preinvex function on coordinates with respect to η_1 and η_2, we have

$$\Omega(p+\lambda_1\eta_1(q,p),r+\lambda_2\eta_2(s,r)) \supseteq (1-\lambda_1)(1-\lambda_2)\Omega(p,r)+(1-\lambda_1)\lambda_2\Omega(p,s) \\ +\lambda_1(1-\lambda_2)\Omega(q,r)+\lambda_1\lambda_2\Omega(q,s). \tag{3}$$

Integrating (3) with respect to (λ_1,λ_2) over $[0,1]\times[0,1]$, we get

$$\int_0^1\int_0^1 \Omega(p+\lambda_1\eta_1(q,p),r+\lambda_2\eta_2(s,r))d\lambda_2 d\lambda_1 \\ \supseteq \int_0^1\int_0^1(1-\lambda_1)(1-\lambda_2)\Omega(p,r)d\lambda_2 d\lambda_1+\int_0^1\int_0^1(1-\lambda_1)\lambda_2\Omega(p,s)d\lambda_2 d\lambda_1 \\ +\int_0^1\int_0^1\lambda_1(1-\lambda_2)\Omega(q,r)d\lambda_2 d\lambda_1+\int_0^1\int_0^1\lambda_1\lambda_2\Omega(q,s)d\lambda_2 d\lambda_1.$$

This implies that

$$\frac{1}{\eta_1(q,p)\eta_2(s,r)}\int_p^{p+\eta_1(q,p)}\int_r^{r+\eta_2(s,r)}\Omega(u,v)dvdu \supseteq \frac{1}{4}[\Omega(p,r)+\Omega(p,s)+\Omega(q,r)+\Omega(q,s)]. \tag{4}$$

Using the definition of an interval-valued coordinated preinvex function and Condition C for η_1,η_2, we get

$$
\begin{aligned}
&\Omega\left(p+\frac{1}{2}\eta_1(q,p), r+\frac{1}{2}\eta_2(s,r)\right)\\
&=\Omega(p+\lambda_1\eta_1(q,p)+\frac{1}{2}\eta_1(p+(1-\lambda_1)\eta_1(q,p), p+\lambda_1\eta_1(q,p)),\ r+\lambda_2\eta_2(s,r)\\
&\quad+\frac{1}{2}\eta_2(r+(1-\lambda_2)\eta_2(s,r), r+\lambda_2\eta_2(s,r)))\\
&\supseteq\frac{1}{4}[\Omega(p+\lambda_1\eta_1(q,p), r+\lambda_2\eta_2(s,r))+\Omega(p+\lambda_1\eta_1(q,p), r+(1-\lambda_2)\eta_2(s,r))\\
&\quad+\Omega(p+(1-\lambda_1)\eta_1(q,p), r+\lambda_2\eta_2(s,r))+\Omega(p+(1-\lambda_1)\eta_1(q,p), r+(1-\lambda_2)\eta_2(s,r))]
\end{aligned}\tag{5}
$$

Thus, integrating (5) with respect to (λ_1, λ_2) over $[0,1]\times[0,1]$, we get

$$
\begin{aligned}
&\int_0^1\int_0^1\Omega\left(p+\frac{1}{2}\eta_1(q,p), r+\frac{1}{2}\eta_2(s,r)\right)d\lambda_2 d\lambda_1\\
&\supseteq\frac{1}{4}\int_0^1\int_0^1[\Omega(p+\lambda_1\eta_1(q,p), r+\lambda_2\eta_2(s,r))+\Omega(p+\lambda_1\eta_1(q,p), r+(1-\lambda_2)\eta_2(s,r))\\
&+\Omega(p+(1-\lambda_1)\eta_1(q,p), r+\lambda_2\eta_2(s,r))+\Omega(p+(1-\lambda_1)\eta_1(q,p), r+(1-\lambda_2)\eta_2(s,r))]d\lambda_2 d\lambda_1.
\end{aligned}
$$

This implies

$$
\Omega\left(p+\frac{1}{2}\eta_1(q,p), r+\frac{1}{2}\eta_2(s,r)\right)\supseteq\frac{1}{\eta_1(q,p)\eta_2(s,r)}\int_p^{p+\eta_1(q,p)}\int_r^{r+\eta_2(s,r)}\Omega(u,v)dvdu. \tag{6}
$$

From (4) and (6), we get the desired result. □

Theorem 7. *Let $X_1\times X_2$ be an invex set with respect to η_1 and η_2. If $\Omega:[p,p+\eta_1(q,p)]\times[r,r+\eta_2(s,r)]\to\mathbb{R}_I^+$ is an interval-valued coordinated preinvex function with respect to η_1 and η_2 such that $\Omega=[\underline{\Omega},\overline{\Omega}]$ and $p<p+\eta_1(q,p)$, $r<r+\eta_2(s,r)$, where $p,q\in X_1$ and $r,s\in X_2$. If η_1,η_2 satisfy Condition C, then we have*

$$
\begin{aligned}
&\frac{1}{\eta_1(q,p)}\int_p^{p+\eta_1(q,p)}\Omega\left(u, r+\frac{1}{2}\eta_2(s,r)\right)du+\frac{1}{\eta_2(s,r)}\int_r^{r+\eta_2(s,r)}\Omega\left(p+\frac{1}{2}\eta_1(q,p), v\right)dv\\
&\supseteq\frac{2}{\eta_1(q,p)\eta_2(s,r)}\int_p^{p+\eta_1(q,p)}\int_r^{r+\eta_2(s,r)}\Omega(u,v)dvdu\\
&\supseteq\frac{1}{2}\left[\frac{1}{\eta_1(q,p)}\int_p^{p+\eta_1(q,p)}(\Omega(u,r)+\Omega(u,r+\eta_2(s,r)))du\right.\\
&\left.+\frac{1}{\eta_2(s,r)}\int_r^{r+\eta_2(s,r)}(\Omega(p,v)+\Omega(p+\eta_1(q,p),v))dv\right].
\end{aligned}\tag{7}
$$

Proof. Since Ω is an interval-valued preinvex function on coordinates $[p,p+\eta_1(q,p)]\times[r,r+\eta_2(s,r)]$, then $\Omega_u:[r,r+\eta_2(s,r)]\to\mathbb{R}_I^+$, $\Omega_u(v)=\Omega(u,v)$ is an interval-valued preinvex function on $[r,r+\eta_2(s,r)]$ for all $u\in[p,p+\eta_1(q,p)]$. From Corollary 1, we have

$$
\Omega_u\left(r+\frac{1}{2}\eta_2(s,r)\right)\supseteq\frac{1}{\eta_2(s,r)}\int_r^{r+\eta_2(s,r)}\Omega_u(v)dv\supseteq\frac{\Omega_u(r)+\Omega_u(r+\eta_2(s,r))}{2}.
$$

This implies

$$
\Omega\left(u, r+\frac{1}{2}\eta_2(s,r)\right)\supseteq\frac{1}{\eta_2(s,r)}\int_r^{r+\eta_2(s,r)}\Omega(u,v)dv\supseteq\frac{\Omega(u,r)+\Omega(u,r+\eta_2(s,r))}{2}. \tag{8}
$$

Integrating (8) over $[p, p+\eta_1(q,p)]$ with respect to u, then dividing by $\eta_1(q,p)$, we get

$$\begin{aligned}
&\frac{1}{\eta_1(q,p)}\int_p^{p+\eta_1(q,p)}\Omega\left(u, r+\frac{1}{2}\eta_2(s,r)\right)du \\
&\supseteq \frac{1}{\eta_1(q,p)\eta_2(s,r)}\int_p^{p+\eta_1(q,p)}\int_r^{r+\eta_2(s,r)}\Omega(u,v)dvdu \\
&\supseteq \frac{1}{2\eta_1(q,p)}\int_p^{p+\eta_1(q,p)}(\Omega(u,r)+\Omega(u,r+\eta_2(s,r)))du. \qquad (9)
\end{aligned}$$

Similarly, $\Omega_v : [p, p+\eta_1(p,q)] \to \mathbb{R}_I^+, \Omega_v(u) = \Omega(u,v)$ is interval-valued preinvex function on $[p, p+\eta_1(p,q)]$ for all $v \in [r, r+\eta_2(s,r)]$. Then, we have

$$\begin{aligned}
&\frac{1}{\eta_2(s,r)}\int_r^{r+\eta_2(s,r)}\Omega\left(p+\frac{1}{2}\eta_1(q,p), v\right)dv \\
&\supseteq \frac{1}{\eta_1(q,p)\eta_2(s,r)}\int_p^{p+\eta_1(q,p)}\int_r^{r+\eta_2(s,r)}\Omega(u,v)dvdu \\
&\supseteq \frac{1}{2\eta_2(s,r)}\int_r^{r+\eta_2(s,r)}(\Omega(p,v)+\Omega(p+\eta_1(q,p),v))dv. \qquad (10)
\end{aligned}$$

By adding (9) and (10), we have

$$\begin{aligned}
&\frac{1}{\eta_1(q,p)}\int_p^{p+\eta_1(q,p)}\Omega\left(u, r+\frac{1}{2}\eta_2(s,r)\right)du + \frac{1}{\eta_2(s,r)}\int_r^{r+\eta_2(s,r)}\Omega\left(p+\frac{1}{2}\eta_1(q,p), v\right)dv \\
&\supseteq \frac{2}{\eta_1(q,p)\eta_2(s,r)}\int_p^{p+\eta_1(q,p)}\int_r^{r+\eta_2(s,r)}\Omega(u,v)dvdu \\
&\supseteq \frac{1}{2}\left[\frac{1}{\eta_1(q,p)}\int_p^{p+\eta_1(q,p)}(\Omega(u,r)+\Omega(u,r+\eta_2(s,r)))du\right. \\
&\left.+\frac{1}{\eta_2(s,r)}\int_r^{r+\eta_2(s,r)}(\Omega(p,v)+\Omega(p+\eta_1(q,p),v))dv\right].
\end{aligned}$$

This completes the proof. □

Example 2. *Let* $[p, p+\eta_1(q,p)] = [\frac{1}{4}, \frac{1}{2}]$, $[r, r+\eta_2(s,r)] = [\frac{1}{4}, \frac{1}{2}]$ *and* $\eta_1(q,p) = q-2p$, $\eta_2(s,r) = s-2r$. *Let* $\Omega : [\frac{1}{4}, \frac{1}{2}] \times [\frac{1}{4}, \frac{1}{2}] \to \mathbb{R}_I^+$ *be defined by* $\Omega(u,v) = [uv, (1-u)(1-v)]$ $\forall\, u \in [\frac{1}{4}, \frac{1}{2}]$ *and* $v \in [\frac{1}{4}, \frac{1}{2}]$. *Then all assumptions of Theorem 7 are satisfied.*

Theorem 8. *Let* $X_1 \times X_2$ *be an invex set with respect to* η_1 *and* η_2. *If* $\Omega : [p, p+\eta_1(q,p)] \times [r, r+\eta_2(s,r)] \to \mathbb{R}_I^+$ *is an interval-valued coordinated preinvex function with respect to* η_1 *and* η_2 *such that* $\Omega = [\underline{\Omega}, \overline{\Omega}]$ *and* $p < p+\eta_1(q,p)$, $r < r+\eta_2(s,r)$, *where* $p, q \in X_1$ *and* $r, s \in X_2$. *If* η_1, η_2 *satisfy Condition C, then we have*

$$\Omega\left(p+\frac{1}{2}\eta_1(q,p),r+\frac{1}{2}\eta_2(s,r))\right)$$
$$\supseteq \frac{1}{2}\left[\frac{1}{\eta_1(q,p)}\int_p^{p+\eta_1(q,p)}\Omega\left(u,r+\frac{1}{2}\eta_2(s,r))\right)du+\frac{1}{\eta_2(s,r)}\int_r^{r+\eta_2(s,r)}\Omega\left(p+\frac{1}{2}\eta_1(q,p),v\right)dv\right]$$
$$\supseteq \frac{1}{\eta_1(q,p)\eta_2(s,r)}\int_p^{p+\eta_1(q,p)}\int_r^{r+\eta_2(s,r)}\Omega(u,v)dvdu$$
$$\supseteq \frac{1}{4}\left[\frac{1}{\eta_1(q,p)}\int_p^{p+\eta_1(q,p)}(\Omega(u,r)+\Omega(u,r+\eta_2(s,r)))du\right.$$
$$\left.+\frac{1}{\eta_2(s,r)}\int_r^{r+\eta_2(s,r)}(\Omega(p,v)+\Omega(p+\eta_1(q,p),v))dv\right]$$
$$\supseteq \frac{1}{4}[\Omega(p,r)+\Omega(p+\eta_1(q,p),r)+\Omega(p,r+\eta_2(s,r))+\Omega(p+\eta_1(q,p),r+\eta_2(s,r))]$$
$$\supseteq \frac{1}{4}[\Omega(p,r)+\Omega(q,r)+\Omega(p,s)+\Omega(q,s)].$$

Proof. Since Ω is an interval-valued preinvex function on coordinates $[p,p+\eta_1(q,p)]\times[r,r+\eta_2(s,r)]$, then from Corollary 1 we get

$$\Omega\left(p+\frac{1}{2}\eta_1(q,p),r+\frac{1}{2}\eta_2(s,r))\right)\supseteq\frac{1}{\eta_1(q,p)}\int_p^{p+\eta_1(q,p)}\Omega\left(u,r+\frac{1}{2}\eta_2(s,r))\right)du, \tag{11}$$

$$\Omega\left(p+\frac{1}{2}\eta_1(q,p),r+\frac{1}{2}\eta_2(s,r))\right)\supseteq\frac{1}{\eta_2(s,r)}\int_r^{r+\eta_2(s,r)}\Omega\left(p+\frac{1}{2}\eta_1(q,p),v\right)dv. \tag{12}$$

Adding (11) and (12), we have

$$\Omega\left(p+\frac{1}{2}\eta_1(q,p),\ r+\frac{1}{2}\eta_2(s,r))\right)$$
$$\supseteq \frac{1}{2}\left[\frac{1}{\eta_1(q,p)}\int_p^{p+\eta_1(q,p)}\Omega\left(u,r+\frac{1}{2}\eta_2(s,r))\right)du+\frac{1}{\eta_2(s,r)}\int_r^{r+\eta_2(s,r)}\Omega\left(p+\frac{1}{2}\eta_1(q,p),v\right)dv\right]. \tag{13}$$

Again from Corollary 1, we get

$$\frac{1}{\eta_1(q,p)}\int_p^{p+\eta_1(q,p)}\Omega(u,r)du\supseteq\frac{\Omega(p,r)+\Omega(p+\eta_1(q,p),r)}{2}, \tag{14}$$
$$\frac{1}{\eta_1(q,p)}\int_p^{p+\eta_1(q,p)}\Omega(u,r+\eta_2(s,r))du\supseteq\frac{\Omega(p,r+\eta_2(s,r))+\Omega(p+\eta_1(q,p),r+\eta_2(s,r))}{2}, \tag{15}$$
$$\frac{1}{\eta_2(s,r)}\int_r^{r+\eta_2(s,r)}\Omega(p,v)dv\supseteq\frac{\Omega(p,r)+\Omega(p,r+\eta_2(s,r))}{2}, \tag{16}$$
$$\frac{1}{\eta_2(s,r)}\int_r^{r+\eta_2(s,r)}\Omega(p+\eta_1(q,p),v)dv\supseteq\frac{\Omega(p+\eta_1(q,p),r)+\Omega(p+\eta_1(q,p),r+\eta_2(s,r))}{2}. \tag{17}$$

Adding (14)–(17), we get

$$\begin{aligned}&\frac{1}{\eta_1(q,p)}\int_p^{p+\eta_1(q,p)}(\Omega(u,r)+\Omega(u,r+\eta_2(s,r)))du\\&+\frac{1}{\eta_2(s,r)}\int_r^{r+\eta_2(s,r)}(\Omega(p,v)+\Omega(p+\eta_1(q,p),v))dv\\&\supseteq\Omega(p,r)+\Omega(p+\eta_1(q,p),r)+\Omega(p,r+\eta_2(s,r))+\Omega(p+\eta_1(q,p),r+\eta_2(s,r)).\end{aligned} \quad (18)$$

By Corollary 1, we also have

$$\begin{aligned}&\Omega(p,r)+\Omega(p+\eta_1(q,p),r)+\Omega(p,r+\eta_2(s,r))+\Omega(p+\eta_1(q,p),r+\eta_2(s,r))\\&\supseteq\Omega(p,r)+\Omega(q,r)+\Omega(p,s)+\Omega(q,s).\end{aligned} \quad (19)$$

From (7), (13), (18), and (19), we get the desired result. □

Remark 4. *If we put $\eta_1(q,p)=q-p$ and $\eta_2(s,r)=s-r$ in Theorem 8, we obtain Theorem 7 of [34].*

Next, we prove H-H type inclusions for the product of two interval-valued coordinated preinvex functions.

Theorem 9. *Let $X_1\times X_2$ be an invex set with respect to η_1 and η_2. If $\Omega,\Upsilon:[p,p+\eta_1(q,p)]\times[r,r+\eta_2(s,r)]\to\mathbb{R}_I^+$ are interval-valued coordinated preinvex functions with respect to η_1 and η_2 such that $\Omega=[\underline{\Omega},\overline{\Omega}]$, $\Upsilon=[\underline{\Upsilon},\overline{\Upsilon}]$ and $p<p+\eta_1(q,p)$, $r<r+\eta_2(s,r)$, where $p,q\in X_1$ and $r,s\in X_2$. If η_1,η_2 satisfy Condition C, then*

$$\begin{aligned}&\frac{1}{\eta_1(q,p)\eta_2(s,r)}\int_p^{p+\eta_1(q,p)}\int_r^{r+\eta_2(s,r)}\Omega(u,v)\Upsilon(u,v)dvdu\\&\supseteq\frac{1}{9}N_1(p,q,r,s)+\frac{1}{18}N_2(p,q,r,s)+\frac{1}{18}N_3(p,q,r,s)+\frac{1}{36}N_4(p,q,r,s),\end{aligned}$$

where
$N_1(p,q,r,s)=\Omega(p,r)\Upsilon(p,r)+\Omega(p+\eta_1(q,p),r)\Upsilon(p+\eta_1(q,p),r)+\Omega(p,r+\eta_2(s,r))\Upsilon(p,r+\eta_2(s,r))+\Omega(p+\eta_1(q,p),r+\eta_2(s,r))\Upsilon(p+\eta_1(q,p),r+\eta_2(s,r))$,

$N_2(p,q,r,s)=\Omega(p,r)\Upsilon(p+\eta_1(q,p),r)+\Omega(p+\eta_1(q,p),r)\Upsilon(p,r)+\Omega(p,r+\eta_2(s,r))\Upsilon(p+\eta_1(q,p),r+\eta_2(s,r))+\Omega(p+\eta_1(q,p),r+\eta_2(s,r))\Upsilon(p,r+\eta_2(s,r))$,

$N_3(p,q,r,s)=\Omega(p,r)\Upsilon(p,r+\eta_2(s,r))+\Omega(p+\eta_1(q,p),r)\Upsilon(p+\eta_1(q,p),r+\eta_2(s,r))+\Omega(p,r+\eta_2(s,r))\Upsilon(p,r)+\Omega(p+\eta_1(q,p),r+\eta_2(s,r))\Upsilon(p+\eta_1(q,p),r)$,

$N_4(p,q,r,s)=\Omega(p,r)\Upsilon(p+\eta_1(q,p),r+\eta_2(s,r))+\Omega(p+\eta_1(q,p),r)\Upsilon(p,r+\eta_2(s,r))+\Omega(p,r+\eta_2(s,r))\Upsilon(p+\eta_1(q,p),r)+\Omega(p+\eta_1(q,p),r+\eta_2(s,r))\Upsilon(p,r)$.

Proof. Since Ω and Υ are interval-valued coordinated preinvex functions on $[p,p+\eta_1(q,p)]\times[r,r+\eta_2(s,r)]$, we have

$$\Omega_u(v):[r,r+\eta_2(s,r)]\to\mathbb{R}_I^+,\ \Omega_u(v)=\Omega(u,v)$$
and
$$\Upsilon_u(v):[r,r+\eta_2(s,r)]\to\mathbb{R}_I^+,\ \Upsilon_u(v)=\Upsilon(u,v)$$

are interval-valued preinvex functions on $[r, r+\eta_2(s,r)]$ for all $u \in [p, p+\eta_1(q,p)]$. Similarly,

$$\Omega_v(u) : [p, p+\eta_1(q,p)] \to \mathbb{R}_I^+,\ \Omega_v(u) = \Omega(u,v)$$
$$\text{and}$$
$$\Upsilon_v(u) : [p, p+\eta_1(q,p)] \to \mathbb{R}_I^+,\ \Upsilon_v(u) = \Upsilon(u,v)$$

are interval-valued preinvex functions on $[p, p+\eta_1(q,p)]$ for all $v \in [r, r+\eta_2(s,r)]$.

From Corollary 2, we get

$$\begin{aligned}
&\frac{1}{\eta_2(s,r)}\int_r^{r+\eta_2(s,r)} \Omega_u(v)\Upsilon_u(v)dv \\
&\supseteq \frac{1}{3}[\Omega_u(r)\Upsilon_u(r) + \Omega_u(r+\eta_2(s,r))\Upsilon_u(r+\eta_2(s,r))] + \frac{1}{6}[\Omega_u(r)\Upsilon_u(r+\eta_2(s,r)) + \Omega_u(r+\eta_2(s,r))\Upsilon_u(r)].
\end{aligned}$$

This implies

$$\begin{aligned}
&\frac{1}{\eta_2(s,r)}\int_r^{r+\eta_2(s,r)} \Omega(u,v)\Upsilon(u,v)dv \\
&\supseteq \frac{1}{3}[\Omega(u,r)\Upsilon(u,r) + \Omega(u,r+\eta_2(s,r))\Upsilon(u,r+\eta_2(s,r))] \\
&\quad + \frac{1}{6}[\Omega(u,r)\Upsilon(u,r+\eta_2(s,r)) + \Omega(u,r+\eta_2(s,r))\Upsilon(u,r)].
\end{aligned} \tag{20}$$

Integrating (20) with respect to u over $[p, p+\eta_1(q,p)]$ and after then dividing by $\eta_1(q,p)$, we find

$$\begin{aligned}
&\frac{1}{\eta_1(q,p)\eta_2(s,r)}\int_p^{p+\eta_1(q,p)}\int_r^{r+\eta_2(s,r)} \Omega(u,v)\Upsilon(u,v)dvdu \\
&\supseteq \frac{1}{3\eta_1(q,p)}\int_p^{p+\eta_1(q,p)} [\Omega(u,r)\Upsilon(u,r) + \Omega(u,r+\eta_2(s,r))\Upsilon(u,r+\eta_2(s,r))]du \\
&\quad + \frac{1}{6\eta_1(q,p)}\int_p^{p+\eta_1(q,p)} [\Omega(u,r)\Upsilon(u,r+\eta_2(s,r)) + \Omega(u,r+\eta_2(s,r))\Upsilon(u,r)]du.
\end{aligned} \tag{21}$$

Again from Corollary 2, we have

$$\begin{aligned}
&\frac{1}{\eta_1(q,p)}\int_p^{p+\eta_1(q,p)} \Omega(u,r)\Upsilon(u,r)du \\
&\supseteq \frac{1}{3}[\Omega(p,r)\Upsilon(p,r) + \Omega(p+\eta_1(q,p),r)\Upsilon(p+\eta_1(q,p),r] \\
&\quad + \frac{1}{6}[\Omega(p,r)\Upsilon(p+\eta_1(q,p),r) + \Omega(p+\eta_1(q,p),r)\Upsilon(p,r)],
\end{aligned} \tag{22}$$

$$\begin{aligned}
&\frac{1}{\eta_1(q,p)}\int_p^{p+\eta_1(q,p)} \Omega(u,r+\eta_2(s,r))\Upsilon(u,r+\eta_2(s,r))du \\
&\supseteq \frac{1}{3}[\Omega(p,r+\eta_2(s,r))\Upsilon(p,r+\eta_2(s,r)) + \Omega(p+\eta_1(q,p),r+\eta_2(s,r))\Upsilon(p+\eta_1(q,p),r+\eta_2(s,r))] \\
&\quad + \frac{1}{6}[\Omega(p,r+\eta_2(s,r))\Upsilon(p+\eta_1(q,p),r+\eta_2(s,r)) + \Omega(p+\eta_1(q,p),r+\eta_2(s,r))\Upsilon(p,r+\eta_2(s,r))],
\end{aligned} \tag{23}$$

$$\frac{1}{\eta_1(q,p)}\int_p^{p+\eta_1(q,p)}\Omega(u,r)Y(u,r+\eta_2(s,r))du$$
$$\supseteq\frac{1}{3}[\Omega(p,r))Y(p,r+\eta_2(s,r))+\Omega(p+\eta_1(q,p),r)Y(p+\eta_1(q,p),r+\eta_2(s,r))]$$
$$+\frac{1}{6}[\Omega(p,r)Y(p+\eta_1(q,p),r+\eta_2(s,r))+\Omega(p+\eta_1(q,p),r)Y(p,r+\eta_2(s,r))], \quad (24)$$

$$\frac{1}{\eta_1(q,p)}\int_p^{p+\eta_1(q,p)}\Omega(u,r+\eta_2(s,r))Y(u,r)du$$
$$\supseteq\frac{1}{3}[\Omega(p,r+\eta_2(s,r))Y(p,r)+\Omega(p+\eta_1(q,p),r+\eta_2(s,r))Y(p+\eta_1(q,p),r]$$
$$+\frac{1}{6}[\Omega(p,r+\eta_2(s,r))Y(p+\eta_1(q,p),r)+\Omega(p+\eta_1(q,p),r+\eta_2(s,r))Y(p,r)]. \quad (25)$$

Substituting (22)–(25) into (21), we obtain the desired result. Similarly, we can obtain the same result by using Corollary 2 for the product $\Omega_v(u)Y_v(u)$ on $[p,p+\eta_1(q,p)]$. □

Remark 5. *If we put $\eta_1(q,p)=q-p$ and $\eta_2(s,r)=s-r$ in Theorem 9, we obtain Theorem 8 of [34].*

Theorem 10. *Let $X_1\times X_2$ be an invex set with respect to η_1 and η_2. If $\Omega, Y:[p,p+\eta_1(q,p)]\times[r,r+\eta_2(s,r)]\to\mathbb{R}_I^+$ are interval-valued coordinated preinvex functions with respect to η_1 and η_2 such that $\Omega=[\underline{\Omega},\overline{\Omega}]$, $Y=[\underline{Y},\overline{Y}]$ and $p<p+\eta_1(q,p)$, $r<r+\eta_2(s,r)$, where $p,q\in X_1$ and $r,s\in X_2$. If η_1,η_2 satisfy Condition C, then we have*

$$4\Omega\left(p+\frac{1}{2}\eta_1(q,p),r+\frac{1}{2}\eta_2(s,r)\right)Y\left(p+\frac{1}{2}\eta_1(q,p),r+\frac{1}{2}\eta_2(s,r)\right)$$
$$\supseteq\frac{1}{\eta_1(q,p)\eta_2(s,r)}\int_p^{p+\eta_1(q,p)}\int_r^{r+\eta_2(s,r)}\Omega(u,v)Y(u,v)dvdu$$
$$+\frac{5}{36}N_1(p,q,r,s)+\frac{7}{36}N_2(p,q,r,s)+\frac{7}{36}N_3(p,q,r,s)+\frac{2}{9}N_4(p,q,r,s),$$

where $N_1(p,q,r,s)$, $N_2(p,q,r,s)$, $N_3(p,q,r,s)$, and $N_4(p,q,r,s)$ are defined as previous.

Proof. Since Ω and Y are interval-valued coordinated preinvex functions, therefore from Corollary 3, we have

$$2\Omega\left(p+\frac{1}{2}\eta_1(q,p),r+\frac{1}{2}\eta_2(s,r)\right)Y\left(p+\frac{1}{2}\eta_1(q,p),r+\frac{1}{2}\eta_2(s,r)\right)$$
$$\supseteq\frac{1}{\eta_1(q,p)}\int_p^{p+\eta_1(q,p)}\Omega(u,r+\frac{1}{2}\eta_2(s,r))Y(u,r+\frac{1}{2}\eta_2(s,r))du$$
$$+\frac{1}{6}\Big[\Omega(p,r+\frac{1}{2}\eta_2(s,r))Y(p,r+\frac{1}{2}\eta_2(s,r))$$
$$+\Omega(p+\eta_1(q,p),r+\frac{1}{2}\eta_2(s,r))Y(p+\eta_1(q,p),r+\frac{1}{2}\eta_2(s,r))\Big]$$
$$+\frac{1}{3}\Big[\Omega(p,r+\frac{1}{2}\eta_2(s,r))Y(p+\eta_1(q,p),r+\frac{1}{2}\eta_2(s,r))$$
$$+\Omega(p+\eta_1(q,p),r+\frac{1}{2}\eta_2(s,r))Y(p,r+\frac{1}{2}\eta_2(s,r))\Big] \quad (26)$$

and

$$
\begin{aligned}
&2\Omega\left(p+\frac{1}{2}\eta_1(q,p),r+\frac{1}{2}\eta_2(s,r)\right)\Upsilon\left(p+\frac{1}{2}\eta_1(q,p),r+\frac{1}{2}\eta_2(s,r)\right)\\
&\supseteq \frac{1}{\eta_2(s,r)}\int_r^{r+\eta_2(s,r)}\Omega(r+\frac{1}{2}\eta_2(s,r),v)\Upsilon(p+\frac{1}{2}\eta_1(q,p),v)dv\\
&\quad+\frac{1}{6}\Big[\Omega(p+\frac{1}{2}\eta_1(q,p),r)\Upsilon(p+\frac{1}{2}\eta_1(q,p),r)\\
&\quad+\Omega(p+\frac{1}{2}\eta_1(q,p),r+\eta_2(s,r))\Upsilon(p+\frac{1}{2}\eta_1(q,p),r+\eta_2(s,r))\Big]\\
&\quad+\frac{1}{3}\Big[\Omega(p+\frac{1}{2}\eta_1(q,p),r)\Upsilon(p+\frac{1}{2}\eta_1(q,p),r+\eta_2(s,r))\\
&\quad+\Omega(p+\frac{1}{2}\eta_1(q,p),r+\eta_2(s,r))\Upsilon(p+\frac{1}{2}\eta_1(q,p),r)\Big]. \qquad (27)
\end{aligned}
$$

Adding (26) and (27), then multiplying both sides of the resultant one by 2, we find

$$
\begin{aligned}
&8\Omega\left(p+\frac{1}{2}\eta_1(q,p),r+\frac{1}{2}\eta_2(s,r)\right)\Upsilon\left(p+\frac{1}{2}\eta_1(q,p),r+\frac{1}{2}\eta_2(s,r)\right)\\
&\supseteq \frac{2}{\eta_1(q,p)}\int_p^{p+\eta_1(q,p)}\Omega(u,r+\frac{1}{2}\eta_2(s,r))\Upsilon(u,r+\frac{1}{2}\eta_2(s,r))du\\
&\quad+\frac{2}{\eta_2(s,r)}\int_r^{r+\eta_2(s,r)}\Omega(r+\frac{1}{2}\eta_2(s,r),v)\Upsilon(p+\frac{1}{2}\eta_1(q,p),v)dv\\
&\quad+\frac{1}{6}\Big[2\Omega(p,r+\frac{1}{2}\eta_2(s,r))\Upsilon(p,r+\frac{1}{2}\eta_2(s,r))\\
&\quad+2\Omega(p+\eta_1(q,p),r+\frac{1}{2}\eta_2(s,r))\Upsilon(p+\eta_1(q,p),r+\frac{1}{2}\eta_2(s,r))\\
&\quad+2\Omega(p+\frac{1}{2}\eta_1(q,p),r)\Upsilon(p+\frac{1}{2}\eta_1(q,p),r)\\
&\quad+2\Omega(p+\frac{1}{2}\eta_1(q,p),r+\eta_2(s,r))\Upsilon(p+\frac{1}{2}\eta_1(q,p),r+\eta_2(s,r))\Big]\\
&\quad+\frac{1}{3}\Big[2\Omega(p,r+\frac{1}{2}\eta_2(s,r))\Upsilon(p+\eta_1(q,p),r+\frac{1}{2}\eta_2(s,r))\\
&\quad+2\Omega(p+\eta_1(q,p),r+\frac{1}{2}\eta_2(s,r))\Upsilon(p,r+\frac{1}{2}\eta_2(s,r))\\
&\quad+2\Omega(p+\frac{1}{2}\eta_1(q,p),r)\Upsilon(p+\frac{1}{2}\eta_1(q,p),r+\eta_2(s,r))\\
&\quad+2\Omega(p+\frac{1}{2}\eta_1(q,p),r+\eta_2(s,r))\Upsilon(p+\frac{1}{2}\eta_1(q,p),r)\Big]. \qquad (28)
\end{aligned}
$$

Now, from Corollary 3, we have

$$
\begin{aligned}
&2\Omega(p,r+\frac{1}{2}\eta_2(s,r))\Upsilon(p,r+\frac{1}{2}\eta_2(s,r))\\
&\supseteq \frac{1}{\eta_2(s,r)}\int_r^{r+\eta_2(s,r)}\Omega(p,v)\Upsilon(p,v)dv\\
&\quad+\frac{1}{6}[\Omega(p,r)\Upsilon(p,r)+\Omega(p,r+\eta_2(s,r))\Upsilon(p,r+\eta_2(s,r))]\\
&\quad+\frac{1}{3}[\Omega(p,r)\Upsilon(p,r+\eta_2(s,r))+\Omega(p,r+\eta_2(s,r))\Upsilon(p,r)], \qquad (29)
\end{aligned}
$$

$$\begin{aligned}
&2\Omega(p+\eta_1(q,p),r+\frac{1}{2}\eta_2(s,r))\Upsilon(p+\eta_1(q,p),r+\frac{1}{2}\eta_2(s,r))\\
&\supseteq \frac{1}{\eta_2(s,r)}\int_r^{r+\eta_2(s,r)}\Omega(p+\eta_1(q,p),v)\Upsilon(p+\eta_1(q,p),v)dv\\
&+\frac{1}{6}[\Omega(p+\eta_1(q,p),r)\Upsilon(p+\eta_1(q,p),r)+\Omega(p+\eta_1(q,p),r+\eta_2(s,r))\Upsilon(p+\eta_1(q,p),r+\eta_2(s,r))]\\
&+\frac{1}{3}[\Omega(p+\eta_1(q,p),r)\Upsilon(p+\eta_1(q,p),r+\eta_2(s,r))+\Omega(p+\eta_1(q,p),r+\eta_2(s,r))\Upsilon(p+\eta_1(q,p),r)],
\end{aligned}\tag{30}$$

$$\begin{aligned}
&2\Omega\left(p+\frac{1}{2}\eta_1(q,p),r\right)\Upsilon\left(p+\frac{1}{2}\eta_1(q,p),r\right)\\
&\supseteq \frac{1}{\eta_1(q,p)}\int_p^{p+\eta_1(q,p)}\Omega(u,r)\Upsilon(u,r)du\\
&+\frac{1}{6}[\Omega(p,r)\Upsilon(p,r)+\Omega(p+\eta_1(q,p),r)\Upsilon(p+\eta_1(q,p),r)]\\
&+\frac{1}{3}[\Omega(p,r)\Upsilon(p+\eta_1(q,p),r)+\Omega(p+\eta_1(q,p),r)\Upsilon(p,r)],
\end{aligned}\tag{31}$$

$$\begin{aligned}
&2\Omega\left(p+\frac{1}{2}\eta_1(q,p),r+\eta_2(s,r)\right)\Upsilon\left(p+\frac{1}{2}\eta_1(q,p),r+\eta_2(s,r)\right)\\
&\supseteq \frac{1}{\eta_1(q,p)}\int_p^{p+\eta_1(q,p)}\Omega(u,r+\eta_2(s,r))\Upsilon(u,r+\eta_2(s,r))du\\
&+\frac{1}{6}[\Omega(p,r+\eta_2(s,r))\Upsilon(p,r+\eta_2(s,r))+\Omega(p+\eta_1(q,p),r+\eta_2(s,r))\Upsilon(p+\eta_1(q,p),r+\eta_2(s,r))]\\
&+\frac{1}{3}[\Omega(p,r+\eta_2(s,r))\Upsilon(p+\eta_1(q,p),r+\eta_2(s,r))+\Omega(p+\eta_1(q,p),r+\eta_2(s,r))\Upsilon(p,r+\eta_2(s,r))],
\end{aligned}\tag{32}$$

$$\begin{aligned}
&2\Omega(p,r+\frac{1}{2}\eta_2(s,r))\Upsilon(p+\eta_1(q,p),r+\frac{1}{2}\eta_2(s,r))\\
&\supseteq \frac{1}{\eta_2(s,r)}\int_r^{r+\eta_2(s,r)}\Omega(p,v)\Upsilon(p+\eta_1(q,p),v)dv\\
&+\frac{1}{6}[\Omega(p,r)\Upsilon(p+\eta_1(q,p),r)+\Omega(p,r+\eta_2(s,r))\Upsilon(p+\eta_1(q,p),r+\eta_2(s,r))]\\
&+\frac{1}{3}[\Omega(p,r)\Upsilon(p+\eta_1(q,p),r+\eta_2(s,r))+\Omega(p,r+\eta_2(s,r))\Upsilon(p+\eta_1(q,p),r)],
\end{aligned}\tag{33}$$

$$\begin{aligned}
&2\Omega(p+\eta_1(q,p),r+\frac{1}{2}\eta_2(s,r))\Upsilon(p,r+\frac{1}{2}\eta_2(s,r))\\
&\supseteq \frac{1}{\eta_2(s,r)}\int_r^{r+\eta_2(s,r)}\Omega(p+\eta_1(q,p),v)\Upsilon(p,v)dv\\
&+\frac{1}{6}[\Omega(p+\eta_1(q,p),r)\Upsilon(p,r)+\Omega(p+\eta_1(q,p),r+\eta_2(s,r))\Upsilon(p,r+\eta_2(s,r))]\\
&+\frac{1}{3}[\Omega(p+\eta_1(q,p),r)\Upsilon(p,r+\eta_2(s,r))+\Omega(p+\eta_1(q,p),r+\eta_2(s,r))\Upsilon(p,r)],
\end{aligned}\tag{34}$$

$$
\begin{aligned}
&2\Omega\left(p+\frac{1}{2}\eta_1(q,p),r\right)\Upsilon\left(p+\frac{1}{2}\eta_1(q,p),r+\eta_2(s,r)\right)\\
&\supseteq \frac{1}{\eta_1(q,p)}\int_p^{p+\eta_1(q,p)}\Omega(u,r)\Upsilon(u,r+\eta_2(s,r))du\\
&+\frac{1}{6}[\Omega(p,r)\Upsilon(p,r+\eta_2(s,r))+\Omega(p+\eta_1(q,p),r)\Upsilon(p+\eta_1(q,p),r+\eta_2(s,r))]\\
&+\frac{1}{3}[\Omega(p,r)\Upsilon(p+\eta_1(q,p),r+\eta_2(s,r))+\Omega(p+\eta_1(q,p),r)\Upsilon(p,r+\eta_2(s,r))],
\end{aligned} \tag{35}
$$

$$
\begin{aligned}
&2\Omega\left(p+\frac{1}{2}\eta_1(q,p),r+\eta_2(s,r)\right)\Upsilon\left(p+\frac{1}{2}\eta_1(q,p),r\right)\\
&\supseteq \frac{1}{\eta_1(q,p)}\int_p^{p+\eta_1(q,p)}\Omega(u,r+\eta_2(s,r))\Upsilon(u,r)du\\
&+\frac{1}{6}[\Omega(p,r+\eta_2(s,r))\Upsilon(p,r)+\Omega(p+\eta_1(q,p),r+\eta_2(s,r))\Upsilon(p+\eta_1(q,p),r)]\\
&+\frac{1}{3}[\Omega(p,r+\eta_2(s,r))\Upsilon(p+\eta_1(q,p),r)+\Omega(p+\eta_1(q,p),r+\eta_2(s,r))\Upsilon(p,r)].
\end{aligned} \tag{36}
$$

Using (29)–(36) in (28), we get

$$
\begin{aligned}
&8\Omega\left(p+\frac{1}{2}\eta_1(q,p),r+\frac{1}{2}\eta_2(s,r)\right)\Upsilon\left(p+\frac{1}{2}\eta_1(q,p),r+\frac{1}{2}\eta_2(s,r)\right)\\
&\supseteq \frac{2}{\eta_1(q,p)}\int_p^{p+\eta_1(q,p)}\Omega(u,r+\frac{1}{2}\eta_2(s,r))\Upsilon(u,r+\frac{1}{2}\eta_2(s,r))du\\
&+\frac{2}{\eta_2(s,r)}\int_r^{r+\eta_2(s,r)}\Omega(r+\frac{1}{2}\eta_2(s,r),v)\Upsilon(p+\frac{1}{2}\eta_1(q,p),v)dv\\
&+\frac{1}{6\eta_2(s,r)}\int_r^{r+\eta_2(s,r)}(\Omega(p,v)\Upsilon(p,v)+\ \Omega(p+\eta_1(q,p),v)\Upsilon(p+\eta_1(q,p),v))dv\\
&+\frac{1}{3\eta_2(s,r)}\int_r^{r+\eta_2(s,r)}(\Omega(p,v)\Upsilon(p+\eta_1(q,p),v)+\Omega(p+\eta_1(q,p),v)\Upsilon(p,v))dv\\
&+\frac{1}{6\eta_1(q,p)}\int_p^{p+\eta_1(q,p)}(\Omega(u,r)\Upsilon(u,r)+\Omega(u,r+\eta_2(s,r))\Upsilon(u,r+\eta_2(s,r)))du\\
&+\frac{1}{3\eta_1(q,p)}\int_p^{p+\eta_1(q,p)}(\Omega(u,r)\Upsilon(u,r+\eta_2(s,r))+\Omega(u,r+\eta_2(s,r))\Upsilon(u,r))du\\
&+\frac{1}{18}N_1(p,q,r,s)+\frac{1}{9}N_2(p,q,r,s)+\frac{1}{9}N_3(p,q,r,s)+\frac{2}{9}N_4(p,q,r,s).
\end{aligned} \tag{37}
$$

Again from Corollary 3, we have

$$
\begin{aligned}
&\frac{2}{\eta_2(s,r)}\int_r^{r+\eta_2(s,r)}\Omega(p+\frac{1}{2}\eta_1(q,p),v)\Upsilon(p+\frac{1}{2}\eta_1(q,p),v)dv\\
&\supseteq \frac{1}{\eta_1(q,p)\eta_2(s,r)}\int_p^{p+\eta_1(q,p)}\int_r^{r+\eta_2(s,r)}\Omega(u,v)\Upsilon(u,v)dvdu\\
&+\frac{1}{6\eta_2(s,r)}\int_r^{r+\eta_2(s,r)}(\Omega(p,v)\Upsilon(p,v)+\Omega(p+\eta_1(q,p),v)\Upsilon(p+\eta_1(q,p),v))dv\\
&+\frac{1}{3\eta_2(s,r)}\int_r^{r+\eta_2(s,r)}(\Omega(p,v)\Upsilon(p+\eta_1(q,p),v)+\Omega(p+\eta_1(q,p),v)\Upsilon(p,v))dv,
\end{aligned} \tag{38}
$$

$$\frac{2}{\eta_1(q,p)}\int_p^{p+\eta_1(q,p)}\Omega(u,r+\frac{1}{2}\eta_2(s,r))Y(u,r+\frac{1}{2}\eta_2(s,r))du$$
$$\supseteq \frac{1}{\eta_1(q,p)\eta_2(s,r)}\int_p^{p+\eta_1(q,p)}\int_r^{r+\eta_2(s,r)}\Omega(u,v)Y(u,v)dvdu$$
$$+\frac{1}{6\eta_1(q,p)}\int_p^{p+\eta_1(q,p)}(\Omega(u,r)Y(u,r)+\Omega(u,r+\eta_2(s,r))Y(u,r+\eta_2(s,r)))du$$
$$+\frac{1}{3\eta_1(q,p)}\int_p^{p+\eta_1(q,p)}(\Omega(u,r)Y(u,r+\eta_2(s,r))+\Omega(u,r+\eta_2(s,r))Y(u,r))du. \quad (39)$$

Using (38) and (39) in (37), we get

$$8\Omega\left(p+\frac{1}{2}\eta_1(q,p),r+\frac{1}{2}\eta_2(s,r)\right)Y\left(p+\frac{1}{2}\eta_1(q,p),r+\frac{1}{2}\eta_2(s,r)\right)$$
$$\supseteq \frac{2}{\eta_1(q,p)\eta_2(s,r)}\int_p^{p+\eta_1(q,p)}\int_r^{r+\eta_2(s,r)}\Omega(u,v)Y(u,v)dvdu$$
$$+\frac{1}{3\eta_2(s,r)}\int_r^{r+\eta_2(s,r)}(\Omega(p,v)Y(p,v)+\Omega(p+\eta_1(q,p),v)Y(p+\eta_1(q,p),v)$$
$$+2\Omega(p,v)Y(p+\eta_1(q,p),v)+2\Omega(p+\eta_1(q,p),v)Y(p,v))dv$$
$$+\frac{1}{3\eta_1(q,p)}\int_p^{p+\eta_1(q,p)}(\Omega(u,r)Y(u,r)+\Omega(u,r+\eta_2(s,r))Y(u,r+\eta_2(s,r))$$
$$+2\Omega(u,r)Y(u,r+\eta_2(s,r))+2\Omega(u,r+\eta_2(s,r))Y(u,r))du$$
$$+\frac{1}{18}N_1(p,q,r,s)+\frac{1}{9}N_2(p,q,r,s)+\frac{1}{9}N_3(p,q,r,s)+\frac{2}{9}N_4(p,q,r,s). \quad (40)$$

Applying Corollary 3 for each integral in right side of (40), we obtain our desired result. □

Remark 6. *If we put $\eta_1(q,p)=q-p$ and $\eta_2(s,r)=s-r$ in Theorem 10, we obtain Theorem 9 of [34].*

4. Conclusions

In this article, we have introduced the concept of interval-valued preinvex functions on coordinates as a generalization of the convex interval-valued functions on coordinates. We have established H-H type inclusions for coordinated preinvex interval-valued functions. Moreover, some new H-H type inclusions for the product of two coordinated preinvex interval-valued functions are investigated. The results obtained in this paper may be extended for other kinds of interval-valued preinvex functions on the coordinates. In the future, we can investigate H-H type and H–H–Fejér type inclusions for interval-valued coordinated preinvex functions via interval-valued fractional integrals on coordinates. We hope that the ideas and results obtained in this article will encourage the readers towards further investigation.

Author Contributions: Formal analysis, K.K.L., S.K.M., J.B. and M.H.; funding acquisition, K.K.L.; investigation, K.K.L., S.K.M., J.B. and M.H.; methodology, J.B.; supervision, K.K.L. and S.K.M.; validation, J.B. and M.H.; writing—original draft preparation, S.K.M. and J.B.; writing—review and editing, J.B. and M.H. All authors have read and agreed to the published version of the manuscript.

Funding: The second author is financially supported by "Research Grant for Faculty" (IoE Scheme) under Dev. Scheme NO. 6031 and Department of Science and Technology, SERB, New Delhi, India through grant no.: MTR/2018/000121, and the third author is financially supported by the Ministry of Science and Technology, Department of Science and Technology, New Delhi, India, through Registration No. DST/INSPIRE Fellowship/[IF190355].

Institutional Review Board Statement: Not applicable.

Informed Consent Statement: Not applicable.

Data Availability Statement: No data were used to support this study.

Acknowledgments: The authors are indebted to the anonymous reviewers for their valuable comments and remarks that helped to improve the presentation and quality of the manuscript.

Conflicts of Interest: The authors declare no conflict of interest.

References

1. Kalsoom, H.; Latif, M.A.; Khan, Z.A.; Vivas-Cortez, M. Some New Hermite-Hadamard-Fejér fractional type inequalities for h-convex and harmonically h-Convex interval-valued Functions. *Mathematics* **2021**, *10*, 74. [CrossRef]
2. Sharma, N.; Bisht, J.; Mishra, S.K.; Hamdi, A. Some majorization integral inequalities for functions defined on rectangles via strong convexity. *J. Inequal. Spec. Funct.* **2019**, *10*, 21–34.
3. Khan, M.B.; Zaini, H.G.; Treanţă, S.; Soliman, M.S.; Nonlaopon, K. Riemann–Liouville fractional integral inequalities for generalized preinvex functions of interval-valued settings based upon pseudo order relation. *Mathematics* **2022**, *10*, 204. [CrossRef]
4. Sharma, N.; Mishra, S.K.; Hamdi, A. A weighted version of Hermite-Hadamard type inequalities for strongly GA-convex functions. *Int. J. Adv. Appl. Sci.* **2020**, *7*, 113–118.
5. Zhao, D.; An, T.; Ye, G.; Torres, D.F.M. On Hermite-Hadamard type inequalities for harmonical h-convex interval-valued functions. *Math. Inequal. Appl.* **2020**, *23*, 95–105.
6. Sharma, N.; Bisht, J.; Mishra, S.K. Hermite-Hadamard type inequalities for functions whose derivatives are strongly $\eta-$convex via fractional integrals. In *Indo-French Seminar on Optimization, Variational Analysis and Applications*; Springer: Berlin, Germany, 2020; pp. 83–102.
7. Hanson, M.A. On sufficiency of the kuhn-tucker conditions. *J. Math. Anal. Appl.* **1981**, *80*, 545–550. [CrossRef]
8. Craven, B.D.; Glover, B.M. Invex functions and duality. *J. Aust. Math. Soc.* **1985**, *39*, 1–20. [CrossRef]
9. Ben-Israel, A.; Mond, B. What is invexity? *ANZIAM J.* **1986**, *28*, 1–9. [CrossRef]
10. Mohan, S.R.; Neogy, S.K. On invex sets and preinvex functions. *J. Math. Anal. Appl.* **1995**, *189*, 901–908. [CrossRef]
11. Weir, T.; Jeyakumar, V. A class of nonconvex functions and mathematical programming. *Bull. Aust. Math. Soc.* **1988**, *38*, 177–189. [CrossRef]
12. Weir, T.; Mond, B. Preinvex functions in multiple objective optimization. *J. Math. Anal. Appl.* **1988**, *136*, 29–38. [CrossRef]
13. Noor, M.A. Hermite-Hadamard integral inequalities for log-preinvex functions. *J. Math. Anal. Approx. Theory* **2007**, *2*, 126–131.
14. Dragomir, S.S. On the Hadamard's inequlality for convex functions on the coordinates in a rectangle from the plane. *Taiwan J. Math.* **2001**, *5*, 775–788. [CrossRef]
15. Latif, M.A.; Dragomir, S.S. Some Hermite-Hadamard type inequalities for functions whose partial derivatives in absloute value are preinvex on the cooordinates. *Facta Univ. Math. Inform.* **2013**, *28*, 257–270.
16. Matłoka, M. On some Hadamard type inequalities for (h_1, h_2)-preinvex functions on the coordinates. *J. Inequal. Appl.* **2013**, *2013*, 1–12. [CrossRef]
17. Matłoka, M. On Some new inequalities for differentiable (h_1, h_2)-preinvex functions on the coordinates. *Math. Stat.* **2014**, *2*, 6–14. [CrossRef]
18. Mehmood, S.; Zafar, F.; Yasmin, N. Hermite-Hadamard-Fejér type inequalities for preinvex functions using fractional integrals. *Mathematics* **2019**, *7*, 467. [CrossRef]
19. Noor, M.A.; Noor, K.I.; Rashid, S. Some new classes of preinvex functions and inequalities. *Mathematics* **2019**, *7*, 29. [CrossRef]
20. Rashid, S.; Latif, M.A.; Hammouch, Z.; Chu, Y.M. Fractional integral inequalities for strongly h-preinvex functions for a kth order differentiable functions. *Symmetry* **2019**, *11*, 1448. [CrossRef]
21. Sharma, N.; Mishra, S.K.; Hamdi, A. Hermite-Hadamard type inequality for ψ-Riemann-Liouville fractional integrals via preinvex functions. *Int. J. Nonlinear Anal. Appl.* **2022**, *13*, 3333–3345.
22. Moore, R.E. *Interval Analysis*; Prentice-Hall: Englewood Cliffs, NJ, USA, 1966.
23. Moore, R.E. *Methods and Applications of Interval Analysis*; SIAM: Philadelphia, PA, USA, 1979.
24. Bhurjee, A.K.; Panda, G. Multi-objective interval fractional programming problems: An approach for obtaining efficient solutions. *Opsearch* **2015**, *52*, 156–167. [CrossRef]
25. Zhang, J.; Liu, S.; Li, L.; Feng, Q. The KKT optimality conditions in a class of generalized convex optimization problems with an interval-valued objective function. *Optim. Lett.* **2014**, *8*, 607–631. [CrossRef]
26. Zhao, D.; An, T.; Ye, G.; Liu, W. Chebyshev type inequalities for interval-valued functions. *Fuzzy Sets Syst.* **2020**, *396*, 82–101. [CrossRef]
27. Guo, Y.; Ye, G.; Zhao, D.; Liu, W. gH-symmetrically derivative of interval-valued functions and applications in interval-valued optimization. *Symmetry* **2019**, *11*, 1203. [CrossRef]
28. Moore, R.E.; Kearfott, R.B.; Cloud, M.J. *Introduction to Interval Analysis*; SIAM: Philadelphia, PA, USA, 2009.
29. Rothwell, E.J.; Cloud, M.J. Automatic error analysis using intervals. *IEEE Trans. Educ.* **2011**, *55*, 9–15. [CrossRef]
30. Snyder, J.M. Interval analysis for computer graphics. In Proceedings of the 19th Annual Conference on Computer Graphics and Interactive Techniques, Chicago, IL, USA, 27–31 July 1992; pp. 121–130.

31. Chalco-Cano, Y.; Lodwick, W.A.; Condori-Equice, W. Ostrowski type inequalities and applications in numerical integration for interval-valued functions. *Soft Comput.* **2015**, *19*, 3293–3300. [CrossRef]
32. Budak, H.; Tunç, T.; Sarikaya, M. Fractional Hermite-Hadamard type inequalities for interval-valued functions. *Proc. Amer. Math. Soc.* **2020**, *148*, 705–718. [CrossRef]
33. Sharma, N.; Singh, S.K.; Mishra, S.K.; Hamdi, A. Hermite-Hadamard type inequalities for interval-valued preinvex functions via Riemann–Liouville fractional integrals. *J. Inequal. Appl.* **2021**, *2021*, 98. [CrossRef]
34. Zhao, D.; Ali, M.A.; Murtaza, G.; Zhang, Z. On the Hermite-Hadamard inequalities for interval-valued coordinated convex functions. *Adv. Differ. Equ.* **2020**, *2020*, 1–14. [CrossRef]
35. Zhao, D.; Zhao, G.; Ye, G.; Liu, W.; Dragomir, S.S. On Hermite-Hadamard type inequalities for coordinated *h*-convex interval-valued functions. *Mathematics* **2021**, *9*, 2352. [CrossRef]
36. Budak, H.; Kara, H.; Ali, M.A.; Khan, S.; Chu, Y. Fractional Hermite-Hadamard-type inequalities for interval-valued coordinated convex functions. *Open Math.* **2021**, *19*, 1081–1097. [CrossRef]
37. Kara, H.; Budak, H.; Ali, M.A.; Sarikaya, M.Z.; Chu, Y.M. Weighted Hermite–Hadamard type inclusions for products of coordinated convex interval-valued functions. *Adv. Differ. Equ.* **2021**, *2021*, 104. [CrossRef]
38. Kara, H.; Ali, M.A.; Budak, H. Hermite-Hadamard type inequalities for interval-valued coordinated convex functions involving generalized fractional integrals. *Math. Methods Appl. Sci.* **2021**, *44*, 104–123. [CrossRef]
39. Lai, K.K.; Bisht, J.; Sharma, N.; Mishra, S.K. Hermite-Hadamard type fractional inclusions for interval-valued preinvex functions. *Mathematics* **2022**, *10*, 264. [CrossRef]
40. Shi, F.; Ye, G.; Zhao, D.; Liu, W. Some fractional Hermite-Hadamard type inequalities for interval-valued coordinated functions. *Adv. Differ. Equ.* **2021**, *2021*, 32. [CrossRef]
41. Tariboon, J.; Ali, M.A.; Budak, H.; Ntouyas, S.K. Hermite-Hadamard inclusions for coordinated interval-valued functions via post-quantum calculus. *Symmetry* **2021**, *13*, 1216. [CrossRef]
42. Du, T.; Zhou, T. On the fractional double integral inclusion relations having exponential kernels via interval-valued coordinated convex mappings. *Chaos Solitons Fractals* **2022**, *156*, 111846. [CrossRef]
43. Khan, M.B.; Santos-García, G.; Zaini, H.G.; Treanţă, S.; Soliman, M.S. Some new concepts related to integral operators and inequalities on coordinates in fuzzy fractional calculus. *Mathematics* **2022**, *10*, 534. [CrossRef]

symmetry

MDPI

Article

Fractional Calculus for Convex Functions in Interval-Valued Settings and Inequalities

Muhammad Bilal Khan [1], Hatim Ghazi Zaini [2], Savin Treanţă [3,*], Gustavo Santos-García [4,*], Jorge E. Macías-Díaz [5,6] and Mohamed S. Soliman [7]

1 Department of Mathematics, COMSATS University Islamabad, Islamabad 44000, Pakistan; bilal42742@gmail.com
2 Department of Computer Science, College of Computers and Information Technology, Taif University, P.O. Box 11099, Taif 21944, Saudi Arabia; h.zaini@tu.edu.sa
3 Department of Applied Mathematics, University Politehnica of Bucharest, 060042 Bucharest, Romania
4 Facultad de Economía y Empresa and Multidisciplinary Institute of Enterprise (IME), University of Salamanca, 37007 Salamanca, Spain
5 Departamento de Matemáticas y Física, Universidad Autónoma de Aguascalientes, Avenida Universidad 940, Ciudad Universitaria, Aguascalientes 20131, Mexico; jemacias@correo.uaa.mx
6 Department of Mathematics, School of Digital Technologies, Tallinn University, Narva Rd. 25, 10120 Tallinn, Estonia
7 Department of Electrical Engineering, College of Engineering, Taif University, P.O. Box 11099, Taif 21944, Saudi Arabia; soliman@tu.edu.sa
* Correspondence: savin.treanta@upb.ro (S.T.); santos@usal.es (G.S.-G.)

Abstract: In this paper, we discuss the Riemann–Liouville fractional integral operator for left and right convex interval-valued functions (left and right convex $I{\cdot}V$-F), as well as various related notions and concepts. First, the authors used the Riemann–Liouville fractional integral to prove Hermite–Hadamard type ($\mathcal{H}$–$\mathcal{H}$ type) inequality. Furthermore, $\mathcal{H}$–$\mathcal{H}$ type inequalities for the product of two left and right convex $I{\cdot}V$-Fs have been established. Finally, for left and right convex $I{\cdot}V$-Fs, we found the Riemann–Liouville fractional integral Hermite–Hadamard type inequality ($\mathcal{H}$–$\mathcal{H}$ Fejér type inequality). The findings of this research show that this methodology may be applied directly and is computationally simple and precise.

Keywords: left and right convex interval-valued function; fractional integral operator; Hermite–Hadamard type inequality; Hermite–Hadamard Fejér type inequality

Citation: Khan, M.B.; Zaini, H.G.; Treanţă, S.; Santos-García, G.; Macías-Díaz, J.E.; Soliman, M.S. Fractional Calculus for Convex Functions in Interval-Valued Settings and Inequalities. *Symmetry* **2022**, *14*, 341. https://doi.org/10.3390/sym14020341

Academic Editor: Clemente Cesarano

Received: 19 January 2022
Accepted: 4 February 2022
Published: 7 February 2022

Publisher's Note: MDPI stays neutral with regard to jurisdictional claims in published maps and institutional affiliations.

1. Introduction

Mathematical inequality, finance, engineering, statistics, and probability all use convex functions in some way. Convex and symmetric convex functions have strong relationships with inequalities. Because of their intriguing features in the mathematical sciences, there are expansive properties and strong links between the symmetric function and different fields of convexity, including convex functions, probability theory, and convex geometry on convex sets. Convex functions have a long and illustrious history in science, and they have been a hot focus of study for more than a century. Several researchers have proposed different convex function guesses, expansions, and variants. Many inequalities or equalities, such as the Ostrowski-type inequality, Hardy-type inequality, Opial-type inequality, Simpson inequality, Fejér-type inequality, and Cebysev-type inequalities, have been established using convex functions. Among these inequalities, the $\mathcal{H}$–$\mathcal{H}$ inequality [1,2], on which many publications have been published, is likely the one that attracts the most attention from scholars. $\mathcal{H}$–$\mathcal{H}$ inequality has been regarded as the most useful inequality in mathematical analysis since its discovery in 1883. It is also known as the conventional $\mathcal{H}$–$\mathcal{H}$ Inequality equation. The expansions and generalizations of the $\mathcal{H}$–$\mathcal{H}$ inequality have piqued the curiosity of a number of mathematicians. For various classes of convex functions and mappings, a number of mathematicians in the fields of pure and applied mathematics have worked to expand, generalize, counterpart, and enhance the $\mathcal{H}$–$\mathcal{H}$ inequality (references [3–13] are a good place to start for interested readers).

Historically, Leibnitz and L'Hospital (1695) are credited with the invention of fractional calculus; however, Riemann, Liouville, and Grunwald–Letnikov, among others, made significant contributions to the field later on. The way that fractional operator speculation deciphers nature's existence in a grand and intentional fashion [14–19] has piqued the curiosity of researchers. By offering an enhanced form of an integral representation for the Appell k-series, Mubeen and Iqbal [20] have contributed to the present research.

Moreover, Khan et al. [21] exploited fuzzy order relations to introduce a new class of convex fuzzy-interval-valued functions (convex *F-I·V-Fs*), known as (h_1, h_2)-convex *F-I·V-Fs*, as well as a novel version of the $\mathcal{H}$–$\mathcal{H}$ type inequality for (h_1, h_2)-convex *F-I·V-Fs* that incorporates the fuzzy interval Riemann integral. Khan et al. went a step further by providing new convex and extended convex *I·V-F* classes, as well as new fractional $\mathcal{H}$–$\mathcal{H}$ type and $\mathcal{H}$–$\mathcal{H}$ type inequalities for left and right (h_1, h_2)-preinvex *I·V-F* [22], left and right p-convex *I·V-Fs* [23], left and right log-h-convex *I·V-Fs* [24], and the references therein. For further analysis of the literature on the applications and properties of fuzzy Riemannian integrals, inequalities, and generalized convex fuzzy mappings, we refer the readers to cited works [25–56] and the references therein.

Motivated and inspired by the fascinating features of symmetry, convexity, and the fractional operator, we study the new $\mathcal{H}$–$\mathcal{H}$ and related $\mathcal{H}$–$\mathcal{H}$ type inequalities for left and right convex *I·V-Fs*, based upon the pseudo order relation and the Riemann–Liouville fractional integral operator.

2. Preliminaries

First, we offer some background information on interval-valued functions, the theory of convexity, interval-valued integration, and interval-valued fractional integration, which will be utilized throughout the article.

We offer some fundamental arithmetic regarding interval analysis in this paragraph, which will be quite useful throughout the article.

$$Y = [Y_*,\ Y^*],\ Q = [Q_*,\ Q^*]\ (Y_* \leq \omega \leq\ Y^*\ and\ Q_* \leq z \leq\ Q^*\ \ \omega,\ z \in \mathbb{R})$$

$$\begin{gathered} Y + Q = [Y_*,\ Y^*] + [Q_*,\ Q^*] = [Y_* + Q_*,\ Y^* + Q^*], \\ Y - Q = [Y_*,\ Y^*] - [Q_*,\ Q^*] = [Y_* - Q_*,\ Y^* - Q^*], \\ Y \times Q = [Y_*,\ Y^*] \times [Q_*,\ Q^*] = [\min\mathcal{K},\ \max\mathcal{K}] \\ \min\mathcal{K} = \min\{Y_*Q_*,\ Y^*Q_*,\ Y_*Q^*,\ Y^*Q^*\},\ \max\mathcal{K} = \max\{Y_*Q_*,\ Y^*Q_*,\ Y_*Q^*,\ Y^*Q^*\} \\ \nu.[Y_*,\ Y^*] = \begin{cases} [\nu Y_*,\ \nu Y^*] & \text{if } \nu > 0, \\ \{0\} & \text{if } \nu = 0, \\ [\nu Y^*, \nu Y_*] & \text{if } \nu < 0. \end{cases} \end{gathered}$$

Let $\mathcal{X}_I$, $\mathcal{X}_I^+$, $\mathcal{X}_I^-$ be the set of all closed intervals of $\mathbb{R}$, the set of all closed positive intervals of $\mathbb{R}$, and the set of all closed negative intervals of $\mathbb{R}$, respectively.

For $[Y_*,\ Y^*],\ [Q_*,\ Q^*] \in \mathcal{X}_I$, the inclusion " $\subseteq$ " is defined by $[Y_*,\ Y^*] \subseteq [Q_*,\ Q^*]$, if and only if, $Q_* \leq Y_*, Y^* \leq Q^*$.

Remark 1. *[21] The left and right relation " $\leq_p$ ", defined on $\mathcal{X}_I$ by $[Y_*,\ Y^*] \leq_p [Q_*,\ Q^*]$. , if and only if, $Y_* \leq Q_*,\ Y^* \leq Q^*$, for all $[Y_*,\ Y^*],\ [Q_*,\ Q^*] \in \mathcal{X}_I$, it is a pseudo order relation. For a given $[Y_*,\ Y^*],\ [Q_*,\ Q^*] \in \mathcal{X}_I$, we say that $[Y_*,\ Y^*] \leq_p [Q_*,\ Q^*]$, if and only if, $Y_* \leq Q_*,\ Y^* \leq Q^*$ or $Y_* \leq Q_*,\ Y^* < Q^*$.*

Theorem 1. *[33] If $Y : [t, s] \subset \mathbb{R} \to \mathcal{X}_I$ is an I·V-F on such that $Y(\omega) = [Y_*(\omega),\ Y^*(\omega)]$, then Y is Riemann integrable over $[t, s]$, if and only if, $Y_*$and Y^* are both Riemann integrable over $[t, s]$, such that*

$$(IR)\int_t^s Y(\omega)d\omega = \left[(R)\int_t^s Y_*(\omega)d\omega,\ (R)\int_t^s Y^*(\omega)d\omega\right].$$

Definition 1. *[28,30] Let $Y \in L([t,s], \mathcal{X}_I^+)$. Then, interval fractional integrals, $\mathcal{I}_{t+}^{\mathfrak{a}}$ and $\mathcal{I}_{s-}^{\mathfrak{a}}$, of order $\mathfrak{a} > 0$ are defined by*

$$\mathcal{I}_{t+}^{\mathfrak{a}}\ Y(\omega) = \frac{1}{\Gamma(\mathfrak{a})}\int_t^{\omega} (\omega - \nu)^{\mathfrak{a}-1} Y(\nu) d\nu, \quad (\omega > t), \tag{1}$$

and

$$\mathcal{I}_{s-}^{\mathfrak{a}}\ Y(\omega) = \frac{1}{\Gamma(\mathfrak{a})}\int_{\omega}^{s} (\nu - \omega)^{\mathfrak{a}-1} Y(\nu) d\nu, \quad (\omega < s), \tag{2}$$

respectively, where $\Gamma(\omega) = \int_0^{\infty} \nu^{\omega-1} e^{-\nu} d\nu$ is the Euler gamma function.

Definition 2. *[31] The I·V-F $Y : K \to \mathcal{X}_I^+$ is named as the left and right convex-I·V- F on convex set K if the coming inequality,*

$$Y(\nu\omega + (1-\nu)z\,) \le_p \nu Y(\omega) + (1 - \nu\zeta) Y(z), \tag{3}$$

holds for all $\omega,\ z \in K$ and $\nu \in [0,\ 1]$ we have. If inequality (3) is reversed, then Y is named as the left and right concave on K. Y is affine, if and only if, it is both left and right convex and left and right concave.

Theorem 2. *[31] Let $Y : K \to \mathcal{X}_I^+$ be an I·V-F, such that*

$$Y(\omega) = [Y_*(\omega),\ Y^*(\omega)],\ \forall\, \omega \in K \tag{4}$$

for all $\omega \in K$. Then, Y is a left and right convex I·V-F on K, if and only if, $Y_*(\omega)$ and $Y^*(\omega)$ both are convex functions.

3. Interval Fractional Hermite–Hadamard Inequalities

The major goal, and the main purpose of this section, is to develop a novel version of the $\mathcal{H}$–$\mathcal{H}$ inequalities in the mode of interval-valued left and right convex functions.

Theorem 3. *Let $Y : [s,\ t] \to \mathcal{X}_I^+$ be a left and right convex I·V-F on $[s,\ t]$ and provided by $Y(\omega) = [Y_*(\omega),\ Y^*(\omega)]$ for all $\omega \in [s,\ t]$. If $Y \in L([s,\ t], \mathcal{X}_I^+)$, then*

$$Y\left(\frac{s+t}{2}\right) \le_p \frac{\Gamma(\mathfrak{a}+1)}{2(t-s)^{\mathfrak{a}}}\left[\mathcal{I}_{s+}^{\mathfrak{a}}\ Y(t) + \mathcal{I}_{t-}^{\mathfrak{a}}\ Y(s)\right] \le_p \frac{Y(s) + Y(t)}{2}. \tag{5}$$

If $Y(\omega)$ is a left and right concave I·V-F, then

$$Y\left(\frac{s+t}{2}\right) \ge_p \frac{\Gamma(\mathfrak{a}+1)}{2(t-s)^{\mathfrak{a}}}\left[\mathcal{I}_{s+}^{\mathfrak{a}}\ Y(t) + \mathcal{I}_{t-}^{\mathfrak{a}}\ Y(s)\right] \ge_p \frac{Y(s) + Y(t)}{2}. \tag{6}$$

Proof. Let $Y : [s,\ t] \to \mathcal{X}_I^+$ be a left and right convex *I·V-F*. Then, by hypothesis, we have:

$$2Y\left(\frac{s+t}{2}\right) \le_p Y(\nu s + (1-\nu)t) + Y((1-\nu)s + \nu t).$$

Therefore, we have

$$2Y_*\left(\tfrac{s+t}{2}\right) \le Y_*(\nu s + (1-\nu)t) + Y_*((1-\nu)s + \nu t),$$
$$2Y^*\left(\tfrac{s+t}{2}\right) \le Y^*(\nu s + (1-\nu)t) + Y^*((1-\nu)s + \nu t).$$

Multiplying both sides by $v^{\mathfrak{a}-1}$ and integrating the obtained result, with respect to v over $(0,1)$, we have

$$2\int_0^1 v^{\mathfrak{a}-1}Y_*\left(\tfrac{s+t}{2}\right)dv$$
$$\leq \int_0^1 v^{\mathfrak{a}-1}Y_*(vs+(1-v)t)dv + \int_0^1 v^{\mathfrak{a}-1}Y_*((1-v)s+vt)dv,$$
$$2\int_0^1 v^{\mathfrak{a}-1}Y^*\left(\tfrac{s+t}{2}\right)dv$$
$$\leq \int_0^1 v^{\mathfrak{a}-1}Y^*(vs+(1-v)t)dv + \int_0^1 v^{\mathfrak{a}-1}Y^*((1-v)s+vt)dv.$$

Let $\omega = vs + (1-v)t$ and $z = (1-v)s + vt$. Then, we have

$$\tfrac{2}{\mathfrak{a}}Y_*\left(\tfrac{s+t}{2}\right) \leq \tfrac{1}{(t-s)^{\mathfrak{a}}}\int_s^t (t-z)^{\mathfrak{a}-1}Y_*(z)dz + \tfrac{1}{(t-s)^{\mathfrak{a}}}\int_s^t (\omega-s)^{\mathfrak{a}-1}Y_*(\omega)d\omega$$

$$\tfrac{2}{\mathfrak{a}}Y_*\left(\tfrac{s+t}{2}\right) \leq \tfrac{1}{(t-s)^{\mathfrak{a}}}\int_s^t (t-z)^{\mathfrak{a}-1}Y^*(z)dz + \tfrac{1}{(t-s)^{\mathfrak{a}}}\int_s^t (\omega-s)^{\mathfrak{a}-1}Y^*(\omega)d\omega,$$

$$\leq \tfrac{\Gamma(\mathfrak{a})}{(t-s)^{\mathfrak{a}}}[\mathcal{I}_{s+}^{\mathfrak{a}} Y_*(t) + \mathcal{I}_{t-}^{\mathfrak{a}} Y_*(s)]$$
$$\leq \tfrac{\Gamma(\mathfrak{a})}{(t-s)^{\mathfrak{a}}}[\mathcal{I}_{s+}^{\mathfrak{a}} Y^*(t) + \mathcal{I}_{t-}^{\mathfrak{a}} Y^*(s)],$$

That is,

$$\tfrac{2}{\mathfrak{a}}\left[Y_*\left(\tfrac{s+t}{2}\right), Y^*\left(\tfrac{s+t}{2}\right)\right] \leq_p \tfrac{\Gamma(\mathfrak{a})}{(t-s)^{\mathfrak{a}}}\left[[\mathcal{I}_{s+}^{\mathfrak{a}} Y_*(t) + \mathcal{I}_{t-}^{\mathfrak{a}} Y_*(s)], [\mathcal{I}_{s+}^{\mathfrak{a}} Y^*(t) + \mathcal{I}_{t-}^{\mathfrak{a}} Y^*(s)]\right]$$

Thus:

$$\tfrac{2}{\mathfrak{a}}Y\left(\tfrac{s+t}{2}\right) \leq_p \tfrac{\Gamma(\mathfrak{a})}{(t-s)^{\mathfrak{a}}}[\mathcal{I}_{s+}^{\mathfrak{a}} Y(t) + \mathcal{I}_{t-}^{\mathfrak{a}} Y(s)] \qquad (7)$$

Similar to the above, we have

$$\tfrac{\Gamma(\mathfrak{a})}{(t-s)^{\mathfrak{a}}}[\mathcal{I}_{s+}^{\mathfrak{a}} Y(t) + \mathcal{I}_{t-}^{\mathfrak{a}} Y(s)] \leq_p \tfrac{Y(s)+Y(t)}{2} \qquad (8)$$

Combining (7) and (8), we have

$$Y\left(\tfrac{s+t}{2}\right) \leq_p \tfrac{\Gamma(\mathfrak{a}+1)}{2(t-s)^{\mathfrak{a}}}[\mathcal{I}_{s+}^{\mathfrak{a}} Y(t) + \mathcal{I}_{t-}^{\mathfrak{a}} Y(s)] \leq_p \tfrac{Y(s)+Y(t)}{2}$$

Hence, we achieve the required result. □

Remark 2. *We may observe from Theorem 3 that:*
Let one take $\alpha = 1$*. Then, from Theorem 1 and (5), we achieve the coming inequality (see [23]):*

$$Y\left(\tfrac{s+t}{2}\right) \leq_p \tfrac{1}{t-s}\int_s^t Y(\omega)d\omega \leq_p \tfrac{Y(s)+Y(t)}{2}$$

If we take $Y_*(\omega) = Y^*(\omega)$*, then from Theorem 3 and (5), we acquire the coming inequality (see [32]):*

$$Y\left(\tfrac{s+t}{2}\right) \leq \tfrac{\Gamma(\mathfrak{a}+1)}{2(t-s)^{\mathfrak{a}}}[\mathcal{I}_{s+}^{\mathfrak{a}} Y(t) + \mathcal{I}_{t-}^{\mathfrak{a}} Y(s)] \leq \tfrac{Y(s)+Y(t)}{2}$$

Let one take $\mathfrak{a} = 1$ *and* $Y_*(\omega) = Y^*(\omega)$*. Then, from Theorem 1 and (5), we achieve classical* $\mathcal{H}$-$\mathcal{H}$ *type inequality.*

Example 1. *Let* $\mathfrak{a} = \tfrac{1}{2}$*,* $\omega \in [2,3]$*, and the I·V-F* $Y : [s,t] = [2,3] \to \mathcal{X}_I^+$*, provided by* $Y(\omega) = [1,2]\left(2 - \omega^{\frac{1}{2}}\right)$*. Since the left and right endpoint functions,* $Y_*(\omega) = 2 - \omega^{\frac{1}{2}}, Y^*(\omega) =$

$2\left(2-\omega^{\frac{1}{2}}\right)$, *are left and right convex functions, then* $Y(\omega)$ *is a left and right convex I·V-F. We clearly see that* $Y \in L([s,\ t], \mathcal{X}_I^+)$, *and*

$$Y_*\left(\frac{s+t}{2}\right) = Y_*\left(\frac{5}{2}\right) = \frac{4-\sqrt{10}}{2}$$
$$Y^*\left(\frac{s+t}{2}\right) = Y^*\left(\frac{5}{2}\right) = 4-\sqrt{10}$$
$$\frac{Y_*(s)+Y_*(t)}{2} = \frac{4-\sqrt{2}-\sqrt{3}}{2}$$
$$\frac{Y^*(s)+Y^*(t)}{2} = 4-\sqrt{2}-\sqrt{3}$$

Note that

$$\frac{\Gamma(\alpha+1)}{2(t-s)^{\alpha}}\left[\mathcal{I}_{s^+}^{\alpha}\ Y_*(t) + \mathcal{I}_{t^-}^{\alpha}\ Y_*(s)\right]$$
$$= \frac{\Gamma\left(\frac{3}{2}\right)}{2}\frac{1}{\sqrt{\pi}}\int_2^3 (3-\omega)^{\frac{-1}{2}}\,.\left(2-\omega^{\frac{1}{2}}\right)d\omega$$
$$+\frac{\Gamma\left(\frac{3}{2}\right)}{2}\frac{1}{\sqrt{\pi}}\int_2^3 (\omega-2)^{\frac{-1}{2}}\,.\left(2-\omega^{\frac{1}{2}}\right)d\omega$$
$$= \frac{1}{4}\left[\frac{7393}{10{,}000} + \frac{9501}{10{,}000}\right]$$
$$= \frac{8447}{20{,}000}.$$
$$\frac{\Gamma(\alpha+1)}{2(t-s)^{\alpha}}\left[\mathcal{I}_{s^+}^{\alpha}\ Y^*(t) + \mathcal{I}_{t^-}^{\alpha}\ Y^*(s)\right]$$
$$= \frac{\Gamma\left(\frac{3}{2}\right)}{2}\frac{1}{\sqrt{\pi}}\int_2^3 (3-\omega)^{\frac{-1}{2}}\,.2\left(2-\omega^{\frac{1}{2}}\right)d\omega$$
$$+\frac{\Gamma\left(\frac{3}{2}\right)}{2}\frac{1}{\sqrt{\pi}}\int_2^3 (\omega-2)^{\frac{-1}{2}}\,.2\left(2-\omega^{\frac{1}{2}}\right)d\omega$$
$$= \frac{1}{2}\left[\frac{7393}{10{,}000} + \frac{9501}{10{,}000}\right]$$
$$= \frac{8447}{10{,}000}$$

Therefore,

$$\left[\frac{4-\sqrt{10}}{2}, 4-\sqrt{10}\right] \leq_p \left[\frac{8447}{20{,}000}, \frac{8447}{10{,}000}\right] \leq_p \left[\frac{4-\sqrt{2}-\sqrt{3}}{2}, 4-\sqrt{2}-\sqrt{3}\right]$$

and Theorem 3 is verified.

The upcoming two results acquire the fractional inequalities for the product of left and right convex *I·V-Fs*.

Theorem 4. *Let* $Y, \mathfrak{G} : [s,\ t] \to \mathcal{X}_I^+$ *be two left and right convex I·V-Fs on* $[s,\ t]$, *provided by* $Y(\omega) = [Y_*(\omega),\ Y^*(\omega)]$ *and* $\mathfrak{G}(\omega) = [\mathfrak{G}_*(\omega),\ \mathfrak{G}^*(\omega)]$ *for all* $\omega \in [s,\ t]$. *If* $Y \times \mathfrak{G} \in L([s,\ t], \mathcal{X}_I^+)$, *then*

$$\frac{\Gamma(\alpha)}{2(t-s)^{\alpha}}\left[\mathcal{I}_{s^+}^{\alpha}\ Y(t)\times\mathfrak{G}(t) + \mathcal{I}_{t^-}^{\alpha} Y(s)\times\mathfrak{G}(s)\right]$$
$$\leq_p \left(\frac{1}{2} - \frac{\alpha}{(\alpha+1)(\alpha+2)}\right)\varphi(s,t) + \left(\frac{\alpha}{(\alpha+1)(\alpha+2)}\right)\nabla(s,t)$$

where $\varphi(s,t) = Y(s)\times\mathfrak{G}(s) + Y(t)\times\mathfrak{G}(t)$, $\nabla(s,t) = Y(s)\times\mathfrak{G}(t) + Y(t)\times\mathfrak{G}(s)$, and $\varphi(s,t) = [\varphi_*(s,t),\ \varphi^*(s,t)]$ and $\nabla(s,t) = [\nabla_*(s,t),\ \nabla^*(s,t)]$.

Proof. Since Y, $\mathfrak{G}$ are both left and right convex *I·V-Fs*, then we have

$$Y_*(\nu s + (1-\nu)t) \leq \nu Y_*(s) + (1-\nu)Y_*(t),$$

$$Y^*(\nu s + (1-\nu)t) \leq \nu Y^*(s) + (1-\nu)Y^*(t).$$

and

$$\mathfrak{G}_*(\nu s + (1-\nu)t) \leq \nu \mathfrak{G}_*(s) + (1-\nu)\mathfrak{G}_*(t),$$

$$\mathfrak{G}^*(\nu s + (1-\nu)t) \leq \nu \mathfrak{G}^*(s) + (1-\nu)\mathfrak{G}^*(t).$$

From the definition of left and right convex $I\cdot V$-Fs, it follows that $0 \leq_p Y(\omega)$ and $0 \leq_p \mathfrak{G}(\omega)$, so

$$\begin{aligned}
Y_*(\nu s + (1-\nu)t) &\times \mathfrak{G}_*(\nu s + (1-\nu)t) \\
&\leq (\nu Y_*(s) + (1-\nu)Y_*(t))(\nu \mathfrak{G}_*(s) + (1-\nu)\mathfrak{G}_*(t)) \\
&= \nu^2 Y_*(s) \times \mathfrak{G}_*(s) + (1-\nu)^2 Y_*(t) \times \mathfrak{G}_*(t) \\
&\quad + \nu(1-\nu)Y_*(s) \times \mathfrak{G}_*(t) + \nu(1-\nu)Y_*(t) \times \mathfrak{G}_*(s) \\
Y^*(\nu s + (1-\nu)t) &\times \mathfrak{G}^*(\nu s + (1-\nu)t) \\
&\leq (\nu Y^*(s) + (1-\nu)Y^*(t))(\nu \mathfrak{G}^*(s) + (1-\nu)\mathfrak{G}^*(t)) \\
&= \nu^2 Y^*(s) \times \mathfrak{G}^*(s) + (1-\nu)^2 Y^*(t) \times \mathfrak{G}^*(t) \\
&\quad + \nu(1-\nu)Y^*(s) \times \mathfrak{G}^*(t) + \nu(1-\nu)Y^*(t) \times \mathfrak{G}^*(s),
\end{aligned} \quad (9)$$

Analogously, we have

$$\begin{aligned}
Y_*((1-\nu)s + \nu t) &\mathfrak{G}_*((1-\nu)s + \nu t) \\
&\leq (1-\nu)^2 Y_*(s) \times \mathfrak{G}_*(s) + \nu^2 Y_*(t) \times \mathfrak{G}_*(t) \\
&\quad + \nu(1-\nu)Y_*(s) \times \mathfrak{G}_*(t) + \nu(1-\nu)Y_*(t) \times \mathfrak{G}_*(s) \\
Y^*((1-\nu)s + \nu t) &\times \mathfrak{G}^*((1-\nu)s + \nu t) \\
&\leq (1-\nu)^2 Y^*(s) \times \mathfrak{G}^*(s) + \nu^2 Y^*(t) \times \mathfrak{G}^*(t) \\
&\quad + \nu(1-\nu)Y^*(s) \times \mathfrak{G}^*(t) + \nu(1-\nu)Y^*(t) \times \mathfrak{G}^*(s).
\end{aligned} \quad (10)$$

Adding (9) and (10), we have

$$\begin{aligned}
Y_*(\nu s + (1-\nu)t) &\times \mathfrak{G}_*(\nu s + (1-\nu)t) \\
+ Y_*((1-\nu)s + \nu t) &\times \mathfrak{G}_*((1-\nu)s + \nu t) \\
&\leq \left[\nu^2 + (1-\nu)^2\right][Y_*(s) \times \mathfrak{G}_*(s) + Y_*(t) \times \mathfrak{G}_*(t)] \\
&\quad + 2\nu(1-\nu)[Y_*(t) \times \mathfrak{G}_*(s) + Y_*(s) \times \mathfrak{G}_*(t)] \\
Y^*(\nu s + (1-\nu)t) &\times \mathfrak{G}^*(\nu s + (1-\nu)t) \\
+ Y^*((1-\nu)s + \nu t) &\times \mathfrak{G}^*((1-\nu)s + \nu t) \\
&\leq \left[\nu^2 + (1-\nu)^2\right][Y^*(s) \times \mathfrak{G}^*(s) + Y^*(t) \times \mathfrak{G}^*(t)] \\
&\quad + 2\nu(1-\nu)[Y^*(t) \times \mathfrak{G}^*(s) + Y^*(s) \times \mathfrak{G}^*(t)].
\end{aligned} \quad (11)$$

Taking the multiplication of (11) by $\nu^{\mathfrak{a}-1}$ and integrating the obtained result, with respect to ν over $(0, 1)$, we have

$$\begin{aligned}
\int_0^1 \nu^{\mathfrak{a}-1} Y_*(\nu s &+ (1-\nu)t) \times \mathfrak{G}_*(\nu s + (1-\nu)t) \\
+ \nu^{\mathfrak{a}-1} Y_*((1-\nu)s &+ \nu t) \times \mathfrak{G}_*((1-\nu)s + \nu t) d\nu \\
&\leq \varphi_*(s,t) \int_0^1 \nu^{\mathfrak{a}-1}\left[\nu^2 + (1-\nu)^2\right]d\nu + 2\nabla_*(s,t)\int_0^1 \nu^{\mathfrak{a}-1}\nu(1-\nu)d\nu \\
\int_0^1 \nu^{\mathfrak{a}-1} Y^*(\nu s &+ (1-\nu)t) \times \mathfrak{G}^*(\nu s + (1-\nu)t) \\
+ \nu^{\mathfrak{a}-1} Y^*((1-\nu)s &+ \nu t) \times \mathfrak{G}^*((1-\nu)s + \nu t) d\nu \\
&\leq \varphi^*(s,t) \int_0^1 \nu^{\mathfrak{a}-1}\left[\nu^2 + (1-\nu)^2\right]d\nu + 2\nabla^*(s,t)\int_0^1 \nu^{\mathfrak{a}-1}\nu(1-\nu)d\nu.
\end{aligned}$$

It follows that

$$\frac{\Gamma(\mathfrak{a})}{(t-s)^{\mathfrak{a}}}\left[\mathcal{I}^{\mathfrak{a}}_{s^+} Y_*(t) \times \mathfrak{G}_*(t) + \mathcal{I}^{\mathfrak{a}}_{t^-} Y_*(s) \times \mathfrak{G}_*(s)\right]$$
$$\leq \frac{2}{\mathfrak{a}}\left(\frac{1}{2} - \frac{\mathfrak{a}}{(\mathfrak{a}+1)(\mathfrak{a}+2)}\right)\varphi_*(s,t) + \frac{2}{\mathfrak{a}}\left(\frac{\mathfrak{a}}{(\mathfrak{a}+1)(\mathfrak{a}+2)}\right)\nabla_*(s,t)$$
$$\frac{\Gamma(\mathfrak{a})}{(t-s)^{\mathfrak{a}}}\left[\mathcal{I}^{\mathfrak{a}}_{s^+} Y^*(t) \times \mathfrak{G}^*(t) + \mathcal{I}^{\mathfrak{a}}_{t^-} Y^*(s) \times \mathfrak{G}^*(s)\right]$$
$$\leq \frac{2}{\mathfrak{a}}\left(\frac{1}{2} - \frac{\mathfrak{a}}{(\mathfrak{a}+1)(\mathfrak{a}+2)}\right)\varphi^*(s,t) + \frac{2}{\mathfrak{a}}\left(\frac{\mathfrak{a}}{(\mathfrak{a}+1)(\mathfrak{a}+2)}\right)\nabla^*(s,t),$$

$$\frac{\Gamma(\mathfrak{a})}{(t-s)^{\mathfrak{a}}}\left[\mathcal{I}^{\mathfrak{a}}_{s^+} Y_*(t) \times \mathfrak{G}_*(t) + \mathcal{I}^{\mathfrak{a}}_{t^-} Y_*(s) \times \mathfrak{G}_*(s)\right]$$
$$\leq \frac{2}{\mathfrak{a}}\left(\frac{1}{2} - \frac{\mathfrak{a}}{(\mathfrak{a}+1)(\mathfrak{a}+2)}\right)\varphi_*(s,t) + \frac{2}{\mathfrak{a}}\left(\frac{\mathfrak{a}}{(\mathfrak{a}+1)(\mathfrak{a}+2)}\right)\nabla_*(s,t)$$
$$\frac{\Gamma(\mathfrak{a})}{(t-s)^{\mathfrak{a}}}\left[\mathcal{I}^{\mathfrak{a}}_{s^+} Y^*(t) \times \mathfrak{G}^*(t) + \mathcal{I}^{\mathfrak{a}}_{t^-} Y^*(s) \times \mathfrak{G}^*(s)\right]$$
$$\leq \frac{2}{\mathfrak{a}}\left(\frac{1}{2} - \frac{\mathfrak{a}}{(\mathfrak{a}+1)(\mathfrak{a}+2)}\right)\varphi^*(s,t) + \frac{2}{\mathfrak{a}}\left(\frac{\mathfrak{a}}{(\mathfrak{a}+1)(\mathfrak{a}+2)}\right)\nabla^*(s,t),$$

That is,

$$\frac{\Gamma(\mathfrak{a})}{(t-s)^{\mathfrak{a}}}\left[\mathcal{I}^{\mathfrak{a}}_{s^+} Y_*(t) \times \mathfrak{G}_*(t) + \mathcal{I}^{\mathfrak{a}}_{t^-} Y_*(s) \times \mathfrak{G}_*(s), \mathcal{I}^{\mathfrak{a}}_{s^+} Y^*(t) \times \mathfrak{G}^*(t) + \mathcal{I}^{\mathfrak{a}}_{t^-} Y^*(s) \times \mathfrak{G}^*(s)\right]$$
$$\leq_p \frac{2}{\mathfrak{a}}\left(\frac{1}{2} - \frac{\mathfrak{a}}{(\mathfrak{a}+1)(\mathfrak{a}+2)}\right)[\varphi_*(s,t), \varphi^*(s,t)] + \frac{2}{\mathfrak{a}}\left(\frac{\mathfrak{a}}{(\mathfrak{a}+1)(\mathfrak{a}+2)}\right)[\nabla_*(s,t), \nabla^*(s,t)]$$

Thus,

$$\frac{\Gamma(\mathfrak{a})}{2(t-s)^{\mathfrak{a}}}\left[\mathcal{I}^{\mathfrak{a}}_{s^+} Y(t) \times \mathfrak{G}(t) + \mathcal{I}^{\mathfrak{a}}_{t^-} Y(s) \times \mathfrak{G}(s)\right]$$
$$\leq_p \left(\frac{1}{2} - \frac{\mathfrak{a}}{(\mathfrak{a}+1)(\mathfrak{a}+2)}\right)\varphi(s,t) + \left(\frac{\mathfrak{a}}{(\mathfrak{a}+1)(\mathfrak{a}+2)}\right)\nabla(s,t)$$

and the theorem has been established. □

Example 2. *Let* $[s,t] = [0,2]$, $\mathfrak{a} = \frac{1}{2}$, $Y(\omega) = \left[\frac{\omega}{2}, \frac{3\omega}{2}\right]$, *and* $\mathfrak{G}(\omega) = [\omega, 3\omega]$. *Since the left and right endpoint functions,* $Y_*(\omega) = \frac{\omega}{2}$, $Y^*(\omega) = \frac{3\omega}{2}$, $\mathfrak{G}_*(\omega) = \omega$ *and* $\mathfrak{G}^*(\omega) = 3\omega$, *are left and right convex functions, then* $Y(\omega)$ *and* $\mathfrak{G}(\omega)$ *are both left and right convex I·V-Fs. We clearly see that* $Y(\omega) \times \mathfrak{G}(\omega) \in L\big([s,t], \mathcal{X}^+_I\big)$, *and*

$$\frac{\Gamma(1+\mathfrak{a})}{2(t-s)^{\mathfrak{a}}}\left[\mathcal{I}^{\mathfrak{a}}_{s^+} Y_*(t) \times \mathfrak{G}_*(t) + \mathcal{I}^{\mathfrak{a}}_{t^-} Y_*(s) \times \mathfrak{G}_*(s)\right]$$
$$= \frac{\Gamma(\frac{3}{2})}{2\sqrt{2}}\frac{1}{\sqrt{\pi}}\int_0^2 (2-\omega)^{\frac{-1}{2}}\left(\frac{1}{2}.\omega^2\right)d\omega + \frac{\Gamma(\frac{3}{2})}{2\sqrt{2}}\frac{1}{\sqrt{\pi}}\int_0^2 (\omega)^{\frac{-1}{2}}\left(\frac{1}{2}.\omega^2\right)d\omega \approx 0.7333,$$
$$\frac{\Gamma(1+\mathfrak{a})}{2(t-s)^{\mathfrak{a}}}\left[\mathcal{I}^{\mathfrak{a}}_{s^+} Y^*(t) \times \mathfrak{G}^*(t) + \mathcal{I}^{\mathfrak{a}}_{t^-} Y^*(s) \times \mathfrak{G}^*(s)\right]$$
$$= \frac{\Gamma(\frac{3}{2})}{2\sqrt{2}}\frac{1}{\sqrt{\pi}}\int_0^2 (2-\omega)^{\frac{-1}{2}}.\frac{9}{2}\omega^2 d\omega + \frac{\Gamma(\frac{3}{2})}{2\sqrt{2}}\frac{1}{\sqrt{\pi}}\int_0^2 (\omega)^{\frac{-1}{2}}.\frac{9}{2}\omega^2 d\omega \approx 6.5997,$$

Note that

$$\left(\frac{1}{2} - \frac{\mathfrak{a}}{(\mathfrak{a}+1)(\mathfrak{a}+2)}\right)\varphi_*(s,t) = [Y_*(s) \times \mathfrak{G}_*(s) + Y_*(t) \times \mathfrak{G}_*(t)] = \frac{11}{15},$$
$$\left(\frac{1}{2} - \frac{\mathfrak{a}}{(\mathfrak{a}+1)(\mathfrak{a}+2)}\right)\varphi^*(s,t) = [Y^*(s) \times \mathfrak{G}^*(s) + Y^*(t) \times \mathfrak{G}^*(t)] = \frac{33}{5},$$
$$\left(\frac{\mathfrak{a}}{(\mathfrak{a}+1)(\mathfrak{a}+2)}\right)\nabla_*(s,t) = [Y_*(s) \times \mathfrak{G}_*(t) + Y_*(t) \times \mathfrak{G}_*(s)] = \frac{2}{15}(0),$$
$$\left(\frac{\mathfrak{a}}{(\mathfrak{a}+1)(\mathfrak{a}+2)}\right)\nabla_*(s,t) = [Y^*(s) \times \mathfrak{G}^*(t) + Y^*(t) \times \mathfrak{G}^*(s)] = \frac{2}{15}(0).$$

Therefore, we have

$$\left(\frac{1}{2} - \frac{\mathfrak{a}}{(\mathfrak{a}+1)(\mathfrak{a}+2)}\right)\varphi(s,t) + \left(\frac{\mathfrak{a}}{(\mathfrak{a}+1)(\mathfrak{a}+2)}\right)\nabla(s,t)$$
$$= \left[\frac{11}{15}, \frac{33}{5}\right] + \frac{2}{15}[0,0] = \left[\frac{11}{15}, \frac{33}{5}\right].$$

It follows that

$$[0.7333,\ 6.5997] \leq_p \left[\frac{11}{15}, \frac{33}{5}\right]$$

and Theorem 4 has been demonstrated.

Theorem 5. *Let $Y, \mathfrak{G} : [s,\ t] \to \mathcal{X}_I^+$ be two left and right convex I·V-Fs, provided by $Y(\omega) = [Y_*(\omega),\ Y^*(\omega)]$ and $\mathfrak{G}(\omega) = [\mathfrak{G}_*(\omega),\ \mathfrak{G}^*(\omega)]$ for all $\omega \in [s,\ t]$. If $Y \times \mathfrak{G} \in L([s,\ t], \mathcal{X}_I^+)$, then*

$$\begin{aligned}\tfrac{1}{\mathfrak{a}}\, Y\left(\tfrac{s+t}{2}\right) \times \mathfrak{G}\left(\tfrac{s+t}{2}\right) \leq_p & \tfrac{\Gamma(\mathfrak{a}+1)}{4(t-s)^{\mathfrak{a}}}\left[\mathcal{I}_{s^+}^{\mathfrak{a}}\ Y(t) \times \mathfrak{G}(t) + \mathcal{I}_{t^-}^{\mathfrak{a}}\ Y(s) \times \mathfrak{G}(s)\right] \\ & + \tfrac{1}{2\mathfrak{a}}\left(\tfrac{1}{2} - \tfrac{\mathfrak{a}}{(\mathfrak{a}+1)(\mathfrak{a}+2)}\right)\nabla(s,t) + \tfrac{1}{2\mathfrak{a}}\left(\tfrac{\mathfrak{a}}{(\mathfrak{a}+1)(\mathfrak{a}+2)}\right)\varphi(s,t)\end{aligned}$$

where $\varphi(s,t) = Y(s) \times \mathfrak{G}(s) + Y(t) \times \mathfrak{G}(t)$, $\nabla(s,t) = Y(s) \times \mathfrak{G}(t) + Y(t) \times \mathfrak{G}(s)$, $\varphi(s,t) = [\varphi_*(s,t),\ \varphi^*(s,t)]$, and $\nabla(s,t) = [\nabla_*(s,t),\ \nabla^*(s,t)]$.

Proof. Consider that $Y, \mathfrak{G} : [s,\ t] \to \mathcal{X}_I^+$ are left and right convex *I·V-Fs*. Then, by hypothesis, we have

$$\begin{aligned} & Y_*\left(\tfrac{s+t}{2}\right) \times \mathfrak{G}_*\left(\tfrac{s+t}{2}\right) \\ & Y^*\left(\tfrac{s+t}{2}\right) \times \mathfrak{G}^*\left(\tfrac{s+t}{2}\right) \\ \leq & \tfrac{1}{4}\left[\begin{array}{c} Y_*(\nu s+(1-\nu)t) \times \mathfrak{G}_*(\nu s+(1-\nu)t) \\ +Y_*(\nu s+(1-\nu)t) \times \mathfrak{G}_*((1-\nu)s+\nu t) \end{array}\right] \\ & +\tfrac{1}{4}\left[\begin{array}{c} Y_*((1-\nu)s+\nu t) \times \mathfrak{G}_*(\nu s+(1-\nu)t) \\ +Y_*((1-\nu)s+\nu t) \times \mathfrak{G}_*((1-\nu)s+\nu t) \end{array}\right] \\ \leq & \tfrac{1}{4}\left[\begin{array}{c} Y^*(\nu s+(1-\nu)t) \times \mathfrak{G}^*(\nu s+(1-\nu)t) \\ +Y^*(\nu s+(1-\nu)t) \times \mathfrak{G}^*((1-\nu)s+\nu t) \end{array}\right] \\ & +\tfrac{1}{4}\left[\begin{array}{c} Y^*((1-\nu)s+\nu t) \times \mathfrak{G}^*(\nu s+(1-\nu)t) \\ +Y^*((1-\nu)s+\nu t) \times \mathfrak{G}^*((1-\nu)s+\nu t) \end{array}\right], \\ \leq & \tfrac{1}{4}\left[\begin{array}{c} Y_*(\nu s+(1-\nu)t) \times \mathfrak{G}_*(\nu s+(1-\nu)t) \\ +Y_*((1-\nu)s+\nu t) \times \mathfrak{G}_*((1-\nu)s+\nu t) \end{array}\right] \\ & +\tfrac{1}{4}\left[\begin{array}{c} (\nu Y_*(s)+(1-\nu)Y_*(t)) \\ \times((1-\nu)\mathfrak{G}_*(s)+\nu\mathfrak{G}_*(t)) \\ +((1-\nu)Y_*(s)+\nu Y_*(t)) \\ \times(\nu\mathfrak{G}_*(s)+(1-\nu)\mathfrak{G}_*(t)) \end{array}\right] \\ \leq & \tfrac{1}{4}\left[\begin{array}{c} Y^*(\nu s+(1-\nu)t) \times \mathfrak{G}^*(\nu s+(1-\nu)t) \\ +Y^*((1-\nu)s+\nu t) \times \mathfrak{G}^*((1-\nu)s+\nu t) \end{array}\right] \\ & +\tfrac{1}{4}\left[\begin{array}{c} (\nu Y^*(s)+(1-\nu)Y^*(t)) \\ \times((1-\nu)\mathfrak{G}^*(s)+\nu\mathfrak{G}^*(t)) \\ +((1-\nu)Y^*(s)+\nu Y^*(t)) \\ \times(\nu\mathfrak{G}^*(s)+(1-\nu)\mathfrak{G}^*(t)) \end{array}\right], \\ = & \tfrac{1}{4}\left[\begin{array}{c} Y_*(\nu s+(1-\nu)t) \times \mathfrak{G}_*(\nu s+(1-\nu)t) \\ +Y_*((1-\nu)s+\nu t) \times \mathfrak{G}_*((1-\nu)s+\nu t) \end{array}\right] \\ & +\tfrac{1}{4}\left[\begin{array}{c} \left\{\nu^2+(1-\nu)^2\right\}\nabla_*(s,t) \\ +\{\nu(1-\nu)+(1-\nu)\nu\}\varphi_*(s,t) \end{array}\right] \\ = & \tfrac{1}{4}\left[\begin{array}{c} Y^*(\nu s+(1-\nu)t) \times \mathfrak{G}^*(\nu s+(1-\nu)t) \\ +Y^*((1-\nu)s+\nu t) \times \mathfrak{G}^*((1-\nu)s+\nu t) \end{array}\right] \\ & +\tfrac{1}{4}\left[\begin{array}{c} \left\{\nu^2+(1-\nu)^2\right\}\nabla^*(s,t) \\ +\{\nu(1-\nu)+(1-\nu)\nu\}\varphi^*(s,t) \end{array}\right]. \end{aligned} \tag{12}$$

Taking the multiplication of (12) with $\nu^{\alpha-1}$ and integrating over $(0,\ 1)$, we get

$$\begin{aligned}
&\tfrac{1}{\alpha}\,Y_*\left(\tfrac{s+t}{2}\right)\times\mathfrak{G}_*\left(\tfrac{s+t}{2}\right)\\
&\leq \tfrac{1}{4(t-s)^{\alpha}}\left[\begin{array}{c}\int_s^t (t-\omega)^{\alpha-1}Y_*(\omega)\times\mathfrak{G}_*(\omega)d\omega\\ +\int_s^t (z-s)^{\alpha-1}Y_*(z)\times\mathfrak{G}_*(z)dz\end{array}\right]\\
&+\tfrac{1}{2\alpha}\left(\tfrac{1}{2}-\tfrac{\alpha}{(\alpha+1)(\alpha+2)}\right)\nabla_*(s,t)+\tfrac{1}{2\alpha}\left(\tfrac{\alpha}{(\alpha+1)(\alpha+2)}\right)\varphi_*(s,t)\\
&=\tfrac{\Gamma(\alpha+1)}{4(t-s)^{\alpha}}\left[\mathcal{I}_{s+}^{\alpha}\ Y_*(t)\times\mathfrak{G}_*(t)+\mathcal{I}_{t-}^{\alpha}\ Y_*(s)\times\mathfrak{G}_*(s)\right]\\
&+\tfrac{1}{2\alpha}\left(\tfrac{1}{2}-\tfrac{\alpha}{(\alpha+1)(\alpha+2)}\right)\nabla_*(s,t)+\tfrac{1}{2\alpha}\left(\tfrac{\alpha}{(\alpha+1)(\alpha+2)}\right)\varphi_*(s,t)\\
&\tfrac{1}{\alpha}\,Y^*\left(\tfrac{s+t}{2}\right)\times\mathfrak{G}^*\left(\tfrac{s+t}{2}\right)\\
&\leq \tfrac{1}{4(t-s)^{\alpha}}\left[\begin{array}{c}\int_s^t (t-\omega)^{\alpha-1}Y^*(\omega)\times\mathfrak{G}^*(\omega)d\omega\\ +\int_s^t (z-s)^{\alpha-1}Y^*(z)\times\mathfrak{G}^*(z)dz\end{array}\right]\\
&+\tfrac{1}{2\alpha}\left(\tfrac{1}{2}-\tfrac{\alpha}{(\alpha+1)(\alpha+2)}\right)\nabla^*(s,t)+\tfrac{1}{2\alpha}\left(\tfrac{\alpha}{(\alpha+1)(\alpha+2)}\right)\varphi^*(s,t)\\
&=\tfrac{\Gamma(\alpha+1)}{4(t-s)^{\alpha}}\left[\mathcal{I}_{s+}^{\alpha}\ Y^*(t)\times\mathfrak{G}^*(t)+\mathcal{I}_{t-}^{\alpha}\ Y^*(s)\times\mathfrak{G}^*(s)\right]\\
&+\tfrac{1}{2\alpha}\left(\tfrac{1}{2}-\tfrac{\alpha}{(\alpha+1)(\alpha+2)}\right)\nabla^*(s,t)+\tfrac{1}{2\alpha}\left(\tfrac{\alpha}{(\alpha+1)(\alpha+2)}\right)\varphi^*(s,t),
\end{aligned}$$

That is,

$$\begin{aligned}
\tfrac{1}{\alpha}\,Y\left(\tfrac{s+t}{2}\right)\times\mathfrak{G}\left(\tfrac{s+t}{2}\right) &\leq_p \tfrac{\Gamma(\alpha+1)}{4(t-s)^{\alpha}}\left[\mathcal{I}_{s+}^{\alpha}\ Y(t)\times\mathfrak{G}(t)+\mathcal{I}_{t-}^{\alpha}\ Y(s)\times\mathfrak{G}(s)\right]\\
&+\tfrac{1}{2\alpha}\left(\tfrac{1}{2}-\tfrac{\alpha}{(\alpha+1)(\alpha+2)}\right)\nabla(s,t)+\tfrac{1}{2\alpha}\left(\tfrac{\alpha}{(\alpha+1)(\alpha+2)}\right)\varphi(s,t).
\end{aligned}$$

Hence, the required result is achieved. □

The upcoming results discuss the $\mathcal{H}$–$\mathcal{H}$ Fejér type inequality left and right convex *I·V-F*. Firstly, we achieve second $\mathcal{H}$–$\mathcal{H}$ Fejér type inequality.

Theorem 6. *Let $Y:[s,\ t]\to\mathcal{X}_I^+$ be a left and right convex I·V-F, with $s<t$, provided by $Y(\omega)=[Y_*(\omega),\ Y^*(\omega)]$ for all $\omega\in[s,\ t]$. Let $Y\in L([s,\ t],\mathcal{X}_I^+)$ and $\mathfrak{C}:[s,\ t]\to\mathbb{R}$, $\mathfrak{C}(\omega)\geq 0$, be symmetric with respect to $\frac{s+t}{2}$. Then,*

$$\left[\mathcal{I}_{s+}^{\alpha}\ Y\mathfrak{C}(t)+\mathcal{I}_{t-}^{\alpha}\ Y\mathfrak{C}(s)\right]\leq_p \frac{Y(s)+Y(t)}{2}\left[\mathcal{I}_{s+}^{\alpha}\ \mathfrak{C}(t)+\mathcal{I}_{t-}^{\alpha}\ \mathfrak{C}(s)\right] \tag{13}$$

If Y is a concave I·V-F, then inequality (13) is reversed.

Proof. Let Y be a left and right convex *I·V-F* and $\nu^{\alpha-1}\mathfrak{C}(\nu s+(1-\nu)t)\geq 0$. Then, we have

$$\begin{aligned}
&\nu^{\alpha-1}Y_*(\nu s+(1-\nu)t)C(\nu s+(1-\nu)t)\\
&\quad\leq \nu^{\alpha-1}(\nu Y_*(s)+(1-\nu)Y_*(t))C(\nu s+(1-\nu)t)\\
&\nu^{\alpha-1}Y^*(\nu s+(1-\nu)t)\mathfrak{C}(\nu s+(1-\nu)t)\\
&\quad\leq \nu^{\alpha-1}(\nu Y^*(s)+(1-\nu)Y^*(t))\mathfrak{C}(\nu s+(1-\nu)t).
\end{aligned} \tag{14}$$

and

$$\begin{aligned}
&\nu^{\alpha-1}Y_*((1-\nu)s+\nu t)C((1-\nu)s+\nu t)\\
&\quad\leq \nu^{\alpha-1}((1-\nu)Y_*(s)+\nu Y_*(t))C((1-\nu)s+\nu t)\\
&\nu^{\alpha-1}Y^*((1-\nu)s+\nu t)\mathfrak{C}((1-\nu)s+\nu t)\\
&\quad\leq \nu^{\alpha-1}((1-\nu)Y^*(s)+\nu Y^*(t))\mathfrak{C}((1-\nu)s+\nu t).
\end{aligned} \tag{15}$$

After adding (14) and (15), and integrating over $[0, 1]$, we get

$$\begin{aligned}
&\int_0^1 v^{\mathfrak{a}-1}Y_*(vs+(1-v)t)\mathfrak{C}(vs+(1-v)t)dv \\
&\qquad +\int_0^1 v^{\mathfrak{a}-1}Y_*((1-v)s+vt)\mathfrak{C}((1-v)s+vt)dv \\
&\quad \leq \int_0^1\left[\begin{array}{c} v^{\mathfrak{a}-1}Y_*(s)\{v\mathfrak{C}(vs+(1-v)t)+(1-v)\mathfrak{C}((1-v)s+vt)\} \\ +v^{\mathfrak{a}-1}Y_*(t)\{(1-v)\mathfrak{C}(vs+(1-v)t)+v\mathfrak{C}((1-v)s+vt)\}\end{array}\right]dv, \\
&\int_0^1 v^{\mathfrak{a}-1}Y^*((1-v)s+vt)\mathfrak{C}((1-v)s+vt)dv \\
&\qquad +\int_0^1 v^{\mathfrak{a}-1}Y^*(vs+(1-v)t)\mathfrak{C}(vs+(1-v)t)dv \\
&\quad \leq \int_0^1\left[\begin{array}{c} v^{\mathfrak{a}-1}Y^*(s)\{v\mathfrak{C}(vs+(1-v)t)+(1-v)\mathfrak{C}((1-v)s+vt)\} \\ +v^{\mathfrak{a}-1}Y^*(t)\{(1-v)\mathfrak{C}(vs+(1-v)t)+v\mathfrak{C}((1-v)s+vt)\}\end{array}\right]dv,
\end{aligned}$$

$$\begin{aligned}
&= Y_*(s)\int_0^1 v^{\mathfrak{a}-1}C(vs+(1-v)t)dv + Y_*(t)\int_0^1 v^{\mathfrak{a}-1}C((1-v)s+vt)dv, \\
&= Y^*(s)\int_0^1 v^{\mathfrak{a}-1}C(vs+(1-v)t)dv + Y^*(t)\int_0^1 v^{\mathfrak{a}-1}C((1-v)s+vt)dv.
\end{aligned}$$

Since $\mathfrak{C}$ is symmetric, then

$$\begin{aligned}
&= [Y_*(s)+Y_*(t)]\int_0^1 \ v^{\mathfrak{a}-1}C((1-v)s+vt)\ dv \\
&= [Y^*(s)+Y^*(t)]\int_0^1 \ v^{\mathfrak{a}-1}C((1-v)s+vt)\ dv.
\end{aligned}$$

$$\begin{aligned}
&= \tfrac{Y_*(s)+Y_*(t)}{2}\tfrac{\Gamma(\mathfrak{a})}{(t-s)^{\mathfrak{a}}}\left[\mathcal{I}_{s+}^{\mathfrak{a}}\ \mathfrak{C}(t)+\mathcal{I}_{t-}^{\mathfrak{a}}\ \mathfrak{C}(s)\right], \\
&= \tfrac{Y^*(s)+Y^*(t)}{2}\tfrac{\Gamma(\mathfrak{a})}{(t-s)^{\mathfrak{a}}}\left[\mathcal{I}_{s+}^{\mathfrak{a}}\ \mathfrak{C}(t)+\mathcal{I}_{t-}^{\mathfrak{a}}\ \mathfrak{C}(s)\right].
\end{aligned} \tag{16}$$

Since

$$\begin{aligned}
&\int_0^1 v^{\mathfrak{a}-1}Y_*(vs+(1-v)t)\mathfrak{C}((1-v)s+vt)dv \\
&\qquad +\int_0^1 v^{\mathfrak{a}-1}Y_*((1-v)s+vt)\mathfrak{C}((1-v)s+vt)dv \\
&\qquad = \tfrac{1}{(t-s)^{\mathfrak{a}}}\ \int_s^t(\omega-s)^{\mathfrak{a}-1}Y_*(s+t-\omega)\mathfrak{C}(\omega)d\omega \\
&\qquad +\tfrac{1}{(t-s)^{\mathfrak{a}}}\ \int_s^t(\omega-s)^{\mathfrak{a}-1}Y_*(\omega)\mathfrak{C}(\omega)d\omega \\
&\qquad = \tfrac{1}{(t-s)^{\mathfrak{a}}}\ \int_s^t(\omega-s)^{\mathfrak{a}-1}Y_*(\omega)\mathfrak{C}(s+t-\omega)d\omega \\
&\qquad +\tfrac{1}{(t-s)^{\mathfrak{a}}}\ \int_s^t(\omega-s)^{\mathfrak{a}-1}Y_*(\omega)\mathfrak{C}(\omega)d\omega \\
&\qquad = \tfrac{\Gamma(\mathfrak{a})}{(t-s)^{\mathfrak{a}}}\left[\mathcal{I}_{s+}^{\mathfrak{a}}\ Y_*\mathfrak{C}(t)+\mathcal{I}_{t-}^{\mathfrak{a}}\ Y_*\mathfrak{C}(s)\right], \\
&\int_0^1 v^{\mathfrak{a}-1}Y^*(vs+(1-v)t)\mathfrak{C}((1-v)s+vt)dv \\
&\qquad +\int_0^1 v^{\mathfrak{a}-1}Y^*((1-v)s+vt)\mathfrak{C}((1-v)s+vt)dv \\
&\qquad = \tfrac{\Gamma(\mathfrak{a})}{(t-s)^{\mathfrak{a}}}\left[\mathcal{I}_{s+}^{\mathfrak{a}}\ Y^*\mathfrak{C}(t)+\mathcal{I}_{t-}^{\mathfrak{a}}\ Y^*\mathfrak{C}(s)\right].
\end{aligned} \tag{17}$$

then, from (16), we have

$$\begin{aligned}
&\tfrac{\Gamma(\mathfrak{a})}{(t-s)^{\mathfrak{a}}}\left[\mathcal{I}_{s+}^{\mathfrak{a}}\ Y^*\mathfrak{C}(t)+\mathcal{I}_{t-}^{\mathfrak{a}}\ Y^*\mathfrak{C}(s)\right] \\
&\qquad \leq \tfrac{Y^*(s)+Y^*(t)}{2}\tfrac{\Gamma(\mathfrak{a})}{(t-s)^{\mathfrak{a}}}\left[\mathcal{I}_{s+}^{\mathfrak{a}}\ \mathfrak{C}(t)+\mathcal{I}_{t-}^{\mathfrak{a}}\ \mathfrak{C}(s)\right] \\
&\qquad \leq \tfrac{Y^*(s)+Y^*(t)}{2}\tfrac{\Gamma(\mathfrak{a})}{(t-s)^{\mathfrak{a}}}\left[\mathcal{I}_{s+}^{\mathfrak{a}}\ \mathfrak{C}(t)+\mathcal{I}_{t-}^{\mathfrak{a}}\ \mathfrak{C}(s)\right], \\
&\tfrac{\Gamma(\mathfrak{a})}{(t-s)^{\mathfrak{a}}}\left[\mathcal{I}_{s+}^{\mathfrak{a}}\ Y^*\mathfrak{C}(t)+\mathcal{I}_{t-}^{\mathfrak{a}}\ Y^*\mathfrak{C}(s)\right] \\
&\qquad \leq \tfrac{Y^*(s)+Y^*(t)}{2}\tfrac{\Gamma(\mathfrak{a})}{(t-s)^{\mathfrak{a}}}\left[\mathcal{I}_{s+}^{\mathfrak{a}}\ \mathfrak{C}(t)+\mathcal{I}_{t-}^{\mathfrak{a}}\ \mathfrak{C}(s)\right] \\
&\qquad \leq \tfrac{Y^*(s)+Y^*(t)}{2}\tfrac{\Gamma(\mathfrak{a})}{(t-s)^{\mathfrak{a}}}\left[\mathcal{I}_{s+}^{\mathfrak{a}}\ \mathfrak{C}(t)+\mathcal{I}_{t-}^{\mathfrak{a}}\ \mathfrak{C}(s)\right],
\end{aligned}$$

That is,

$$\frac{\Gamma(\mathfrak{a})}{(t-s)^{\mathfrak{a}}}\left[\left[\mathcal{I}_{s+}^{\mathfrak{a}}\ Y_*\mathfrak{C}(t)+\mathcal{I}_{t-}^{\mathfrak{a}}\ Y_*\mathfrak{C}(s)\right],\ \mathcal{I}_{s+}^{\mathfrak{a}}\ Y^*\mathfrak{C}(t)+\mathcal{I}_{t-}^{\mathfrak{a}}\ Y^*\mathfrak{C}(s)\right]$$

$$\leq_p \frac{\Gamma(\mathfrak{a})}{(t-s)^{\mathfrak{a}}}\left[\frac{Y_*(s)+Y_*(t)}{2},\ \frac{Y^*(s)+Y^*(t)}{2}\right]\left[\mathcal{I}_{s^+}^{\mathfrak{a}}\ \mathfrak{C}(t)+\mathcal{I}_{t^-}^{\mathfrak{a}}\ \mathfrak{C}(s)\right]$$
$$\leq_p \frac{\Gamma(\mathfrak{a})}{(t-s)^{\mathfrak{a}}}\left[\frac{Y_*(s)+Y_*(t)}{2},\ \frac{Y^*(s)+Y^*(t)}{2}\right]\left[\mathcal{I}_{s^+}^{\mathfrak{a}}\ \mathfrak{C}(t)+\mathcal{I}_{t^-}^{\mathfrak{a}}\ \mathfrak{C}(s)\right],$$

Hence,

$$\left[\mathcal{I}_{s^+}^{\mathfrak{a}}\ Y\mathfrak{C}(t)\ \leq_p\ \mathcal{I}_{t^-}^{\mathfrak{a}}\ Y\mathfrak{C}(s)\right]\leq_p \frac{Y(s)+Y(t)}{2}\left[\mathcal{I}_{s^+}^{\mathfrak{a}}\ \mathfrak{C}(t)+\mathcal{I}_{t^-}^{\mathfrak{a}}\ \mathfrak{C}(s)\right]$$
$$\leq_p \frac{Y(s)+Y(t)}{2}\left[\mathcal{I}_{s^+}^{\mathfrak{a}}\ \mathfrak{C}(t)+\mathcal{I}_{t^-}^{\mathfrak{a}}\ \mathfrak{C}(s)\right].$$

Now, we first obtain the $\mathcal{H}$–$\mathcal{H}$ Fejér type inequality for the left and right convex *I·V-F*. □

Theorem 7. *Let $Y : [s,\ t] \to \mathcal{X}_I^+$ be a left and right convex I·V-F, with $s < t$, and defined by $Y(\omega) = [Y_*(\omega),\ Y^*(\omega)]$ for all $\omega \in [s,\ t]$. If $Y \in L([s,\ t], \mathcal{X}_I^+)$ and $\mathfrak{C} : [s,\ t] \to \mathbb{R}$, $\mathfrak{C}(\omega) \geq 0$ are symmetric with respect to $\frac{s+t}{2}$, then*

$$Y\left(\frac{s+t}{2}\right)\left[\mathcal{I}_{s^+}^{\mathfrak{a}}\ \mathfrak{C}(t)+\mathcal{I}_{t^-}^{\mathfrak{a}}\ \mathfrak{C}(s)\right]\leq_p \left[\mathcal{I}_{s^+}^{\mathfrak{a}}\ Y\mathfrak{C}(t)+\mathcal{I}_{t^-}^{\mathfrak{a}}\ Y\mathfrak{C}(s)\right] \tag{18}$$

If Y is a concave I·V-F, then inequality (18) is reversed.

Proof. Since Y is a left and right convex *I·V-F*, then we have

$$\begin{aligned} Y_*\left(\tfrac{s+t}{2}\right) &\leq \tfrac{1}{2}(Y_*(\nu s+(1-\nu)t)+Y_*((1-\nu)s+\nu t)) \\ Y^*\left(\tfrac{s+t}{2}\right) &\leq \tfrac{1}{2}(Y^*(\nu s+(1-\nu)t)+Y^*((1-\nu)s+\nu t)), \end{aligned} \tag{19}$$

Since $\mathfrak{C}(\nu s+(1-\nu)t) = \mathfrak{C}((1-\nu)s+\nu t)$, then by multiplying (19) by $\nu^{\mathfrak{a}-1}\mathfrak{C}((1-\nu)s+\nu t)$ and integrating it, with respect to ν over $[0,\ 1]$, we obtain

$$\begin{aligned} &Y_*\left(\tfrac{s+t}{2}\right)\int_0^1 \nu^{\mathfrak{a}-1}\mathfrak{C}((1-\nu)s+\nu t)d\nu \\ &\quad\leq \tfrac{1}{2}\begin{pmatrix} \int_0^1 \nu^{\mathfrak{a}-1}Y_*(\nu s+(1-\nu)t)\mathfrak{C}((1-\nu)s+\nu t)d\nu \\ +\int_0^1 \nu^{\mathfrak{a}-1}Y_*((1-\nu)s+\nu t)\mathfrak{C}((1-\nu)s+\nu t)d\nu \end{pmatrix}, \\ &Y^*\left(\tfrac{s+t}{2}\right)\int_0^1 \mathfrak{C}((1-\nu)s+\nu t)d\nu \\ &\quad\leq \tfrac{1}{2}\begin{pmatrix} \int_0^1 \nu^{\mathfrak{a}-1}Y^*(\nu s+(1-\nu)t)\mathfrak{C}((1-\nu)s+\nu t)d\nu \\ +\int_0^1 \nu^{\mathfrak{a}-1}Y^*((1-\nu)s+\nu t)\mathfrak{C}((1-\nu)s+\nu t)d\nu \end{pmatrix} \end{aligned} \tag{20}$$

Let $\omega = (1-\nu)s+\nu t$. Then, we have

$$\begin{aligned} &\int_0^1 \nu^{\mathfrak{a}-1}Y_*(\nu s+(1-\nu)t)\mathfrak{C}((1-\nu)s+\nu t)d\nu \\ &\quad+\int_0^1 \nu^{\mathfrak{a}-1}Y_*((1-\nu)s+\nu t)\mathfrak{C}((1-\nu)s+\nu t)d\nu \\ &\quad= \tfrac{1}{(t-s)^{\mathfrak{a}}}\int_s^t (\omega-s)^{\mathfrak{a}-1}Y_*(s+t-\omega)\mathfrak{C}(\omega)d\omega \\ &\quad+\tfrac{1}{(t-s)^{\mathfrak{a}}}\int_s^t (\omega-s)^{\mathfrak{a}-1}Y_*(\omega)\mathfrak{C}(\omega)d\omega \\ &\quad= \tfrac{1}{(t-s)^{\mathfrak{a}}}\int_s^t (\omega-s)^{\mathfrak{a}-1}Y_*(\omega)\mathfrak{C}(s+t-\omega)d\omega \\ &\quad+\tfrac{1}{(t-s)^{\mathfrak{a}}}\int_s^t (\omega-s)^{\mathfrak{a}-1}Y_*(\omega)\mathfrak{C}(\omega)d\omega \\ &\quad= \tfrac{\Gamma(\mathfrak{a})}{(t-s)^{\mathfrak{a}}}\left[\mathcal{I}_{s^+}^{\mathfrak{a}}\ Y_*\mathfrak{C}(t)+\mathcal{I}_{t^-}^{\mathfrak{a}}\ Y_*\mathfrak{C}(s)\right], \\ &\int_0^1 \nu^{\mathfrak{a}-1}Y^*(\nu s+(1-\nu)t)\mathfrak{C}((1-\nu)s+\nu t)d\nu \\ &\quad+\int_0^1 \nu^{\mathfrak{a}-1}Y^*((1-\nu)s+\nu t)\mathfrak{C}((1-\nu)s+\nu t)d\nu \\ &\quad= \tfrac{\Gamma(\mathfrak{a})}{(t-s)^{\mathfrak{a}}}\left[\mathcal{I}_{s^+}^{\mathfrak{a}}\ Y^*\mathfrak{C}(t)+\mathcal{I}_{t^-}^{\mathfrak{a}}\ Y^*\mathfrak{C}(s)\right]. \end{aligned} \tag{21}$$

Then, from (21), we have

$$\frac{\Gamma(\mathfrak{a})}{(t-s)^{\mathfrak{a}}}Y_*\left(\tfrac{s+t}{2}\right)\left[\mathcal{I}_{s^+}^{\mathfrak{a}}\ \mathfrak{C}(t)+\mathcal{I}_{t^-}^{\mathfrak{a}}\ \mathfrak{C}(s)\right] \leq \frac{\Gamma(\mathfrak{a})}{(t-s)^{\mathfrak{a}}}\left[\mathcal{I}_{s^+}^{\mathfrak{a}}\ Y_*\mathfrak{C}(t)+\mathcal{I}_{t^-}^{\mathfrak{a}}\ Y_*\mathfrak{C}(s)\right]$$
$$\frac{\Gamma(\mathfrak{a})}{(t-s)^{\mathfrak{a}}}Y^*\left(\tfrac{s+t}{2}\right)\left[\mathcal{I}_{s^+}^{\mathfrak{a}}\ \mathfrak{C}(t)+\mathcal{I}_{t^-}^{\mathfrak{a}}\ \mathfrak{C}(s)\right] \leq \frac{\Gamma(\mathfrak{a})}{(t-s)^{\mathfrak{a}}}\left[\mathcal{I}_{s^+}^{\mathfrak{a}}\ Y^*\mathfrak{C}(t)+\mathcal{I}_{t^-}^{\mathfrak{a}}\ Y^*\mathfrak{C}(s)\right]$$

from which, we have

$$\frac{\Gamma(\mathfrak{a})}{(t-s)^{\mathfrak{a}}}\left[Y_*\left(\tfrac{s+t}{2}\right),\ Y^*\left(\tfrac{s+t}{2}\right)\right]\left[\mathcal{I}_{s^+}^{\mathfrak{a}}\ \mathfrak{C}(t)+\mathcal{I}_{t^-}^{\mathfrak{a}}\ \mathfrak{C}(s)\right]$$
$$\leq_p \frac{\Gamma(\mathfrak{a})}{(t-s)^{\mathfrak{a}}}\left[\mathcal{I}_{s^+}^{\mathfrak{a}}\ Y_*\mathfrak{C}(t)+\mathcal{I}_{t^-}^{\mathfrak{a}}\ Y_*\mathfrak{C}(s),\ \mathcal{I}_{s^+}^{\mathfrak{a}}\ Y^*\mathfrak{C}(t)+\mathcal{I}_{t^-}^{\mathfrak{a}}\ Y^*\mathfrak{C}(s)\right],$$

That is,

$$\frac{\Gamma(\mathfrak{a})}{(t-s)^{\mathfrak{a}}}Y\left(\frac{s+t}{2}\right)\left[\mathcal{I}_{s^+}^{\mathfrak{a}}\ \mathfrak{C}(t)+\mathcal{I}_{t^-}^{\mathfrak{a}}\ \mathfrak{C}(s)\right]$$
$$\leq_p \frac{\Gamma(\mathfrak{a})}{(t-s)^{\mathfrak{a}}}\left[\mathcal{I}_{s^+}^{\mathfrak{a}}\ Y\mathfrak{C}(t)+\mathcal{I}_{t^-}^{\mathfrak{a}}\ Y\mathfrak{C}(s)\right].$$

This completes the proof. □

Example 3. *We consider the I·V-F* $Y : [0,\ 2] \to \mathcal{X}_I^+$, *defined by* $Y(\omega) = \left[(2-\sqrt{\omega}), 2(2-\sqrt{\omega})\right]$. *Since endpoint functions* $Y_*(\omega)$, $Y^*(\omega)$ *are convex functions, then* $Y(\omega)$ *is a left and right convex I·V-F. If*

$$\mathfrak{C}(\omega) = \begin{cases} \sqrt{\omega}, & \omega \in [0,1], \\ \sqrt{2-\omega}, & \omega \in (1,\ 2], \end{cases}$$

then $\mathfrak{C}(2-\omega) = \mathfrak{C}(\omega) \geq 0$ *for all* $\omega \in [0,\ 2]$. *Since* $Y_*(\omega) = 2-\sqrt{\omega}$ *and* $Y^*(\omega) = 2(2-\sqrt{\omega})$, *if* $\mathfrak{a} = \frac{1}{2}$, *then we compute the following:*

$$\left[\mathcal{I}_{s^+}^{\mathfrak{a}}\ Y\mathfrak{C}(t)\tilde{+}\mathcal{I}_{t^-}^{\mathfrak{a}}\ Y\mathfrak{C}(s)\right] \leq_p \frac{Y(s)+Y(t)}{2}\left[\mathcal{I}_{s^+}^{\mathfrak{a}}\ \mathfrak{C}(t)+\mathcal{I}_{t^-}^{\mathfrak{a}}\ \mathfrak{C}(s)\right]$$

$$\begin{aligned} \tfrac{Y_*(s)+Y_*(t)}{2}\left[\mathcal{I}_{s^+}^{\mathfrak{a}}\ \mathfrak{C}(t)+\mathcal{I}_{t^-}^{\mathfrak{a}}\ \mathfrak{C}(s)\right] &= \tfrac{\pi}{\sqrt{2}}\left(\tfrac{4-\sqrt{2}}{2}\right) \\ \tfrac{Y^*(s)\tilde{+}Y^*(t)}{2}\left[\mathcal{I}_{s^+}^{\mathfrak{a}}\ \mathfrak{C}(t)+\mathcal{I}_{t^-}^{\mathfrak{a}}\ \mathfrak{C}(s)\right] &= \tfrac{\pi}{\sqrt{2}}\left(4-\sqrt{2}\right), \end{aligned} \tag{22}$$

$$\begin{aligned} \tfrac{Y_*(s)+Y_*(t)}{2}\left[\mathcal{I}_{s^+}^{\mathfrak{a}}\ \mathfrak{C}(t)+\mathcal{I}_{t^-}^{\mathfrak{a}}\ \mathfrak{C}(s)\right] &= \tfrac{\pi}{\sqrt{2}}\left(\tfrac{4-\sqrt{2}}{2}\right) \\ \tfrac{Y^*(s)+Y^*(t)}{2}\left[\mathcal{I}_{s^+}^{\mathfrak{a}}\ \mathfrak{C}(t)+\mathcal{I}_{t^-}^{\mathfrak{a}}\ \mathfrak{C}(s)\right] &= \tfrac{\pi}{\sqrt{2}}\left(4-\sqrt{2}\right), \end{aligned} \tag{23}$$

$$\begin{aligned} \left[\mathcal{I}_{s^+}^{\mathfrak{a}}\ Y_*\mathfrak{C}(t)+\mathcal{I}_{t^-}^{\mathfrak{a}}\ Y_*\mathfrak{C}(s)\right] &= \tfrac{1}{\sqrt{\pi}}\left(2\pi+\tfrac{4-8\sqrt{2}}{3}\right), \\ \left[\mathcal{I}_{s^+}^{\mathfrak{a}}\ Y^*\mathfrak{C}(t)+\mathcal{I}_{t^-}^{\mathfrak{a}}\ Y^*\mathfrak{C}(s)\right] &= \tfrac{2}{\sqrt{\pi}}\left(2\pi+\tfrac{4-8\sqrt{2}}{3}\right). \end{aligned} \tag{24}$$

From (22)–(24), (13) we have

$$\frac{1}{\sqrt{\pi}}\left[\left(2\pi+\frac{4-8\sqrt{2}}{3}\right),\ 2\left(2\pi+\frac{4-8\sqrt{2}}{3}\right)\right] \leq_p \frac{\pi}{\sqrt{2}}\left[\frac{4-\sqrt{2}}{2},\ 4-\sqrt{2}\right] = \frac{\pi}{\sqrt{2}}\left[\frac{4-\sqrt{2}}{2},\ 4-\sqrt{2}\right].$$

Hence, Theorem 6 is verified.

For Theorem 7, we have

$$\begin{aligned} Y_*\left(\tfrac{s+t}{2}\right)\left[\mathcal{I}_{s^+}^{\mathfrak{a}}\ \mathfrak{C}(t)+\mathcal{I}_{t^-}^{\mathfrak{a}}\ \mathfrak{C}(s)\right] &= \sqrt{\pi}, \\ Y^*\left(\tfrac{s+t}{2}\right)\left[\mathcal{I}_{s^+}^{\mathfrak{a}}\ \mathfrak{C}(t)+\mathcal{I}_{t^-}^{\mathfrak{a}}\ \mathfrak{C}(s)\right] &= 2\sqrt{\pi}. \end{aligned} \tag{25}$$

From (24) and (25), we have

$$\sqrt{\pi}[1,\,2] \;\leq\; {}_{p}\frac{1}{\sqrt{\pi}}\left[2\pi+\frac{4-8\sqrt{2}}{3},\; 2\left(2\pi+\frac{4-8\sqrt{2}}{3}\right)\right]$$

Hence, (18) has been verified.

Remark 3. *If one takes $\mathfrak{C}(\omega)=1$, then, from (13) and (18), we acquire (5).*

Let us take $\mathfrak{a}=1$. Then, we achieve the coming inequality (see [22]).

$$\Upsilon\left(\frac{s+t}{2}\right) \leq_p \frac{1}{\int_s^t \mathfrak{C}(\omega)d\omega}\int_s^t \Upsilon(\omega)\mathfrak{C}(\omega)d\omega \leq_p \frac{\Upsilon(s)+\Upsilon(t)}{2}$$

If we take $\Upsilon_*(\omega)=\Upsilon^*(\omega)$, then from (13) and (18), we acquire the coming inequality (see [33]).

$$\Upsilon\left(\frac{s+t}{2}\right)\left[\mathcal{I}_{s^+}^{\mathfrak{a}}\,\mathfrak{C}(t)+\mathcal{I}_{t^-}^{\mathfrak{a}}\,\mathfrak{C}(s)\right] \leq_p \left[\mathcal{I}_{s^+}^{\mathfrak{a}}\,\Upsilon\mathfrak{C}(t)+\mathcal{I}_{t^-}^{\mathfrak{a}}\,\Upsilon\mathfrak{C}(s)\right]$$
$$\leq_p \frac{\Upsilon(s)+\Upsilon(t)}{2}\left[\mathcal{I}_{s^+}^{\mathfrak{a}}\,\mathfrak{C}(t)+\mathcal{I}_{t^-}^{\mathfrak{a}}\,\mathfrak{C}(s)\right]$$

If one takes $\Upsilon_*(\omega)=\Upsilon^*(\omega)$ with $\mathfrak{a}=1$, then from (13) and (18), we achieve the classical $\mathcal{H}$–$\mathcal{H}$ Fejér inequality (see [26]).

4. Conclusions

In applied sciences, convex functions and fractional calculus are essential. The new interval-valued left and right convex functions are presented in this article. Some novel Riemann–Liouville fractional integral $\mathcal{H}$–$\mathcal{H}$ and Fejér-type inequalities are provided, utilizing the idea of interval-valued left and right convex functions and some supplementary interval analysis findings. Our results are a generalization of a number of previously published findings. In the future, we will use generalized interval and fuzzy Riemann–Liouville fractional operators to investigate this concept for generalized left and right convex *I·V-Fs* and *F-I·V-Fs* by using interval Katugampola fractional integrals and fuzzy Katugampola fractional integrals. For applications, see [53–56].

Author Contributions: Conceptualization, M.B.K.; methodology, M.B.K.; validation, S.T., H.G.Z., and M.S.S.; formal analysis, G.S.-G.; investigation, M.S.S.; resources, S.T. and J.E.M.-D.; data curation, H.G.Z.; writing—original draft preparation, H.G.Z., M.B.K., and G.S.-G.; writing—review and editing, S.T. and M.B.K.; visualization, J.E.M.-D., and H.G.Z.; supervision, M.S.S. and M.B.K.; project administration, M.B.K.; funding acquisition, M.S.S., G.S.-G., and H.G.Z. All authors have read and agreed to the published version of the manuscript.

Funding: This research received no external funding.

Data Availability Statement: Not applicable.

Acknowledgments: The authors would like to thank the Rector, COMSATS University Islamabad, Islamabad, Pakistan, for providing excellent research. This work was funded by Taif University Researchers Supporting Project (number TURSP-2020/345), Taif University, Taif, Saudi Arabia. Moreover, the work of Santos-García was also partially supported by the Spanish project TRACES TIN2015-67522-C3-3-R.

Conflicts of Interest: The authors declare no conflict of interest.

References

1. Niculescu, C.P.; Persson, L.E. *Convex Functions and Their Applications*; Springer: New York, NY, USA, 2006.
2. Hadamard, J. Étude sur les Propriétés des Fonctions Entières en Particulier d'une Fonction Considérée par Riemann. *J. Math. Pures. Appl.* **1893**, *58*, 171–215.

3. Özdemir, M.E.; Avci, M.; Set, E. On Some Inequalities of Hermite-Hadamard Type via M-Convexity. *Appl. Math. Lett.* **2010**, *23*, 1065–1070. [CrossRef]
4. Butt, S.I.; Tariq, M.; Aslam, A.; Ahmad, H.; Nofel, T.A. Hermite–Hadamard Type Inequalities via Generalized Harmonic Exponential Convexity. *J. Funct. Spaces* **2021**, *2021*, 5533491. [CrossRef]
5. İşcan, I. Hermite-Hadamard Type Inequalities for Harmonically Convex Functions. *Hacet. J. Math. Stat.* **2013**, *43*, 935–942. [CrossRef]
6. Butt, S.I.; Kashuri, A.; Tariq, M.; Nasir, J.; Aslam, A.; Geo, W. Hermite–Hadamard–Type Inequalities via N–Polynomial Exponential–Type Convexity and Their Applications. *Adv. Differ. Equ.* **2020**, *2020*, 508. [CrossRef]
7. Butt, S.I.; Kashuri, A.; Tariq, M.; Nasir, J.; Aslam, A.; Geo, W. N–Polynomial Exponential–Type P–Convex Function with Some Related Inequalities and Their Application. *Heliyon* **2020**, *6*, e05420. [CrossRef]
8. Ahmad, H.; Tariq, M.; Sahoo, S.K.; Baili, J.; Cesarano, C. New Estimations of Hermite–Hadamard Type Integral Inequalities for Special Functions. *Fractal Fract.* **2021**, *5*, 144. [CrossRef]
9. Tariq, M.; Nasir, J.; Sahoo, S.K.; Mallah, A.A. A Note on Some Ostrowski Type Inequalities via Generalized Exponentially Convex Functions. *J. Math. Anal. Model* **2021**, *2*, 1–15. [CrossRef]
10. Sahoo, S.K.; Ahmad, H.; Tariq, M.; Kodamasingh, B.; Aydi, H.; de la Sen, M. Hermite–Hadamard Type Inequalities Involving K-Fractional Operator for (H,M)-Convex Functions. *Symmetry* **2021**, *13*, 1686. [CrossRef]
11. Oader, T.G.H. Some Inequalities for M-Convex Functions. *Stud. Univ. Babes-Bolyai Math.* **1993**, *38*, 21–28.
12. Dragomir, S.S.; Pearce, C.E.M. Selected Topics on Hermite-Hadamard Type Inequalities and Applications, RGMIA Monographs. 2000. Available online: http://rgmia.vu.edu.au/monographs/hermitehadamard.html (accessed on 1 July 2021).
13. Tariq, M.; Ahmad, H.; Sahoo, S.K. The Hermite-Hadamard Type Inequality and Its Estimations via Generalized Convex Functions of Raina Type. *Math. Model. Numer. Simul. Appl. (MMNSA)* **2021**, *1*, 32–43. [CrossRef]
14. Atangana, A. Modelling the Spread of COVID-19 with New Fractal-Fractional Operators: Can the Lockdown Save Mankind Before Vaccination? *Chaos Solitons Fractals* **2020**, *136*, 109860. [CrossRef] [PubMed]
15. Danane, J.; Allali, K.; Hammouch, Z. Mathematical Analysis of a Fractional Differential Model of HBV Infection with Antibody Immune Response. *Chaos Solitons Fractals* **2020**, *136*, 109787. [CrossRef]
16. Singh, J.; Kumar, D.; Hammouch, Z.; Atangana, A. A Fractional Epidemiological Model for Computer Viruses Pertaining to a New Fractional Derivative. *Appl. Math. Comput.* **2018**, *316*, 504–515. [CrossRef]
17. Kumar, S.; Kumar, A.; Samet, B.; Dutta, H. A Study on Fractional Host Parasitoid Population Dynamical Model to Describe Insect Species. *Numer. Methods Part. Differ. Equ.* **2020**, *37*, 1673–1692. [CrossRef]
18. Sulaiman, T.A.; Bulut, H.; Baskonus, H.M. Optical Solitons to the Fractional Perturbed NLSE in Nano-Fibers. *Discret. Cont. Dyn. Syst.* **2020**, *3*, 925–936.
19. Veeresha, P.; Baskonus, H.M.; Prakasha, D.G.; Gao, W.; Yel, G. Regarding New Numerical Solution of Fractional Schistosomiasis Disease Arising in Biological Phenomena. *Chaos Solitons Fractals* **2020**, *133*, 109–661. [CrossRef]
20. Mubeen, S.; Iqbal, S.; Rahman, G. Contiguous Function Relations and an Integral Representation for Appell K-Series F1,K. *Int. J. Math. Res.* **2015**, *4*, 53–63. [CrossRef]
21. Khan, M.B.; Noor, M.A.; Noor, K.I.; Chu, Y.M. New Hermite-Hadamard Type Inequalities for -Convex Fuzzy-Interval-Valued Functions. *Adv. Differ. Equ.* **2021**, *2021*, 6–20. [CrossRef]
22. Khan, M.B.; Noor, M.A.; Noor, K.I.; Nisar, K.S.; Ismail, K.A.; Elfasakhany, A. Some Inequalities for LR-$$\left ({h} _ {1},{h} _ {2}\right) $$ h 1, h 2-Convex Interval-Valued Functions by Means of Pseudo Order Relation. *Int. J. Comput. Intell. Syst.* **2021**, *14*, 180. [CrossRef]
23. Khan, M.B.; Mohammed, P.O.; Noor, M.A.; Baleanu, D.; Guirao, J. Some New Fractional Estimates of Inequalities for LR-P-Convex Interval-Valued Functions by Means of Pseudo Order Relation. *Axioms* **2021**, *10*, 175. [CrossRef]
24. Khan, M.B.; Noor, M.A.; Al-Bayatti, H.M.; Noor, K.I. Some New Inequalities for LR-log-h-Convex Interval-Valued Functions by Means of Pseudo Order Relation. *Appl. Math. Inf. Sci.* **2021**, *15*, 459–470.
25. Kunt, M.; İşcan, İ. Hermite–Hadamard–Fejer Type Inequalities for P-Convex Functions. *Arab. J. Math. Sci.* **2017**, *23*, 215–230. [CrossRef]
26. Fej'er, L. Uberdie Fourierreihen II. Math. Naturwise. Anz, Ungar. *Akad. Wiss* **1906**, *24*, 369–390.
27. Noor, M.A.; Noor, K.I.; Awan, M.U.; Costache, S. Some Integral Inequalities for Harmonically H-Convex Functions. *Politehn. Univ. Bucharest Sci. Bull. Ser. A Appl. Math. Phys.* **2015**, *77*, 5–16.
28. Lupulescu, V. Fractional Calculus for Interval-Valued Functions. *Fuzzy Sets Syst.* **2015**, *265*, 63–85. [CrossRef]
29. Moore, R.E. *Interval Analysis*; Prentice Hall: Englewood Cliffs, NJ, USA, 1966.
30. Budak, H.; Tunç, T.; Sarikaya, M. Fractional Hermite-Hadamard-Type Inequalities for Interval-Valued Functions. *Proc. Am. Math. Soc.* **2020**, *148*, 705–718. [CrossRef]
31. Zhang, D.; Guo, C.; Chen, D.; Wang, G. Jensen's Inequalities for Set-Valued and Fuzzy Set-Valued Functions. *Fuzzy Sets Syst.* **2021**, *404*, 178–204. [CrossRef]
32. Sarikaya, M.Z.; Set, E.; Yaldiz, H.; Başak, N. Hermite-Hadamard's Inequalities for Fractional Integrals and Related Fractional Inequalities. *Math. Comput. Model.* **2013**, *57*, 2403–2407. [CrossRef]
33. Işcan, I. Hermite-Hadamard-Fejer Type Inequalities for Convex Functions via Fractional Integrals. *Stud. Univ. Babes-Bolyai, Mathematica* **2015**, *60*, 355–366.

34. Chen, F. A Note on Hermite-Hadamard Inequalities for Products of Convex Functions via Riemann-Liouville Fractional Integrals. *Ital. J. Pure Appl. Math.* **2014**, *33*, 299–306.
35. Khan, M.B.; Treanţă, S.; Budak, H. Generalized P-Convex Fuzzy-Interval-Valued Functions and Inequalities Based upon the Fuzzy-Order Relation. *Fractal Fract.* **2022**, *6*, 63. [CrossRef]
36. Khan, M.B.; Srivastava, H.M.; Mohammed, P.O.; Macías-Díaz, J.E.; Hamed, Y.S. Some New Versions of Integral Inequalities for Log-Preinvex Fuzzy-Interval-Valued Functions through Fuzzy Order Relation. *Alex. Eng. J.* **2022**, *6*, 7089–7101. [CrossRef]
37. Khan, M.B.; Srivastava, H.M.; Mohammed, P.O.; Guirao, J.L.; Jawa, T.M. Fuzzy-Interval Inequalities for Generalized Preinvex Fuzzy Interval Valued Functions. *Math. Biosci. Eng.* **2022**, *19*, 812–835. [CrossRef]
38. Khan, M.B.; Mohammed, P.O.; Noor, M.A.; Hamed, Y.S. New Hermite-Hadamard Inequalities in Fuzzy-Interval Fractional Calculus and Related Inequalities. *Symmetry* **2021**, *13*, 673. [CrossRef]
39. Khan, M.B.; Mohammed, P.O.; Noor, M.A.; Alsharif, A.M.; Noor, K.I. New Fuzzy-Interval Inequalities in Fuzzy-Interval Fractional Calculus by Means of Fuzzy Order Relation. *AIMS Math.* **2021**, *6*, 10964–10988. [CrossRef]
40. Khan, M.B.; Noor, M.A.; Mohammed, P.O.; Guirao, J.L.; Noor, K.I. Some Integral Inequalities for Generalized Convex Fuzzy-Interval-Valued Functions via Fuzzy Riemann Integrals. *Int. J. Comput. Intell. Syst.* **2021**, *14*, 1–15. [CrossRef]
41. Khan, M.B.; Noor, M.A.; Al-Shomrani, M.M.; Abdullah, L. Some Novel Inequalities for LR-H-Convex Interval-Valued Functions by Means of Pseudo-Order Relation. *Math. Methods Appl. Sci.* **2022**, *45*, 1310–1340. [CrossRef]
42. Khan, M.B.; Noor, M.A.; Abdullah, L.; Chu, Y.M. Some New Classes of Preinvex Fuzzy-Interval-Valued Functions and Inequalities. *Int. J. Comput. Intell. Syst.* **2021**, *14*, 1403–1418. [CrossRef]
43. Khan, M.B.; Noor, M.A.; Abdeljawad, T.; Mousa, A.A.A.; Abdalla, B.; Alghamdi, S.M. LR-Preinvex Interval-Valued Functions and Riemann-Liouville Fractional Integral Inequalities. *Fractal Fract.* **2021**, *5*, 243. [CrossRef]
44. Liu, P.; Khan, M.B.; Noor, M.A.; Noor, K.I. New Hermite-Hadamard and Jensen Inequalities for Log-S-Convex Fuzzy-Interval-Valued Functions in the Second Sense. *Complex Intell. Syst.* **2021**, *2021*, 1–15. [CrossRef]
45. Sana, G.; Khan, M.B.; Noor, M.A.; Mohammed, P.O.; Chu, Y.M. Harmonically Convex Fuzzy-Interval-Valued Functions and Fuzzy-Interval Riemann–Liouville Fractional Integral Inequalities. *Int. J. Comput. Intell. Syst.* **2021**, *14*, 1809–1822. [CrossRef]
46. Khan, M.B.; Mohammed, P.O.; Noor, M.A.; Abualnaja, K.M. Fuzzy Integral Inequalities on Coordinates of Convex Fuzzy Interval-Valued Functions. *Math. Biosci. Eng.* **2021**, *18*, 6552–6580. [CrossRef]
47. Khan, M.B.; Treanţă, S.; Soliman, M.S.; Nonlaopon, K.; Zaini, H.G. Some Hadamard–Fejér Type Inequalities for LR-Convex Interval-Valued Functions. *Fractal Fract.* **2022**, *6*, 6. [CrossRef]
48. Khan, M.B.; Srivastava, H.M.; Mohammed, P.O.; Nonlaopon, K.; Hamed, Y.S. Some New Jensen, Schur and Hermite-Hadamard Inequalities for Log Convex Fuzzy Interval-Valued Functions. *AIMS Math.* **2022**, *7*, 4338–4358. [CrossRef]
49. Khan, M.B.; Mohammed, P.O.; Machado, J.A.T.; Guirao, J.L. Integral Inequalities for Generalized Harmonically Convex Functions in Fuzzy-Interval-Valued Settings. *Symmetry* **2021**, *13*, 2352. [CrossRef]
50. Khan, M.B.; Srivastava, H.M.; Mohammed, P.O.; Baleanu, D.; Jawa, T.M. Fuzzy-Interval Inequalities for Generalized Convex Fuzzy-Interval-Valued Functions via Fuzzy Riemann Integrals. *AIMS Math.* **2022**, *7*, 1507–1535. [CrossRef]
51. Macías-Díaz, J.E.; Khan, M.B.; Noor, M.A.; Abd Allah, A.M.; Alghamdi, S.M. Hermite-Hadamard Inequalities for Generalized Convex Functions in Interval-Valued Calculus. *AIMS Math.* **2022**, *7*, 4266–4292. [CrossRef]
52. Khan, M.B.; Zaini, H.G.; Treanţă, S.; Soliman, M.S.; Nonlaopon, K. Riemann–Liouville Fractional Integral Inequalities for Generalized Pre-Invex Functions of Interval-Valued Settings Based upon Pseudo Order Relation. *Mathematics* **2022**, *10*, 204. [CrossRef]
53. Konwar, N.; Debnath, P. Continuity and Banach Contraction Principle in Intuitionistic Fuzzy N-Normed Linear Spaces. *J. Intell. Fuzzy Syst.* **2017**, *33*, 2363–2373. [CrossRef]
54. Konwar, N.; Davvaz, B.; Debnath, P. Approximation of New Bounded Operators in Intuitionistic Fuzzy N-Banach Spaces. *J. Intell. Fuzzy Syst.* **2018**, *35*, 6301–6312. [CrossRef]
55. Srivastava, H.M.; Sahoo, S.K.; Mohammed, P.O.; Baleanu, D.; Kodamasingh, B. Hermite–Hadamard Type Inequalities for Interval-Valued Preinvex Functions via Fractional Integral Operators. *Int. J. Comput. Intell. Syst.* **2022**, *15*, 1–12. [CrossRef]
56. Sahoo, S.K.; Tariq, M.; Ahmad, H.; Aly, A.A.; Felemban, B.F.; Thounthong, P. Some Hermite–Hadamard-Type Fractional Integral Inequalities Involving Twice-Differentiable Mappings. *Symmetry* **2021**, *13*, 2209. [CrossRef]

symmetry

MDPI

Article

Some Fuzzy Riemann–Liouville Fractional Integral Inequalities for Preinvex Fuzzy Interval-Valued Functions

Muhammad Bilal Khan [1], **Hatim Ghazi Zaini** [2], **Jorge E. Macías-Díaz** [3,4,*], **Savin Treanţă** [5,*] and **Mohamed S. Soliman** [6]

1 Department of Mathematics, COMSATS University Islamabad, Islamabad 44000, Pakistan; bilal42742@gmail.com
2 Department of Computer Science, College of Computers and Information Technology, Taif University, P.O. Box 11099, Taif 21944, Saudi Arabia; h.zaini@tu.edu.sa
3 Departamento de Matemáticas y Física, Universidad Autónoma de Aguascalientes, Avenida, Universidad 940, Ciudad Universitaria, Aguascalientes 20131, Mexico
4 Department of Mathematics, School of Digital Technologies, Tallinn University, Narva Rd. 25, 10120 Tallinn, Estonia
5 Department of Applied Mathematics, University Politehnica of Bucharest, 060042 Bucharest, Romania
6 Department of Electrical Engineering, College of Engineering, Taif University, P.O. Box 11099, Taif 21944, Saudi Arabia; soliman@tu.edu.sa
* Correspondence: jemacias@correo.uaa.mx (J.E.M.-D.); savin.treanta@upb.ro (S.T.)

Abstract: The main objective of this study is to introduce new versions of fractional integral inequalities in fuzzy fractional calculus utilizing the introduced preinvexity. Due to the behavior of its definition, the idea of preinvexity plays a significant role in the subject of inequalities. The concepts of preinvexity and symmetry have a tight connection thanks to the significant correlation that has developed between both in recent years. In this study, we attain the Hermite-Hadamard ($H{\cdot}H$) and Hermite-Hadamard-Fejér ($H{\cdot}H$ Fejér) type inequalities for preinvex fuzzy-interval-valued functions (preinvex $F{\cdot}I{\cdot}V{\cdot}Fs$) via Condition C and fuzzy Riemann–Liouville fractional integrals. Furthermore, we establish some refinements of fuzzy fractional $H{\cdot}H$ type inequality. There are also some specific examples of the reported results for various preinvex functions deduced. To support the newly introduced ideal, we have provided some nontrivial and logical examples. The results presented in this research are a significant improvement over earlier results. This paper's awe-inspiring notions and formidable tools may energize and revitalize future research on this worthwhile and fascinating topic.

Keywords: preinvex fuzzy interval-valued function; fuzzy fractional integral operator; Hermite-Hadamard type inequality; Hermite-Hadamard Fejér type inequality

Citation: Khan, M.B.; Zaini, H.G.; Macías-Díaz, J.E.; Treanţă, S.; Soliman, M.S. Some Fuzzy Riemann–Liouville Fractional Integral Inequalities for Preinvex Fuzzy Interval-Valued Functions. *Symmetry* **2022**, *14*, 313. https://doi.org/10.3390/sym14020313

Academic Editor: Alexander Zaslavski

Received: 4 January 2022
Accepted: 21 January 2022
Published: 3 February 2022

1. Introduction

Convex function theory has a wide range of potential applications in a variety of unique and fascinating disciplines of study. Furthermore, this theory is useful in a variety of fields, including physics, information theory, coding theory, engineering, optimization, and inequality theory. This theory is currently making a significant contribution to the extensions and improvements of a wide range of mathematical and practical fields. Many authors analyzed, celebrated, and executed their work on the concept of convexity, and used fruitful methodologies and novel ideas to extend its many variations in helpful ways. In the literature, several new families of classical convex functions have been proposed. The references [1–5] are provided for the benefit of the readers. Many authors and scientists have always attempted to contribute to the theory of inequality by producing high-quality work. Integral inequalities on convex functions, both derivative and integration, have likewise been a hot and engaging area of study in recent years. The theory of inequalities has significant applications in the field of applied analysis, such as geometric function theory, impulsive diffusion equations, coding theory, numerical analysis, and fractional calculus, to name a few. Sun [6] and co-workers [7] recently used the local fractional integral operator to generalize the Hermite-Hadamard condition for harmonically convex and s-preinvex functions. The references [8–13] are provided for the benefit of the readers.

Several writers have recently proposed novel inequalities for various types of convexities, preinvexities, statistical theory, and other topics. Several discussions show a tight connection between inequality theory and convex functions. Hanson examined the invex function in the context of bi-function $\varphi(.,.)$ for the first time in 1981 (see [14]). Following Hanson's work, Ben-Israel and Mond attempted to delve deeper into linked invexity, introducing the concepts of invex sets and preinvex functions for the first time (see [15]). Under certain conditions, the preinvex and invex functions in the form of differentiability are comparable, according to Mohan and Neogy [16]. Antczak [17] discovered and analyzed the features of preinvex functions for the first time in 2005.

Note that fuzzy mappings ($F{\cdot}Ms$) are fuzzy-interval-valued functions. On the other hand, the concept of convex $F{\cdot}Ms$ from $\mathbb{R}^n$ to the set of fuzzy numbers was introduced by Nanda and Kar [18], Syau [19], and Furukawa [20]. They also explored Lipschitz continuity of fuzzy valued mappings and created other types of convex $F{\cdot}Ms$, such as logarithmic convex $F{\cdot}Ms$ and quasi-convex $F{\cdot}Ms$. Based on Goetschel and Voxman's concept of ordering [21], Yan and Xu [22] introduced the conceptions of epigraphs and convexity of $F{\cdot}Ms$, as well as the properties of convex $F{\cdot}Ms$ and quasi-convex $F{\cdot}Ms$. Khan et al. [23–26] extended the class of convex $F{\cdot}Ms$ and defined h-convex and (h_1, h_2)-convex $F{\cdot}I{\cdot}V{\cdot}Fs$ using fuzzy partial order relation. Moreover, they introduced $H{\cdot}H$, $H{\cdot}H$ Fejér, $H{\cdot}H$ fractional, $H{\cdot}H$ fractional Fejér for h-convex and (h_1, h_2)-convex $F{\cdot}I{\cdot}V{\cdot}Fs$ via fuzzy Riemannian and fuzzy Riemann–Liouville fractional integrals. Noor [27] proposed and investigated the notion of fuzzy preinvex mapping on the invex set. He also showed how to express the fuzzy optimality conditions of differentiable preinvex fuzzy mappings using variational inequalities. Recently Khan et al. [28] generalized the concept of preinvex fuzzy mappings in terms of (h_1, h_2)-preinvex $F{\cdot}I{\cdot}V{\cdot}Fs$. Moreover, they established relation between $H{\cdot}H$ inequalities and (h_1, h_2)-preinvex $F{\cdot}I{\cdot}V{\cdot}Fs$ by using fuzzy Riemannian integrals. Recently Khan et al. [29–33] proposed the concepts of strongly preinvex $F{\cdot}I{\cdot}V{\cdot}Fs$, higher strongly preinvex $F{\cdot}I{\cdot}V{\cdot}Fs$, generalized strongly preinvex $F{\cdot}I{\cdot}V{\cdot}Fs$ and characterized their optimality conditions by introducing different variational like inequalities. Moreover, they proposed $H{\cdot}H$ inequalities for strongly preinvex $F{\cdot}I{\cdot}V{\cdot}Fs$ by utilizing fuzzy Riemannian.

At one step forward, Khan et al. introduced new classes of convex and generalized convex $F{\cdot}I{\cdot}V{\cdot}Fs$, and derived new $H{\cdot}H$ type inequalities for log-s-convex $F{\cdot}I{\cdot}V{\cdot}Fs$ in the second sense [34], log-h-convex $F{\cdot}I{\cdot}V{\cdot}Fs$ [35] and the references therein. We refer to the readers for further analysis of literature on the applications and properties of fuzzy-interval, and inequalities and generalized convex $F{\cdot}Ms$, see [36–56] and the references therein.

The goal of this study is to complete the fuzzy Riemann–Liouville fractional integrals for $F{\cdot}I{\cdot}V{\cdot}Fs$ and use these integrals to get the $H{\cdot}H$ inequalities. These integrals are also used to derive $H{\cdot}H$ type inequalities for preinvex $F{\cdot}I{\cdot}V{\cdot}Fs$.

2. Preliminaries

Let $\mathcal{K}_C$ be the space of all closed and bounded intervals of $\mathbb{R}$ and $\eta \in \mathcal{K}_C$ be defined by

$$\eta = [\eta_*, \eta^*] = \{\omega \in \mathbb{R} |\ \eta_* \leq \omega \leq \eta^*\}, \quad (\eta_*, \eta^* \in \mathbb{R})$$

if $\eta_* = \eta^*$ then, η is said to be degenerate. In this article, all intervals will be non-degenerate intervals. If $\eta_* \geq 0$, then $[\eta_*, \eta^*]$ is called positive interval. The set of all positive interval is denoted by $\mathcal{K}_C^+$ and defined as $\mathcal{K}_C^+ = \{[\eta_*, \eta^*] : [\eta_*, \eta^*] \in \mathcal{K}_C \text{ and } \eta_* \geq 0\}$.

Let $\varsigma \in \mathbb{R}$ and $\varsigma\eta$ be defined by

$$\varsigma{\cdot}\eta = \begin{cases} [\varsigma\eta_*, \varsigma\eta^*] & \text{if } \varsigma \geq 0, \\ [\varsigma\eta^*, \varsigma\eta_*] & \text{if } \varsigma < 0. \end{cases} \tag{1}$$

Then the Minkowski difference $\xi - \eta$, addition $\eta + \xi$ and $\eta \times \xi$ for $\eta, \xi \in \mathcal{K}_C$ are defined by

$$\begin{aligned} [\xi_*, \xi^*] - [\eta_*, \eta^*] &= [\xi_* - \eta_*, \ \xi^* - \eta^*], \\ [\xi_*, \xi^*] + [\eta_*, \eta^*] &= [\xi_* + \eta_*, \ \xi^* + \eta^*], \end{aligned} \tag{2}$$

and

$$[\xi_*, \xi^*] \times [\eta_*, \eta^*] = [min\{\xi_*\eta_*, \xi^*\eta_*, \xi_*\eta^*, \xi^*\eta^*\}, max\{\xi_*\eta_*, \xi^*\eta_*, \xi_*\eta^*, \xi^*\eta^*\}]$$

The inclusion "$\subseteq$" means that

$$\xi \subseteq \eta \text{ if and only if, } [\xi_*, \xi^*] \subseteq [\eta_*, \eta^*], \text{ if and only if } \eta_* \le \xi_*, \ \xi^* \le \eta^* \tag{3}$$

Remark 2.1. [38] The relation "$\le_I$" defined on $\mathcal{K}_C$ by

$$[\nabla_*, \nabla^*] \le_I [\eta_*, \eta^*] \text{ if and only if } \nabla_* \le \eta_*, \nabla^* \le \eta^*, \tag{4}$$

for all $[\nabla_*, \nabla^*], [\eta_*, \eta^*] \in \mathcal{K}_C$, it is an order relation. For given $[\nabla_*, \nabla^*], [\eta_*, \eta^*] \in \mathcal{K}_C$, we say that $[\nabla_*, \nabla^*] \le_I [\eta_*, \eta^*]$ if and only if $\nabla_* \le \eta_*$, $\nabla^* \le \eta^*$ or $\nabla_* \le \eta_*$, $\nabla^* < \eta^*$.

A fuzzy subset A of $\mathbb{R}$ is characterize by a mapping $\zeta : \mathbb{R} \to [0,1]$ called the membership function, for each fuzzy set and $\theta \in (0, 1]$, then θ-level sets of ζ is denoted and defined as follows $\zeta_\theta = \{u \in \mathbb{R} |\ \zeta(u) \ge \theta\}$. If $\theta = 0$, then $supp(\zeta) = \{\omega \in \mathbb{R} \mid \zeta(\omega)\rangle 0\}$ is called support of ζ. By $[\zeta]^0$ we define the closure of $supp(\psi)$.

Let $\mathbb{F}(\mathbb{R})$ be the family of all fuzzy sets and $\zeta \in \mathbb{F}(\mathbb{R})$ denote the family of all nonempty sets. $\zeta \in \mathbb{F}(\mathbb{R})$ be a fuzzy set. Then we define the following:

(1) ζ is said to be normal if there exists $\omega \in \mathbb{R}$ and $\zeta(\omega) = 1$;
(2) ζ is said to be upper semi continuous on $\mathbb{R}$ if for given $\omega \in \mathbb{R}$, there exist $\varepsilon > 0$ there exist $\delta > 0$ such that $\zeta(\omega) - \zeta(y) < \varepsilon$ for all $y \in \mathbb{R}$ with $|\omega - y| < \delta$;
(3) ζ is said to be fuzzy convex if ζ_θ is convex for every $\theta \in [0,1]$;
(4) ζ is compactly supported if $supp(\zeta)$ is compact.

A fuzzy set is called a fuzzy number or fuzzy interval if it has properties (1), (2), (3) and (4). We denote by $\mathbb{F}_0$ the family of all intervals.

Let $\zeta \in \mathbb{F}_0$ be a fuzzy-interval, if and only if, θ-levels $[\zeta]^\theta$ is a nonempty compact convex set of $\mathbb{R}$. From these definitions, we have

$$[\zeta]^\theta = [\zeta_*(\theta), \zeta^*(\theta)],$$

where

$$\zeta_*(\theta) = inf\{\omega \in \mathbb{R} |\ \zeta(\omega) \ge \theta\}, \zeta^*(\theta) = sup\{\omega \in \mathbb{R} |\ \zeta(\omega) \ge \theta\}. \tag{5}$$

Proposition 2.2. [47] If $\zeta, \eta \in \mathbb{F}_0$ then relation "$\preccurlyeq$" defined on $\mathbb{F}_0$ by

$$\zeta \preccurlyeq \eta \text{ if and only if, } [\zeta]^\theta \le_I [\eta]^\theta, \text{ for all } \theta \in [0,1], \tag{6}$$

this relation is known as partial order relation.

For $\zeta, \eta \in \mathbb{F}_0$ and $\varsigma \in \mathbb{R}$, the sum $\zeta \tilde{+} \eta$, product $\zeta \tilde{\times} \eta$, scalar product $\varsigma.\zeta$ and sum with scalar are defined by:

Then, for all $\theta \in [0, 1]$, we have

$$[\zeta \tilde{+} \eta]^\theta = [\zeta]^\theta + [\eta]^\theta, \tag{7}$$

$$[\zeta \tilde{\times} \eta]^\theta = [\zeta]^\theta \times [\eta]^\theta, \tag{8}$$

$$[\varsigma.\zeta]^\theta = \varsigma.[\zeta]^\theta. \tag{9}$$

$$[\varsigma \tilde{+} \zeta]^{\theta} = \varsigma + [\zeta]^{\theta}. \tag{10}$$

For $\psi \in \mathbb{F}_0$ such that $\zeta = \eta \tilde{+} \psi$, then by this result we have existence of Hukuhara difference of ζ and η, and we say that ψ is the H-difference of ζ and η, and denoted by $\zeta \tilde{-} \eta$. If H-difference exists, then

$$(\psi)^*(\theta) = (\zeta \tilde{-} \eta)^*(\theta) = \zeta^*(\theta) - \eta^*(\theta),\ (\psi)_*(\theta) = (\zeta \tilde{-} \eta)_*(\theta) = \zeta_*(\theta) - \eta_*(\theta)$$

Definition 2.3. [36] A fuzzy map $\Psi : [u, v] \subset \mathbb{R} \to \mathbb{F}_0$ is called $F{\cdot}I{\cdot}V{\cdot}F$. For each $\theta \in [0, 1]$, whose θ-levels define the family of $I{\cdot}V{\cdot}F$ $\Psi_\theta : [u, v] \subset \mathbb{R} \to \mathcal{K}_C$ are given by $\Psi_\theta(\omega) = [\Psi_*(\omega, \theta), \Psi^*(\omega, \theta)]$ for all $\omega \in [u, v]$. Here, for each $\theta \in [0, 1]$, the left and right real valued functions $\Psi_*(\omega, \theta)$, $\Psi^*(\omega, \theta) : [u, v] \to \mathbb{R}$ are also called lower and upper functions of Ψ.

Remark 2.4. If $\Psi : [u, v] \subset \mathbb{R} \to \mathbb{F}_0$ is a $F{\cdot}I{\cdot}V{\cdot}F$, then $\Psi(\omega)$ is called continuous function at $\omega \in [u, v]$, if for each $\theta \in [0, 1]$, both left and right real valued functions $\Psi_*(\omega, \theta)$ and $\Psi^*(\omega, \theta)$ are continuous at $\omega \in [u, v]$.

The following FI Riemann–Liouville fractional integral operators were introduced by Allahviranloo et al. [40]:

Definition 2.5. Let $\beta > 0$ and $L([\mu, v], \mathbb{F}_0)$ be the collection of all Lebesgue measurable $F{\cdot}I{\cdot}V{\cdot}Fs$ on $[\mu, v]$. Then the fuzzy left and right Riemann–Liouville fractional integral of $\Psi \in L([\mu, v], \mathbb{F}_0)$ with order $\beta > 0$ are defined by

$$\mathcal{I}^{\beta}_{\mu^+} \Psi(\omega) = \frac{1}{\Gamma(\beta)} \int_{\mu}^{\omega} (\omega - \varsigma)^{\beta - 1} \Psi(\varsigma) d\varsigma,\ (\omega > \mu) \tag{11}$$

and

$$\mathcal{I}^{\beta}_{v^-} \Psi(\omega) = \frac{1}{\Gamma(\beta)} \int_{\omega}^{v} (\varsigma - \omega)^{\beta - 1} \Psi(\varsigma) d\varsigma,\ (\omega < v), \tag{12}$$

respectively, where $\Gamma(\omega) = \int_0^\infty \varsigma^{\omega - 1} e^{-\varsigma} d\varsigma$ is the Euler gamma function. The fuzzy left and right Riemann–Liouville fractional integral ω based on left and right end point functions can be defined, that is

$$\begin{aligned} \left[\mathcal{I}^{\beta}_{\mu^+} \Psi(\omega)\right]^{\theta} &= \tfrac{1}{\Gamma(\beta)} \int_{\mu}^{\omega} (\omega - \varsigma)^{\beta - 1} \Psi_\theta(\varsigma) d\varsigma \\ &= \tfrac{1}{\Gamma(\beta)} \int_{\mu}^{\omega} (\omega - \varsigma)^{\beta - 1} [\Psi_*(\varsigma, \theta), \Psi^*(\varsigma, \theta)] d\varsigma,\ (\omega > \mu) \end{aligned} \tag{13}$$

where

$$\mathcal{I}^{\beta}_{\mu^+} \Psi_*(\omega, \theta) = \frac{1}{\Gamma(\beta)} \int_{\mu}^{\omega} (\omega - \varsigma)^{\beta - 1} \Psi_*(\varsigma, \theta) d\varsigma,\ (\omega > \mu), \tag{14}$$

and

$$\mathcal{I}^{\beta}_{\mu^+} \Psi^*(\omega, \theta) = \frac{1}{\Gamma(\beta)} \int_{\mu}^{\omega} (\omega - \varsigma)^{\beta - 1} \Psi^*(\varsigma, \theta) d\varsigma,\ (\omega > \mu), \tag{15}$$

Similarly, the left and right end point functions can be used to define the right Riemann–Liouville fractional integral Ψ of ω.

Definition 2.6. [18]. The $F{\cdot}I{\cdot}V{\cdot}F$ $\Psi : [u, v] \to \mathbb{F}_0$ is called convex $F{\cdot}I{\cdot}V{\cdot}F$ on $[u, v]$ if

$$\Psi(\varsigma\omega + (1 - \varsigma) y) \preccurlyeq \varsigma \Psi(\omega) \tilde{+} (1 - \varsigma) \Psi(y), \tag{16}$$

for all $\omega,\ y \in\ [u,\ v]\ ,\ \varsigma \in\ [0,\ 1]\ $, where for all $\Psi(\omega)\ \succcurlyeq \widetilde{0}$ for all $\omega \in\ [u,\ v]$. If (16) is reversed, then Ψ is called concave $F{\cdot}I{\cdot}V{\cdot}F$ on $[u,\ v]$. Ψ is affine if and only if, it is both convex and concave $F{\cdot}I{\cdot}V{\cdot}F$.

Definition 2.7. [27]. The $F{\cdot}I{\cdot}V{\cdot}F\ \Psi:\ [u,\ v]\ \to \mathbb{F}_0$ is called preinvex $F{\cdot}I{\cdot}V{\cdot}F$ on invex interval $[u,\ v]$ if

$$\Psi(\omega+\ (1-\varsigma)\varphi(\omega,y))\ \preccurlyeq \varsigma\Psi(\omega)\widetilde{+}(1-\varsigma)\Psi(y)\ , \tag{17}$$

for all $\omega,\ y \in\ [u,\ v]\ ,\ \varsigma \in\ [0,\ 1]$, where $\Psi(\omega)\ \succcurlyeq \widetilde{0}$ for all $\omega \in\ [u,\ v]$ and $\varphi:\ [u,\ v]\ \times\ [u,\ v] \to \mathbb{R}$. If (17) is reversed then, Ψ is called preconcave $F{\cdot}I{\cdot}V{\cdot}F$ on $[u,\ v]$. Ψ is affine if and only if, it is both preinvex and preconcave $F{\cdot}I{\cdot}V{\cdot}F$.

We need the following assumption regarding the function $\varphi:\ [u,\ v]\ \times\ [u,\ v]\ \to \mathbb{R}$, which plays an important role in upcoming main results.

Condition C. [16]

$$\varphi(y,\omega+\tau\varphi(y,\omega))\ =\ (1-\tau)\varphi(y,\omega)\ ,$$

$$\varphi(\omega,\omega+\tau\varphi(y,\omega))\ =-\tau\varphi(y,\omega)$$

Note that $\forall\ \omega,\ y \in\ [u,\ v]$ and $\varsigma \in\ [0,\ 1]$, then from Condition C we have

$$\varphi(\omega+\tau_2\varphi(y,\omega)\ ,\omega+\tau_1\varphi(y,\omega))\ =\ (\tau_2-\tau_1)\varphi(y,\omega)$$

Clearly for $\tau = 0$, we have $\xi(y,\omega) = 0$ if and only if $y=\omega$, for all $\omega,\ y \in\ [u,\ v]$. For the application of Condition C, see [27–33].

Theorem 2.8. [28] *Let $[u,\ v]$ be an invex set with resoect to bifunvtion φ and $\Psi:\ [u,\ v]\ \to \mathbb{F}_C(\mathbb{R})$ be a $F{\cdot}I{\cdot}V{\cdot}F$ with $\Psi(\omega)\ \succcurlyeq \widetilde{0}$, whose θ-levels define the family of $I{\cdot}V{\cdot}Fs$ $\Psi_\theta:\ [u,\ v]\ \subset \mathbb{R} \to \mathcal{K}_C{}^+$ are given by*

$$\Psi_\theta(\omega)\ =\ [\Psi_*(\omega,\theta)\ ,\ \Psi^*(\omega,\theta)]\ ,\ \forall\ \omega \in\ [u,\ v] \tag{18}$$

for all $\omega \in\ [u,\ v]$ and for all $\theta \in\ [0,\ 1]$. Then, Ψ is preinvex F·I·V·F on $[u,\ v]$, if and only if, for all $\theta \in\ [0,\ 1]\ ,\ \Psi_*(\omega,\ \theta)$ and $\Psi^*(\omega,\ \theta)$ both are preinvex functions.

Remark 2.9. If $\varphi(\omega,y)\ =\omega-y$, then we obtain inequality (16).

If $\Psi_*(\omega,\theta)\ =\Psi^*(\omega,\theta)$ with $\theta=1$, then from (17), we obtain the definition of classical preinvex function, see [16].

If $\Psi_*(\omega,\theta)\ =\Psi^*(\omega,\theta)$ with $\varphi(\omega,y)\ =\omega-y$ and $\theta=1$, then from (17), we obtain the definition of classical convex function.

3. Fuzzy-Interval Fractional Hermite-Hadamard Inequalities

The major goal of this section is to build a new version of fractional $H{\cdot}H$ and $H{\cdot}H$ Fejér type inequality in the mode of preinvex $F{\cdot}I{\cdot}V{\cdot}Fs$, which is a classical studied topic. We also study some related inequalities. In what follows, we denote by $L([u,\ u+\varphi(v,u)]\ ,\mathbb{F}_0)$ the family of Lebesgue measureable $F{\cdot}I{\cdot}V{\cdot}Fs$.

Theorem 3.1. *Let $\Psi:\ [u,\ u+\varphi(v,u)]\ \to \mathbb{F}_0$ be a preinvex $F{\cdot}I{\cdot}V{\cdot}F$ on $[u,\ u+\varphi(v,u)]$, whose θ-levels define the family of $I{\cdot}V{\cdot}Fs$ $\Psi_\theta:\ [u,\ u+\varphi(v,u)]\ \subset \mathbb{R} \to \mathcal{K}_C{}^+$ are given by $\Psi_\theta(\omega) = [\Psi_*(\omega,\theta)\ ,\ \Psi^*(\omega,\theta)]$ for all $\omega \in\ [u,\ u+\varphi(v,u)]$ and for all $\theta \in\ [0,\ 1]$. If φ satisfies Condition C and $\Psi \in L([u,\ u+\varphi(v,u)]\ ,\mathbb{F}_0)$, then*

$$\Psi\left(\frac{2u+\varphi(v,u)}{2}\right)\ \preccurlyeq \frac{\Gamma(\beta+1)}{2(\varphi(v,u))^\beta}\left[\mathcal{I}^\beta_{u^+}\ \Psi(u+\varphi(v,u))\widetilde{+}\mathcal{I}^\beta_{u+\varphi(v,u)^-}\ \Psi(u)\right]\ \preccurlyeq \frac{\Psi(u)\widetilde{+}\Psi(u+\varphi(v,u))}{2} \preccurlyeq \frac{\Psi(u)\widetilde{+}\Psi(v)}{2} \tag{19}$$

If $\Psi(\omega)$ is preconcave $F{\cdot}I{\cdot}V{\cdot}F$ then

$$\Psi\left(\frac{2u+\varphi(\nu,u)}{2}\right) \succcurlyeq \frac{\Gamma(\beta+1)}{2(\varphi(\nu,u))^{\beta}}\left[\mathcal{I}_{u^+}^{\beta}\ \Psi(u+\varphi(\nu,u))\widetilde{+}\mathcal{I}_{u+\varphi(\nu,u)^-}^{\beta}\ \Psi(u)\right] \succcurlyeq \frac{\Psi(u)\widetilde{+}\Psi(u+\varphi(\nu,u))}{2} \succcurlyeq \frac{\Psi(u)\widetilde{+}\Psi(\nu)}{2} \quad (20)$$

Proof. Let $\Psi:\ [u,\ u+\varphi(\nu,u)]\ \rightarrow \mathbb{F}_0$ be a preinvex $F{\cdot}I{\cdot}V{\cdot}F$. If Condition C holds then, by hypothesis, we have that

$$2\Psi\left(\frac{2u+\varphi(\nu,u)}{2}\right) \preccurlyeq \Psi(u+\ (1-\varsigma)\varphi(\nu,u))\widetilde{+}\Psi(u+\varsigma\varphi(\nu,u))$$

Therefore, for every $\theta\,[0,1]$, we have

$$2\Psi_*\left(\tfrac{2u+\varphi(\nu,u)}{2},\ \theta\right)\ \leq \Psi_*(u+\ (1-\varsigma)\varphi(\nu,u)\ ,\ \theta)\ +\Psi_*(u+\varsigma\varphi(\nu,u)\ ,\ \theta)\ ,$$

$$2\Psi^*\left(\tfrac{2u+\varphi(\nu,u)}{2},\ \theta\right)\ \leq \Psi^*(u+\ (1-\varsigma)\varphi(\nu,u)\ ,\ \theta)\ +\Psi^*(u+\varsigma\varphi(\nu,u)\ ,\theta)\ .$$

Multiplying both sides by $\varsigma^{\beta-1}$ and integrating the obtained result with respect to ς over $(0,1)$, we have

$$2\int_0^1 \varsigma^{\beta-1}\Psi_*\left(\tfrac{2u+\varphi(\nu,u)}{2},\ \theta\right)d\varsigma$$

$$\leq \int_0^1 \varsigma^{\beta-1}\Psi_*(u+\ (1-\varsigma)\varphi(\nu,u)\ ,\theta)d\varsigma + \int_0^1 \varsigma^{\beta-1}\Psi_*(u+\varsigma\varphi(\nu,u)\ ,\ \theta)d\varsigma,$$

$$2\int_0^1 \varsigma^{\beta-1}\Psi^*\left(\tfrac{2u+\varphi(\nu,u)}{2},\theta\right)d\varsigma$$

$$\leq \int_0^1 \varsigma^{\beta-1}\Psi^*(u+\ (1-\varsigma)\varphi(\nu,u)\ ,\ \theta)d\varsigma + \int_0^1 \varsigma^{\beta-1}\Psi^*(u+\varsigma\varphi(\nu,u)\ ,\theta)d\varsigma.$$

Let $\omega = u+\ (1-\varsigma)\varphi(\nu,u)$ and $y = u+\varsigma\varphi(\nu,u)$. Then we have

$$\tfrac{2}{\beta}\Psi_*\left(\tfrac{2u+\varphi(\nu,u)}{2},\ \theta\right)\ \leq \tfrac{1}{(\varphi(\nu,u))^{\beta}}\int_u^{u+\varphi(\nu,u)}(u+\varphi(\nu,u)\ -y)^{\beta-1}\Psi_*(y,\theta)dy$$

$$+\tfrac{1}{(\varphi(\nu,u))^{\beta}}\int_u^{u+\varphi(\nu,u)}(\omega-u)^{\beta-1}\Psi_*(\omega,\theta)d\omega$$

$$\tfrac{2}{\beta}\Psi_*\left(\tfrac{2u+\varphi(\nu,u)}{2},\ \theta\right)\ \leq \tfrac{1}{(\varphi(\nu,u))^{\beta}}\int_u^{u+\varphi(\nu,u)}(u+\varphi(\nu,u)\ -y)^{\beta-1}\Psi^*(y,\theta)dy$$

$$+\tfrac{1}{(\varphi(\nu,u))^{\beta}}\int_u^{u+\varphi(\nu,u)}(\omega-u)^{\beta-1}\Psi^*(\omega,\theta)d\omega,$$

$$\leq \tfrac{\Gamma(\beta)}{(\varphi(\nu,u))^{\beta}}\left[\mathcal{I}_{u^+}^{\beta}\ \Psi_*(u+\varphi(\nu,u)\ ,\ \theta)\ +\mathcal{I}_{u+\varphi(\nu,u)^-}^{\beta}\ \Psi_*(u,\ \theta)\right]$$

$$\leq \tfrac{\Gamma(\beta)}{(\varphi(\nu,u))^{\beta}}\left[\mathcal{I}_{u^+}^{\beta}\ \Psi^*(u+\varphi(\nu,u)\ ,\ \theta)\ +\mathcal{I}_{u+\varphi(\nu,u)^-}^{\beta}\ \Psi^*(u,\ \theta)\right],$$

That is

$$\tfrac{2}{\beta}\left[\Psi_*\left(\tfrac{2u+\varphi(\nu,u)}{2},\ \theta\right),\ \Psi^*\left(\tfrac{2u+\varphi(\nu,u)}{2},\ \theta\right)\right]$$

$$\leq_I \tfrac{\Gamma(\beta)}{(\varphi(\nu,u))^{\beta}}\left[\mathcal{I}_{u^+}^{\beta}\ \Psi_*(u+\varphi(\nu,u)\ ,\ \theta)\ +\mathcal{I}_{u+\varphi(\nu,u)^-}^{\beta}\ \Psi_*(u,\ \theta)\ ,\ \mathcal{I}_{u^+}^{\beta}\ \Psi^*(u+\varphi(\nu,u)\ ,\ \theta)\ +\mathcal{I}_{\nu^-}^{\beta}\ \Psi^*(u+\varphi(\nu,u)\ ,\ \theta)\right]$$

Thus,

$$\frac{2}{\beta}\Psi\left(\frac{2u+\varphi(\nu,u)}{2}\right) \preccurlyeq \frac{\Gamma(\beta)}{(\varphi(\nu,u))^{\beta}}\left[\mathcal{I}^{\beta}_{u^+}\Psi(u+\varphi(\nu,u))\tilde{+}\mathcal{I}^{\beta}_{u+\varphi(\nu,u)^-}\Psi(u)\right] \tag{21}$$

In a similar way as above, we have

$$\frac{\Gamma(\beta)}{(\varphi(\nu,u))^{\beta}}\left[\mathcal{I}^{\beta}_{u^+}\Psi(u+\varphi(\nu,u))\tilde{+}\mathcal{I}^{\beta}_{u+\varphi(\nu,u)^-}\Psi(u)\right] \preccurlyeq \frac{\Psi(u)\tilde{+}\Psi(u+\varphi(\nu,u))}{2} \preccurlyeq \frac{\Psi(u)\tilde{+}\Psi(\nu)}{2}. \tag{22}$$

Combining (21) and (22), we have

$$\Psi\left(\frac{2u+\varphi(\nu,u)}{2}\right) \preccurlyeq \frac{\Gamma(\beta+1)}{2(\varphi(\nu,u))^{\beta}}\left[\mathcal{I}^{\beta}_{u^+}\Psi(u+\varphi(\nu,u))\tilde{+}\mathcal{I}^{\beta}_{u+\varphi(\nu,u)^-}\Psi(u)\right] \preccurlyeq \frac{\Psi(u)\tilde{+}\Psi(u+\varphi(\nu,u))}{2} \preccurlyeq \frac{\Psi(u)\tilde{+}\Psi(\nu)}{2}$$

Hence, the required result. □

Remark 3.2. From Theorem 3.1 we clearly see that

If $\varphi(\omega,y) = \omega - y$, then from Theorem 3.1, we get following result in fuzzy fractional calculus, see [23].

$$\Psi\left(\frac{u+\nu}{2}\right) \preccurlyeq \frac{\Gamma(\beta+1)}{2(\nu-u)^{\beta}}\left[\mathcal{I}^{\beta}_{u^+}\Psi(\nu)\tilde{+}\mathcal{I}^{\beta}_{\nu^-}\Psi(u)\right] \preccurlyeq \frac{\Psi(u)\tilde{+}\Psi(\nu)}{2}$$

Let $\beta = 1$. Then Theorem 3.1 reduces to the result for preinvex $F{\cdot}I{\cdot}V{\cdot}F$ given in [28]:

$$\Psi\left(\frac{2u+\varphi(\nu,u)}{2}\right) \preccurlyeq \frac{1}{\varphi(\nu,u)}\int_u^{u+\varphi(\nu,u)}\Psi(\omega)d\omega \preccurlyeq \frac{\Psi(u)\ \tilde{+}\ \Psi(\nu)}{2}.$$

Let $\beta = 1$ and $\varphi(\omega,y) = \omega - y$. Then Theorem 3.1 reduces to the result for convex $F{\cdot}I{\cdot}V{\cdot}F$ given in [26]:

$$\Psi\left(\frac{u+\nu}{2}\right) \preccurlyeq \frac{1}{\nu-u}\int_u^{\nu}\Psi(\omega)d\omega \preccurlyeq \frac{\Psi(u)\ \tilde{+}\ \Psi(\nu)}{2}$$

Let $\beta = 1 = \theta$ and $\Psi_*(\omega,\theta) = \Psi^*(\omega,\theta)$ with $\varphi(\omega,y) = \omega - y$. Then from Theorem 3.1 we obtain classical $H{\cdot}H$ Fejér type inequality.

Example 3.3. Let $\beta = \frac{1}{2}$, $\omega \in [2, 2+\varphi(3,2)]$, and the $F{\cdot}I{\cdot}V{\cdot}F$ $\Psi : [u,\ u+\varphi(\nu,u)] = [2, 2+\varphi(3,2)] \to \mathbb{F}_0$, defined by

$$\Psi(\omega)(\theta) = \begin{cases} \frac{\theta}{2-\omega^{\frac{1}{2}}} & \theta \in \left[0,\ 2-\omega^{\frac{1}{2}}\right] \\ \frac{2\left(2-\omega^{\frac{1}{2}}\right)-\theta}{2-\omega^{\frac{1}{2}}} & \theta \in \left(2-\omega^{\frac{1}{2}},\ 2\left(2-\omega^{\frac{1}{2}}\right)\right] \\ 0 & \textit{otherwise}, \end{cases}$$

Then, for each $\theta \in [0,\ 1]$, we have $\Psi_\theta(\omega) = \left[\theta\left(2-\omega^{\frac{1}{2}}\right),\ (2-\theta)\left(2-\omega^{\frac{1}{2}}\right)\right]$. Since left and right end point functions $\Psi_*(\omega,\theta) = \theta\left(2-\omega^{\frac{1}{2}}\right)$, $\Psi^*(\omega,\theta) = (2-\theta)\left(2-\omega^{\frac{1}{2}}\right)$, are preinvex functions with respect to $\varphi(\nu,u) = \nu - u$, for each $\theta \in [0,1]$, then $\Psi(\omega)$ is preinvex $F{\cdot}I{\cdot}V{\cdot}F$. We clearly see that $\Psi \in L([u,\ u+\varphi(\nu,u)], \mathbb{F}_0)$ and

$$\Psi_*\left(\frac{2u+\varphi(\nu,u)}{2},\ \theta\right) = \Psi_*\left(\frac{5}{2},\ \theta\right) = \theta\frac{4-\sqrt{10}}{2}$$

$$\Psi^*\left(\frac{2u+\varphi(v,u)}{2},\theta\right) = \Psi^*\left(\frac{5}{2},\theta\right) = (2-\theta)\frac{4-\sqrt{10}}{2}$$

$$\frac{\Psi_*(u,\theta) + \Psi_*(u+\varphi(v,u)\,,\theta)}{2} = \theta\left(\frac{4-\sqrt{2}-\sqrt{3}}{2}\right)$$

$$\frac{\Psi^*(u,\theta) + \Psi^*(u+\varphi(v,u)\,,\theta)}{2} = (2-\theta)\left(\frac{4-\sqrt{2}-\sqrt{3}}{2}\right)$$

Note that

$$\frac{\Gamma(\beta+1)}{2(\varphi(v,u))^\beta}\left[\mathcal{I}^\beta_{u^+}\,\Psi_*(u+\varphi(v,u)\,,\theta) + \mathcal{I}^\beta_{u+\varphi(v,u)^-}\,\Psi_*(u,\theta)\right]$$
$$= \frac{\Gamma\left(\frac{3}{2}\right)}{2}\frac{1}{\sqrt{\pi}}\int_2^{2+\varphi(3,2)}(3-\omega)^{\frac{-1}{2}}\,.\,\theta\left(2-\omega^{\frac{1}{2}}\right)d\omega$$
$$+ \frac{\Gamma\left(\frac{3}{2}\right)}{2}\frac{1}{\sqrt{\pi}}\int_2^{2+\varphi(3,2)}(\omega-2)^{\frac{-1}{2}}\,.\,\theta\left(2-\omega^{\frac{1}{2}}\right)d\omega$$
$$= \frac{1}{4}\theta\left[\frac{7393}{10,000}+\frac{9501}{10,000}\right]$$
$$= \theta\frac{8447}{20,000}$$

$$\frac{\Gamma(\beta+1)}{2(\varphi(v,u))^\beta}\left[\mathcal{I}^\beta_{u^+}\,\Psi^*(u+\varphi(v,u)\,,\theta) + \mathcal{I}^\beta_{u+\varphi(v,u)^-}\,\Psi^*(u,\theta)\right]$$
$$= \frac{\Gamma\left(\frac{3}{2}\right)}{2}\frac{1}{\sqrt{\pi}}\int_2^{2+\varphi(3,2)}(3-\omega)^{\frac{-1}{2}}\,.\,(2-\theta)\left(2-\omega^{\frac{1}{2}}\right)d\omega$$
$$+ \frac{\Gamma\left(\frac{3}{2}\right)}{2}\frac{1}{\sqrt{\pi}}\int_2^{2+\varphi(3,2)}(\omega-2)^{\frac{-1}{2}}\,.\,(2-\theta)\left(2-\omega^{\frac{1}{2}}\right)d\omega$$
$$= \frac{1}{4}(2-\theta)\left[\frac{7393}{10,000}+\frac{9501}{10,000}\right]$$
$$= (2-\theta)\frac{8447}{20,000}$$

Therefore

$$\left[\theta\frac{4-\sqrt{10}}{2},\,(2-\theta)\frac{4-\sqrt{10}}{2}\right] \leq_I \left[\theta\frac{8447}{20,000},\,(2-\theta)\frac{8447}{20,000}\right] \leq_I \left[\theta\left(\frac{4-\sqrt{2}-\sqrt{3}}{2}\right),\,(2-\theta)\left(\frac{4-\sqrt{2}+\sqrt{3}}{2}\right)\right]$$

and Theorem 3.1 is verified.

It is well known fact that $H{\cdot}H$ Fejér type inequality is a generalization of $H{\cdot}H$ type inequality. In Theorem 3.4 and Theorem 3.5, we obtain second and first fuzzy fractional $H{\cdot}H$ Fejér type inequalities for introduced preinvex $F{\cdot}I{\cdot}V{\cdot}F$.

Theorem 3.4. *Let $\Psi : [u,\ u+\varphi(v,u)] \to \mathbb{F}_0$ be a preinvex $F{\cdot}I{\cdot}V{\cdot}F$ with $u < v$, whose θ-levels define the family of $I{\cdot}V{\cdot}F$ $\Psi_\theta : [u,\ u+\varphi(v,u)] \subset \mathbb{R} \to \mathcal{K}_C^{\ +}$ are given by $\Psi_\theta(\omega) = [\Psi_*(\omega,\theta), \Psi^*(\omega,\theta)]$ for all $\omega \in [u,\ u+\varphi(v,u)]$ and for all $\theta \in [0,\ 1]$. Let $\Psi \in$*

$L([u,\ u+\varphi(\nu,u)],\mathbb{F}_0)$ and $\Omega:\ [u,\ u+\varphi(\nu,u)]\ \to\mathbb{R},\ \Omega(\omega)\ \geq 0,$ symmetric with respect to $\frac{2u+\varphi(\nu,u)}{2}$. If φ satisfies Condition C, then

$$\left[\mathcal{I}^{\beta}_{u^+}\ \Psi\Omega(u+\varphi(\nu,u))\widetilde{+}\mathcal{I}^{\beta}_{u+\varphi(\nu,u)^-}\ \Psi\Omega(u)\right]$$

$$\preccurlyeq \frac{\Psi(u)\widetilde{+}\Psi(u+\varphi(\nu,u))}{2}\left[\mathcal{I}^{\beta}_{u^+}\ \Omega(u+\varphi(\nu,u))\ +\mathcal{I}^{\beta}_{u+\varphi(\nu,u)^-}\ \Omega(u)\right] \tag{23}$$

$$\preccurlyeq \frac{\Psi(u)\widetilde{+}\Psi(\nu)}{2}\left[\mathcal{I}^{\beta}_{u^+}\ \Omega(u+\varphi(\nu,u))\widetilde{+}\mathcal{I}^{\beta}_{u+\varphi(\nu,u)^-}\ \Omega(u)\right]$$

If Ψ is preconcave $F{\cdot}I{\cdot}V{\cdot}F$, then inequality (23) is reversed.

Proof. Let Ψ be a preinvex $F{\cdot}I{\cdot}V{\cdot}F$ and $\varsigma^{\beta-1}\Omega(u+\ (1-\varsigma)\varphi(\nu,u))\ \geq 0$. Then, for each $\theta\in\ [0,\ 1]$, we have

$$\begin{gathered}\varsigma^{\beta-1}\Psi_*(u+\ (1-\varsigma)\varphi(\nu,u)\ ,\ \theta)\Omega(u+\ (1-\varsigma)\varphi(\nu,u))\\ \leq \varsigma^{\beta-1}(\varsigma\Psi_*(u,\ \theta)\ +\ (1-\varsigma)\Psi_*(u+\varphi(\nu,u)\ ,\ \theta))\Omega(u+\ (1-\varsigma)\varphi(u+\varphi(\nu,u)\ ,u))\\ \varsigma^{\beta-1}\Psi^*(u+\ (1-\varsigma)\varphi(\nu,u)\ ,\ \theta)\Omega(u+\ (1-\varsigma)\varphi(\nu,u))\\ \leq \varsigma^{\beta-1}(\varsigma\Psi^*(u,\ \theta)\ +\ (1-\varsigma)\Psi^*(u+\varphi(\nu,u)\ ,\ \theta))\Omega(u+\ (1-\varsigma)\varphi(u+\varphi(\nu,u)\ ,u)).\end{gathered} \tag{24}$$

and

$$\begin{gathered}\varsigma^{\beta-1}\Psi_*(u+\varsigma\varphi(\nu,u)\ ,\ \theta)\Omega(u+\varsigma\varphi(\nu,u))\\ \leq \varsigma^{\beta-1}((1-\varsigma)\Psi_*(u,\ \theta)\ +\varsigma\Psi_*(u+\varphi(\nu,u)\ ,\ \theta))\Omega(u+\varsigma\varphi(\nu,u))\\ \varsigma^{\beta-1}\Psi^*(u+\varsigma\varphi(\nu,u)\ ,\ \theta)\Omega(u+\varsigma\varphi(\nu,u))\\ \leq \varsigma^{\beta-1}((1-\varsigma)\Psi^*(u,\ \theta)\ +\varsigma\Psi^*(u+\varphi(\nu,u)\ ,\ \theta))\Omega(u+\varsigma\varphi(\nu,u))\end{gathered} \tag{25}$$

After adding (24) and (25), and integrating over $[0,\ 1]$, we get

$$\int_0^1\varsigma^{\beta-1}\Psi_*(u+\ (1-\varsigma)\varphi(\nu,u)\ ,\ \theta)\Omega(u+\ (1-\varsigma)\varphi(\nu,u))d\varsigma$$
$$+\int_0^1\varsigma^{\beta-1}\Psi_*(u+\varsigma\varphi(\nu,u)\ ,\ \theta)\Omega(u+\varsigma\varphi(\nu,u))d\varsigma$$
$$\leq\int_0^1\left[\begin{array}{c}\varsigma^{\beta-1}\Psi_*(u,\ \theta)\{\varsigma\Omega(u+\ (1-\varsigma)\varphi(\nu,u))\ +\ (1-\varsigma)\Omega(u+\varsigma\varphi(\nu,u))\}\\ +\varsigma^{\beta-1}\Psi_*(u+\varphi(\nu,u)\ ,\ \theta)\{(1-\varsigma)\Omega(u+\ (1-\varsigma)\varphi(\nu,u))\ +\varsigma\Omega(u+\varsigma\varphi(\nu,u))\}\end{array}\right]d\varsigma,$$
$$\int_0^1\varsigma^{\beta-1}\Psi^*(u+\varsigma\varphi(\nu,u)\ ,\ \theta)\Omega(u+\varsigma\varphi(\nu,u))d\varsigma$$
$$+\int_0^1\varsigma^{\beta-1}\Psi^*(u+\ (1-\varsigma)\varphi(\nu,u)\ ,\ \theta)\Omega(u+\ (1-\varsigma)\varphi(\nu,u))d\varsigma$$
$$\leq\int_0^1\left[\begin{array}{c}\varsigma^{\beta-1}\Psi^*(u,\ \theta)\{\varsigma\Omega(u+\ (1-\varsigma)\varphi(\nu,u))\ +\ (1-\varsigma)\Omega(u+\varsigma\varphi(\nu,u))\}\\ +\varsigma^{\beta-1}\Psi^*(u+\varphi(\nu,u)\ ,\ \theta)\{(1-\varsigma)\Omega(u+\ (1-\varsigma)\varphi(\nu,u))\ +\varsigma\Omega(u+\varsigma\varphi(\nu,u))\}\end{array}\right]d\varsigma,$$
$$=\Psi_*(u,\ \theta)\int_0^1\ \varsigma^{\beta-1}\Omega(u+\ (1-\varsigma)\varphi(\nu,u))\ d\varsigma+\Psi_*(u+\varphi(\nu,u)\ ,\ \theta)\int_0^1\ \varsigma^{\beta-1}\Omega(u+\varsigma\varphi(\nu,u))\ d\varsigma,$$
$$=\Psi^*(u,\ \theta)\int_0^1\ \varsigma^{\beta-1}\Omega(u+\ (1-\varsigma)\varphi(\nu,u))\ d\varsigma+\Psi^*(u+\varphi(\nu,u)\ ,\ \theta)\int_0^1\ \varsigma^{\beta-1}\Omega(u+\varsigma\varphi(\nu,u))\ d\varsigma.$$

Since Ω is symmetric, then

$$= [\Psi_*(u,\ \theta)\ + \Psi_*(u+\varphi(\nu,u)\ ,\ \theta)] \int_0^1\ \varsigma^{\beta-1}\Omega(u+\varsigma\varphi(\nu,u))\ d\varsigma$$

$$= [\Psi^*(u,\ \theta)\ + \Psi^*(u+\varphi(\nu,u)\ ,\ \theta)] \int_0^1\ \varsigma^{\beta-1}\Omega(u+\varsigma\varphi(\nu,u))\ d\varsigma.$$

$$= \frac{\Psi_*(u,\theta)\ +\Psi_*(u+\varphi(\nu,u)\ ,\theta)}{2}\frac{\Gamma(\beta)}{(\varphi(\nu,u))^\beta}\left[\mathcal{I}^\beta_{u^+}\ \Omega(u+\varphi(\nu,u))\ +\mathcal{I}^\beta_{u+\varphi(\nu,u)^-}\ \Omega(u)\right], \tag{26}$$

$$= \frac{\Psi^*(u,\theta)\ +\Psi^*(u+\varphi(\nu,u)\ ,\theta)}{2}\frac{\Gamma(\beta)}{(\varphi(\nu,u))^\beta}\left[\mathcal{I}^\beta_{u^+}\ \Omega(u+\varphi(\nu,u))\ +\mathcal{I}^\beta_{u+\varphi(\nu,u)^-}\ \Omega(u)\right].$$

Since

$$\begin{aligned}
&\int_0^1 \varsigma^{\beta-1}\Psi_*(u+\ (1-\varsigma)\varphi(\nu,u)\ ,\ \theta)\Omega(u+\varsigma\varphi(\nu,u))d\varsigma \\
&\quad+\int_0^1 \varsigma^{\beta-1}\Psi_*(u+\varsigma\varphi(\nu,u)\ ,\ \theta)\Omega(u+\varsigma\varphi(\nu,u))d\varsigma \\
&= \frac{1}{(\varphi(\nu,u))^\beta}\ \int_u^{u+\varphi(\nu,u)}(\omega-u)^{\beta-1}\Psi_*(2u+\varphi(\nu,u)\ -\omega,\theta)\Omega(\omega)d\omega \\
&\quad+\frac{1}{(\varphi(\nu,u))^\beta}\ \int_u^{u+\varphi(\nu,u)}(\omega-u)^{\beta-1}\Psi_*(\omega,\theta)\Omega(\omega)d\omega \\
&= \frac{1}{(\varphi(\nu,u))^\beta}\ \int_u^{u+\varphi(\nu,u)}(\omega-u)^{\beta-1}\Psi_*(\omega,\theta)\Omega(2u+\varphi(\nu,u)\ -\omega)d\omega \\
&\quad+\frac{1}{(\varphi(\nu,u))^\beta}\ \int_u^{u+\varphi(\nu,u)}(\omega-u)^{\beta-1}\Psi_*(\omega,\theta)\Omega(\omega)d\omega \\
&= \frac{\Gamma(\beta)}{(\varphi(\nu,u))^\beta}\left[\mathcal{I}^\beta_{u^+}\ \Psi_*\Omega(\nu)\ +\mathcal{I}^\beta_{\nu^-}\ \Psi_*\Omega(u)\right], \\
&\int_0^1 \varsigma^{\beta-1}\Psi^*(u+\ (1-\varsigma)\varphi(\nu,u)\ ,\ \theta)\Omega(u+\varsigma\varphi(\nu,u))d\varsigma \\
&\quad+\int_0^1 \varsigma^{\beta-1}\Psi^*(u+\varsigma\varphi(\nu,u)\ ,\ \theta)\Omega(u+\varsigma\varphi(\nu,u))d\varsigma \\
&= \frac{\Gamma(\beta)}{(\varphi(\nu,u))^\beta}\left[\mathcal{I}^\beta_{u^+}\ \Psi^*\Omega(u+\varphi(\nu,u))\ +\mathcal{I}^\beta_{u+\varphi(\nu,u)^-}\ \Psi^*\Omega(u)\right].
\end{aligned} \tag{27}$$

Then from (26), we have

$$\begin{aligned}
&\frac{\Gamma(\beta)}{(\varphi(\nu,u))^\beta}\left[\mathcal{I}^\beta_{u^+}\ \Psi_*\Omega(u+\varphi(\nu,u))\ +\mathcal{I}^\beta_{u+\varphi(\nu,u)^-}\ \Psi_*\Omega(u)\right] \\
&\le \frac{\Psi_*(u,\theta)\ +\Psi_*(u+\varphi(\nu,u)\ ,\theta)}{2}\frac{\Gamma(\beta)}{(\varphi(\nu,u))^\beta}\left[\mathcal{I}^\beta_{u^+}\ \Omega(u+\varphi(\nu,u))\ +\mathcal{I}^\beta_{u+\varphi(\nu,u)^-}\ \Omega(u)\right] \\
&\le \frac{\Psi_*(u,\theta)\ +\Psi_*(u+\varphi(\nu,u)\ ,\theta)}{2}\frac{\Gamma(\beta)}{(\varphi(\nu,u))^\beta}\left[\mathcal{I}^\beta_{u^+}\ \Omega(u+\varphi(\nu,u))\ +\mathcal{I}^\beta_{u+\varphi(\nu,u)^-}\ \Omega(u)\right], \\
&\frac{\Gamma(\beta)}{(\varphi(\nu,u))^\beta}\left[\mathcal{I}^\beta_{u^+}\ \Psi^*\Omega(u+\varphi(\nu,u))\ +\mathcal{I}^\beta_{u+\varphi(\nu,u)^-}\ \Psi^*\Omega(u)\right] \\
&\le \frac{\Psi^*(u,\theta)\ +\Psi^*(u+\varphi(\nu,u)\ ,\theta)}{2}\frac{\Gamma(\beta)}{(\varphi(\nu,u))^\beta}\left[\mathcal{I}^\beta_{u^+}\ \Omega(u+\varphi(\nu,u))\ +\mathcal{I}^\beta_{u+\varphi(\nu,u)^-}\ \Omega(u)\right] \\
&\le \frac{\Psi^*(u,\theta)\ +\Psi^*(u+\varphi(\nu)\ ,\theta)}{2}\frac{\Gamma(\beta)}{(\varphi(\nu,u))^\beta}\left[\mathcal{I}^\beta_{u^+}\ \Omega(u+\varphi(\nu,u))\ +\mathcal{I}^\beta_{u+\varphi(\nu,u)^-}\ \Omega(u)\right],
\end{aligned}$$

that is

$$\frac{\Gamma(\beta)}{(\varphi(\nu,u))^{\beta}}\left[\left[\mathcal{I}_{u^+}^{\beta}\ \Psi_*\Omega(u+\varphi(\nu,u))\ +\mathcal{I}_{u+\varphi(\nu,u)^-}^{\beta}\ \Psi_*\Omega(u)\right],\mathcal{I}_{u^+}^{\beta}\ \Psi^*\Omega(u+\varphi(\nu,u))\ +\mathcal{I}_{u+\varphi(\nu,u)^-}^{\beta}\ \Psi^*\Omega(u)\right]$$

$$\leq_I \frac{\Gamma(\beta)}{(\varphi(\nu,u))^{\beta}}\left[\frac{\Psi_*(u,\theta)\ +\Psi_*(u+\varphi(\nu,u)\ ,\theta)}{2},\ \frac{\Psi^*(u,\theta)\ +\Psi^*(u+\varphi(\nu,u)\ ,\theta)}{2}\right]\left[\mathcal{I}_{u^+}^{\beta}\ \Omega(u+\varphi(\nu,u))\ +\mathcal{I}_{u+\varphi(\nu,u)^-}^{\beta}\ \Omega(u)\right]$$

$$\leq_I \frac{\Gamma(\beta)}{(\varphi(\nu,u))^{\beta}}\left[\frac{\Psi_*(u,\theta)\ +\Psi_*(\nu,\theta)}{2},\ \frac{\Psi^*(u,\theta)\ +\Psi^*(\nu,\theta)}{2}\right]\left[\mathcal{I}_{u^+}^{\beta}\ \Omega(u+\varphi(\nu,u))\ +\mathcal{I}_{u+\varphi(\nu,u)^-}^{\beta}\ \Omega(u)\right]$$

hence

$$\left[\mathcal{I}_{u^+}^{\beta}\ \Psi\Omega(u+\varphi(\nu,u))\ \tilde{+}\,\mathcal{I}_{u+\varphi(\nu,u)^-}^{\beta}\ \Psi\Omega(u)\right]$$

$$\preccurlyeq \frac{\Psi(u)\tilde{+}\Psi(u+\varphi(\nu,u))}{2}\left[\mathcal{I}_{u^+}^{\beta}\ \Omega(u+\varphi(\nu,u))\ +\mathcal{I}_{u+\varphi(\nu,u)^-}^{\beta}\ \Omega(u)\right]$$

$$\preccurlyeq \frac{\Psi(u)\tilde{+}\Psi(\nu)}{2}\left[\mathcal{I}_{u^+}^{\beta}\ \Omega(u+\varphi(\nu,u))\tilde{+}\,\mathcal{I}_{u+\varphi(\nu,u)^-}^{\beta}\ \Omega(u)\right]$$

□

Theorem 3.5. *Let* $\Psi:\ [u,\ u+\varphi(\nu,u)]\ \to\mathbb{F}_0$ *be a preinvex F·I·V·F with* $u<\nu$, *whose* θ*-levels define the family of I·V·Fs* $\Psi_\theta:\ [u,\ u+\varphi(\nu,u)]\ \subset\mathbb{R}\to\mathcal{K}_C{}^+$ *are given by* $\Psi_\theta(\omega)=[\Psi_*(\omega,\theta)\ ,\ \Psi^*(\omega,\theta)]$ *for all* $\omega\in\ [u,\ u+\varphi(\nu,u)]$ *and for all* $\theta\in\ [0,\ 1]$*. If* $\Psi\in L([u,\ u+\varphi(\nu,u)],\mathbb{F}_0)$ *and* $\Omega:\ [u,\ u+\varphi(\nu,u)]\ \to\mathbb{R},\ \Omega(\omega)\ \geq0$, *symmetric with respect to* $\frac{2u+\varphi(\nu,u)}{2}$*. If* φ *satisfies Condition C and then*

$$\Psi\left(\frac{2u+\varphi(\nu,u)}{2}\right)\left[\mathcal{I}_{u^+}^{\beta}\ \Omega(u+\varphi(\nu,u))\ +\mathcal{I}_{u+\varphi(\nu,u)^-}^{\beta}\ \Omega(u)\right]$$
$$\preccurlyeq\ \left[\mathcal{I}_{u^+}^{\beta}\ \Psi\Omega(u+\varphi(\nu,u))\tilde{+}\mathcal{I}_{u+\varphi(\nu,u)^-}^{\beta}\ \Psi\Omega(u)\right]. \quad (28)$$

If Ψ is preconcave *F·I·V·F*, then inequality (28) is reversed.

Proof. Since Ψ is a preinvex *F·I·V·F*, then for $\theta\in\ [0,\ 1]$, we have

$$\Psi_*\left(\frac{2u+\varphi(\nu,u)}{2},\ \theta\right)\ \leq\tfrac{1}{2}(\Psi_*(u+\ (1-\varsigma)\varphi(\nu,u)\ ,\ \theta)\ +\Psi_*(u+\varsigma\varphi(\nu,u)\ ,\ \theta))$$
$$\Psi^*\left(\frac{2u+\varphi(\nu,u)}{2},\ \theta\right)\ \leq\tfrac{1}{2}(\Psi^*(u+\ (1-\varsigma)\varphi(\nu,u)\ ,\ \theta)\ +\Psi^*(u+\varsigma\varphi(\nu,u)\ ,\ \theta))\ , \quad (29)$$

Since $\Omega(u+\ (1-\varsigma)\varphi(\nu,u))\ =\ \Omega(u+\varsigma\varphi(\nu,u))$, then by multiplying (29) by $\varsigma^{\beta-1}\Omega(u+\varsigma\varphi(\nu,u))$ and integrate it with respect to ς over $[0,\ 1]$, we obtain

$$\Psi_*\left(\frac{2u+\varphi(\nu,u)}{2},\ \theta\right)\int_0^1\varsigma^{\beta-1}\Omega(u+\varsigma\varphi(\nu,u))d\varsigma$$
$$\leq\frac{1}{2}\left(\begin{array}{c}\int_0^1\varsigma^{\beta-1}\Psi_*(u+\ (1-\varsigma)\varphi(\nu,u)\ ,\ \theta)\Omega(u+\varsigma\varphi(\nu,u))d\varsigma\\ +\int_0^1\varsigma^{\beta-1}\Psi_*(u+\varsigma\varphi(\nu,u)\ ,\ \theta)\Omega(u+\varsigma\varphi(\nu,u))d\varsigma\end{array}\right),$$
$$\Psi^*\left(\frac{2u+\varphi(\nu,u)}{2},\ \theta\right)\int_0^1\Omega(u+\varsigma\varphi(\nu,u))d\varsigma$$
$$\leq\frac{1}{2}\left(\begin{array}{c}\int_0^1\varsigma^{\beta-1}\Psi^*(u+\ (1-\varsigma)\varphi(\nu,u)\ ,\ \theta)\Omega(u+\varsigma\varphi(\nu,u))d\varsigma\\ +\int_0^1\varsigma^{\beta-1}\Psi^*(u+\varsigma\varphi(\nu,u)\ ,\ \theta)\Omega(u+\varsigma\varphi(\nu,u))d\varsigma\end{array}\right). \quad (30)$$

Let $\omega = u + \varsigma\varphi(\nu, u)$. Then we have

$$\begin{aligned}
&\int_0^1 \varsigma^{\beta-1}\Psi_*(u + (1-\varsigma)\varphi(\nu,u), \theta)\Omega(u+\varsigma\varphi(\nu,u))d\varsigma \\
&\quad + \int_0^1 \varsigma^{\beta-1}\Psi_*(u+\varsigma\varphi(\nu,u), \theta)\Omega(u+\varsigma\varphi(\nu,u))d\varsigma \\
&= \frac{1}{(\varphi(\nu,u))^\beta} \int_u^{u+\varphi(\nu,u)} (\omega-u)^{\beta-1}\Psi_*(2u+\varphi(\nu,u) - \omega, \theta)\Omega(\omega)d\omega \\
&\quad + \frac{1}{(\varphi(\nu,u))^\beta} \int_u^{u+\varphi(\nu,u)} (\omega-u)^{\beta-1}\Psi_*(\omega,\theta)\Omega(\omega)d\omega \\
&= \frac{1}{(\varphi(\nu,u))^\beta} \int_u^{u+\varphi(\nu,u)} (\omega-u)^{\beta-1}\Psi_*(\omega,\theta)\Omega(2u+\varphi(\nu,u) - \omega)d\omega \\
&\quad + \frac{1}{(\varphi(\nu,u))^\beta} \int_u^{u+\varphi(\nu,u)} (\omega-u)^{\beta-1}\Psi_*(\omega,\theta)\Omega(\omega)d\omega \\
&= \frac{\Gamma(\beta)}{(\varphi(\nu,u))^\beta}\left[\mathcal{I}_{u^+}^\beta\ \Psi_*\Omega(u+\varphi(\nu,u)) + \mathcal{I}_{u+\varphi(\nu,u)^-}^\beta\ \Psi_*\Omega(u)\right], \\
&\int_0^1 \varsigma^{\beta-1}\Psi^*(u + (1-\varsigma)\varphi(\nu,u), \theta)\Omega(u+\varsigma\varphi(\nu,u))d\varsigma \\
&\quad + \int_0^1 \varsigma^{\beta-1}\Psi^*(u+\varsigma\varphi(\nu,u), \theta)\Omega(u+\varsigma\varphi(\nu,u))d\varsigma \\
&= \frac{\Gamma(\beta)}{(\varphi(\nu,u))^\beta}\left[\mathcal{I}_{u^+}^\beta\ \Psi^*\Omega(u+\varphi(\nu,u)) + \mathcal{I}_{u+\varphi(\nu,u)^-}^\beta\ \Psi^*\Omega(u)\right].
\end{aligned} \tag{31}$$

Then from (31), we have

$$\begin{aligned}
&\frac{\Gamma(\beta)}{(\varphi(\nu,u))^\beta}\Psi_*\left(\frac{2u+\varphi(\nu,u)}{2}, \theta\right)\left[\mathcal{I}_{u^+}^\beta\ \Omega(u+\varphi(\nu,u)) + \mathcal{I}_{u+\varphi(\nu,u)^-}^\beta\ \Omega(u)\right] \\
&\quad \le \frac{\Gamma(\beta)}{(\varphi(\nu,u))^\beta}\left[\mathcal{I}_{u^+}^\beta\ \Psi_*\Omega(u+\varphi(\nu,u)) + \mathcal{I}_{u+\varphi(\nu,u)^-}^\beta\ \Psi_*\Omega(u)\right] \\
&\frac{\Gamma(\beta)}{(\varphi(\nu,u))^\beta}\Psi^*\left(\frac{2u+\varphi(\nu,u)}{2}, \theta\right)\left[\mathcal{I}_{u^+}^\beta\ \Omega(u+\varphi(\nu,u)) + \mathcal{I}_{u+\varphi(\nu,u)^-}^\beta\ \Omega(u)\right] \\
&\quad \le \frac{\Gamma(\beta)}{(\varphi(\nu,u))^\beta}\left[\mathcal{I}_{u^+}^\beta\ \Psi^*\Omega(u+\varphi(\nu,u)) + \mathcal{I}_{u+\varphi(\nu,u)^-}^\beta\ \Psi^*\Omega(u)\right],
\end{aligned}$$

from which, we have

$$\begin{aligned}
&\frac{\Gamma(\beta)}{(\varphi(\nu,u))^\beta}\left[\Psi_*\left(\frac{2u+\varphi(\nu,u)}{2}, \theta\right), \Psi^*\left(\frac{2u+\varphi(\nu,u)}{2}, \theta\right)\right]\left[\mathcal{I}_{u^+}^\beta\ \Omega(u+\varphi(\nu,u)) + \mathcal{I}_{u+\varphi(\nu,u)^-}^\beta\ \Omega(u)\right] \\
&\le_I \frac{\Gamma(\beta)}{(\varphi(\nu,u))^\beta}\left[\mathcal{I}_{u^+}^\beta\ \Psi_*\Omega(u+\varphi(\nu,u)) + \mathcal{I}_{u+\varphi(\nu,u)^-}^\beta\ \Psi_*\Omega(u), \mathcal{I}_{u^+}^\beta\ \Psi^*\Omega(u+\varphi(\nu,u)) + \mathcal{I}_{u+\varphi(\nu,u)^-}^\beta\ \Psi^*\Omega(u)\right],
\end{aligned}$$

that is

$$\begin{aligned}
&\frac{\Gamma(\beta)}{(\varphi(\nu,u))^\beta}\Psi\left(\frac{2u+\varphi(\nu,u)}{2}\right)\left[\mathcal{I}_{u^+}^\beta\ \Omega(u+\varphi(\nu,u)) + \mathcal{I}_{u+\varphi(\nu,u)^-}^\beta\ \Omega(u)\right] \\
&\quad \preccurlyeq \frac{\Gamma(\beta)}{(\varphi(\nu,u))^\beta}\left[\mathcal{I}_{u^+}^\beta\ \Psi\Omega(u+\varphi(\nu,u))\tilde{+}\mathcal{I}_{u+\varphi(\nu,u)^-}^\beta\ \Psi\Omega(u)\right]
\end{aligned}$$

This completes the proof. □

Example 3.6. We consider the $F{\cdot}I{\cdot}V{\cdot}F$ $\Psi : [0, 2] \to \mathbb{F}_0$ defined by,

$$\Psi(\omega)(\sigma) = \begin{cases} \frac{\sigma}{2-\sqrt{\omega}}, & \sigma \in \left[0, 2-\sqrt{\omega}\right], \\ \frac{2\left(2-\sqrt{\omega}\right)-\sigma}{2-\sqrt{\omega}}, & \sigma \in \left(2-\sqrt{\omega}, 2\left(2-\sqrt{\omega}\right)\right], \\ 0, & otherwise. \end{cases}$$

Then, for each $\theta \in [0, 1]$, we have $\Psi_\theta(\omega) = \left[\theta\left(2-\sqrt{\omega}\right), (2-\theta)\left(2-\sqrt{\omega}\right)\right]$. Since end point functions $\Psi_*(\omega,\theta)$, $\Psi^*(\omega,\theta)$ are preinvex functions with respect to $\varphi(\nu,u) = \nu - u$ for each $\theta \in [0,1]$, then $\Psi(\omega)$ is preinvex $F{\cdot}I{\cdot}V{\cdot}F$. If

$$\Omega(\omega) = \begin{cases} \sqrt{\omega}, & \sigma \in [0,1], \\ \sqrt{2-\omega}, & \sigma \in (1, 2], \end{cases}$$

then $\Omega(2-\omega) = \Omega(\omega) \geq 0$, for all $\omega \in [0, 2]$. Since $\Psi_*(\omega,\theta) = \theta\left(2-\sqrt{\omega}\right)$ and $\Psi^*(\omega,\theta) = (2-\theta)\left(2-\sqrt{\omega}\right)$. If $\beta = \frac{1}{2}$, then we compute the following:

$$\left[\mathcal{I}^{\beta}_{u^+}\ \Psi\Omega(u+\varphi(\nu,u))\tilde{+}\mathcal{I}^{\beta}_{u+\varphi(\nu,u)^-}\ \Psi\Omega(u)\right] \preccurlyeq \frac{\Psi(u)\tilde{+}\Psi(u+\varphi(\nu,u))}{2}\left[\begin{array}{c}\mathcal{I}^{\beta}_{u^+}\ \Omega(u+\varphi(\nu,u)) \\ +\mathcal{I}^{\beta}_{u+\varphi(\nu,u)^-}\ \Omega(u)\end{array}\right]$$

$$\preccurlyeq \frac{\Psi(u)\tilde{+}\Psi(\nu)}{2}\left[\mathcal{I}^{\beta}_{u^+}\ \Omega(u+\varphi(\nu,u)) + \mathcal{I}^{\beta}_{u+\varphi(\nu,u)^-}\ \Omega(u)\right] \tag{32}$$

$$\frac{\Psi_*(u)+\Psi_*(u+\varphi(\nu,u))}{2}\left[\mathcal{I}^{\beta}_{u^+}\ \Omega(u+\varphi(\nu,u)) + \mathcal{I}^{\beta}_{u+\varphi(\nu,u)^-}\ \Omega(u)\right] = \frac{\pi}{\sqrt{2}}\theta\left(\frac{4-\sqrt{2}}{2}\right)$$

$$\frac{\Psi^*(u)\tilde{+}\Psi^*(u+\varphi(\nu,u))}{2}\left[\mathcal{I}^{\beta}_{u^+}\ \Omega(u+\varphi(\nu,u)) + \mathcal{I}^{\beta}_{u+\varphi(\nu,u)^-}\ \Omega(u)\right] = \frac{\pi}{\sqrt{2}}(2-\theta)\left(\frac{4-\sqrt{2}}{2}\right),$$

$$\frac{\Psi_*(u)+\Psi_*(\nu)}{2}\left[\mathcal{I}^{\beta}_{u^+}\ \Omega(u+\varphi(\nu,u)) + \mathcal{I}^{\beta}_{u+\varphi(\nu,u)^-}\ \Omega(u)\right] = \frac{\pi}{\sqrt{2}}\theta\left(\frac{4-\sqrt{2}}{2}\right)$$

$$\frac{\Psi^*(u)\tilde{+}\Psi^*(\nu)}{2}\left[\mathcal{I}^{\beta}_{u^+}\ \Omega(u+\varphi(\nu,u)) + \mathcal{I}^{\beta}_{u+\varphi(\nu,u)^-}\ \Omega(u)\right] = \frac{\pi}{\sqrt{2}}(2-\theta)\left(\frac{4-\sqrt{2}}{2}\right), \tag{33}$$

$$\left[\mathcal{I}^{\beta}_{u^+}\ \Psi_*\Omega(u+\varphi(\nu,u)) + \mathcal{I}^{\beta}_{u+\varphi(\nu,u)^-}\ \Psi_*\Omega(u)\right] = \frac{1}{\sqrt{\pi}}\theta\left(2\pi + \frac{4-8\sqrt{2}}{3}\right),$$

$$\left[\mathcal{I}^{\beta}_{u^+}\ \Psi^*\Omega(u+\varphi(\nu,u)) + \mathcal{I}^{\beta}_{u+\varphi(\nu,u)^-}\ \Psi^*\Omega(u)\right] = \frac{1}{\sqrt{\pi}}(2-\theta)\left(2\pi + \frac{4-8\sqrt{2}}{3}\right). \tag{34}$$

From (32), (33) and (34), we have

$$\frac{1}{\sqrt{\pi}}\left[\theta\left(2\pi + \frac{4-8\sqrt{2}}{3}\right), (2-\theta)\left(2\pi + \frac{4-8\sqrt{2}}{3}\right)\right] \leq_I \frac{\pi}{\sqrt{2}}\left[\theta\left(\frac{4-\sqrt{2}}{2}\right), (2-\theta)\left(\frac{4-\sqrt{2}}{2}\right)\right]$$

$$= \frac{\pi}{\sqrt{2}}\left[\theta\left(\frac{4-\sqrt{2}}{2}\right), (2-\theta)\left(\frac{4-\sqrt{2}}{2}\right)\right]$$

for each $\theta \in [0, 1]$. Hence, Theorem 10 is verified.

For Theorem 11, we have

$$\Psi_*\left(\frac{2u+\varphi(\nu,u)}{2}, \theta\right)\left[\mathcal{I}^{\beta}_{u^+}\ \Omega(u+\varphi(\nu,u)) + \mathcal{I}^{\beta}_{u+\varphi(\nu,u)^-}\ \Omega(u)\right] = \theta\sqrt{\pi},$$

$$\Psi^*\left(\frac{2u+\varphi(\nu,u)}{2}, \theta\right)\left[\mathcal{I}^{\beta}_{u^+}\ \Omega(u+\varphi(\nu,u)) + \mathcal{I}^{\beta}_{u+\varphi(\nu,u)^-}\ \Omega(u)\right] = (2-\theta)\sqrt{\pi}. \tag{35}$$

From (34) and (35), we have $\sqrt{\pi}[\theta,\ (2-\theta)] \leq_I \frac{1}{\sqrt{\pi}}[\theta(2\pi+\frac{4-8\sqrt{2}}{3}),(2-\theta)(2\pi+\frac{4-8\sqrt{2}}{3})]$, for each $\theta \in\ [0,\ 1]$.

Remark 3.7. If $\Omega(\omega)\ = 1$. Then from Theorem 3.4 and Theorem 3.5, we get Theorem 3.1.

Let $\beta = 1$. Then we obtain following $H{\cdot}H$ Fejér type inequality for preinvex $F{\cdot}I{\cdot}V{\cdot}F$, see [28].

$$\Psi\left(\frac{2u+\varphi(\nu,u)}{2}\right) \preccurlyeq \frac{1}{\int_u^{u+\varphi(\nu,u)}\Omega(\omega)d\omega}\ (FR)\int_u^{u+\varphi(\nu,u)}\Psi(\omega)\Omega(\omega)d\omega \preccurlyeq \frac{\Psi(u)\ +\Psi(\nu)}{2}$$

If $\Psi_*(\omega,\ \theta)\ = \Psi^*(\omega,\ \theta)$ with $\varphi(\omega,y)\ = \omega - y$ and $\Omega(\omega)\ = \beta = 1 = \theta$. Then from Theorem 3.4 and Theorem 3.5, we get the classical $H{\cdot}H$ inequality.

If $\Psi_*(\omega,\ \theta)\ = \Psi^*(\omega,\ \theta)$ with $\varphi(\omega,y)\ = \omega - y$ and $\beta = 1$, then from Theorem 3.4 and Theorem 3.5, we obtain the classical $H{\cdot}H$ Fejér inequality, see [46].

From Theorems 3.8 and 3.9, now we get several fuzzy-interval fractional integral inequalities linked to fuzzy-interval fractional $H{\cdot}H$ type inequality for the product of preinvex $F{\cdot}I{\cdot}V{\cdot}Fs$.

Theorem 3.8. *Let $\Psi,\Phi\ :\ [u,\ u+\varphi(\nu,u)]\ \to \mathbb{F}_0$ be two preinvex $F{\cdot}I{\cdot}V{\cdot}Fs$ on $[u,\ u+\varphi(\nu,u)]$, whose θ-levels $\Psi_\theta,\ \Phi_\theta : [u,\ u+\varphi(\nu,u)]\ \subset \mathbb{R} \to \mathcal{K}_C{}^+$ are defined by $\Psi_\theta(\omega)\ = [\Psi_*(\omega,\theta)\ ,\ \Psi^*(\omega,\theta)]$ and $\Phi_\theta(\omega)\ =\ [\Phi_*(\omega,\theta)\ ,\ \Phi^*(\omega,\theta)]$ for all $\omega \in\ [u,\ u+\varphi(\nu,u)]$ and for all $\theta \in\ [0,\ 1]$. If $\Psi\widetilde{\times}\Phi \in\ L([u,\ u+\varphi(\nu,u)]\ ,\mathbb{F}_0)$ and φ satisfies Condition C, then*

$$\frac{\Gamma(\beta)}{2(\varphi(\nu,u))^\beta}\left[\mathcal{I}_{u^+}^\beta\ \Psi(u+\varphi(\nu,u))\widetilde{\times}\Phi(u+\varphi(\nu,u))\widetilde{+}\mathcal{I}_{u+\varphi(\nu,u)^-}^\beta\Psi(u)\widetilde{\times}\Phi(u)\right]$$
$$\preccurlyeq\ \left(\tfrac{1}{2} - \tfrac{\beta}{(\beta+1)(\beta+2)}\right)\Delta\ (u,u+\varphi(\nu,u))\widetilde{+}\left(\tfrac{\beta}{(\beta+1)(\beta+2)}\right)\nabla\ (u,u+\varphi(\nu,u))$$

where $\Delta\ (u,u+\varphi(\nu,u))\ =\ \Psi(u)\widetilde{\times}\Phi(u)\ \widetilde{+}\ \Psi(u+\varphi(\nu,u))\widetilde{\times}\Phi(u+\varphi(\nu,u))$, $\nabla\ (u,u+\varphi(\nu,u))\ =\ \Psi(u)\widetilde{\times}\Phi(u+\varphi(\nu,u))\ \widetilde{+}\ \Psi(u+\varphi(\nu,u))\widetilde{\times}\Phi(u)$, and $\Delta_\theta(u,u+\varphi(\nu,u))\ = [\Delta_*((u,u+\varphi(\nu,u))\ ,\ \theta)\ ,\ \Delta^*((u,u+\varphi(\nu,u))\ ,\ \theta)]$ and $\nabla_\theta(u,\nu)\ = [\nabla_*((u,u+\varphi(\nu,u)),\theta),\nabla^*((u,u+\varphi(\nu,u))\ ,\ \theta)]$.

Proof. Since $\Psi,\ \Phi$ both are preinvex $F{\cdot}I{\cdot}V{\cdot}Fs$ and Condition C holds φ for then, for each $\theta \in\ [0,\ 1]$ we have

$$\begin{aligned}\Psi_*(u+\ (1-\varsigma)\varphi(\nu,u)\ ,\ \theta)\ &= \Psi_*(u+\varphi(\nu,u)\ +\varsigma\varphi(u,u+\varphi(\nu,u))\ ,\ \theta)\\ &\leq \varsigma\Psi_*(u,\theta)\ +\ (1-\varsigma)\Psi_*(u+\varphi(\nu,u)\ ,\ \theta)\\ \Psi^*(u+\ (1-\varsigma)\varphi(\nu,u)\ ,\ \theta)\ &= \Psi^*(u+\varphi(\nu,u)\ +\varsigma\varphi(u,u+\varphi(\nu,u))\ ,\ \theta)\\ &\leq \varsigma\Psi^*(u,\theta)\ +\ (1-\varsigma)\Psi^*(u+\varphi(\nu,u)\ ,\ \theta).\end{aligned}$$

and

$$\begin{aligned}\Phi_*(u+\ (1-\varsigma)\varphi(\nu,u)\ ,\ \theta)\ &= \Phi_*(u+\varphi(\nu,u)\ +\varsigma\varphi(u,u+\varphi(\nu,u))\ ,\ \theta)\\ &\leq \varsigma\Phi_*(u,\theta)\ +\ (1-\varsigma)\Phi_*(u+\varphi(\nu,u)\ ,\ \theta)\\ \Phi^*(u+\ (1-\varsigma)\varphi(\nu,u)\ ,\ \theta)\ &= \Phi^*(u+\varphi(\nu,u)\ +\varsigma\varphi(u,u+\varphi(\nu,u))\ ,\ \theta)\\ &\leq \varsigma\Phi^*(u,\theta)\ +\ (1-\varsigma)\Phi^*(u+\varphi(\nu,u)\ ,\ \theta).\end{aligned}$$

From the definition of preinvex $F{\cdot}I{\cdot}V{\cdot}Fs$ it follows that $\widetilde{0} \preccurlyeq \Psi(\omega)$ and $\widetilde{0} \preccurlyeq \Phi(\omega)$, so

$$\begin{aligned}
&\Psi_*(u+\ (1-\varsigma)\varphi(\nu,u)\ ,\ \theta)\ \times\Phi_*(u+\ (1-\varsigma)\varphi(\nu,u)\ ,\ \theta)\\
&\leq\ (\varsigma\Psi_*(u,\theta)\ +\ (1-\varsigma)\Psi_*(u+\varphi(\nu,u)\ ,\ \theta))(\varsigma\Phi_*(u,\theta)\ +\ (1-\varsigma)\Phi_*(u+\varphi(\nu,u)\ ,\ \theta))\\
&=\varsigma^2\Psi_*(u,\theta)\ \times\Phi_*(u,\theta)\ +(1-\varsigma)^2\Psi_*(u+\varphi(\nu,u)\ ,\ \theta)\ \times\Phi_*(u+\varphi(\nu,u)\ ,\ \theta)\\
&+\varsigma(1-\varsigma)\Psi_*(u,\theta)\ \times\Phi_*(u+\varphi(\nu,u)\ ,\ \theta)\ +\varsigma(1-\varsigma)\Psi_*(u+\varphi(\nu,u)\ ,\ \theta)\ \times\Phi_*(u,\theta)\\
&\Psi^*(u+\ (1-\varsigma)\varphi(\nu,u)\ ,\ \theta)\ \times\Phi^*(u+\ (1-\varsigma)\varphi(\nu,u)\ ,\ \theta)\\
&\leq\ (\varsigma\Psi^*(u,\theta)\ +\ (1-\varsigma)\Psi^*(u+\varphi(\nu,u)\ ,\ \theta))(\varsigma\Phi^*(u,\theta)\ +\ (1-\varsigma)\Phi^*(u+\varphi(\nu,u)\ ,\ \theta))\\
&=\varsigma^2\Psi^*(u,\theta)\ \times\Phi^*(u,\theta)\ +(1-\varsigma)^2\Psi^*(u+\varphi(\nu,u)\ ,\ \theta)\ \times\Phi^*(u+\varphi(\nu,u)\ ,\ \theta)\\
&+\varsigma(1-\varsigma)\Psi^*(u,\theta)\ \times\Phi^*(u+\varphi(\nu,u)\ ,\ \theta)\ +\varsigma(1-\varsigma)\Psi^*(u+\varphi(\nu,u)\ ,\ \theta)\ \times\Phi^*(u,\theta),
\end{aligned}\tag{36}$$

Analogously, we have

$$\begin{aligned}
&\Psi_*(u+\varsigma\varphi(\nu,u)\ ,\ \theta)\Phi_*(u+\varsigma\varphi(\nu,u)\ ,\ \theta)\\
&\leq(1-\varsigma)^2\Psi_*(u,\theta)\ \times\Phi_*(u,\theta)\ +\varsigma^2\Psi_*(u+\varphi(\nu,u)\ ,\ \theta)\ \times\Phi_*(u+\varphi(\nu,u)\ ,\ \theta)\\
&+\varsigma(1-\varsigma)\Psi_*(u,\theta)\ \times\Phi_*(u+\varphi(\nu,u)\ ,\ \theta)\ +\varsigma(1-\varsigma)\Psi_*(u+\varphi(\nu,u)\ ,\ \theta)\ \times\Phi_*(u,\theta)\\
&\Psi^*(u+\varsigma\varphi(\nu,u)\ ,\ \theta)\ \times\Phi^*(u+\varsigma\varphi(\nu,u)\ ,\ \theta)\\
&\leq(1-\varsigma)^2\Psi^*(u,\theta)\ \times\Phi^*(u,\theta)\ +\varsigma^2\Psi^*(u+\varphi(\nu,u)\ ,\ \theta)\ \times\Phi^*(u+\varphi(\nu,u)\ ,\ \theta)\\
&+\varsigma(1-\varsigma)\Psi^*(u,\theta)\ \times\Phi^*(u+\varphi(\nu,u)\ ,\ \theta)\ +\varsigma(1-\varsigma)\Psi^*(u+\varphi(\nu,u)\ ,\ \theta)\ \times\Phi^*(u,\theta).
\end{aligned}\tag{37}$$

Adding (36) and (37), we have

$$\begin{aligned}
&\Psi_*(u+\ (1-\varsigma)\varphi(\nu,u)\ ,\ \theta)\ \times\Phi_*(u+\ (1-\varsigma)\varphi(\nu,u)\ ,\ \theta)\\
&+\Psi_*(u+\varsigma\varphi(\nu,u)\ ,\ \theta)\ \times\Phi_*(u+\varsigma\varphi(\nu,u)\ ,\ \theta)\\
&\leq\ \left[\varsigma^2+(1-\varsigma)^2\right][\Psi_*(u,\theta)\ \times\Phi_*(u,\theta)\ +\Psi_*(u+\varphi(\nu,u)\ ,\ \theta)\ \times\Phi_*(u+\varphi(\nu,u)\ ,\ \theta)]\\
&+2\varsigma(1-\varsigma)[\Psi_*(u+\varphi(\nu,u)\ ,\ \theta)\ \times\Phi_*(u,\theta)\ +\Psi_*(u,\theta)\ \times\Phi_*(u+\varphi(\nu,u)\ ,\ \theta)]\\
&\Psi^*(u+\ (1-\varsigma)\varphi(\nu,u)\ ,\ \theta)\ \times\Phi^*(u+\ (1-\varsigma)\varphi(\nu,u)\ ,\ \theta)\\
&+\Psi^*(u+\varsigma\varphi(\nu,u)\ ,\ \theta)\ \times\Phi^*(u+\varsigma\varphi(\nu,u)\ ,\ \theta)\\
&\leq\ \left[\varsigma^2+(1-\varsigma)^2\right][\Psi^*(u,\theta)\ \times\Phi^*(u,\theta)\ +\Psi^*(u+\varphi(\nu,u)\ ,\ \theta)\ \times\Phi^*(u+\varphi(\nu,u)\ ,\ \theta)]\\
&+2\varsigma(1-\varsigma)[\Psi^*(u+\varphi(\nu,u)\ ,\ \theta)\ \times\Phi^*(u,\theta)\ +\Psi^*(u,\theta)\ \times\Phi^*(u+\varphi(\nu,u)\ ,\ \theta)].
\end{aligned}\tag{38}$$

Taking multiplication of (38) by $\varsigma^{\beta-1}$ and integrating the obtained result with respect to ς over (0,1), we have

$$\begin{aligned}
&\int_0^1\varsigma^{\beta-1}\Psi_*(u+\ (1-\varsigma)\varphi(\nu,u)\ ,\ \theta)\ \times\Phi_*(u+\ (1-\varsigma)\varphi(\nu,u)\ ,\ \theta)\\
&\quad+\varsigma^{\beta-1}\Psi_*(u+\varsigma\varphi(\nu,u)\ ,\ \theta)\ \times\Phi_*(u+\varsigma\varphi(\nu,u)\ ,\ \theta)d\varsigma\\
&\quad\leq\Delta_*((u,u+\varphi(\nu,u))\ ,\ \theta)\int_0^1\varsigma^{\beta-1}\left[\varsigma^2+(1-\varsigma)^2\right]d\varsigma\\
&\quad+2\nabla_*((u,u+\varphi(\nu,u))\ ,\ \theta)\int_0^1\varsigma^{\beta-1}\varsigma(1-\varsigma)d\varsigma\\
&\int_0^1\varsigma^{\beta-1}\Psi^*(u+\ (1-\varsigma)\varphi(\nu,u)\ ,\ \theta)\ \times\Phi^*(u+\ (1-\varsigma)\varphi(\nu,u)\ ,\ \theta)\\
&\quad+\varsigma^{\beta-1}\Psi^*(u+\varsigma\varphi(\nu,u)\ ,\ \theta)\ \times\Phi^*(u+\varsigma\varphi(\nu,u)\ ,\ \theta)d\varsigma\\
&\quad\leq\Delta^*((u,u+\varphi(\nu,u))\ ,\ \theta)\int_0^1\varsigma^{\beta-1}\left[\varsigma^2+(1-\varsigma)^2\right]d\varsigma\\
&\quad+2\nabla^*((u,u+\varphi(\nu,u))\ ,\ \theta)\int_0^1\varsigma^{\beta-1}\varsigma(1-\varsigma)d\varsigma.
\end{aligned}$$

It follows that,

$$\frac{\Gamma(\beta)}{(\varphi(v,u))^{\beta}}\left[\mathcal{I}_{u^+}^{\beta}\ \Psi_*(u+\varphi(v,u)\,,\,\theta)\ \times\Phi_*(u+\varphi(v,u)\,,\,\theta)\ +\mathcal{I}_{u+\varphi(v,u)^-}^{\beta}\ \Psi_*(u,\theta)\ \times\Phi_*(u,\theta)\right]$$
$$\leq \tfrac{2}{\beta}\left(\tfrac{1}{2}-\tfrac{\beta}{(\beta+1)(\beta+2)}\right)\Delta_*((u,u+\varphi(v,u))\,,\,\theta)\ +\tfrac{2}{\beta}\left(\tfrac{\beta}{(\beta+1)(\beta+2)}\right)\nabla_*((u,u+\varphi(v,u))\,,\,\theta)$$
$$\frac{\Gamma(\beta)}{(\varphi(v,u))^{\beta}}\left[\mathcal{I}_{u^+}^{\beta}\ \Psi^*(u+\varphi(v,u)\,,\,\theta)\ \times\Phi^*(u+\varphi(v,u)\,,\,\theta)\ +\mathcal{I}_{u+\varphi(v,u)^-}^{\beta}\ \Psi^*(u,\theta)\ \times\Phi^*(u,\theta)\right]$$
$$\leq \tfrac{2}{\beta}\left(\tfrac{1}{2}-\tfrac{\beta}{(\beta+1)(\beta+2)}\right)\Delta^*((u,u+\varphi(v,u))\,,\,\theta)\ +\tfrac{2}{\beta}\left(\tfrac{\beta}{(\beta+1)(\beta+2)}\right)\nabla^*((u,u+\varphi(v,u))\,,\,\theta),$$

that is

$$\frac{\Gamma(\beta)}{(\varphi(v,u))^{\beta}}[\mathcal{I}_{u^+}^{\beta}\ \Psi_*(u+\varphi(v,u)\,,\,\theta)\ \times\Phi_*(u+\varphi(v,u)\,,\,\theta)\ +\mathcal{I}_{u+\varphi(v,u)^-}^{\beta}\ \Psi_*(u,\theta)\ \times\Phi_*(u,\theta)\,,$$
$$\mathcal{I}_{u^+}^{\beta}\ \Psi^*(u+\varphi(v,u)\,,\,\theta)\ \times\Phi^*(u+\varphi(v,u)\,,\,\theta)\ +\mathcal{I}_{u+\varphi(v,u)^-}^{\beta}\ \Psi^*(u,\theta)\ \times\Phi^*(u,\,\theta)]$$
$$\leq_I \tfrac{2}{\beta}\left(\tfrac{1}{2}-\tfrac{\beta}{(\beta+1)(\beta+2)}\right)[\Delta_*((u,u+\varphi(v,u))\,,\,\theta)\,,\,\Delta^*((u,u+\varphi(v,u))\,,\,\theta)]$$
$$+\tfrac{2}{\beta}\left(\tfrac{\beta}{(\beta+1)(\beta+2)}\right)[\nabla_*((u,u+\varphi(v,u))\,,\,\theta)\,,\,\nabla^*((u,u+\varphi(v,u))\,,\,\theta)]$$

Thus,

$$\frac{\Gamma(\beta)}{2(\varphi(v,u))^{\beta}}\left[\mathcal{I}_{u^+}^{\beta}\ \Psi(u+\varphi(v,u))\tilde{\times}\Phi(u+\varphi(v,u))\tilde{+}\mathcal{I}_{u+\varphi(v,u)^-}^{\beta}\ \Psi(u)\tilde{\times}\Phi(u)\right]$$
$$\preccurlyeq\ \left(\tfrac{1}{2}-\tfrac{\beta}{(\beta+1)(\beta+2)}\right)\Delta\,(u,u+\varphi(v,u))\tilde{+}\left(\tfrac{\beta}{(\beta+1)(\beta+2)}\right)\nabla\,(u,u+\varphi(v,u))$$

and the theorem has been established. □

Theorem 3.9. *Let $\Psi,\Phi:[u,\ u+\varphi(v,u)]\to\mathbb{F}_0$ be two preinvex F·I·V·Fs, whose θ-levels define the family of I·V·Fs $\Psi_\theta,\ \Phi_\theta:[u,\ u+\varphi(v,u)]\subset\mathbb{R}\to\mathcal{K}_C{}^+$ are given by $\Psi_\theta(\omega)=[\Psi_*(\omega,\theta)\,,\,\Psi^*(\omega,\theta)]$ and $\Phi_\theta(\omega)=[\Phi_*(\omega,\theta)\,,\,\Phi^*(\omega,\theta)]$ for all $\omega\in[u,\ u+\varphi(v,u)]$ and for all $\theta\in[0,\ 1]$. If $\Psi\tilde{\times}\Phi\in L([u,\ u+\varphi(v,u)]\,,\mathbb{F}_0)$ and φ satisfies Condition C, then*

$$\frac{1}{\beta}\Psi\left(\frac{2u+\varphi(v,u)}{2}\right)\tilde{\times}\Phi\left(\frac{2u+\varphi(v,u)}{2}\right)$$
$$\preccurlyeq\frac{\Gamma(\beta+1)}{4(\varphi(v,u))^{\beta}}\left[\mathcal{I}_{u^+}^{\beta}\ \Psi(u+\varphi(v,u))\tilde{\times}\Phi(u+\varphi(v,u))\tilde{+}\mathcal{I}_{u+\varphi(v,u)^-}^{\beta}\ \Psi(u)\tilde{\times}\Phi(u)\right]$$
$$\tilde{+}\frac{1}{2\beta}\left(\frac{1}{2}-\frac{\beta}{(\beta+1)(\beta+2)}\right)\nabla\,(u,u+\varphi(v,u))\tilde{+}\frac{1}{2\beta}\left(\frac{\beta}{(\beta+1)(\beta+2)}\right)\Delta\,(u,u+\varphi(v,u)).$$

where $\Delta\,(u,u+\varphi(v,u))=\Psi(u)\tilde{\times}\Phi(u)\ \tilde{+}\ \Psi(u+\varphi(v,u))\tilde{\times}\Phi(u+\varphi(v,u))$, $\nabla\,(u,v)=\Psi(u)\tilde{\times}\Phi(u+\varphi(v,u))\ \tilde{+}\ \Psi(u+\varphi(v,u))\tilde{\times}\Phi(u)$, and $\Delta_\theta(u,u+\varphi(v,u))=[\Delta_*((u,u+\varphi(u+\varphi(v,u)))\,,\,\theta)\,,\,\Delta^*((u,u+\varphi(v,u))\,,\,\theta)]$ and $\nabla_\theta(u,u+\varphi(v,u))=[\nabla_*((u,u+\varphi(v,u))\,,\,\theta)\,,\,\nabla^*((u,u+\varphi(v,u))\,,\,\theta)]$.

Proof. Consider $\Psi,\Phi:[u,\ u+\varphi(v,u)]\to\mathbb{F}_0$ are preinvex *F·I·V·Fs*. Then by hypothesis, for each $\theta\in[0,\ 1]$, we have

$$
\begin{aligned}
&\Psi_*\left(\tfrac{2u+\varphi(\nu,u)}{2},\theta\right) \times \Phi_*\left(\tfrac{2u+\varphi(\nu,u)}{2},\theta\right)\\
&\Psi^*\left(\tfrac{2u+\varphi(\nu,u)}{2},\theta\right) \times \Phi^*\left(\tfrac{2u+\varphi(\nu,u)}{2},\theta\right)\\
&\leq \tfrac{1}{4}\left[\begin{array}{c} \Psi_*(u+(1-\varsigma)\varphi(\nu,u),\theta) \times \Phi_*(u+(1-\varsigma)\varphi(\nu,u),\theta) \\ +\Psi_*(u+(1-\varsigma)\varphi(\nu,u),\theta) \times \Phi_*(u+\varsigma\varphi(\nu,u),\theta) \end{array}\right]\\
&\quad+\tfrac{1}{4}\left[\begin{array}{c} \Psi_*(u+\varsigma\varphi(\nu,u),\theta) \times \Phi_*(u+(1-\varsigma)\varphi(\nu,u),\theta) \\ +\Psi_*(u+\varsigma\varphi(\nu,u),\theta) \times \Phi_*(u+\varsigma\varphi(\nu,u),\theta) \end{array}\right]\\
&\leq \tfrac{1}{4}\left[\begin{array}{c} \Psi^*(u+(1-\varsigma)\varphi(\nu,u),\theta) \times \Phi^*(u+(1-\varsigma)\varphi(\nu,u),\theta) \\ +\Psi^*(u+(1-\varsigma)\varphi(\nu,u),\theta) \times \Phi^*(u+\varsigma\varphi(\nu,u),\theta) \end{array}\right]\\
&\quad+\tfrac{1}{4}\left[\begin{array}{c} \Psi^*(u+\varsigma\varphi(\nu,u),\theta) \times \Phi^*(u+(1-\varsigma)\varphi(\nu,u),\theta) \\ +\Psi^*(u+\varsigma\varphi(\nu,u),\theta) \times \Phi^*(u+\varsigma\varphi(\nu,u),\theta) \end{array}\right],\\
&\leq \tfrac{1}{4}\left[\begin{array}{c} \Psi_*(u+(1-\varsigma)\varphi(\nu,u),\theta) \times \Phi_*(u+(1-\varsigma)\varphi(\nu,u),\theta) \\ +\Psi_*(u+\varsigma\varphi(\nu,u),\theta) \times \Phi_*(u+\varsigma\varphi(\nu,u),\theta) \end{array}\right]\\
&\quad+\tfrac{1}{4}\left[\begin{array}{c} (\varsigma\Psi_*(u,\theta)+(1-\varsigma)\Psi_*(u+\varphi(\nu,u),\theta)) \\ \times((1-\varsigma)\Phi_*(u,\theta)+\varsigma\Phi_*(u+\varphi(\nu,u),\theta)) \\ +((1-\varsigma)\Psi_*(u,\theta)+\varsigma\Psi_*(u+\varphi(\nu,u),\theta)) \\ \times(\varsigma\Phi_*(u,\theta)+(1-\varsigma)\Phi_*(u+\varphi(\nu,u),\theta)) \end{array}\right]\\
&\leq \tfrac{1}{4}\left[\begin{array}{c} \Psi^*(u+(1-\varsigma)\varphi(\nu,u),\theta) \times \Phi^*(u+(1-\varsigma)\varphi(\nu,u),\theta) \\ +\Psi^*(u+\varsigma\varphi(\nu,u),\theta) \times \Phi^*(u+\varsigma\varphi(\nu,u),\theta) \end{array}\right]\\
&\quad+\tfrac{1}{4}\left[\begin{array}{c} (\varsigma\Psi^*(u,\theta)+(1-\varsigma)\Psi^*(u+\varphi(\nu,u),\theta)) \\ \times((1-\varsigma)\Phi^*(u,\theta)+\varsigma\Phi^*(u+\varphi(\nu,u),\theta)) \\ +((1-\varsigma)\Psi^*(u,\theta)+\varsigma\Psi^*(u+\varphi(\nu,u),\theta)) \\ \times(\varsigma\Phi^*(u,\theta)+(1-\varsigma)\Phi^*(u+\varphi(\nu,u),\theta)) \end{array}\right],\\
&= \tfrac{1}{4}\left[\begin{array}{c} \Psi_*(u+(1-\varsigma)\varphi(\nu,u),\theta) \times \Phi_*(u+(1-\varsigma)\varphi(\nu,u),\theta) \\ +\Psi_*(u+\varsigma\varphi(\nu,u),\theta) \times \Phi_*(u+\varsigma\varphi(\nu,u),\theta) \end{array}\right]\\
&\quad+\tfrac{1}{4}\left[\begin{array}{c} \left\{\varsigma^2+(1-\varsigma)^2\right\}\nabla_*((u,u+\varphi(\nu,u)),\theta) \\ +\{\varsigma(1-\varsigma)+(1-\varsigma)\varsigma\}\Delta_*((u,u+\varphi(\nu,u)),\theta) \end{array}\right]\\
&= \tfrac{1}{4}\left[\begin{array}{c} \Psi^*(u+(1-\varsigma)\varphi(\nu,u),\theta) \times \Phi^*(u+(1-\varsigma)\varphi(\nu,u),\theta) \\ +\Psi^*(u+\varsigma\varphi(\nu,u),\theta) \times \Phi^*(u+\varsigma\varphi(\nu,u),\theta) \end{array}\right]\\
&\quad+\tfrac{1}{4}\left[\begin{array}{c} \left\{\varsigma^2+(1-\varsigma)^2\right\}\nabla^*((u,u+\varphi(\nu,u)),\theta) \\ +\{\varsigma(1-\varsigma)+(1-\varsigma)\varsigma\}\Delta^*((u,u+\varphi(\nu,u)),\theta) \end{array}\right].
\end{aligned}
\tag{39}
$$

Taking multiplication of (39) with $\varsigma^{\beta-1}$ and integrating over $(0,\ 1)$, we get

$$\frac{1}{\beta}\,\Psi_*\left(\frac{2u+\varphi(\nu,u)}{2},\theta\right)\ \times\Phi_*\left(\frac{2u+\varphi(\nu,u)}{2},\theta\right)$$

$$\leq \frac{1}{4(\varphi(\nu,u))^{\beta}}\left[\begin{array}{c}\int_u^{u+\varphi(\nu,u)}(u+\varphi(\nu,u)\ -\omega)^{\beta-1}\Psi_*(\omega,\theta)\ \times\Phi_*(\omega,\theta)d\omega\\ +\int_u^{u+\varphi(\nu,u)}(y-u)^{\beta-1}\Psi_*(y,\theta)\ \times\Phi_*(y,\theta)dy\end{array}\right]$$

$$+\frac{1}{2\beta}\left(\frac{1}{2}-\frac{\beta}{(\beta+1)(\beta+2)}\right)\nabla_*((u,u+\varphi(\nu,u))\,,\,\theta)\ +\frac{1}{2\beta}\left(\frac{\beta}{(\beta+1)(\beta+2)}\right)\Delta_*((u,u+\varphi(\nu,u))\,,\,\theta)$$

$$=\frac{\Gamma(\beta+1)}{4(\varphi(\nu,u))^{\beta}}\left[\mathcal{I}_{u^+}^{\beta}\ \Psi_*(u+\varphi(\nu,u))\ \times\Phi_*(u+\varphi(\nu,u))\ +\mathcal{I}_{u+\varphi(\nu,u)^-}^{\beta}\ \Psi_*(u)\ \times\Phi_*(u)\right]$$

$$+\frac{1}{2\beta}\left(\frac{1}{2}-\frac{\beta}{(\beta+1)(\beta+2)}\right)\nabla_*((u,u+\varphi(\nu,u))\,,\,\theta)\ +\frac{1}{2\beta}\left(\frac{\beta}{(\beta+1)(\beta+2)}\right)\Delta_*((u,u+\varphi(\nu,u))\,,\,\theta)$$

$$\frac{1}{\beta}\,\Psi^*\left(\frac{2u+\varphi(\nu,u)}{2},\theta\right)\ \times\Phi^*\left(\frac{2u+\varphi(\nu,u)}{2},\theta\right)$$

$$\leq \frac{1}{4(\varphi(\nu,u))^{\beta}}\left[\begin{array}{c}\int_u^{u+\varphi(\nu,u)}(u+\varphi(\nu,u)\ -\omega)^{\beta-1}\Psi^*(\omega,\theta)\ \times\Phi^*(\omega,\theta)d\omega\\ +\int_u^{u+\varphi(\nu,u)}(y-u)^{\beta-1}\Psi^*(y,\theta)\ \times\Phi^*(y,\theta)dy\end{array}\right]$$

$$+\frac{1}{2\beta}\left(\frac{1}{2}-\frac{\beta}{(\beta+1)(\beta+2)}\right)\nabla^*((u,u+\varphi(\nu,u))\,,\,\theta)\ +\frac{1}{2\beta}\left(\frac{\beta}{(\beta+1)(\beta+2)}\right)\Delta^*((u,u+\varphi(\nu,u))\,,\,\theta)$$

$$=\frac{\Gamma(\beta+1)}{4(\varphi(\nu,u))^{\beta}}\left[\mathcal{I}_{u^+}^{\beta}\ \Psi^*(u+\varphi(\nu,u))\ \times\Phi^*(u+\varphi(\nu,u))\ +\mathcal{I}_{u+\varphi(\nu,u)^-}^{\beta}\ \Psi^*(u)\ \times\Phi^*(u)\right]$$

$$+\frac{1}{2\beta}\left(\frac{1}{2}-\frac{\beta}{(\beta+1)(\beta+2)}\right)\nabla^*((u,u+\varphi(\nu,u))\,,\,\theta)\ +\frac{1}{2\beta}\left(\frac{\beta}{(\beta+1)(\beta+2)}\right)\Delta^*((u,u+\varphi(\nu,u))\,,\,\theta)\,,$$

that is

$$\frac{1}{\beta}\,\Psi\left(\frac{2u+\varphi(\nu,u)}{2}\right)\widetilde{\times}\Phi\left(\frac{2u+\varphi(\nu,u)}{2}\right)$$

$$\preccurlyeq\frac{\Gamma(\beta+1)}{4(\varphi(\nu,u))^{\beta}}\left[\mathcal{I}_{u^+}^{\beta}\ \Psi(u+\varphi(\nu,u))\widetilde{\times}\Phi(u+\varphi(\nu,u))\widetilde{+}\mathcal{I}_{u+\varphi(\nu,u)^-}^{\beta}\ \Psi(u)\widetilde{\times}\Phi(u)\right]$$

$$\widetilde{+}\frac{1}{2\beta}\left(\frac{1}{2}-\frac{\beta}{(\beta+1)(\beta+2)}\right)\nabla\ (u,u+\varphi(\nu,u))\widetilde{+}\frac{1}{2\beta}\left(\frac{\beta}{(\beta+1)(\beta+2)}\right)\Delta\ (u,u+\varphi(\nu,u))$$

Hence, the required result. □

Example 3.10. Let $[u,u+\varphi(\nu,u)]\ =\ [0,\varphi(2,0)]$, $\beta=\frac{1}{2}$, $\Psi(\omega)\ =\ [\omega,2\omega]$, and $\Phi(\omega)=[\omega,3\omega]$.

$$\Psi(\omega)(\theta)\ =\ \begin{cases}\frac{\theta}{\omega} & \theta\in\ [0,\ \omega]\\ \frac{2\omega-\theta}{\omega} & \theta\in\ (\omega,\ 2\omega]\\ 0 & otherwise,\end{cases}$$

$$\Phi(\omega)(\theta)\ =\ \begin{cases}\frac{\theta}{2\omega} & \theta\in\ [0,\ 2\omega]\\ \frac{4\omega-\theta}{2\omega} & \theta\in\ (2\omega,\ 4\omega]\\ 0 & otherwise.\end{cases}$$

Then, for each $\theta\ \in\ \ [0,\ 1]$, we have $\Psi_\theta(\omega)\ \ =\ \ [\theta\omega,\ (2-\theta)\omega]$ and $\Phi_\theta(\omega)=[2\theta\omega,2(2-\theta)\omega]$. Since left and right end point functions $\Psi_*(\omega,\theta)\ =\theta\omega$, $\Psi^*(\omega,\ \theta)\ =(2-\theta)\omega$, $\Phi_*(\omega,\theta)\ =2\theta\omega$ and $\Phi^*(\omega,\ \theta)\ =2(2-\theta)\omega$ are preinvex functions with respect to $\varphi(\nu,u)\ =\nu-u$ and for each $\theta\in\ [0,1]$, then $\Psi(\omega)$ and $\Phi(\omega)$ both are preinvex $F{\cdot}I{\cdot}V{\cdot}F$. We clearly see that $\Psi(\omega)\widetilde{\times}\Phi(\omega)\ \in L([u,\ u+\varphi(\nu,u)]\ ,\mathbb{F}_0)$ and

$$\frac{\Gamma(1+\beta)}{2(\varphi(\nu,u))^{\beta}}\left[\mathcal{I}^{\beta}_{u^{+}}\ \Psi_{*}(u+\varphi(\nu,u))\ \times\Phi_{*}(u+\varphi(\nu,u))\ +\mathcal{I}^{\beta}_{u+\varphi(\nu,u)^{-}}\ \Psi_{*}(u)\ \times\Phi_{*}(u)\right]$$

$$=\frac{\Gamma\left(\frac{3}{2}\right)}{2\sqrt{2}}\frac{1}{\sqrt{\pi}}\int_{0}^{\varphi(2,0)}(2-\omega)^{\frac{-1}{2}}\ \left(2\theta^{2}\omega^{2}\right)d\omega+\frac{\Gamma\left(\frac{3}{2}\right)}{2\sqrt{2}}\frac{1}{\sqrt{\pi}}\int_{0}^{\varphi(2,0)}(\omega)^{\frac{-1}{2}}\ \left(2\theta^{2}\omega^{2}\right)d\omega\approx 2.93332\theta^{2},$$

$$\frac{\Gamma(1+\beta)}{2(\varphi(\nu,u))^{\beta}}\left[\mathcal{I}^{\beta}_{u^{+}}\ \Psi^{*}(u+\varphi(\nu,u))\ \times\Phi^{*}(u+\varphi(\nu,u))\ +\mathcal{I}^{\beta}_{u+\varphi(\nu,u)^{-}}\ \Psi^{*}(u)\ \times\Phi^{*}(u)\right]$$

$$=\frac{\Gamma\left(\frac{3}{2}\right)}{2\sqrt{2}}\frac{1}{\sqrt{\pi}}\int_{0}^{\varphi(2,0)}(2-\omega)^{\frac{-1}{2}}\ .2(2-\theta)^{2}\omega^{2}d\omega+\frac{\Gamma\left(\frac{3}{2}\right)}{2\sqrt{2}}\frac{1}{\sqrt{\pi}}\int_{0}^{\varphi(2,0)}(\omega)^{\frac{-1}{2}}\ .2(2-\theta)^{2}\omega^{2}d\omega$$

$$\approx 2.9332(2-\theta)^{2},$$

Note that

$$\left(\frac{1}{2}-\frac{\beta}{(\beta+1)(\beta+2)}\right)\Delta_{*}(u,u+\varphi(\nu,u))\ =\ [\Psi_{*}(u)\ \times\Phi_{*}(u)\ +\Psi_{*}(u+\varphi(\nu,u))\ \times\Phi_{*}(u+\varphi(\nu,u))]$$

$$=\tfrac{11}{30}.8\theta^{2},$$

$$\left(\frac{1}{2}-\frac{\beta}{(\beta+1)(\beta+2)}\right)\Delta^{*}(u,u+\varphi(\nu,u))$$

$$=\ [\Psi^{*}(u)\ \times\Phi^{*}(u)\ +\Psi^{*}(u+\varphi(\nu,u))\ \times\Phi^{*}(u+\varphi(\nu,u))]\ =\tfrac{11}{30}.8(2-\theta)^{2},$$

$$\left(\frac{\beta}{(\beta+1)(\beta+2)}\right)\nabla_{*}(u,u+\varphi(\nu,u))\ =\ [\Psi_{*}(u)\ \times\Phi_{*}(u+\varphi(\nu,u))\ +\Psi_{*}(u+\varphi(\nu,u))\ \times\Phi_{*}(u)]$$

$$=\tfrac{2}{15}(0)\ ,\left(\frac{\beta}{(\beta+1)(\beta+2)}\right)\nabla_{*}(u,u+\varphi(\nu,u))\ =\ [\Psi^{*}(u)\ \times\Phi^{*}(u+\varphi(\nu,u))\ +\Psi^{*}(u+\varphi(\nu,u))\ \times\Phi^{*}(u)]$$

$$=\tfrac{2}{15}(0)\ .$$

Therefore, we have

$$\left(\frac{1}{2}-\frac{\beta}{(\beta+1)(\beta+2)}\right)\Delta_{\theta}((u,u+\varphi(\nu,u))\ ,\ \theta)\ +\ \left(\frac{\beta}{(\beta+1)(\beta+2)}\right)\nabla_{\theta}((u,u+\varphi(\nu,u))\ ,\ \theta)$$

$$=\tfrac{11}{30}\left[8\theta^{2},8(2-\theta)^{2}\right]\ +\tfrac{2}{15}[0,0]\ \approx\ \left[2.93332\theta^{2},2.9332(2-\theta)^{2}\right].$$

It follows that

$$\left[2.93332\theta^{2},2.9332(2-\theta)^{2}\right]\leq_{I}\left[2.93332\theta^{2},2.9332(2-\theta)^{2}\right],$$

and Theorem 3.7. has been demonstrated.

4. Conclusions and Future Plan

In this article, we established relation between integral inequalities and preinvex $F{\cdot}I{\cdot}V{\cdot}Fs$ using fuzzy Riemann–Liouville fractional integrals and Condition C. We addressed $H{\cdot}H$ type inequalities and $H{\cdot}H$ Fejér type inequalities for introduced preinvex $F{\cdot}I{\cdot}V{\cdot}F$. Moreover, some related fuzzy fractional inequalities were also obtained. We gave useful examples to verify the validity of presented results. In future, we will try to explore this concept for generalized preinvex $F{\cdot}I{\cdot}V{\cdot}Fs$ and using fuzzy Riemann–Liouville fractional integrals, we will try to get new inequalities for preinvex $F{\cdot}I{\cdot}V{\cdot}Fs$. We believe that the implications and methodologies presented in this article will energize and encourage scholars to pursue a more intriguing follow-up in this field. Finally, we think that our findings may be applied to other fractional calculus models having Mittag-Liffler functions in their kernels, such as Atangana-Baleanue and Prabhakar fractional operators. This consideration has been kept as an open problem for academics interested in this topic. Researchers that are interested might follow the steps outlined in references [52,53].

Author Contributions: Conceptualization, M.B.K.; methodology, M.B.K.; validation, S.T., M.S.S. and H.G.Z.; formal analysis, J.E.M.-D.; investigation, M.S.S.; resources, S.T.; data curation, H.G.Z.; writing—original draft preparation, M.B.K., J.E.M.-D. and H.G.Z.; writing—review and editing, M.B.K. and S.T.; visualization, H.G.Z.; supervision, M.B.K. and M.S.S.; project administration, M.B.K.; funding acquisition, J.E.M.-D., M.S.S. and H.G.Z. All authors have read and agreed to the published version of the manuscript.

Funding: This research received no external funding.

Institutional Review Board Statement: Not applicable.

Informed Consent Statement: Not applicable.

Data Availability Statement: Not applicable.

Acknowledgments: The authors would like to thank the Rector, COMSATS University Islamabad, Islamabad, Pakistan, for providing excellent research. This work was funded by Taif University Researchers Supporting Project number (TURSP-2020/345), Taif University, Taif, Saudi Arabia and this work was also supported by Consejo Nacional de Ciencia y Tecnología, Grant No. A1-S-45928.

Conflicts of Interest: The authors declare no conflict of interest.

References

1. Xi, B.-Y.; Qi, F. Some Integral Inequalities of Hermite-Hadamard Type for Convex Functions with Applications to Means. *J. Funct. Spaces Appl.* **2012**, *2012*, 980438. [CrossRef]
2. Niculescu, C.P.; Persson, L.E. *Convex Functions and Their Applications*; Springer: Berlin/Heidelberg, Germany, 2006.
3. Ozcan, S.; Iscan, I. Some new Hermite-Hadamard type integral inequalities for s-convex functions and theirs applications. *J. Inequal. Appl.* **2019**, *1*, 201. [CrossRef]
4. Sahoo, S.K.; Ahmad, H.; Tariq, M.; Kodamasingh, B.; Aydi, H.; De la Sen, M. Hermite-Hadamard type inequalities involving k-fractional operator for (h, m)-convex functions. *Symmetry* **2021**, *13*, 1686. [CrossRef]
5. Tariq, M.; Sahoo, S.K.; Nasir, J.; Aydi, H.; Alsamir, H. Some Ostrowski type inequalities via n-polynomial exponentially s-convex functions and their applications. *AIMS Math.* **2021**, *6*, 13272–13290. [CrossRef]
6. Sun, W.; Xu, R. Some new Hermite-Hadamard type inequalities for generalized harmonically convex functions involving local fractional integrals. *AIMS Math.* **2021**, *6*, 10679–10695. [CrossRef]
7. Sun, W. Hermite-Hadamard type local fractional integral inequalities for generalized s-preinvex functions and their generalization. *Fractals* **2021**, *29*, 2150098. [CrossRef]
8. Khan, M.A.; Chu, Y.M.; Khan, T.U.; Khan, J. Some new inequalities of Hermite-Hadamard type for s-convex functions with applications. *Open Math.* **2017**, *15*, 1414–1430. [CrossRef]
9. Du, T.; Awan, M.U.; Kashuri, A.; Zhao, S. Some k-fractional extensions of the trapezium inequalities through generalized relative semi-(m,h)-preinvexity. *Appl. Anal.* **2021**, *100*, 642–662. [CrossRef]
10. Butt, S.I.; Tariq, M.; Aslam, A.; Ahmad, H.; Nofel, T.A. Hermite-Hadamard type inequalities via generalized harmonic exponential convexity and applications. *J. Funct. Space.* **2021**, *2021*, 5533491. [CrossRef]
11. Sahoo, S.K.; Tariq, M.; Ahmad, H.; Nasir, J.; Aydi, H.A.; Mukheimer, A. New Ostrowski-Type Fractional Integral Inequalities via Generalized Exponential-Type Convex Functions and Applications. *Symmetry* **2021**, *13*, 1429. [CrossRef]
12. Tariq, M.; Nasir, J.; Sahoo, S.K.; Mallah, A.A. A note on some Ostrowski type inequalities via Generalized Exponentially Convexity. *J. Math. Anal. Model.* **2021**, *2*, 1–15. [CrossRef]
13. Tariq, M.; Sahoo, S.K.; Nasir, J.; Awan, S.K. Some Ostrowski Type Integral Inequalities using Hypergeometric Functions. *J. Fract. Calc. Nonlinear Syst.* **2021**, *2*, 24–41. [CrossRef]
14. Hanson, M.A. On sufficiency of the Kuhn-Tucker conditions. *J. Math. Anal. Appl.* **1981**, *80*, 545–550. [CrossRef]
15. Ben-Isreal, A.; Mond, B. What is invexity? *Anziam. J.* **1986**, *28*, 1–9. [CrossRef]
16. Mohan, S.R.; Neogy, S.K. On Invex Sets and Preinvex Functions. *J. Math. Anal. Appl.* **1995**, *189*, 901–908. [CrossRef]
17. Antczak, T. Mean value in invexity analysis. *Nonlinear Anal. Theory Methods Appl.* **2005**, *60*, 1473–1484. [CrossRef]
18. Nanda, S.; Kar, K. Convex fuzzy mappings. *Fuzzy Sets Syst.* **1992**, *48*, 129–132. [CrossRef]
19. Syau, Y.-R. On convex and concave fuzzy mappings. *Fuzzy Sets Syst.* **1999**, *103*, 163–168. [CrossRef]
20. Furukawa, N. Convexity and local Lipschitz continuity of fuzzy-valued mappings. *Fuzzy Sets Syst.* **1998**, *93*, 113–119. [CrossRef]
21. Goetschel, R., Jr.; Voxman, W. Elementary fuzzy calculus. *Fuzzy Sets Syst.* **1986**, *18*, 31–43. [CrossRef]
22. Yan, H.; Xu, J. A class of convex fuzzy mappings. *Fuzzy Sets Syst.* **2002**, *129*, 47–56. [CrossRef]

23. Khan, M.B.; Mohammed, P.O.; Noor, M.A.; Hamed, Y.S. New Hermite–Hadamard Inequalities in Fuzzy-Interval Fractional Calculus and Related Inequalities. *Symmetry* **2021**, *13*, 673. [CrossRef]
24. Khan, M.B.; Mohammed, P.O.; Noor, M.A.; Alsharif, A.M.; Noor, K.I. New fuzzy-interval inequalities in fuzzy-interval fractional calculus by means of fuzzy order relation. *AIMS Math.* **2021**, *6*, 10964–10988. [CrossRef]
25. Khan, M.B.; Noor, M.A.; Mohammed, P.O.; Guirao, J.L.; Noor, K.I. Some Integral Inequalities for Generalized Convex Fuzzy-Interval-Valued Functions via Fuzzy Riemann Integrals. *Int. J. Comput. Intell. Syst.* **2021**, *14*, 158. [CrossRef]
26. Khan, M.B.; Noor, M.A.; Noor, K.I.; Chu, Y.M. New Hermite-Hadamard type inequalities for (h1, h2)-convex fuzzy-interval-valued functions. *Adv. Differ. Equations* **2021**, *2021*, 6–20. [CrossRef]
27. Noor, M.A. Fuzzy preinvex functions. *Fuzzy Sets Syst.* **1994**, *64*, 95–104. [CrossRef]
28. Khan, M.B.; Noor, M.A.; Abdullah, L.; Chu, Y.M. Some new classes of preinvex fuzzy-interval-valued functions and inequalities. *Int. J. Comput. Intell. Syst.* **2021**, *14*, 1403–1418. [CrossRef]
29. Khan, M.B.; Srivastava, H.M.; Mohammed, P.O.; Guirao, J.L.G. Fuzzy Mixed Variational-like and Integral Inequalities for Strongly Preinvex Fuzzy Mappings. *Symmetry* **2021**, *13*, 1816. [CrossRef]
30. Khan, M.B.; Noor, M.A.; Noor, K.I.; Chu, Y.M. Higher-order strongly preinvex fuzzy mappings and fuzzy mixed variational-like inequalities. *Int. J. Comput. Intell. Syst.* **2021**, *14*, 1856–1870. [CrossRef]
31. Khan, M.B.; Noor, M.A.; Noor, K.I.; Almusawa, H.; Nisar, K.S. Exponentially preinvex fuzzy mappings and fuzzy exponentially mixed variational-like inequalities. *Int. J. Anal. Appl.* **2021**, *19*, 518–541.
32. Liu, P.; Khan, M.B.; Noor, M.A.; Noor, K.I. On Strongly Generalized Preinvex Fuzzy Mappings. *J. Math.* **2021**, *2021*, 6657602. [CrossRef]
33. Khan, M.B.; Noor, M.A.; Noor, K.I.; Ab Ghani, A.T.; Abdullah, L. Extended Perturbed Mixed Variational-Like Inequalities for Fuzzy Mappings. *J. Math.* **2021**, *2021*, 6652930. [CrossRef]
34. Liu, P.; Khan, M.B.; Noor, M.A.; Noor, K.I. New Hermite–Hadamard and Jensen inequalities for log-convex fuzzy-interval-valued functions in the second sense. *Complex Intell. Syst.* **2021**, *2021*, 1–15. [CrossRef]
35. Khan, M.B.; Noor, M.A.; Abdullah, L.; Noor, M.A.; Noor, K.I. New Hermite–Hadamard and Jensen Inequalities for Log-h-Convex Fuzzy-Interval-Valued Functions. *Int. J. Comput. Intell. Syst.* **2021**, *14*, 155. [CrossRef]
36. Bede, B.; Gal, S.G. Generalizations of the differentiability of fuzzy-number-valued functions with applications to fuzzy dif-ferential equations. *Fuzzy Sets Syst.* **2005**, *151*, 581–599. [CrossRef]
37. Kaleva, O. Fuzzy differential equations. *Fuzzy Sets Syst.* **1987**, *24*, 301–317. [CrossRef]
38. Kulish, U.; Miranker, W. *Computer Arithmetic in Theory and Practice*; Academic Press: Cambridge, MA, USA, 2014.
39. Awan, M.U.; Noor, M.; Noor, K.I.; Costache, S. Some Integral Inequalities for Harmonically logarithmic h-convex functions. *Sohag J. Math.* **2018**, *5*, 57–62. [CrossRef]
40. Allahviranloo, T.; Salahshour, S.; Abbasbandy, S. Explicit solutions of fractional differential equations with uncertainty. *Soft Comput.* **2011**, *16*, 297–302. [CrossRef]
41. Hadamard, J. Étude sur les propriétés des fonctions entières et en particulier d'une fonction considérée par Riemann. *J. Math. Pures Appl.* **1893**, *7*, 171–215.
42. Hermite, C. Sur deux limites d'une intégrale définie. *Mathesis* **1883**, *3*, 82–97.
43. Moore, R.E. *Interval Analysis*; Prentice Hall: Hoboken, NJ, USA, 1966.
44. Stefanini, L.; Bede, B. Generalized Hukuhara differentiability of interval-valued functions and interval differential equations. *Nonlinear Anal.* **2010**, *71*, 1311–1328. [CrossRef]
45. Sarikaya, M.Z.; Set, E.; Yaldiz, H.; Basak, N. Hermite–Hadamard's inequalities for fractional integrals and related fractional inequalities. *Math. Comput. Model.* **2013**, *57*, 2403–2407. [CrossRef]
46. Fejer, L. Uberdie Fourierreihen II. Math. Naturwise. Anz. *Ungar Akad Wiss.* **1906**, *24*, 369–390.
47. Costa, T.; Román-Flores, H. Some integral inequalities for fuzzy-interval-valued functions. *Inf. Sci.* **2017**, *420*, 110–125. [CrossRef]
48. Khan, M.B.; Treanţă, S.; Soliman, M.S.; Nonlaopon, K.; Zaini, H.G. Some Hadamard–Fejér Type Inequalities for LR-Convex Interval-Valued Functions. *Fractal Fract.* **2022**, *6*, 6. [CrossRef]
49. Macías-Díaz, J.E.; Khan, M.B.; Noor, M.A.; Mousa, A.A.A.; Alghamdi, S.M. Hermite-Hadamard inequalities for generalized convex functions in interval-valued calculus. *AIMS Math.* **2022**, *7*, 4266–4292. [CrossRef]
50. Khan, M.B.; Noor, M.A.; Al-Shomrani, M.M.; Abdullah, L. Some Novel Inequalities for LR-h-Convex Interval-Valued Func-tions by Means of Pseudo Order Relation. *Math. Meth. Appl. Sci.* **2021**, *45*, 1310–1340. [CrossRef]
51. Khan, M.B.; Noor, M.A.; Abdeljawad, T.; Abdalla, B.; Althobaiti, A. Some fuzzy-interval integral inequalities for harmonically convex fuzzy-interval-valued functions. *AIMS Math.* **2022**, *7*, 349–370. [CrossRef]
52. Fernandez, A.; Mohammed, P. Hermite-Hadamard inequalities in fractional calculus defined using Mittag-Leffler kernels. Math. *Meth. Appl. Sci.* **2020**, *2020*, 8414–8431.
53. Mohammed, P.O.; Abdeljawad, T. Integral inequalities for a fractional operator of a function with respect to another function with nonsingular kernel. *Adv. Differ. Equ.* **2020**, *2020*, 363. [CrossRef]
54. Khan, M.B.; Zaini, H.G.; Treanţă, S.; Soliman, M.S.; Nonlaopon, K. Riemann–Liouville Fractional Integral Inequalities for Generalized Pre-Invex Functions of Interval-Valued Settings Based upon Pseudo Order Relation. *Mathematics* **2022**, *10*, 204. [CrossRef]

55. Todorcevic, V. *Harmonic Quasiconformal Mappings and Hyperbolic Type Metrics*; Springer Nature: Basingstoke, UK, 2019.
56. Debnath, P.; Konwar, N.; Radenovic, S. *Metric Fixed Point Theory: Applications in Science, Engineering and Behavioural Science*; Springer: Berlin/Heidelberg, Germany, 2021.

symmetry

MDPI

Article

Multiobjective Convex Optimization in Real Banach Space

Kin Keung Lai [1,*,†], Mohd Hassan [2,†], Jitendra Kumar Maurya [3,†], Sanjeev Kumar Singh [2,†] and Shashi Kant Mishra [2,†]

1 International Business School, Shaanxi Normal University, Xi'an 710119, China
2 Department of Mathematics, Institute of Science, Banaras Hindu University, Varanasi 221005, India; mohd.hassan10@bhu.ac.in (M.H.); sanjeevk.singh1@bhu.ac.in (S.K.S.); shashikant.mishra@bhu.ac.in (S.K.M.)
3 Kashi Naresh Government Postgraduate College, Bhadohi 221304, India; jitendrak.maurya1@bhu.ac.in
* Correspondence: mskklai@outlook.com
† These authors contributed equally to this work.

Abstract: In this paper, we consider convex multiobjective optimization problems with equality and inequality constraints in real Banach space. We establish saddle point necessary and sufficient Pareto optimality conditions for considered problems under some constraint qualifications. These results are motivated by the symmetric results obtained in the recent article by Cobos Sánchez et al. in 2021 on Pareto optimality for multiobjective optimization problems of continuous linear operators. The discussions in this paper are also related to second order symmetric duality for nonlinear multiobjective mixed integer programs for arbitrary cones due to Mishra and Wang in 2005. Further, we establish Karush–Kuhn–Tucker optimality conditions using saddle point optimality conditions for the differentiable cases and present some examples to illustrate our results. The study in this article can also be seen and extended as symmetric results of necessary and sufficient optimality conditions for vector equilibrium problems on Hadamard manifolds by Ruiz-Garzón et al. in 2019.

Keywords: multiobjective programming; nonlinear programming; convex optimization; saddle point

Citation: Lai, K.K.; Hassan, M.; Maurya, J.K.; Singh, S.K.; Mishra, S.K. Multiobjective Convex Optimization in Real Banach Space. *Symmetry* **2021**, *13*, 2148. https://doi.org/10.3390/sym13112148

Academic Editors: Octav Olteanu and Savin Treanta

Received: 8 October 2021
Accepted: 27 October 2021
Published: 10 November 2021

Publisher's Note: MDPI stays neutral with regard to jurisdictional claims in published maps and institutional affiliations.

1. Introduction

Consider the general multiobjective optimization problem

$$\text{(MOP)} \ \min f(x) = (f_1(x), \cdots, f_p(x)), \ \text{subject to } g(x) \leqq 0, \ h(x) = 0, \tag{1}$$

where the functions $f : X \to \mathbb{R}^p$, $g : X \to \mathbb{R}^q$, and $h : X \to \mathbb{R}^r$ are real vector valued functions and X is real Banach space.

Multiobjective optimization problem (MOP) arises when two or more objective functions are simultaneously optimized over a feasible region. The multiobjective optimization has been considerably analyzed and studied by many researchers, see for instance [1–6]. Multiobjective optimization problems play a crucial role in various fields like economics, engineering, management sciences [2,7–11], and many more places in daily life.

To deal with the multiobjective optimization problems, we have to find Pareto optimal solutions. These solutions are non-dominated by one another. A solution is called non-dominated or Pareto optimal if none of the objective functions can be improved in value without reducing one or more objective values. One of the best techniques to deal with multiobjective optimization problems is scalarization. Wendell and Lee [12] developed the scalarization technique to deal with multiobjective optimization problems. Wendell and Lee [12] generalized the results on efficient points for multiobjective optimization problems to nonlinear optimization problems. The multiobjective problem is converted into a single objective problem in the scalarization technique.

The saddle point optimality conditions are briefly explained in [13], Rooyen et al. [14] constructed a Langrangian function for the convex multiobjective problem and established a relationship between saddle point optimality conditions and Pareto optimal solutions.

Cobos-Sànchez et al. [15] proposed Pareto optimality conditions for multiobjective optimization problems of continuous linear operators. Recently, Treanta [16] studied robust saddle point criterion in second order partial differential equations and partial differential inequations.

Rooyen et al. [14] discussed necessary and sufficient optimality conditions for (MOP) without any constraint qualification in Euclidean space. Recently, Antczak and Abdulaleem [17] studied optimality and duality results for E-differentiable functions. Barbu and Precupanu [18] studied the saddle point optimality conditions of convex optimization problem for real Banach space. Valyi [19] proposed the concept of approximate saddle point condition for convex multiobjective optimization problems. Further Rong and Wu [20] generalized the results of Valyi [19] with set valued maps.

Karush–Kuhn–Tucker (KKT) optimality conditions [21] play a pivotal role to solve scalar optimization problem as well as multiobjective optimization problems. Recently Lai et al. [3] discussed unconstrained multiobjective optimization problems. Further, Guu et al. [22] studied strong KKT type sufficient optimality conditions for semi-infinite programming problems.

Motivated by the work of Barbu and Precupanu [18], Rooyen et al. [14] and Wendell and Lee [12], we extend the results related to saddle point optimality conditions and Karush–Kuhn–Tucker optimality conditions from single objective function to multiobjective function with the help of Slater's constraint qualifications [13]. We also present some illustrative examples to support the theory.

The organization of this paper is as follows: In Section 2, we recall some preliminaries and basic results. In Section 3, results on saddle point and Karush–Kuhn–Tucker necessary optimality conditions for multiobjective optimization problems are extended. Further, we establish the relationship between the Pareto solution and the saddle point for the Lagrange function using Slater's constraint qualification. The last section is dedicated to conclusions and future remarks.

2. Preliminaries

In this section, we recall some notions and preliminary results which will be used in this paper. $\mathbb{R}$ denotes the set of real numbers. Let X be real Banach Space and X^* be its dual space. Let $x, y \in \mathbb{R}^n$, then following inequalities represent their meaning as follows:

$$\begin{aligned} x \geqq y &\implies x_i \geqq y_i \\ x \geq y &\implies x_i \geqq y_i,\ x \neq y, \\ x > y &\implies x_i > y_i, \\ x = y &\implies x_i = y_i. \end{aligned}$$

We denote the feasible region as

$$S = \{x \in X : \ g(x) \ \leqq 0, \ h(x) \ = 0\}.$$

To deal with the multiobjective optimization problems (MOP), we require some basic definitions.

Definition 1 (Ref. [2]). *A decision vector $\bar{x} \in S$ is global Pareto optimal solution (global efficient solution) if there does not exist another decision vector $x \in S$ such that*

$$f(x) \leq f(\bar{x}).$$

Consider the following scalarized multiobjective optimization problem (SMOP) corresponding to (*MOP*):

$$(SMOP) \quad \min \sum_{i=1}^{p} f_i(x)$$

subject to $f(x) \leqq f(\bar{x}),\ g(x) \leqq 0,\ h(x) = 0,$ where $\bar{x}$ is any feasible point of (MOP).

Now, we recall the result from [2], which relate the solution of (*MOP*) and (*SMOP*).

Theorem 1 (Ref. [7]). *A feasible point $\bar{x} \in S$ is a Pareto optimal solution of the (MOP) if and only if $\bar{x}$ is an optimal solution of the (SMOP).*

Definition 2 (Ref. [13]). *A subset of the linear space X is said to be convex if for every distinct pair x and y of subset, it contains $\lambda x + (1-\lambda)y,\ \forall\, \lambda \in [0,1]$.*

Definition 3 (Ref. [13]). *A function f is said to be convex on X if the inequality*

$$f(\lambda x + (1-\lambda)y) \leqq \lambda f(x) + (1-\lambda) f(y)$$

holds for all $x,\ y \in X$ and for every $\lambda \in [0,1]$.

Definition 4 (Ref. [18]). *The function $f : X \to \overline{\mathbb{R}} = [-\infty, +\infty]$ is said to be proper convex if $f(x) > -\infty\ \forall\, x \in X$ and if f is not the constant function then $+\infty$ (that is, $f \not\equiv +\infty$).*
If f is a convex function, $Dom(f)$ denotes the effective domain of f, which is as follows:

$$Dom(f) = \{x \in X : f(x) < +\infty\}.$$

If f is proper, then $Dom(f)$ is finite. Conversely, if A is a nonempty convex subset of X and f is a finite and convex function on A, then one can obtain a proper convex function on X by setting $f(x) = +\infty$ if $x \in X \setminus A$.

Definition 5 (Ref. [18]). *The function $f : X \to \overline{\mathbb{R}}$ is called lower semi continuous at $\bar{x}$ if*

$$f(\bar{x}) = \lim_{x \to \bar{x}} inf f(x).$$

Corollary 1 (Ref. [18]). *If A_1 and A_2 are two non-empty disjoint convex sets of $\mathbb{R}^n$, there exist a non zero element $c = (c_1, \cdots, c_n) \in \mathbb{R}^n \setminus \{0\}$ such that*

$$\sum_{i=1}^{n} c_i u_i \leqq \sum_{i=1}^{n} c_i v_1,\ \forall\, u = (u_i) \in A_1,\ \forall\, v = (v_i) \in A_2.$$

Definition 6 (Ref. [18]). *Given the proper convex function $f : X \to]-\infty, +\infty]$, the subdifferential of such a function is the mapping $\partial f : X \to X^*$ defined by*

$$\partial f(x) = \{x^* \in X^* : f(u) - f(x) \geqq (u - x, x^*), \forall\, u \in X\},$$

where X^* is dual of X and (.,.) denote the canonical pairing between X and X^*. The element $x^* \in \partial f(x)$ called subgradient of f at x.

Corollary 2 (Ref. [18]). *If f is a proper convex function on X, then the minimum (global) of f over X is attained at the point $\bar{x} \in X$ if and only if $0 \in \partial f(\bar{x})$.*

Theorem 2 (Ref. [18]). *If the functions f_1 and f_2 are finite at a point in which at least one is continuous then*

$$\partial(f_1 + f_2)(x) = \partial f_1(x) + \partial f_2(x)\ \forall\, x \in X.$$

Definition 7. *Slater's constraint qualification*

1. *There exists a point $\bar{x} \in S$ such that $g_j(\bar{x}) < 0$, $\forall j = 1, \ldots, q$, and*
2. *The equality constraints satisfy interiority conditions, if*

$$0 \in \{(h_1(x), h_2(x), \cdots, h_r(x)); x \in X_0\}.$$

3. Saddle Point and Karush–Kuhn–Tucker Optimality Conditions

In this section, we established saddle point and Karush–Kuhn–Tucker type optimality conditions for considered (MOP) in Banach space.

Theorem 3. *Let $f_1, \cdots, f_p, g_1, \cdots, g_q$ be proper convex functions and $h_1, \cdots, h_r$ be affine functions. If $\bar{x}$ is a Pareto optimal solution of the (MOP). Then, there exist real numbers $\lambda_1^f, \ldots, \lambda_p^f, \lambda_1^g, \cdots, \lambda_q^g, \lambda_1^h, \cdots, \lambda_r^h$ not all zero and have the properties:*

$$\sum_{i=1}^{p} \lambda_i^f f_i(\bar{x}) \leqq \sum_{i=1}^{p} \lambda_i^f f_i(x) + \sum_{j=1}^{q} \lambda_j^g g_j(x) + \sum_{k=1}^{r} \lambda_k^h h_k(x), \ \forall\, x \in X_0,$$
$$\lambda_i^f \geqq 0, \ \forall\, i = 1, \ldots, p, \ \lambda_j^g \geqq 0, \ \forall\, j = 1, \ldots, q, \ \lambda_j^g g_j(\bar{x}) = 0, \tag{2}$$
$$\text{where } X_0 = \bigcap_{i=1}^{p} Dom(f_i) \cap \bigcap_{j=1}^{q} Dom(g_j).$$

Proof. Let $\bar{x}$ be an Pareto optimal solution of the consistent problem (MOP). Then, from Theorem 1 $\bar{x}$ is an optimal solution of the problem

$$(SMOP) \ \min \sum_{i=1}^{p} f_i(x)$$
$$\text{subject to } f_i(x) \leqq f_i(\bar{x}) \ \forall\, i = 1, \cdots, p,$$
$$g_j(x) \leqq 0 \ (j = 1, \cdots, q), \ h_k(x) = 0 \ (k = 1, \cdots, r).$$

Now, we consider the subset

$$B = \Bigg\{ \sum_{i=1}^{p} f_i(x) - \sum_{i=1}^{p} f_i(\bar{x}) + \alpha_0^f, f_1(x) - f_1(\bar{x}) + \alpha_1^f, \cdots, f_p(x) - f_p(\bar{x}) + \alpha_p^f,$$
$$g_1(x) + \alpha_1^g, \cdots, g_q(x) + \alpha_q^g, h_1(x), \cdots, h_r(x); \ x \in X_0, \ \alpha_i^f > 0 \, \forall\, i, \ \alpha_j^g > 0 \, \forall\, j \Bigg\}. \tag{3}$$

It is easy to see that the set B does not contain origin as well as it is a non-void convex subset of $\mathbb{R}^{1+p+q+r}$. Since origin is a nonempty convex set, then from Corollary 1 there exist a homogeneous hyperplane, that is there exist $1 + p + q + r$ real numbers not all zero $\hat{\lambda}_0^f, \hat{\lambda}_1^f, \ldots, \hat{\lambda}_p^f, \lambda_1^g, \ldots, \lambda_q^g, \lambda_1^h, \ldots, \lambda_r^h$, such that

$$\hat{\lambda}_0^f \Bigg\{ \sum_{i=1}^{p} f_i(x) - \sum_{i=1}^{p} f_i(\bar{x}) + \alpha_0^f \Bigg\} + \sum_{i=1}^{p} \hat{\lambda}_i^f \Big\{ f_i(x) - f_i(\bar{x}) + \alpha_i^f \Big\}$$
$$+ \sum_{j=1}^{q} \lambda_j^g \Big\{ g_j(x) + \alpha_j^g \Big\} + \sum_{k=1}^{r} \lambda_k^h h_k(x) \geqq 0, \tag{4}$$

$\forall\, x \in X_0$, $\alpha_i^f > 0$ $(i = 0, 1, \ldots, p)$, $\alpha_j^g > 0$ $(j = 1, \ldots, q)$, taking $x = \bar{x}$, $\alpha_j^g \downarrow 0$ $(\forall\, j)$, $\alpha_i^f \downarrow 0$ for $i \neq l$ and $\alpha_l^f \uparrow \infty$. Again taking $x = \bar{x}$, $\alpha_i^f \downarrow 0$ $(\forall\, i)$, $\alpha_j^g \downarrow 0$ for $j \neq l$ and $\alpha_l^g \uparrow \infty$, we get

$$\hat{\lambda}_0^f \geqq 0,\ \hat{\lambda}_i^f \geqq 0 \text{ and } \lambda_i^g \geqq 0.$$

Thus, relation (4) becomes

$$\hat{\lambda}_0^f\left\{\sum_{i=1}^{p} f_i(x) - \sum_{i=1}^{p} f_i(\bar{x})\right\} + \sum_{i=1}^{p} \hat{\lambda}_i^f\{f_i(x) - f_i(\bar{x})\} + \sum_{j=1}^{q} \lambda_j^g g_j(x) + \sum_{k=1}^{r} \lambda_k^h h_k(x) \geqq 0,$$

$$\Longrightarrow \sum_{i=1}^{p} f_i(x)\left\{\hat{\lambda}_0^f + \hat{\lambda}_i^f\right\} + \sum_{j=1}^{q} \lambda_j^g g_j(x) + \sum_{k=1}^{r} \lambda_k^h h_k(x) \geqq \sum_{i=1}^{p} f_i(\bar{x})\left\{\hat{\lambda}_0^f + \hat{\lambda}_i^f\right\},$$

$$\Longrightarrow \sum_{i=1}^{p} \lambda_i^f f_i(x) + \sum_{j=1}^{q} \lambda_j^g g_j(x) + \sum_{k=1}^{r} \lambda_k^h h_k(x) \geqq \sum_{i=1}^{p} \lambda_i^f f_i(\bar{x}), \tag{5}$$

where $\lambda_i^f = \hat{\lambda}_0^f + \hat{\lambda}_i^f$. Since $\bar{x}$ is feasible, therefore

$$\lambda_j^g g_j(\bar{x}) \leqq 0,\ \forall\, j, \tag{6}$$

substituting $x = \bar{x}$ in inequality (5), we get

$$\sum_{j=1}^{q} \lambda_j^g g_j(\bar{x}) \geqq 0. \tag{7}$$

Now, from (6) and (7) we have $\lambda_j^g g_j(\bar{x}) = 0$, $\forall\, j = 1, \ldots, q$, which completes the proof. □

Example 1. *Consider the problem*

$$\min f(x) = (f_1(x), f_2(x)),\ \text{subject to } g(x) \leqq 0,$$

where $f_1(x) = \begin{cases} x_1^2, & \text{if } -3 \leqq x_1, x_2 \leqq 3, \\ +\infty, & \text{otherwise} \end{cases}$, $f_2(x) = \begin{cases} x_2^2, & \text{if } -3 \leqq x_1, x_2 \leqq 3, \\ +\infty, & \text{otherwise} \end{cases}$,
and $g(x) = \begin{cases} (x_1-1)^2 + (x_2-1)^2 - 1, & \text{if } -3 \leqq x_1, x_2 \leqq 3, \\ +\infty, & \text{otherwise} \end{cases}$.

Therefore, feasible region $S = \{(x_1, x_2) \in \mathbb{R}^2 : (x_1-1)^2 + (x_2-1)^2 \leqq 1\}$ *and common effective domain* $X_0 = \bigcap_{i=1}^{2} Dom(f_i) \cap Dom(g) = \{(x_1, x_2) \in \mathbb{R}^n : -1 \leqq x_1, x_2 \leqq 1\}$. *Since,* $\bar{x} = (1, 0)$ *is a Pareto optimal solution, then for* $\lambda_1^f = 0$, $\lambda_2^f > 0$, $\lambda^g = 0$, *the following inequality satisfies*

$$\begin{aligned} \lambda_1^f f_1(\bar{x}) + \lambda_2^f f_2(\bar{x}) &= 0 \leqq \lambda_1^f x_1^2 + \lambda_2^f x_2^2 + \lambda^g[(x_1-1)^2 + (x_2-1)^2 - 1] \\ &= \lambda_1^f f_1(x) + \lambda_2^f f_2(x) + \lambda^g g(x), \forall\, x \in X_0. \end{aligned}$$

Hence, result is verified.

Thus, it is natural to call the function

$$L(x, \lambda^f, \lambda^g, \lambda^h) = \sum_{i=1}^{p} \lambda_i^f f_i(x) + \sum_{j=1}^{q} \lambda_j^g g_j(x) + \sum_{k=1}^{r} \lambda_k^h h_k(x), \tag{8}$$

$\lambda^f = (\lambda_i^f) \in \mathbb{R}^p$, $\lambda^g = (\lambda_j^g) \in \mathbb{R}^q$ and $\lambda^h = (\lambda_k^h) \in \mathbb{R}^r$.

Remark 1. *The necessary conditions (2) with $\bar{x} \in S$ are equivalent to the fact that the point $(\bar{x}, \lambda^f, \lambda^g, \lambda^h)$ is a saddle point for the Lagrange function (8) on $X_0 \times \mathbb{R}^p \times \mathbb{R}^q \times \mathbb{R}^r$, with respect to minimization on X_0 and maximization on $\mathbb{R}^p \times \mathbb{R}^q \times \mathbb{R}^r$, that is,*

$$\sum_{i=1}^{p} \lambda_i^f f_i(\bar{x}) + \sum_{j=1}^{q} \lambda_j^g g_j(\bar{x}) + \sum_{k=1}^{r} \lambda_k^h h_k(\bar{x}) \leqq \sum_{i=1}^{p} \lambda_i^f f_i(x) + \sum_{j=1}^{q} \lambda_j^g g_j(x) + \sum_{k=1}^{r} \lambda_k^h h_k(x)$$

$$\Longrightarrow L(\bar{x}, \lambda^f, \lambda^g, \lambda^h) \leqq L(x, \lambda^f, \lambda^g, \lambda^h), \forall\, \bar{x} \in X_0, \tag{9}$$

and for every $(x, \lambda^f, \lambda^g, \lambda^h) \in X \times \mathbb{R}^p \times \mathbb{R}^q \times \mathbb{R}^r$.

Remark 2. *The necessary optimality conditions (2) with $\lambda^f \neq 0$, and $\bar{x} \in S$ are also sufficient for $\bar{x}$ to be a Pareto optimal solution to (MOP). If $\lambda^f = 0$, then optimality conditions concern only the constraints functions, without giving any piece of information from the function which is minimized.*

Theorem 4. *Let $f_1, \cdots, f_p, g_1, \cdots, g_q$ be proper convex functions and let $h_1, \cdots, h_r$ be affine functions such that Slater's constraint qualification satisfied at a feasible point $\bar{x}$ of (MOP). Then, the point $\bar{x}$ is a Pareto optimal solution for (MOP) if and only if there exist $p + q + r$ real numbers $\lambda_1^f, \cdots, \lambda_p^f, \lambda_1^g, \cdots, \lambda_q^g, \lambda_1^h, \cdots, \lambda_r^h$, such that*

$$\sum_{i=1}^{p} \lambda_i^f f_i(\bar{x}) \leqq \sum_{i=1}^{p} \lambda_i^f f_i(x) + \sum_{j=1}^{q} \lambda_j^g g_j(x) + \sum_{k=1}^{r} \lambda_k^h h_k(x), \tag{10}$$

$$\text{and } \lambda^f \geqq 0,\ \lambda^f \neq 0,\ \lambda^g \geqq 0,\ \lambda_j^g g_j(\bar{x}) = 0\ \forall\, j = 1, \cdots, q.$$

Proof. Let $\bar{x}$ be a Pareto optimal solution of (MOP). Then, from above Theorem 3, there exist $\lambda_1^f, \cdots, \lambda_p^f, \lambda_1^g, \cdots, \lambda_q^g, \lambda_1^h, \cdots, \lambda_r^h$ not all zero such that (2) hold. If we suppose $\lambda^f = 0$, taking $x = \bar{x} \in S$, then from (2) we get $\sum_{j=1}^{q} \lambda_j^g g_j(\bar{x}) \geqq 0$. Since $\lambda_i^f \geqq 0$ *and* $g_j(\bar{x}) < 0\ (\forall\, j)$, we must have $\lambda_j^g = 0\ (\forall j)$, therefore from (2) we have

$$\sum_{k=1}^{r} \lambda_k^h h_k(x) \geqq 0\ \forall\, x \in X_0,$$

and all components of λ^h are not zero, which is contradiction of the interiority conditions of Slater's constraint qualification. Hence $\lambda^f \neq 0$, that is, we can take some components of λ^f are greater than zero.

Conversely, suppose $\bar{x}$ is not Pareto optimal solution of (MOP), then there exist $x^*(\neq \bar{x}) \in S$, which is a Pareto optimal solution for (MOP), that is

$$f(x^*) \leq f(\bar{x}). \tag{11}$$

Now, from relation (10) for $x^* \in S$, we have

$$\sum_{i=1}^{p} \lambda_i^f f_i(\bar{x}) \leqq \sum_{i=1}^{p} \lambda_i^f f_i(x^*),$$

which is contradiction of inequality (11). Hence, $\bar{x}$ is a Pareto optimal solution for (MOP). Since $f(x)$ is a proper convex function, then $f(x)$ is necessarily finite. □

Theorem 5. *Under the assumptions of Theorem 4, $\bar{x} \in X$ is a Pareto optimal solution of (MOP) if and only if there exist $\lambda^f = (\lambda_1^f, \cdots, \lambda_p^f) \in \mathbb{R}^p$, $\lambda^g = (\lambda_1^g, \cdots, \lambda_q^g) \in \mathbb{R}^q$ and $\lambda^h =$*

$(\lambda_1^h, \cdots, \lambda_r^h) \in \mathbb{R}^r$ *such that* $(\bar{x}, \lambda^f, \lambda^g, \lambda^h)$ *is a saddle point for the Lagrange function on* $X_0 \times \mathbb{R}^p \times \mathbb{R}^q \times \mathbb{R}^r$, *that is*

$$\sum_{i=1}^{p} \lambda_i^f f_i(\bar{x}) + \sum_{j=1}^{q} \lambda_j^g g_j(\bar{x}) + \sum_{k=1}^{r} \lambda_k^h h_k(\bar{x}) \leqq \sum_{i=1}^{p} \lambda_i^f f_i(x) + \sum_{j=1}^{q} \lambda_j^g g_j(x) + \sum_{k=1}^{r} \lambda_k^h h_k(x)$$

for all $(x, \lambda^f, \lambda^g, \lambda^h) \in X_0 \times \mathbb{R}^p \times \mathbb{R}^q \times \mathbb{R}^r$.

Proof. Thus, the proof is obvious from Theorem 4. □

Now, we establish optimality conditions where differentiability of all functions is essential. The following result extends the Karush–Kuhn–Tucker theorem for the lower-semicontinuous multiobjective functions.

Theorem 6. *Under the hypothesis of Theorem 4, if we suppose that the function* f_i *is lower-semicontinuous and* g_j, h_k *are continuous real functions, then the optimality conditions for* $\bar{x} \in S$ *is equivalent to the conditions*

$$0 \in \sum_{i=1}^{p} \lambda_i^f \partial f_i(\bar{x}) + \sum_{j=1}^{q} \lambda_j^g \partial g_j(\bar{x}) + \sum_{k=1}^{r} \lambda_k^h \nabla h_k(\bar{x}). \tag{12}$$

Proof. From Equation (10), if $\bar{x} \in S$ is the minimum point of the function, then

$$\sum_{i=1}^{p} \lambda_i^f f_i(\bar{x}) \leqq \sum_{i=1}^{p} \lambda_i^f f_i(x) + \sum_{j=1}^{q} \lambda_j^g g_j(x) + \sum_{k=1}^{r} \lambda_k^h h_k(x). \tag{13}$$

Since $g_j(\bar{x}) \leqq 0$, $h_k(\bar{x}) = 0$. Then, inequality (13) takes the form

$$\sum_{i=1}^{p} \lambda_i^f f_i(\bar{x}) + \sum_{j=1}^{q} \lambda_j^g g_j(\bar{x}) + \sum_{k=1}^{r} \lambda_k^h h_k(\bar{x}) \leqq \sum_{i=1}^{p} \lambda_i^f f_i(x) + \sum_{j=1}^{q} \lambda_j^g g_j(x) + \sum_{k=1}^{r} \lambda_k^h h_k(x).$$

Now, from Corollary 2, the minimum point of Lagrange function is solution of the equation

$$0 \in \partial\left(\sum_{i=1}^{p} \lambda_i^f f_i + \sum_{j=1}^{q} \lambda_j^g g_j + \sum_{k=1}^{r} \lambda_k^h h_k \right)(\bar{x}).$$

Making use of previous results and additive property of subdifferential, we get

$$0 \in \sum_{i=1}^{p} \lambda_i^f \partial f_i(\bar{x}) + \sum_{j=1}^{q} \lambda_j^g \partial g_j(\bar{x}) + \sum_{k=1}^{r} \lambda_k^h \partial h_k(\bar{x}).$$

We know that $h_k(\bar{x})$ be an affine function, then

$$\partial h_k(\bar{x}) = \nabla h_k(\bar{x}).$$

Hence, we get the required result. □

Example 2. *Consider the following problem*

$$min\ f(x) = (f_1(x), f_2(x)),\ \textit{subject to}\ g(x) \leqq 0,\ \textit{at a feasible point}\ \bar{x} = (0,0).$$

where, $f_1(x) = |x_1|$, $f_2(x) = |x_2|$, *and* $g(x) = |x_1| + |x_2| - 1$.

Since, $\bar{x}$ is a Pareto optimal solution for the considered problem as well as satisfying Slater's constraints qualification because $g(\bar{x}) < 0$, then $\lambda^f = (\lambda_1^f, \lambda_2^f) \neq 0$, $\lambda^f \geqq 0$ and $\lambda^g g(\bar{x}) = 0 \implies \lambda^g = 0$. Now from the definition of subdifferential, we get

$$\partial f_1(\bar{x}) = \{(\xi, 0) \in \mathbb{R}^2 : -1 \leqq \xi \leqq 1\}, \partial f_2(\bar{x}) = \{(0, \xi) \in \mathbb{R}^2 : -1 \leqq \xi \leqq 1\},$$

which implies that

$$0 \in \lambda_1^f \partial f_1(\bar{x}) + \lambda_2^f \partial f_2(\bar{x}) + \lambda^g \partial g(\bar{x}).$$

Hence, the result is verified.

Remark 3. *Since h_k are affine, then there exist a continuous linear functional $x_k^* \in X^*$ and a real number $\alpha_k \in \mathbb{R}$ such that $h_k = x_k^* + \alpha_k$, therefore we have $\nabla h_k = x_k^*$ and above condition becomes*

$$0 \in \sum_{i=1}^{p} \lambda_i^f \partial f_i(\bar{x}) + \sum_{j=1}^{q} \lambda_j^g \partial g_j(\bar{x}) + \sum_{k=1}^{r} \lambda_k^h x_k^*(\bar{x}). \tag{14}$$

Now, if we consider only the case of the constraint given by inequalities, that is,

$$S_1 = \{x \in X : g_j(x) \leqq 0, \forall j = 1, \cdots, q\}.$$

Then, Slater's constraints qualification is as follows:
There exist a point $\bar{x} \in \bigcap_{i=1}^{p} Dom(f_i)$ such that $g_j(\bar{x}) < 0$, $\forall j = 1, \cdots, q$.

Theorem 7. *Let $f_1, \cdots, f_p$ be a proper convex lower-semicontinuous function and $g_1, \cdots, g_q$ be real convex continuous functions satisfying the Slater's constraint qualification (7) at a feasible point $\bar{x}$. Then, the point $\bar{x} \in S_1$ is a Pareto optimal solution for (MOP) if and only if there exists $\lambda^f = (\lambda_1^f, \cdots, \lambda_p^f)$, $\lambda^g = (\lambda_1^g, \cdots, \lambda_q^g)$ such that*

$$0 \in \sum_{i=1}^{p} \lambda_i^f \partial f_i(\bar{x}) + \sum_{j=1}^{q} \lambda_j^g \partial g_j(\bar{x}), \tag{15}$$

$$\lambda^f \geqq 0,\ \lambda^f \neq 0,\ \lambda_j^g \geqq 0,\ \lambda_j^g g_j(\bar{x}) = 0,\ \forall j = 1, \cdots, q. \tag{16}$$

Proof. Suppose $\bar{x} \in S$ is a Pareto optimal solution of problem (MOP) then, from equation

$$\sum_{i=1}^{p} \lambda_i^f f_i(\bar{x}) \leqq \sum_{i=1}^{p} \lambda_i^f f_i(x) + \sum_{j=1}^{q} \lambda_j^g g_j(x). \tag{17}$$

By Slater's constraint qualification there exists $\bar{x} \in S$, such that

$$\sum_{i=1}^{p} \lambda_i^f f_i(\bar{x}) + \sum_{j=1}^{q} \lambda_j^g g_j(\bar{x}) \leqq \sum_{i=1}^{p} \lambda_i^f f_i(x) + \sum_{j=1}^{q} \lambda_j^g g_j(x).$$

Now from Corollary (2) the minimum point of the Langrange function is the solutuon of the relation

$$0 \in \partial \left(\sum_{i=1}^{p} \lambda_i^f f_i + \sum_{j=1}^{q} \lambda_j^g g_j + \sum_{k=1}^{r} \lambda_k^h h_k \right)(\bar{x}).$$

Using the additive property of subdifferential, we get

$$0 \in \sum_{i=1}^{p} \lambda_i^f \partial f_i(\bar{x}) + \sum_{j=1}^{q} \lambda_j^g \partial g_j(\bar{x}) + \sum_{k=1}^{r} \lambda_k^h \partial h_k(\bar{x}).$$

$$\lambda^f \geqq 0,\ \lambda^f \neq 0,\ \lambda_j^g \geqq 0,\ \lambda_j^g g_j(\bar{x}) = 0,\ \forall\, j = 1, \cdots, q.$$

Conversely, suppose $\bar{x}$ is not pareto optimal solution of (MOP), then there exists $x^*(\neq \bar{x}) \in S$ which is Pareto optimal solution for MOP that is

$$f(x^*) \leq f(\bar{x}). \tag{18}$$

Now, from relation (10) for $x^* \in S$

$$\sum_{i=1}^{p} \lambda_i^f f_i(\bar{x}) \ \leqq\ \sum_{i=1}^{p} \lambda_i^f f_i(x^*),$$

which is contradiction to inequality (18). Hence $\bar{x}$ is a pareto optimal solution for MOP. Since $f(x)$ is a proper convex function, therefore $f(x)$ is necessarily finite. □

Corollary 3. *Let $f_1, \cdots, f_p, g_1, \cdots, g_q$ be real convex and differentiable functions on X which satisfy (1). Then, a feasible point $\bar{x}$ is a Pareto solution of problem (MOP) with* (1) *given by (15) if and only if there exist real numbers $\lambda_1^f, \cdots, \lambda_p^f, \lambda_1^g, \cdots, \lambda_q^g$ such that*

$$\sum_{i=1}^{p} \lambda_i^f \nabla f_i(\bar{x}) + \sum_{j=1}^{q} \lambda_j^g \nabla g_j(\bar{x}) = 0, \tag{19}$$

$$\lambda^f \geqq 0,\ \lambda^f \neq 0,\ \lambda_j^g \ \geqq\ 0,\ \lambda_j^g g_j(\bar{x}) = 0,\ \forall\, j = 1, \cdots, q.$$

4. Conclusions

In this paper, we have established saddle point optimality conditions for a convex MOP in real Banach space. We recall Slater's constraint qualification from [18] and derive saddle point necessary and sufficient Pareto optimality condition for the considered problem where multipliers of objective functions never vanished simultaneously. We have deduced Karush–Kuhn–Tucker optimality conditions from saddle point optimality conditions for the subdifferentiable case and present some examples to verify our results. We have characterized saddle point optimality conditions for Pareto points to convex MOPs in real Banach space which is more general as well as proofing technique is different from Ehrgott and Wiecek [23]. Further, we have concluded Karush–Kuhn–Tucker optimality conditions for smooth and nonsmooth cases from saddle point optimality conditions that is a new thing as compared to Ehrgott and Wiecek. Our derived Karush–Kuhn–Tucker optimality conditions are the same as in Miettinen [2] and Haeser and Ramos [24]. That is why our paper includes novelty from Ehrgott and Wiecek [23] in some senses. Further, these results can be extended for convex semi-infinite programming problems [25,26]. In the future, we can extend these results to interval-valued optimality conditions and can deduce some applications motivated by the recent article by Treanta [27]. Further, we can extend these results on vector equilibrium on Hadamard manifolds motivated by Ruiz-Garzòn et al. [28].

Author Contributions: Writing—original draft preparation, K.K.L., M.H., J.K.M., S.K.S. and S.K.M.; writing—review and editing, K.K.L., M.H., J.K.M., S.K.S. and S.K.M.; funding acquisition, K.K.L. All authors have read and agreed to the published version of the manuscript.

Funding: The second author is financially supported by CSIR-UGC JRF, New Delhi, India, through Reference no.: 1009/(CSIR-UGC NET JUNE 2018). The fourth author is financially supported by CSIR-UGC JRF, New Delhi, India, through Reference no.: 1272/(CSIR-UGC NET DEC.2016). The fifth author is financially supported by "Research Grant for Faculty" (IoE Scheme) under Dev. Scheme NO. 6031.

Institutional Review Board Statement: Not applicable.

Informed Consent Statement: Not applicable.

Data Availability Statement: No data were used to support this study.

Acknowledgments: The authors are indebted to the anonymous reviewers for their valuable comments and remarks that helped to improve the presentation and quality of the manuscript.

Conflicts of Interest: The authors declare no conflict of interest.

References

1. Branke, J.; Deb, K.; Miettinen, K.; Słowiński, S. *Multiobjective Optimization: Interactive and Evolutionary Approaches*; Springer: Berlin/Heidelberg, Germany, 2008.
2. Miettinen, K.M. *Nonlinear Multiobjective Optimization*; Kluwer Academic Publishers: Boston, MA, USA, 1999.
3. Lai, K.K.; Mishra, S.K.; Panda, G.; Ansary, M.A.; Ram, B. On q-steepest descent method for unconstrained multiobjective optimization problems. *AIMS Math.* **2020**, *5*, 5521–5540.
4. Tzou, J.; Wetton, B. Optimal covering points and curves. *AIMS Math.* **2019**, *4*, 1796–1804. [CrossRef]
5. Sawaragi, Y.; Nakayama, H.; Tanino, T. *Theory of Multiobjective Optimization*; Academic Press Inc.: Orlando, FL, USA, 1985.
6. Mishra, S.K.; Wang, S.Y. Second order symmetric duality for nonlinear multiobjective mixed integer programming. *Eur. J. Oper. Res.* **2005**, *161*, 673–682. [CrossRef]
7. Ehrgott, M. *Multicriteria Optimization*; Springer: Berlin, Germany, 2005.
8. Moreno-Pulido, S.; Garcia-Pacheco, F.J.; Cobos-Sanchez, C.; Sanchez-Alzola, A. Exact Solutions to the Maxmin Problem max $\|Ax\|$ Subject to $\|Bx\| \leq 1$. *Mathematics* **2020**, *8*, 85. [CrossRef]
9. Garcia-Pacheco, F.J.; Cobos-Sanchez, C.; Moreno-Pulido, S.; Sanchez-Alzola, A. Exact solutions to $\max\limits_{\|x\|=1} \sum_{i=1}^{\infty} \|T_i(x)\|^2$ with applications to Physics, Bioengineering and Statistics. *Comm. Nonlinear Sci. Numer. Simul.* **2020**, *82*, 105054. [CrossRef]
10. Sánchez, C.C.; Garcia-Pacheco, F.J.; Guerrero-Rodriguez, J.M.; Garcia-Barrachina, L. Solving an IBEM with supporting vector analysis to design quiet TMS coils. *Eng. Anal. Bound. Elem.* **2020**, *117*, 1–12. [CrossRef]
11. Sánchez-Alzola, A.; García-Pacheco, F.J.; Naranjo-Guerra, E.; Moreno-Pulido, S. Supporting vectors for the ℓ_1-norm and the ℓ_∞-norm and an application. *Math. Sci.* **2021**, *15*, 173–187. [CrossRef]
12. Wendell, R.E.; Lee, D.N. Efficiency in multiple objective optimization problems. *Math. Program.* **1977**, *12*, 406–414. [CrossRef]
13. Mangasarian, O.L. *Nonlinear Programming*; McGraw-Hill: New York, NY, USA, 1969.
14. Van Rooyen, M.; Zhou, X.; Zlobec, S. A saddle-point characterization of Pareto optima. *Math. Program.* **1994**, *67*, 77–88. [CrossRef]
15. Cobos-Sánchez, C.; Vilchez-Membrilla, J.A.; Campos-Jiménez, A.; García-Pacheco, F.J. Pareto Optimality for Multioptimization of Continuous Linear Operators. *Symmetry* **2021**, *13*, 661. [CrossRef]
16. Treanţă, S. Robust saddle-point criterion in second-order partial differential equation and partial differential inequation constrained control problems. *Int. J. Robust Nonlinear Control* **2021**. [CrossRef]
17. Antczak, T.; Abdulaleem, N. Optimality and duality results for E-differentiable multiobjective fractional programming problems under E-convexity. *J. Ineq. Appl.* **2019**, *2019*, 1–24. [CrossRef]
18. Barbu, V.; Precupanu, T. *Convexity and Optimization in Banach Spaces*; Springer: Dordrecht, The Netherlands; New York, NY, USA, 2012.
19. Valyi, I. Approximate saddle-point theorems in vector optimization. *J. Optim. Theory Appl.* **1987**, *55*, 435–448. [CrossRef]
20. Rong, W.D.; Wu, N.Y. ϵ- weak minimal solutions of vector optimization problems with set-valued maps. *J. Optim. Theory Appl.* **2000**, *106*, 569–579. [CrossRef]
21. Kuhn, H.W.; Tucker, A.W. *Nonlinear Programming*; University of California Press: Berkeley, CA, USA; Los Angeles, CA, USA, 1951.
22. Guu, S.M.; Singh, Y.; Mishra, S.K. On strong KKT type sufficient optimality conditions for multiobjective semi-infinite programming problems with vanishing constraints. *J. Ineq. Appl.* **2017**, *2017*, 1–9. [CrossRef]
23. Ehrgott, M.; Wiecek, M.M. Saddle points and Pareto points in multiple objective programming. *J. Glob. Optim.* **2005**, *32*, 11–33. [CrossRef]
24. Haeser, G.; Ramos, A. Constraint Qualifications for Karush–Kuhn–Tucker Conditions in Multiobjective Optimization. *J. Optim. Theory Appl.* **2020**, *187*, 469–487. [CrossRef]
25. Hettich, R.; Kortanek, K.O. Semi-Infinite Programming: Theory, Methods, and Applications. *SIAM Rev.* **1993**, *35*, 380–429. [CrossRef]
26. Li, W.; Nahak, C.; Singer, I. Constraint qualifications for semi-infinite systems of convex inequalities. *SIAM J. Optim.* **2000**, *11*, 31–52. [CrossRef]
27. Treanţă, S. LU-Optimality Conditions in Optimization Problems With Mechanical Work Objective Functionals. *IEEE Trans. Neural Networks Learn. Syst.* **2021**. [CrossRef]
28. Ruiz-Garzón, G.; Osuna-Gómez, R.; Ruiz-Zapatero, J. Necessary and sufficient optimality conditions for vector equilibrium problems on Hadamard manifolds. *Symmetry* **2019**, *11*, 1037. [CrossRef]

symmetry MDPI

Article

The Well Posedness for Nonhomogeneous Boussinesq Equations

Yan Liu [1] and Baiping Ouyang [2,*]

1 Department of Mathematics, Guangdong University of Finance, Guangzhou 510521, China; 26-046@gduf.edu.cn
2 School of Data Science, Guangzhou Huashang College, Guangzhou 511300, China
* Correspondence: oytengfei79@gdhsc.edu.cn

Abstract: This paper is devoted to studying the Cauchy problem for non-homogeneous Boussinesq equations. We built the results on the critical Besov spaces $(\theta, u) \in L^\infty_T(\dot{B}^{N/p}_{p,1}) \times L^\infty_T(\dot{B}^{N/p-1}_{p,1}) \bigcap L^1_T(\dot{B}^{N/p+1}_{p,1})$ with $1 < p < 2N$. We proved the global existence of the solution when the initial velocity is small with respect to the viscosity, as well as the initial temperature approaches a positive constant. Furthermore, we proved the uniqueness for $1 < p \leq N$. Our results can been seen as a version of symmetry in Besov space for the Boussinesq equations.

Keywords: non homogenous boussinesq equations; global well-posedness; littlewood-paley decomposition

Citation: Liu, Y.; Ouyang, B. The Well Posedness for Nonhomogeneous Boussinesq Equations. *Symmetry* **2021**, *13*, 2110. https://doi.org/10.3390/sym13112110

Academic Editors: Octav Olteanu and Savin Treanta

Received: 19 October 2021
Accepted: 30 October 2021
Published: 6 November 2021

1. Introduction

This paper discusses the global well-posedness of Boussinesq equations. We assume that the viscosity and thermal conductivity are temperature dependent. The coupled mass flow and heat flow of the viscous incompressible fluid are controlled by Boussinesq approximation. The equations we study are as follows:

$$\begin{cases} u_t - div(\nu(\theta)\nabla u) + u \cdot \nabla u + \alpha\theta g + \nabla p = 0, \\ div(u) = 0, \\ \theta_t - div(\kappa(\theta)\nabla\theta) + u \cdot \nabla\theta = 0. \end{cases} \tag{1}$$

Here $u(t,x)$ denotes the velocity of the fluid , $(t,x) \in R^+ \times R^N$, $N \geq 2$ is the spatial dimension; $p(t,x)$ is the hydrostatic pressure; $\theta(t,x)$ is the temperature; $g(t,x)$ is the external force by a unit of mass; $\nu(\theta)$ is the kinematic viscosity; $\kappa(\theta)$ is the thermal conductivity; α is a positive constant which is dependent on the coefficient of volume expansion. The Boussinesq system has important roles in the atmospheric sciences, for more details, one could refer to [1,2].

The homogeneous Boussinesq equations corresponding to the special case where coefficients ν and κ are positive constants:

$$\begin{cases} u_t - \nu\triangle u + u \cdot \nabla u + \alpha\theta g + \nabla p = 0, \\ div(u) = 0, \\ \theta_t - \kappa\triangle\theta + u \cdot \nabla\theta = 0. \end{cases} \tag{2}$$

The global well-posedness of (2) with $\nu > 0, \kappa > 0$ is well-known (see [3]). However, for the case of $\nu = 0$ and $\kappa = 0$ in (2), the global existence of solution is still an outstanding open problem in the mathematical fluid mechanics (see [4–6]). Recently, some authors obtain the global well-posedness of (2) with partial viscosity cases (i.e., either the zero diffusivity case: $\kappa = 0$ and $\nu > 0$, or the zero viscosity case: $\kappa > 0$ and $\nu = 0$) (see [6–12]).

Some attentions have been paid to the nonhomogeneous case (1). In [13], the authors investigated the initial-boundary problems of (1) and obtained the global well-posedness.

In [14], they studied an optimum control problem of mathematical model describing steady non-isothermal creep of incompressible fluid through local Lipschitz bounded region. In [15], they studied an optimal control problem for the mathematical model that describes steady non-isothermal creeping flows of an incompressible fluid through a locally Lipschitz bounded domain. In [16], the initial-boundary value problem of completely incompressible Navier-Stokes equations with viscosity coefficient ν and heat conductivity κ varying with temperature by the power law of Chapman-Enskog are studied. When $\kappa = 0$, the method used in [16] is not applicable. We must seek new methods to overcome the difficulty.

The purpose of this paper is to study the well-posedness of the Boussinesq system (1). Equations (1) corresponds to the physical environment which we can't ignore the variation of fluid viscosity (and thermal conductivity) with temperature (for more details see [17] and the references therein). The existing literature has more discussion on the constant viscosity and less discussions on the viscosity of temperature. This paper will provide some methods for studying other problems when viscosity relates to temperature. In the present paper, we consider the system (1) without thermal conductivity, and with the viscosity ν dependent on θ. The main difficulty is that we can not use the results obtained previously for the constant viscosity. We firstly use the method of iteration, then we transform the problem into a constant viscosity problem. This is the biggest innovation of this paper. Since the Besov space is more meticulous than the traditional Sobolev space, the results obtained in this paper are no longer correct in the Sobolev space. In the present paper, we study the following equations:

$$\begin{cases} u_t - div(\nu(\theta)\nabla u) + u \cdot \nabla u + \alpha\theta g + \nabla p = 0, \\ div(u) = 0, \\ \theta_t + u \cdot \nabla\theta = 0, \\ t = 0, u = u_0, \theta = \theta_0. \end{cases} \tag{3}$$

In order to have a clear idea of our purpose, we shall recall some research history for the following Navier-Stokes equations:

$$\begin{cases} \partial_t\rho + \nabla \cdot (\rho u) = 0, \\ \partial_t(\rho u) + \nabla \cdot (\rho u \times u) - \mu\Delta u = \rho f, \\ \nabla \cdot u = 0. \end{cases} \tag{4}$$

In [18], Fujita & Kato proved the global existence and uniqueness of problem (4) in the critical Sobolev space $\dot{H}^{\frac{N}{2}} \times (\dot{H}^{\frac{N}{2}-1})^N$. Precisely, if (ρ, u) is a solution of (4), with initial data $(\rho_0(x), u_0(x))$, then:

$$\rho_\lambda(t,x) = \rho(\lambda^2 t, \lambda x), \quad u_\lambda(t,x) = \lambda u(\lambda^2 t, \lambda x)$$

is also the solution of (4) with initial data $(\rho_{0,\lambda}(x), u_{0,\lambda}(x)) = (\rho_0(\lambda x), \lambda u_0(\lambda x))$.

Subsequently, in [19], Danchin generalized the results by Fujita & Kato [18] in Besov space $(\dot{B}_{2,1}^{\frac{N}{2}-1})^N$; see also [20–24]. Some ideas of this paper came from [19,20]. Some new results about the equations may be found in [25–30].

We suppose that the initial data $\theta_0 > 0$. In the present paper, we shall establish the well-posedness of the non-homogeneous Bounssinesq Equation (3) in $\dot{B}_{p,1}^{N/p}$ (see the definition in Section 2). Since the Besov spaces are symmetry, the results obtained in this paper have the property of symmetry. We shall restrict our work to solutions such that the temperature θ is a small perturbation of a constant temperature $\overline{\theta}$. As we know, there are inevitable errors in the process of modeling or measurement. We are looking forward to understanding the impact of these errors on the behavior of the solutions. This paper solves this problem well. There are few relevant studies at present. Without loss of generality, in the following, we take $\overline{\theta} = 1, \nu \in C^\infty$ and $\nu(\overline{\theta}) = \nu(1) = \underline{\nu}$. Therefore, Equation (3) can be rewritten as:

$$\begin{cases} u_t - \underline{\nu}\Delta u + u \cdot \nabla u + \nabla p = G, \\ div(u) = 0, \\ \theta_t + u \cdot \nabla \theta = 0, \\ t = 0, u = u_0, \theta = \theta_0, \end{cases} \tag{5}$$

where,

$$G = \nabla \cdot [(\nu(\theta) - \underline{\nu})\nabla u] - \alpha\theta g. \tag{6}$$

We write:

$$\widetilde{\nu}(\theta + 1) = \nu(\theta) \quad and \quad \widetilde{\nu}(\underline{\theta}) = 1. \tag{7}$$

Let us now state our main results.

Theorem 1. *Let $1 < p < 2N$, then for $(\theta_0, u_0) \in (\dot{B}^{N/p}_{p,1}) \times (\dot{B}^{N/p-1}_{p,1})^N$, $g \in L^1_T(\dot{B}^{N/p-1}_{p,1}) \bigcap L^2_T(\dot{B}^{N/p}_{p,1})$ there exists $T(\theta_0, u_0) > 0$, such that the problem (5) admits a solution (θ, u) with:*

$$\theta \in C([0,T), \dot{B}^{N/p}_{p,1}) \bigcap L^\infty_T(\dot{B}^{N/p}_{p,1}),$$

$$u \in C([0,T), \dot{B}^{N/p-1}_{p,1}) \bigcap L^\infty_T(\dot{B}^{N/p-1}_{p,1}) \bigcap L^1_T(\dot{B}^{N/p+1}_{p,1}).$$

Moreover, if there exist a small constant ε, such that:

$$\|u_0\|_{L^\infty_T(\dot{B}^{N/p-1}_{p,1})} + \|g\|_{L^1_T(\dot{B}^{N/p-1}_{p,1})} \leq \varepsilon\underline{\mu},$$

then $T = +\infty$. If $1 < p \leq N$, the solution is unique.

The present paper is structured as follows: in the next section, we show some preliminaries. In Section 3, we show the existence of the solution. The uniqueness is presented in Section 4. Some conclusions are included in Section 5.

Remark 1. *Throughout this paper, C stands for a 'harmless' uniform constant, and we sometimes use the notation $A \lesssim B$ as an equivalent of $A \leq CB$. The notation $A \approx B$ means that $A \lesssim B$ and $B \lesssim A$.*

2. Some Results on Besov Spaces

2.1. Littlewood-Paley Theory

At the beginning, we shall recall the Littlewood-Paley decomposition.

Take $\chi, \phi \in C^\infty(R^N)$ supported on $B = \{\xi \in R^N, |\xi| \leq 4/3\}$ and $\Gamma = \{\xi \in R^N, 3/4 \leq |\xi| \leq 8/3\}$ respectively, such that:

$$\sum_{j\in\mathbb{Z}} \phi(2^{-j}\xi) = 1, \quad \chi = 1 - \sum_{j\geq 0} \phi(2^{-j}\xi), \quad \forall\xi \neq 0. \tag{8}$$

Denoting:

$$\Delta_j u = F^{-1}(\phi(2^{-j}\cdot)\hat{u}(\cdot)) = 2^{Nj}\int_{R^N} \psi(2^j y)u(x-y)dy, \quad \text{for } j \in \mathbb{Z},$$

and:

$$S_j u = \sum_{k\leq j-1} \Delta_k u = 2^{Nj}\int_{R^N} \psi_1(2^j y)u(x-y)dy,$$

where $\hat{u} = \mathcal{F}(u)$ denote the Fourier transformation of u, $\psi = \mathcal{F}^{-1}(\phi(\cdot))$, and $\psi_1 = \mathcal{F}^{-1}(\chi(\cdot))$. The formal decomposition:

$$u = \sum_{j=-\infty}^{\infty} \Delta_j u, \tag{9}$$

is called homogenous Littlewood-Paley decomposition. This dyadic decomposition has a nice quasi-orthogonality, and we have:

$$\Delta_i \Delta_j u \equiv 0, \quad \text{if}, \quad |i-j| \geq 2, \quad \text{and} \tag{10}$$

$$\Delta_i (S_{j-1} u \Delta_j u) \equiv 0, \quad \text{if}, \quad |i-j| \geq 5. \tag{11}$$

The details of Littlewood-Paley decomposition can be found in [31,32].

2.2. The Homogeneous Besov Spaces

In the following, we shall define the functional spaces in which we shall work in.

Definition 1. *For $s \in R$, $(p,r) \in [1,+\infty] \times [1,+\infty]$, and $u \in \mathcal{S}'(R^N)$. Define:*

$$\dot{B}^s_{p,r} = \{u \in \mathcal{S}'(R^N), \|u\|_{\dot{B}^s_{p,r}} < +\infty\},$$

where:

$$\|u\|_{\dot{B}^s_{p,r}} = \begin{cases} \left(\sum_{j\in\mathbb{Z}} 2^{rjs} \|\Delta_j u\|^r_{L^p}\right)^{\frac{1}{r}}, & r < +\infty, \\ \sup_j 2^{js} \|\Delta_j u\|_{L^p}, & r = +\infty. \end{cases}$$

Let us now recall some classical properties for these Besov spaces (see [23,24])

Proposition 1. *The following properties hold:*
(i) There exists a uniform constant C, such that,

$$C^{-1}\|u\|_{\dot{B}^s_{p,r}} \leq \|\nabla u\|_{\dot{B}^{s-1}_{p,r}} \leq C\|u\|_{\dot{B}^s_{p,r}}, \tag{12}$$

(ii) Sobolev embedding: for $p_1 \leq p_2$ and $r_1 \leq r_2$, then,

$$\dot{B}^s_{p_1,r_1} \hookrightarrow \dot{B}^{s-N(\frac{1}{p_1}-\frac{1}{p_2})}_{p_2,r_2}, \tag{13}$$

(iii) For $s > 0$, $\dot{B}^s_{p,r} \cap L^\infty$ is an algebra. Moreover, for any $p \in [1,+\infty]$, then,

$$\dot{B}^{N/p}_{p,1} \hookrightarrow \dot{B}^{N/p}_{p,\infty} \bigcap L^\infty. \tag{14}$$

(iv) Interpolation: $[\dot{B}^{s_1}_{p,r}, \dot{B}^{s_2}_{p,r}]_{\theta,r'} = \dot{B}^{\theta s_1+(1-\theta)s_2}_{p,r'}$.

Through this paper, we shall use the product law in Besov spaces. These product laws are proved in [20,33].

Proposition 2. *Let $(p,p_1,p_2) \in [1,+\infty]^3$ such that:*

$$\frac{1}{p} \leq \frac{1}{p_1} + \frac{1}{p_2},$$

We get:

(i) If:

$$s_1 + s_2 + Ninf\left(0, 1 - \frac{1}{p_1} - \frac{1}{p_2}\right) > 0, \quad s_1 < \frac{N}{p_1} \quad and \quad s_2 < \frac{N}{p_2},$$

there holds,

$$\|uv\|_{\dot{B}^{s_1+s_2-N(\frac{1}{p_1}+\frac{1}{p_2}-\frac{1}{p})}_{p,r}} \lesssim \|u\|_{\dot{B}^{s_1}_{p_1,r}} \|v\|_{\dot{B}^{s_2}_{p_2,\infty}}, \tag{15}$$

furthermore, if $s_1 = \frac{N}{p_1}$ *and* $s_2 = \frac{N}{p_2}$, *we take* $r = 1$.

(ii) If $|s| < |\frac{N}{p}|$ *and* $p \geq 2$, *then we get:*

$$\|uv\|_{\dot{B}^s_{p,r}} \lesssim \|u\|_{\dot{B}^s_{p,r}} \|v\|_{\dot{B}^{N/p}_{p,\infty} \cap L^\infty}. \tag{16}$$

(iii) If $s_1 + s_2 = 0$, $s_1 \in (-\frac{N}{p_1}, \frac{N}{p_1}]$ *and* $\frac{1}{p_1} + \frac{1}{p_2} \leq 1$, *then:*

$$\|uv\|_{\dot{B}^{-N(\frac{1}{p_1}+\frac{1}{p_2}-\frac{1}{p})}_{p,\infty}} \lesssim \|u\|_{\dot{B}^{s_1}_{p_1,1}} \|v\|_{\dot{B}^{s_2}_{p_2,\infty}}. \tag{17}$$

Additionally, we need the definition of $\tilde{L}^\alpha_T(\dot{B}^s_{p,r})$ introduced in [19,20,31].

Definition 2. *Let* $(r, \alpha, p) \in [1, +\infty]^3$, $T \in [0, +\infty]$ *and* $s \in R$. *We set:*

$$\|u\|_{\tilde{L}^\alpha_T(\dot{B}^s_{p,r})} \triangleq \left(\sum_{j\in\mathbb{Z}} 2^{jrs} \left(\int_0^T \|\Delta_j u(t)\|^\alpha_{L^p} dt\right)^{r/\alpha}\right)^{1/r}.$$

By virtue of the Minkowski inequality, we get:

$$\|u\|_{\tilde{L}^\alpha_T(\dot{B}^s_{p,r})} \leq \|u\|_{L^\alpha_T(\dot{B}^s_{p,r})}, \quad \text{if } \alpha \leq r. \tag{18}$$

Thus,

$$\|u\|_{L^\alpha_T(\dot{B}^s_{p,r})} \leq \|u\|_{\tilde{L}^\alpha_T(\dot{B}^s_{p,r})}, \quad \text{if } r \leq \alpha. \tag{19}$$

Moreover, for $\theta \in (0, 1]$, we have:

$$\|u\|_{\tilde{L}^\alpha_T(\dot{B}^s_{p,r})} \leq \|u\|^\theta_{\tilde{L}^{\alpha_1}_T(\dot{B}^{s_1}_{p,r})} \|u\|^{1-\theta}_{\tilde{L}^{\alpha_2}_T(\dot{B}^{s_2}_{p,r})}, \tag{20}$$

with,

$$\frac{1}{\alpha} = \frac{\theta}{\alpha_1} + \frac{1-\theta}{\alpha_2}, \quad \text{and} \quad s = \theta s_1 + (1-\theta)s_2.$$

2.3. Estimates for Linear Transport Equation

In the following, we recall some estimates for the following linear transport equation:

$$\begin{cases} \partial_t g + \nabla \cdot (vg) = F, \\ g(0, x) = g_0. \end{cases} \tag{21}$$

The following results will hold, (see proof in [19,24,33]).

Proposition 3. *Let* $(p, r) \in [1, +\infty]^2$ *and* s *be such that* $-1 - Ninf(\frac{1}{p'}, \frac{1}{p}) < s < 1 + \frac{N}{p}$ *where* p' *is the conjugate of* p. *Let* v *be a free divergence vector such that* $\nabla v \in L^1(0, T; \dot{B}^{N/p}_{p,r} \cap L^\infty)$. *Suppose that* $g_0 \in \dot{B}^s_{p,r}$ *and* $F \in L^1(0, T, \dot{B}^s_{p,r})$, *and* g *be a solution of* (21) *then holds:*

$$\|g\|_{\tilde{L}^\infty_T(\dot{B}^s_{p,r})} \leq \exp\left(C\|\nabla v\|_{L^1_T(\dot{B}^{N/p}_{p,r} \cap L^\infty)}\right)\left(\|g_0\|_{\dot{B}^s_{p,r}} + \int_0^T \|F(t)\|_{\dot{B}^s_{p,r}} dt\right). \tag{22}$$

Proposition 4. *Let $p \in (1, +\infty)$ and $-1 - N inf(\frac{1}{p}, \frac{1}{p'}) < s < \frac{N}{p}$, where p' is the conjugate exponent of p. Let $u_0 \in \dot{B}^s_{p,r}$, $F \in \tilde{L}^1_T(\dot{B}^s_{p,r})$ and v be a free divergence vector such that $\nabla v \in L^1(0, T; \dot{B}^{N/p}_{p,r} \bigcap L^\infty)$, then Let u be a solution of the following system:*

$$\begin{cases} \partial_t u + v \cdot \nabla u - \nu \Delta u + \nabla P = F, \\ \nabla \cdot u = 0, \\ u(0, x) = u_0, \end{cases} \tag{23}$$

where ν is a positive constant. Then there exists a constant C such that the following estimates hold:

$$\|u\|_{\tilde{L}^\infty_T(\dot{B}^s_{p,r})} + \nu \|u\|_{\tilde{L}^1_T(\dot{B}^{s+2}_{p,r})} + \|\nabla P\|_{\tilde{L}^1_T(\dot{B}^s_{p,r})}$$

$$\leq \exp\left(C\|\nabla v\|_{\tilde{L}^1_T(\dot{B}^{N/p}_{p,r} \bigcap L^\infty)}\right)\left(\|u_0\|_{\dot{B}^s_{p,r}} + C\|F\|_{\tilde{L}^1_T(\dot{B}^s_{p,r})}\right). \tag{24}$$

3. The Existence of the Solution

In this section we shall prove the existence of the solution for (5). We state the results as following.

Theorem 2. *Let $1 < p < 2N$, then for $(\theta_0, u_0) \in (\dot{B}^{N/p}_{p,1}) \times (\dot{B}^{N/p-1}_{p,1})^N$, $g \in L^1_T(\dot{B}^{N/p-1}_{p,1}) \bigcap L^2_T(\dot{B}^{N/p}_{p,1})$ there exists $T(\theta_0, u_0) > 0$, such that the problem (5) admits a solution (θ, u) with:*

$$\theta \in C([0, T), \dot{B}^{N/p}_{p,1}) \bigcap L^\infty_T(\dot{B}^{N/p}_{p,1}),$$

$$u \in C([0, T), \dot{B}^{N/p-1}_{p,1}) \bigcap L^\infty_T(\dot{B}^{N/p-1}_{p,1}) \bigcap L^1_T(\dot{B}^{N/p+1}_{p,1}).$$

Moreover, if there exist a small constant ε, such that:

$$\|u_0\|_{L^\infty_T(\dot{B}^{N/p-1}_{p,1})} + \|g\|_{L^1_T \dot{B}^{N/p-1}_{p,1}} \leq \varepsilon \underline{\mu},$$

then $T = +\infty$.

Proof. We shall prove this results by iteration. Denoting,

$$\sum_{j \leq n} \Delta_j \theta = \theta^n, \quad \sum_{j \leq n} \Delta_j u = u^n, \quad \sum_{j \leq n} \Delta_j p = p^n.$$

We shall build an approximate smooth solution (θ^n, u^n, p^n) of (5) satisfying,

$$\begin{cases} \partial_t \theta^{n+1} + u^n \cdot \nabla \theta^{n+1} = 0, \\ \partial_t u^{n+1} + u^n \cdot \nabla u^{n+1} - \underline{\nu} \Delta u^{n+1} + \nabla p^{n+1} = G^n, \\ \nabla \cdot u^{n+1} = 0, \\ (\theta^1, u^1) = S_2(\theta_0, u_0), \\ (\tau^{n+1}, u^{n+1})|_{t=0} = S_{n+2}(\theta_0, u_0), \end{cases} \tag{25}$$

where,

$$G^n = \nabla \cdot [(\widetilde{\nu}(\theta^n + 1) - \underline{\nu})\nabla u^n] - \alpha \theta^n g. \tag{26}$$

Obviously, from Propositions 3 and 4, we know that there exist a T such that (25) admits a unique smooth solution in $t \in [0, T]$. Then, the proof of Theorem 2 is divided into two steps:

(1) The uniform a priori estimates for (θ^n, u^n).

(2) The proof of the convergence of the sequences.
We begin to obtain the uniform estimates for (θ^n, u^n)
Denoting:

$$I_0 \triangleq \|\theta_0\|_{\dot{B}^{N/p}_{p,1}} + \|u_0\|_{\dot{B}^{N/p-1}_{p,1}}, \tag{27}$$

and,

$$E^n_T = \|\theta^n\|_{\tilde{L}^\infty_T(\dot{B}^{N/p}_{p,1})} + \|u^n\|_{\tilde{L}^\infty_T(\dot{B}^{N/p-1}_{p,1})} + \underline{\mu}\|u^n\|_{\tilde{L}^1_T(\dot{B}^{N/p+1}_{p,1})}.$$

Let:

$$\chi_T = \tilde{L}^\infty_T(\dot{B}^{N/p}_{p,1}) \times (\tilde{L}^\infty_T(\dot{B}^{N/p-1}_{p,1}) \bigcap \tilde{L}^1_T(\dot{B}^{N/p+1}_{p,1}))^N.$$

Now, we shall prove that $\{(\theta^n, u^n)_{n\in\mathbb{Z}}\}$ is uniformly bounded in χ_T. Moreover, $\forall n \in \mathbb{Z}$, we have the following conclusion:

$$\textbf{claim:}\quad E^n_T \le 4I_0. \tag{28}$$

We shall prove these by induction. For $n = 0$, they are valid obviously. We assume that for a fixed n, $(\theta^n, u^n) \in \chi_T$ is valid and the claim holds, we shall show that for $n+1$, $(\theta^{n+1}, u^{n+1}) \in \chi_T$ and the claim are also valid.

From (25), by Propositions 3 and 4, we have:

$$\|\theta^{n+1}\|_{\tilde{L}^\infty_T(\dot{B}^{N/p}_{p,1})} \le e^{\int_0^T c\|\nabla u^n\|_{\dot{B}^{N/p}_{p,1}}dt} \|\theta^{n+1}_0\|_{\dot{B}^{N/p}_{p,1}}, \tag{29}$$

and:

$$\begin{aligned}\|u^{n+1}\|_{\tilde{L}^\infty_T(\dot{B}^{N/p-1}_{p,1})} &+ \underline{\nu}\|u^{n+1}\|_{\tilde{L}^1_T(\dot{B}^{N/p+1}_{p,1})} + \|\nabla p^n\|_{\tilde{L}^1_T(\dot{B}^{N/p-1}_{p,1})} \\ &\le e^{\int_0^T c\|\nabla u^n\|_{\dot{B}^{N/p}_{p,1}}dt}\Big(\int_0^T \|G^n\|_{\dot{B}^{N/p-1}_{p,1}}dt + \|u_0\|_{\dot{B}^{N/p-1}_{p,1}}\Big).\end{aligned} \tag{30}$$

By the induction hypothesis, taking $T_1 < T$ small enough, such that:

$$e^{c\|u^n\|_{\tilde{L}^1_{T_1}(\dot{B}^{N/p+1}_{p,1})}} \le 2, \tag{31}$$

then, we obtain:

$$\|\theta^{n+1}\|_{\tilde{L}^\infty_{T_1}(\dot{B}^{N/p}_{p,1})} \le 2\|\theta_0\|_{\dot{B}^{N/p}_{p,1}}. \tag{32}$$

From (30) and (31), we have:

$$\begin{aligned}\|u^{n+1}\|_{\tilde{L}^\infty_{T_1}(\dot{B}^{N/p-1}_{p,1})} &+ \underline{\nu}\|u^{n+1}\|_{\tilde{L}^1_{T_1}(\dot{B}^{N/p+1}_{p,1})} + \|\nabla p^n\|_{\tilde{L}^1_{T_1}(\dot{B}^{N/p-1}_{p,1})} \\ &\le 2\Big(\int_0^{T_1} \|G^n\|_{\dot{B}^{N/p-1}_{p,1}}dt + \|u_0\|_{\dot{B}^{N/p-1}_{p,1}}\Big).\end{aligned} \tag{33}$$

We now want to deal with $\int_0^{T_1} \|G^n\|_{\dot{B}^{N/p-1}_{p,1}}dt$. Owing to Taylor's formula and Proposition 2, for $1 < p < 2N$, we obtain:

$$\begin{aligned}\|\nabla\cdot[(\widetilde{\nu}(\theta^n+1) - \underline{\nu})\nabla u^n]\|_{\tilde{L}^1_{T_1}(\dot{B}^{N/p-1}_{p,1})} &\lesssim \\ \|[(\widetilde{\nu}(\theta^n+1) - \underline{\nu})\nabla u^n]\|_{\tilde{L}^1_{T_1}(\dot{B}^{N/p}_{p,1})}& \\ &\lesssim (\|\theta^n\|_{\tilde{L}^\infty_{T_1}(\dot{B}^{N/p}_{p,1})}\|u^n\|_{\tilde{L}^1_{T_1}(\dot{B}^{N/p+1}_{p,1})}.\end{aligned} \tag{34}$$

Combining (26) and (34), and using (15), we can get:

$$\|G^n\|_{\tilde{L}^1_{T_1}(\dot{B}^{N/p-1}_{p,1})} \lesssim \|\theta^n\|_{\tilde{L}^\infty_{T_1}(\dot{B}^{N/p}_{p,1})}\|u^n\|_{\tilde{L}^1_{T_1}(\dot{B}^{N/p+1}_{p,1})} + \alpha\|\theta^n\|_{\tilde{L}^\infty_{T_1}(\dot{B}^{N/p}_{p,1})}\|g\|_{\tilde{L}^1_{T_1}(\dot{B}^{N/p-1}_{p,1})}$$

$$\lesssim 4I_0\|u^n\|_{\tilde{L}^1_{T_1}(\dot{B}^{N/p+1}_{p,1})} + \alpha I_0\|g\|_{\tilde{L}^1_{T_1}(\dot{B}^{N/p-1}_{p,1})}. \quad (35)$$

Therefore, by the induction hypothesis, taking T_1 small enough, such that:

$$4I_0\|u^n\|_{\tilde{L}^1_{T_1}(\dot{B}^{N/p+1}_{p,1})} + \alpha I_0\|g\|_{\tilde{L}^1_{T_1}(\dot{B}^{N/p-1}_{p,1})} \leq I_0, \quad (36)$$

Then, from (32), (33), (35), and (36), we proved the claim that:

$$(\boldsymbol{\tau}^{\mathbf{n+1}}, \mathbf{u}^{\mathbf{n+1}}) \in \chi_{\mathbf{T_1}}. \quad (37)$$

Repeating the progress above, we see that if there exists a constant ε small enough such that:

$$\|u_0\|_{L^\infty_T(\dot{B}^{N/p-1}_{p,1})} + \|g\|_{\tilde{L}^1_T(\dot{B}^{N/p-1}_{p,1})} \leq \varepsilon\underline{\nu},$$

then, the results presented above will be valid globally. (37) will be valid for all T. Thus, we have proved the claim (28).

We begin to get the convergence of the sequences.

To verify the convergence of the sequences of (θ^n, u^n), we shall consider the time derivative of the solution. We first show the following Lemma.

Lemma 1. *Let* $0 < \eta < inf(1, \frac{2N}{p})$,$1 < p < 2N$, *be such that* $1 + \eta < \frac{2N}{p}$. *Then* ∇p^n *is uniformly bounded in* $L_T^{\frac{2}{2-\eta}}(\dot{B}_{p,1}^{\frac{N}{p}-1-\eta})$.

Proof. Since $g \in L^1_T(\dot{B}^{N/p-1}_{p,1}) \bigcap L^2_T(\dot{B}^{N/p}_{p,1})$,we can easily get $g \in L_T^{\frac{2}{2-\eta}}(\dot{B}^{N/p-1-\eta}_{p,1})$ by interpolation.

Applying $\nabla\cdot$ on the second equation of (25), noting $\nabla \cdot u^n = 0$, then we get:

$$\nabla \cdot (\nabla p^{n+1}) = \nabla \cdot [\nabla \cdot [\widetilde{\nu}(\theta^n + 1) - \underline{\nu})\nabla u^n]] + \nabla \cdot (\underline{\nu}\triangle u^{n+1}) - \nabla \cdot [u^n \cdot \nabla u^{n+1}] + \alpha\nabla \cdot [\theta^n g]. \quad (38)$$

By the first step we have proved that:

$$u^n \in (\tilde{L}^\infty_T(\dot{B}^{N/p-1}_{p,1}) \bigcap \tilde{L}^1_T(\dot{B}^{N/p+1}_{p,1}))^N,$$

From (19) and (20), we get $u^n \in L^2_T(\dot{B}^{N/p}_{p,1})$ by interpolation. Similarly, we also have: $u^n \in L_T^{\frac{2}{2-\eta}}(\dot{B}_{p,1}^{\frac{N}{p}+1-\eta})$; $u^n \in L_T^{\frac{2}{1-\eta}}(\dot{B}_{p,1}^{\frac{N}{p}-\eta})$ with $0 < \eta < inf(1, \frac{2N}{p})$.

By Taylor's formula, we obtain that:

$$\|\nabla \cdot \nabla \cdot [(\widetilde{\nu}(\theta^n + 1) - \underline{\nu})\nabla u^n]\|_{L_T^{\frac{2}{2-\eta}}(\dot{B}_{p,1}^{\frac{N}{p}-2-\eta})}$$

$$\lesssim \|\nabla \cdot [(\widetilde{\nu}(\theta^n + 1) - \underline{\nu})\nabla u^n\|_{L_T^{\frac{2}{2-\eta}}(\dot{B}_{p,1}^{\frac{N}{p}-1-\eta})}$$

$$\lesssim \|(\widetilde{\nu}(\theta^n + 1) - \underline{\nu})\nabla u^n\|_{L_T^{\frac{2}{2-\eta}}(\dot{B}_{p,1}^{\frac{N}{p}-\eta})}$$

$$\lesssim \|\theta^n\|_{L^\infty_T(\dot{B}_{p,\infty}^{\frac{N}{p}})}\|u^n\|_{L_T^{\frac{2}{2-\eta}}(\dot{B}_{p,1}^{\frac{N}{p}+1-\eta})}$$

$$\lesssim \|\theta^n\|_{L^\infty_T(\dot{B}_{p,1}^{\frac{N}{p}})}\|u^n\|_{L_T^{\frac{2}{2-\eta}}(\dot{B}_{p,1}^{\frac{N}{p}+1-\eta})}. \quad (39)$$

in deriving (39), we have used (14) and (15).

Since $u^{n+1} \in L_T^{\frac{2}{2-\eta}}(\dot{B}_{p,1}^{\frac{N}{p}+1-\eta})$, we can easily obtain:

$$\Delta u^{n+1} \in L_T^{\frac{2}{2-\eta}}(\dot{B}_{p,1}^{\frac{N}{p}-1-\eta}). \tag{40}$$

Using (14) and (15) we have:

$$\begin{aligned}\|u^n \cdot \nabla u^{n+1}\|_{L_T^{\frac{2}{2-\eta}}(\dot{B}_{p,1}^{\frac{N}{p}-1-\eta})} &\lesssim \|u^n \otimes u^{n+1}\|_{L_T^{\frac{2}{2-\eta}}(\dot{B}_{p,1}^{\frac{N}{p}-\eta})} \\ &\lesssim \|u^n\|_{L_T^{\frac{2}{1-\eta}}(\dot{B}_{p,1}^{\frac{N}{p}-\eta})} \|u^{n+1}\|_{L_T^2(\dot{B}_{p,1}^{\frac{N}{p}})}.\end{aligned} \tag{41}$$

We now begin to bound the last item $\|\theta^n g\|_{L_T^{\frac{2}{2-\eta}}(\dot{B}_{p,1}^{\frac{N}{p}-1-\eta})}$.

Using (15), we have:

$$\|\theta^n g\|_{L_T^{\frac{2}{2-\eta}}(\dot{B}_{p,1}^{\frac{N}{p}-1-\eta})} \lesssim \|\theta^n\|_{L_T^\infty(\dot{B}_{p,1}^{\frac{N}{p}})} \|g\|_{L_T^{\frac{2}{2-\eta}}(\dot{B}_{p,1}^{\frac{N}{p}-1-\eta})}. \tag{42}$$

Combining (38) and (42), we obtain the desired result. □

In order to use the Ascoli Theorem, it suffices to estimate the derivatives of θ^n and u^n.

Proposition 5. *For the sequence* $(\theta^n, u^n)_{n\in N}$

(i) The sequence $(\partial_t\theta^n)_{n\in\mathbb{N}}$ *is uniformly bounded in* $L_T^2(\dot{B}_{p,1}^{\frac{N}{p}-1})$.

(ii) The sequence $(\partial_t u^n)_{n\in\mathbb{N}}$ *is uniformly bounded in* $L_T^{\frac{2}{2-\eta}}(\dot{B}_{p,1}^{\frac{N}{p}-1-\eta})$, *for:*

$$0 < \eta < inf(1, \frac{2N}{p} - 1) \quad and \quad 1 < p < 2N.$$

Proof. From (25), we have:

$$\partial_t\theta^{n+1} = -u^n \cdot \nabla\theta^{n+1}. \tag{43}$$

Recall that $(\theta^{n+1}, u^n) \in L_T^\infty(\dot{B}_{p,1}^{N/p}) \times (L_T^2(\dot{B}_{p,1}^{N/p}))^N$, from (43), we have:

$$\partial_t\theta^{n+1} \in L_T^2(\dot{B}_{p,1}^{N/p-1}). \tag{44}$$

Similarly, we get:

$$\partial_t u^{n+1} = -u^n \cdot \nabla u^{n+1} + \underline{\nu}\Delta u^{n+1} - \nabla p^{n+1} + G^n. \tag{45}$$

Then we get the desired result (ii) from Lemma 1. □

Now we turn to the proof of the existence of the solution. According to Proposition 5, Cauchy-Schwarz inequality and Hölder's inequality, we deduce the following Corollary.

Corollary 1. *For the sequence* (θ^n, u^n)*:*

(i) The sequence $(\theta^n)_{n\in\mathbb{N}}$ *is uniformly bounded in* $C^{\frac{1}{2}}([0,T], \dot{B}_{p,1}^{\frac{N}{p}-1})$,

(ii) The sequence $(u^n)_{n\in\mathbb{N}}$ *is uniformly bounded in* $C^{\frac{\eta}{2}}(\dot{B}_{p,1}^{\frac{N}{p}-1-\eta})^N$, *for,*

$$0 < \eta < inf(1, \frac{2N}{p} - 1).$$

According to Corollary 1, the sequence $(\theta^n, u^n)_{n\in N}$ is uniformly bounded in $C^{\frac{1}{2}}([0,T], \dot{B}_{p,1}^{\frac{N}{p}-1}) \times C^{\frac{\eta}{2}}(\dot{B}_{p,1}^{\frac{N}{p}-1-\eta})^N$, thus is uniformly bounded in $C([0,T], \dot{B}_{p,1}^{\frac{N}{p}-1}) \times C([0,T], \dot{B}_{p,1}^{\frac{N}{p}-1-\eta})^N$. We recall that the injection of $\dot{B}^{s+\varepsilon}_{pq,loc}$ in $\dot{B}^{s}_{pq,loc}$ is compact for all $\varepsilon > 0$. (See the proof in [34]). Using the uniform estimates and applying the Ascoli's Theorem, there exists a subsequence $(\theta^{n'}, u^{n'})$, which converges to (θ, u). We gather that (θ, u) is a solution of (25) belongs to:

$$(C([0,T], \dot{B}_{p,1}^{N/p}) \bigcap L_T^\infty(\dot{B}_{p,1}^{N/p})) \times (C([0,T], \dot{B}_{p,1}^{N/p-1}) \bigcap L_T^\infty(\dot{B}_{p,1}^{N/p-1}) \bigcap L_T^1(\dot{B}_{p,1}^{N/p+1})).$$

□

4. The Uniqueness of the Solution

In this section we shall prove the uniqueness of the solution for (5). We shall only establish the uniqueness when $p = N$, the case when $1 < p < N$ follows by injection.

We state the results as following.

Theorem 3. *Let $(\theta^i, u^i, p^i), (i = 1, 2)$ be two solutions solve (5) with the same initial data (θ_0, u_0). Assume that:*

$$g \in L^1([0,T], \dot{B}^0_{N,1}),$$

$$\theta^i \in C([0,T], \dot{B}^1_{N,1}) \bigcap L^\infty([0,T], \dot{B}^1_{N,1}), \tag{46}$$

$$u^i \in C([0,T], \dot{B}^0_{N,1}) \bigcap L^\infty([0,T], \dot{B}^0_{N,1}) \bigcap L^1([0,T], \dot{B}^2_{N,1}), \tag{47}$$

$$\nabla p^i \in L^1([0,T], \dot{B}^0_{N,1}), \tag{48}$$

there exists a constant ε small enough, if we have:

$$\|\theta^1\|_{L_T^\infty(\dot{B}^1_{N,1})} \leq \varepsilon, \tag{49}$$

then $(\theta^1, u^1, \nabla p^1) = (\theta^2, u^2, \nabla p^2)$.

Proof. Let $(\theta^i, u^i, \nabla p^i)$ $(i = 1, 2)$ be two solutions to the system (5), we denote:

$$(\delta\theta, \delta u, \delta\nabla p) = (\theta^1 - \theta^2, u^1 - u^2, \nabla p^1 - \nabla p^2), \tag{50}$$

then we have:

$$\begin{cases} \partial_t \delta\theta + u^2 \cdot \nabla\delta\theta + \delta u \nabla\theta^1 = 0, \\ \partial_t \delta u + u^1 \cdot \nabla\delta u - \underline{\nu}\Delta\delta u + \nabla\delta p = K, \\ \nabla \cdot (\delta u) = 0, \\ (\delta\theta, \delta u)|_{t=0} = (0,0), \end{cases} \tag{51}$$

where,

$$K = \nabla \cdot [(\nu(\theta^1) - \underline{\nu})\nabla u^1] - \nabla \cdot [(\nu(\theta^2) - \underline{\nu})\nabla u^2] + \delta u \cdot \nabla u^2 + \delta\theta g. \tag{52}$$

We shall prove the uniqueness in the space $\mathfrak{D}_T$ with:

$$\mathfrak{D}_T = (C([0,T], \dot{B}^0_{N,\infty}) \bigcap L^\infty([0,T], \dot{B}^0_{N,\infty})) \times (C([0,T], \dot{B}^{-1}_{N,\infty}) \bigcap L^\infty([0,T], \dot{B}^{-1}_{N,\infty}) \bigcap L^1([0,T], \dot{B}^1_{N,\infty}) \times L^1([0,T], \dot{B}^{-1}_{N,\infty})). \tag{53}$$

Firstly,we have to state that $(\delta\theta, \delta u, \delta\nabla p) \in \mathfrak{D}_T$.

According to our assumption on (θ^i, u^i), the estimates of paraproduct yield $\partial_t\theta^i \in L_T^2(\dot{B}^0_{N,1})$. Therefore $\bar{\theta}^i = \theta^i - \theta_0$ belongs to $C^{\frac{1}{2}}([0,T], \dot{B}^0_{N,1})$. Which clearly entails by embedding:

$$\delta\theta \in C([0,T], \dot{B}^0_{N,1}).$$

We now define:

$$u^i = u_L + \bar{u^i}, \nabla p^i = \nabla p^i_L + \nabla \bar{p^i}.$$

The quantities u_L and ∇p_L are defined by the system below:

$$\begin{cases} \partial_t u_L - \underline{\nu}\Delta u + \nabla p_L = 0, \\ \nabla \cdot u_L = 0, \\ u_L|_{t=0} = u_0. \end{cases}$$

Thanks to Proposition 2.6 above and Proposition 2.1 in [32], we have:

$$u_L \in C([0,T], \dot{B}^0_{N,1}) \bigcap L^1([0,T], \dot{B}^2_{N,1}),$$

and,

$$\nabla p_L \in L^1([0,T], \dot{B}^0_{N,1}).$$

We obviously have $\bar{u^i}|_{t=0} = 0$ and $(\bar{u^i}, \nabla \bar{p^i})$ verify:

$$\begin{cases} \partial_t \bar{u^i} - \underline{\nu}\Delta \bar{u^i} + \nabla \bar{p^i} = K(\theta^i, u^i), \\ \nabla \cdot \bar{u^i} = 0, \\ \bar{u^i}|_{t=0} = u_0, \end{cases}$$

where $K(\theta^i, u^i) = -u^i \cdot \nabla u^i + \nabla \cdot [(\widetilde{\nu}(\theta^n + 1) - \underline{\nu})\nabla u^n] - \alpha \theta^n g$.

The product and composition laws in Besov Spaces insure that $K(\theta^i, u^i)$ belongs to $L^1_T(\dot{B}^{-1}_{N,1})$, thus we can easily get $K(\theta^i, u^i)$ belongs to $L^1_T(\dot{B}^{-1}_{N,\infty})$.

The Proposition 2.6 above and Proposition 2.1 in [32] yield:

$$\bar{u^i} \in (C([0,T], \dot{B}^{-1}_{N,\infty}) \bigcap L^\infty([0,T], \dot{B}^{-1}_{N,\infty}) \bigcap L^1([0,T], \dot{B}^1_{N,\infty}),$$

and,

$$\nabla \bar{p^i} \in L^1([0,T], \dot{B}^{-1}_{N,\infty}).$$

Since

$$\delta\theta = (\theta^2 - \theta_0) - (\theta^1 - \theta_0), \delta u = \bar{u^2} - \bar{u^1} \quad and \quad \nabla \delta p = \nabla \bar{p^2} - \nabla \bar{p^1},$$

on combining the above discussions, we can conclude:

$$(\delta\theta, \delta u, \delta \nabla p) \in \mathfrak{D}_T.$$

To get the estimates of $\|(\delta\theta, \delta u, \delta\nabla p)\|_{\mathfrak{D}_T}$, by Proposition 4, we have:

$$\|\delta u\|_{\tilde{L}^\infty_T(\dot{B}^{-1}_{N,\infty})} + \underline{\nu}\|\delta u\|_{\tilde{L}^1_T(\dot{B}^1_{N,\infty})} + \|\delta \nabla p\|_{\tilde{L}^1_T(\dot{B}^{-1}_{N,\infty})} \lesssim exp\left(\int_0^T \|\nabla u^1\|_{\dot{B}^1_{N,\infty} \cap L^\infty} dt\right) \int_0^T \|K\|_{\dot{B}^{-1}_{N,\infty}} dt. \tag{54}$$

Noting (53), and using Proposition 2, we have:

$$\begin{aligned} &\|\nabla \cdot [(\widetilde{\nu}(\theta^1) - \underline{\nu})\nabla u^1] - \|\nabla \cdot [(\widetilde{\nu}(\theta^2) - \underline{\nu})\nabla u^2]\|_{\tilde{L}^1_T(\dot{B}^{-1}_{N,\infty})} \\ &\qquad \lesssim \|\nabla \cdot [(\widetilde{\nu}(\theta^1) - \underline{\nu})\nabla u^1] - \nabla \cdot [(\widetilde{\nu}(\theta^1) - \underline{\nu})\nabla u^2]\|_{\tilde{L}^1_T(\dot{B}^{-1}_{N,\infty})} \\ &\qquad + \|\nabla \cdot [(\widetilde{\nu}(\theta^1) - \underline{\nu})\nabla u^2] - \nabla \cdot [(\widetilde{\nu}(\theta^2) - \underline{\nu})\nabla u^2]\|_{\tilde{L}^1_T(\dot{B}^{-1}_{N,\infty})} \\ &\qquad \lesssim \|\theta^1\|_{\tilde{L}^\infty_T(\dot{B}^1_{N,1})}\|\delta u\|_{\tilde{L}^1_T(\dot{B}^1_{N,\infty})} + \|\delta\theta\|_{\tilde{L}^\infty_T(\dot{B}^0_{N,\infty})}\|u^2\|_{\tilde{L}^1_T(\dot{B}^2_{N,1})}) \end{aligned} \tag{55}$$

and,

$$\|\delta u \cdot \nabla u^2\|_{\tilde{L}^1_T(\dot{B}^{-1}_{N,\infty})} \lesssim \|\delta u\|_{\tilde{L}^\infty_T(\dot{B}^{-1}_{N,\infty})}\|u^2\|_{\tilde{L}^1_T(\dot{B}^2_{N,1})}. \tag{56}$$

Now, we shall estimate the term $\delta\theta$. By Proposition 3,

$$\|\delta\theta\|_{\tilde{L}^{\infty}_T(\dot{B}^0_{N,\infty})} \leq exp\left(\int_0^T \|\nabla u^2\|_{\dot{B}^1_{N,\infty}\cap L^\infty} dt\right) \int_0^T \|\delta u \nabla\theta^1\|_{\dot{B}^0_{N,\infty}} dt, \tag{57}$$

Using $(51)_3$ and (13), we get:

$$\int_0^T \|\delta u \nabla\theta^1\|_{\dot{B}^0_{N,\infty}} dt = \int_0^T \|\nabla\cdot(\delta u\theta^1)\|_{\dot{B}^0_{N,\infty}} dt$$
$$= \int_0^T \|\delta u\theta^1\|_{\dot{B}^1_{N,\infty}} dt \lesssim \int_0^T \|\delta u\theta^1\|_{\dot{B}^1_{N,1}} dt \tag{58}$$

If we choose $s_1 = 1, s_2 = 1, p_1 = p_2 = p = N$ in (15), we obtain:

$$\int_0^T \|\delta u\theta^1\|_{\dot{B}^1_{N,1}} dt \lesssim \int_0^T \|\delta u\|_{\dot{B}^1_{N,\infty}} \|\theta^1\|_{\dot{B}^1_{N,1}} dt \lesssim \|\theta^1\|_{\tilde{L}^{\infty}_T(\dot{B}^1_{N,1})} \|\delta u\|_{\tilde{L}^1_T(\dot{B}^1_{N,\infty})}. \tag{59}$$

We now begin to bound $\int_0^T \alpha\|\delta\theta g\|_{\tilde{L}^1_T(\dot{B}^{-1}_{N,\infty})}$,

$$\int_0^T \alpha\|\delta\theta g\|_{\tilde{L}^1_T(\dot{B}^{-1}_{N,\infty})} \lesssim \alpha\|\delta\theta\|_{\tilde{L}^{\infty}_T(\dot{B}^0_{N,\infty})} \|g\|_{\tilde{L}^1_T(\dot{B}^0_{N,1})}. \tag{60}$$

in deriving (60), we have used (17).

Write:

$$\gamma(T) \triangleq \|\delta\theta\|_{\tilde{L}^{\infty}_T(\dot{B}^0_{N,\infty})} + \|\delta u\|_{\tilde{L}^{\infty}_T(\dot{B}^{-1}_{N,\infty})} + \underline{\mu}\|\delta u\|_{\tilde{L}^1_T(\dot{B}^1_{N,\infty})} + \|\delta\nabla p\|_{\tilde{L}^1_T(\dot{B}^{-1}_{N,\infty})}. \tag{61}$$

Then from (54)–(60), we get:

$$\gamma(T) \lesssim \|\theta^1\|_{\tilde{L}^{\infty}_T(\dot{B}^1_{N,1})} \|\delta u\|_{\tilde{L}^1_T(\dot{B}^1_{N,\infty})} + \|\delta\theta\|_{\tilde{L}^{\infty}_T(\dot{B}^0_{N,\infty})} \|u^2\|_{\tilde{L}^1_T(\dot{B}^2_{N,1})}$$
$$+ \|\delta u\|_{\tilde{L}^{\infty}_T(\dot{B}^{-1}_{N,\infty})} \|u^2\|_{\tilde{L}^1_T(\dot{B}^2_{N,1})} + \alpha\|\delta\theta\|_{\tilde{L}^{\infty}_T(\dot{B}^0_{N,\infty})} \|g\|_{\tilde{L}^1_T(\dot{B}^0_{N,1})}. \tag{62}$$

Taking T small enough, such that for any small positive constant ε_0, we have:

$$\|\nabla u^2\|_{\tilde{L}^1_T(\dot{B}^1_{N,1})} + \|g\|_{L^1_T(\dot{B}^0_{N,1})} \leq \frac{1}{2}\varepsilon_0. \tag{63}$$

Thus, we have:

$$\gamma(T) \leq \frac{1}{2}\gamma(T). \tag{64}$$

we get,

$$\gamma(T) \equiv 0,$$

which yields uniqueness of the solutions. □

5. Conclusions

In this paper, we studied the Cauchy problem for non-homogeneous Boussinesq equations. We proved the global existence of the solution when the initial velocity are small with respect to the viscosity, as well as the initial temperature approaches a positive constant on the critical Besov spaces $(\theta, u) \in L^{\infty}_T(\dot{B}^{N/p}_{p,1}) \times L^{\infty}_T(\dot{B}^{N/p-1}_{p,1}) \cap L^1_T(\dot{B}^{N/p+1}_{p,1})$ with $1 < p < 2N$. Furthermore, we proved the uniqueness for $1 < p \leq N$. When $N \leq p \leq 2N$, the uniqueness is difficult. We can't get any result following the method proposed in this paper. We will consider the uniqueness for $N \leq p \leq 2N$ in the future. We can also obtain similar results for other fluid equations.

Author Contributions: Writing—original draft, Y.L. and B.O. All authors have read and agreed to the published version of the manuscript.

Funding: This research was funded by Key projects of universities in Guangdong Province (NATURAL SCIENCE) (2019KZDXM042) and the Research Fundations of Guangzhou Huashang College (2021HSKT01,2020HSDS01).

Institutional Review Board Statement: Not applicable.

Informed Consent Statement: Not applicable.

Data Availability Statement: Not applicable.

Acknowledgments: The authors would like to deeply thank all the reviewers for their insightful and constructive comments.

Conflicts of Interest: The authors declare no conflict of interest.

References

1. Drazin, P.G.; Reid, W.H. *Hydrodynamic Stability*; Cambridge University Press: Cambridge, UK, 1981.
2. Majda, A. *Introduction to PDEs and Waves for the Atmosphere and Ocean*; Courant Lecture Notes in Mathematics; AMS/CIMS: Providence, RI, USA, 2003; Volume 9.
3. Cannon, J.R.; Benedetto, E.D. *The Initial Problem for the Boussinesq Equations with Data in L^p*; Lecture Note in Mathematics; Springer: Berlin, Germany, 1980; Volume 771, pp. 129–144.
4. Chae, D.; Nam, H.-S. Local existence and blow-up criterion for the Boussinesq equations. *Proc. R. Soc. Edinb.* **1997**, *127A*, 935–946. [CrossRef]
5. Chae, D.; Kim, S.-K.; Nam, H.-S. Local existence and blow-up criterion of Holder continuous solutions of the Boussinesq equations. *Nagoya Math. J.* **1999**, *155*, 58–80. [CrossRef]
6. Taniuchi, Y. A note on the blow-up criterion for the inviscid 2-D Boussinesq equations. *Lect. Notes Pure Appl. Math.* **2002**, *223*, 131–140.
7. Chae, D. Global regularity for the 2D Boussinesq equations with partial viscosity terms. *Adv. Math.* **2006**, *203*, 497–513. [CrossRef]
8. Danchin, R.; Paicu, M. Existence and uniqueness results for the Boussinesq system with data in Lorentz spaces. *Physica D* **2008**, *237*, 1444–1460. [CrossRef]
9. Danchin, R.; Paicu, M. Global well-posedness issues for the inviscid Boussinesq system with Yudovich's type data. *Commun. Math. Phys.* **2009**, *290*, 1–14. [CrossRef]
10. Hou, T.Y.; Li, C. Global well-posedness of the viscous Boussinesq equations. *Discret. Contin. Dyn. Syst.* **2005**, *12*, 1–12. [CrossRef]
11. Liu, X.; Wang, M.; Zhang, Z. Local Well-Posedness and Blowup Criterion of the Boussinesq Equations in Critical Besov Spaces. *J. Math. Fluid Mech.* **2010**, *12*, 280–292.
12. Abidi, H.; Hmidi, T. On the global well-posedness for Boussinesq system. *J. Differ. Equ.* **2007**, *233*, 199–220. [CrossRef]
13. Sebastian, A.L.; Jose, L.B. The initial value problem for a genneralized Boussinesq model. *Nonlinear Anal.* **1999**, *36*, 457–480.
14. Baranovskii, E.S.; Domnich, A.A. Model of a Nonuniformly Heated Viscous Flow through a Bounded Domain. *Differ. Equ.* **2020**, *56*, 304–314. [CrossRef]
15. Baranovskii, E.S.; Domnich, A.A.; Artemov, M.A. Optimal Boundary Control of Non-Isothermal Viscous Fluid Flow. *Fluids* **2019**, *4*, 133. [CrossRef]
16. Guo, Z.H.; Li, Q.Y. Global existence and large time behaviors of the solutions to the full incompressible Navier-Stokes equations with temperature-dependent coefficients. *J. Differ. Equ.* **2021**, *274*, 876–923. [CrossRef]
17. Lorca, S.A.; Boldrini, J.L. Stationary solutions for genneralized Boussinesq model. *J. Differ. Equ.* **1996**, *124*, 389–406. [CrossRef]
18. Fujita, H.; Kato, T. On the Navier-Stokes initial value problem I. *Arch. Ration. Mech. Anal.* **1964**, *16*, 269–315. [CrossRef]
19. Danchin, R. Global existence in critical spaces for compressible Navier-Stokes equations. *Invent. Math.* **2000**, *141*, 579–614. [CrossRef]
20. Abidi, H.; Paicu, M. Global Existence for the Magnetohydrodynamic system in critical spaces. *Proc. R. Soc. Edinb.* **2008**, *138A*, 447–476. [CrossRef]
21. Chen, Q.; Miao, C.; Zhang, Z. On the well-posedness for the viscous shallow water equations. *SIAM J. Math. Anal.* **2008**, *40*, 443–474. [CrossRef]
22. Danchin, R. Local theory in Critical spaces for compressible viscous and heat conductive gases. *Commun. Partial Differ. Equ.* **2001**, *26*, 1183–1233. [CrossRef]
23. Danchin, R. Global existence in critical spaces for flows of compressible viscous and heat-conductive gases. *Arch. Ration. Mech. Anal.* **2001**, *160*, 1–39. [CrossRef]
24. Danchin, R. Density-dependent incompressible viscous fluids in critical spaces. *Proc. R. Soc. Edinb.* **2003**, *133A*, 1311–1334. [CrossRef]
25. Deng, W.; Wu, J.; Zhang, P. Stability of Couette flow for 2D Boussinesq system with vertical dissipation. *J. Funct. Anal.* **2021**, *281*, 109255. [CrossRef]

26. Qiu, H.; Du, Y.; Yao, Z. A note on the regularity criterion of the two-dimensional Newton CBoussinesq equations. *Nonlinear Anal. Real World Appl.* **2011**, *12*, 2012–2015. [CrossRef]
27. Qiu, H.; Du, Y.; Yao, Z. Blow-up criteria for 3D Boussinesq equations in the multiplier space. *Commun. Nonlinear Sci. Numer. Simul.* **2011**, *16*, 1820–1824. [CrossRef]
28. Qiu, H.; Du, Y.; Yao, Z. A blow-up criterion for 3D Boussinesq equations in Besov spaces. *Nonlinear Anal. Theory Methods Appl.* **2010**, *73*, 806–815. [CrossRef]
29. Chen, W.; Ikehata, R. The Cauchy problem for the Moore-Gibson-Thompson equation in the dissipative case. *J. Differ. Equ.* **2021**, *292*, 176–219. [CrossRef]
30. Chen, W.; Palmieri, A. Weakly coupled system of semilinear wave equations with distinct scale-invariant terms in the linear part. *Z. Angew. Math. Phys.* **2019**, *70*, 67. [CrossRef]
31. Chemin, J.-Y. *Perfect Incompressible Fluids*; Oxford University Press: New York, NY, USA, 1998.
32. Chemin, J.-Y. Théorèmes D'unicité Pour le Systèème de Navie-Stockes Tridimensionnel. *J. Anal.* **1999**, *77*, 27–50.
33. Abidi, H.; Paicu, M. Éxistence globale pour un fluide inhomogène. *Ann. Inst. Fourier* **2007**, *57*, 883–917. [CrossRef]
34. Runst, T.; Sickel, W. Sobolev spaces of fractional order, Nemytskii operators, and nonlinear partial differential equations. In *Nonlinear Analysis and Applications*; Walter de Wruyter: Berlin, Germany, 1996; Volume 3.

MDPI
St. Alban-Anlage 66
4052 Basel
Switzerland
Tel. +41 61 683 77 34
Fax +41 61 302 89 18
www.mdpi.com

Symmetry Editorial Office
E-mail: symmetry@mdpi.com
www.mdpi.com/journal/symmetry